Democratisation in Britain

British Studies Series

General Editor JEREMY BLACK

Published

Alan Boom **The British Economy in the Twentieth Century**
John Charmley **A History of Conservative Politics, 1900–1996**
David Childs **Britain since 1939 (2nd edn)**
John Davis **A History of Britain, 1885–1939**
David Eastwood **Government and Community in the English Provinces, 1700–1870**
Philip Edwards **The Making of the Modern English State, 1460–1660**
W.H. Fraser **A History of British Trade Unionism, 1700–1998**
John Garrard **Democratisation in Britain: Elites, Civil Society and Reform since 1800**
Brian Hill **The Early Parties and Politics in Britain, 1688–1832**
Katrina Honeyman **Women, Gender and Industrialisation in England, 1700–1870**
Kevin Jefferys **Retreat from New Jerusalem: British Politics, 1951–1964**
T.A. Jenkins **The Liberal Ascendancy, 1830–1886**
David Loades **Power in Tudor England**
Ian Machin **The Rise of Democracy in Britain, 1830–1918**
Alexander Murdoch **British History, 1660–1832: National Identity and Local Culture**
Anthony Musson and W. M. Ormrod **The Evolution of English Justice: Law, Politics and Society in the Fourteenth Century**
Murray G.H. Pittock **Inventing and Resisting Britain: Cultural Identities in Britain and Ireland, 1685–1789**
Nick Smart **The National Government, 1931–40**
Andrew Thorpe **A History of the British Labour Party (2nd edn)**

British Studies Series
Series Standing Order
ISBN 0–333–71691–4 hardcover
ISBN 0–333–69332–9 paperback
(outside North America only)

You can receive future titles in this series as they are published by placing a standing order. Please contact your bookseller or, in case of difficulty, write to us at the address below with your name and address, the title of the series and an ISBN quoted above.

Customer Services Department, Macmillan Distribution Ltd
Houndmills, Basingstoke, Hampshire RG21 6XS, England

Democratisation in Britain

Elites, Civil Society and Reform since 1800

John Garrard

palgrave

First published 2002 by
PALGRAVE
Houndmills, Basingstoke, Hampshire RG21 6XS and
175 Fifth Avenue, New York, N. Y. 10010
Companies and representatives throughout the world

PALGRAVE is the new global academic imprint of St. Martin's Press LLC
Scholarly and Reference Division and Palgrave Publishers Ltd (formerly
Macmillan Press Ltd).

ISBN 0–333–64639–8 hardback
ISBN 0–333–64640–1 paperback

This book is printed on paper suitable for recycling and
made from fully managed and sustained forest sources.

A catalogue record for this book is available
from the British Library.

Library of Congress Cataloging-in-Publication Data
Garrard, John.
    Democratisation in Britain : elites, civil society and reform since
    1800 / John Garrard.
        p. cm. — (British studies series)
    Includes bibliographical references and index.
    ISBN 0–333–64639–8
        1. Democratization—Great Britain—History. 2. Elite (Social
    sciences)—Great Britain—Political activity—History. 3. Working
    class—Great Britain—Political activity—History. 4. Civil society—
    Great Britain—History. 5. Great Britain—Politics and government.
    I. Title. II. Series.

JN210 .G37 2001
306.2'0941—dc21
                                                                    2001036529

10 9 8 7 6 5 4 3 2 1
11 10 09 08 07 06 05 04 03 02

Printed in China

For Eve and David

'If great changes accomplished by the people are dangerous, although sometimes salutary, great changes accomplished by an aristocracy, at the desire of the people, are at once salutary and safe.'

—**Lord John Russel**
1822 quoted Ellis Archer Wasson,
'The Great Whigs and Parliamentary
Reform 1809–30', *Journal of British Studies*,
24 (1985) 434–64

'...the Cato Street conspirators, while plotting in a garret the assassination of the Cabinet, found it necessary to appoint one of their number as Chairman...and...take the question of beheading Castlereagh...in proper form, with a vote upon the substantive motion.'

—**E.P. Thompson**,
The Making of the English Working Class

Contents

Acknowledgements

For help, support, encouragement and comments along the way, all of them generous, at least the following: David Garrard, Eve Garrard, Bill Williams, Peter Shapely, Neville Kirk, Frank O'Gorman, Sandra Hayton, Jon Tonge, Pat Garside, Frank Neil, Richard Popplewell, Tom Clitheroe, all the members of my 1996 democratisation class, Ralph White, Vera Tolz, David Walsh, Geoff Harris, David Marquand, Simon Gunn, Martin Bull, Martin Alexander, Eric Evans, Declan McHugh, Gideon Baker, David Green, Martin Gorski and Joss Evans. The mistakes I managed by myself, and have copyright on every one.

JOHN GARRARD

Democratisation and Liberalisation: A Legislative Diary

Not all the legislation outlined here is unambiguously democratising in effect, still less in intention. Some, indeed, is partly aimed at counter-weighting electoral popularisation. Nor is legislation the only democratising and liberalising factor. The list also includes landmark legislation creating the legal framework facilitating civil association.

1688 'The Glorious Revolution'

1689 Bill of Rights Defines the limits of royal power on the basis of perceived usurpations by James II. Framework for constitutional monarchy which slowly emerged.

1689 Toleration Act Dissenters no longer legally obliged to attend Anglican services; licensing system for their chapels; schools legally sanctioned; limits powers of Anglican courts.

1793 First legislation offering legal registration to friendly societies.

1824 Repeal of Anti-Combination Laws (1799) Legalises trade unions, though activities constrained by restoration of the Law of Conspiracy in 1825.

1828 Repeal of Test and Corporation Acts Removes legal obstacles to Dissenters holding civil office; as much symbolic as actual since the Acts had long ceased to be effective barriers. Disabilities remain for Catholics and Jews.

1829 Catholic Emancipation Removes legal barriers to Catholics holding any civil office except those directly involving the Crown.

Accompanied by Act raising Irish county franchise from 40 shilling freehold to £10 household.

1832 Franchise Reform Act

Enfranchisement: Franchise formally defined as male.

England and Wales: In *counties*, adds £10 copyholders and £50 tenants-at-will to existing 40 shilling freeholders. In *boroughs*, enfranchises £10 male householder and occupier provided he occupies relevant property within the borough and has resided in or within seven miles of borough for at least 12 months, and has not received poor relief in the past year. Destroys all existing wide and narrow qualifications, though leaves holders in possession of their vote until death or removal.

Electorate 1831: 439 200; 1833: 656 000; rise 49 per cent
Ratio enfranchised: 1 in 5 adult males

Scotland: In *counties*, reduces property-owning qualification from £100 to £10, and adds £10 leaseholders (if lease not less than £57) and £50 leaseholders (if lease not less than 19 years); also tenants of property worth £50. In *burghs*, in place of £100 property-owning qualification, enfranchises £10 householder on same basis as in England. Abolishes old system whereby town council elected a delegate who had one vote in election.

Electorate 1831: 4500; 1833: 60 000; rise 1233 per cent.
Ratio enfranchised: 1 in 8 adult males

Ireland: In *counties*, adds £10 leaseholders (with leases of 20 + years) to £10 property owners permitted to vote after 1829. In *boroughs*, enfranchises £10 householders on same basis as in England and Scotland, and abolishes existing franchises, though holders retain qualifications during lifetimes.

Electorate 1831: 49 000; 1832: 90 000; rise 84 per cent.
Ratio enfranchised: 1 in 20 adult males

Overall Electorate: 1831 492 700; 1833: 806 000;
Rise 64 per cent
Pencentage enfranchised 1833: 14.5 per cent

Redistribution

England and Wales: 56 boroughs lost representation altogether; 30 boroughs reduced from 2 to 1 MP; 22 new boroughs created with 2 MPs; 19 new boroughs created with 1 MP; county representation increased by 65 after reallocation of small borough seats. Nevertheless, small boroughs still dominate borough representation.

Scotland: gets 8 new seats; counties retain existing 30 seats; borough representation increased from 15 to 23.

Ireland: county representation unchanged at 64; representation of Belfast, Limerick, Galway and Waterford increased from 1 to 2, as is that of Dublin University.

1835 Municipal Corporations Act 178 unelected English and Welsh corporations automatically replaced by councils elected by adult male direct ratepayers, subject to 30 months qualification period; other towns permitted to petition for incorporation.

1836 Newspaper stamp duty reduced from 4d to 1d.

1850 Irish Franchise Act Occupier-based franchise and new registration system increases post-Famine electorate from 45 000 to 163 000.

1850 Small Tenements Act Allows municipal rating of cheap houses, and gives compounded ratepayers the right to vote in council elections. Permissive, but, where adopted, could double local electorate.

1852 Parliament empowers itself to create Royal Commissions of Enquiry to investigate petitions about electoral fraud in constituencies.

1854 Corrupt Practices Act Attempts precise definitions of various types of electoral corruption, including bribery, intimidation and undue influence, with penalties for each; requires itemised accounts for constituency election expenditure to be submitted to election auditors.

1853 Newspaper advertising duty removed.

1855 Newspaper stamp duty removed.

1856 Industrial and Provident Societies Act Co-ops given the same legal status and privileges as friendly societies.

1858   Jews admitted to Parliament.

1859   Abolition of Property Qualification for MPs.

1862   Limited liability status available to co-ops. Expanded further in 1876 and 1893.

1867/8 Franchise Reform Acts

In *boroughs*, enfranchises adult male householder of 12 months standing within the borough of registration; £10 lodgers resident at their address for 12 months ; electorate increases 138 per cent.

In *counties*: enfranchises adult-male £5 lease and copyholders, and £12 occupiers of 12 months standing in England, Wales and Scotland, but not Ireland; electorate increased by 38 per cent.

Personal payment of rates retained only for Scotland.

Overall electorate 1866: 1 357 519; 1868: 2 476 745; increase 82.5 per cent; little effect in Ireland.

Limited *redistribution*: small boroughs lose 45 seats. 25 seats to more populous counties. Manchester, Leeds, Birmingham and Liverpool increase representation from 2 to 3 seats, though (the 'minority clause') each elector only has two votes. 11 towns become constituencies. Scotland receives 7 extra seats.

1868 Corrupt Practices Act   Election petition trials removed from Parliament to the courts.

1869   Courts confirm parliamentary franchise as specifically male.

1869 Municipal Franchise Act   Allows municipal vote to all ratepayers, direct and indirect, regardless of whether town has adopted Small Tenements Act; allows vote to unmarried adult female ratepayers. Qualification period reduced to 12 months.

1870 Education Act   Women given ratepaying voting rights, and right to stand in Education Board elections.

1875   Peaceful picketing legalised; strikes secured from breach of contract proceedings until Taff Vale case 1899.

1872 Ballot Act   Voting becomes secret. Demise of hustings in favour of polling booths.

1874   First working-class MPs.

1875 Public Health Act   Complete network of elected sanitary authorities established across country, including rural areas where authority vested in boards of guardians.

1883 Corrupt and Illegal Practices Act   Distinguishes between corrupt and illegal electoral behaviour, with high penalties on the former. Curbs election expenditure. Seen as decisive.

1884/5 Franchise Reform and Redistribution Acts

Standardises adult male householder and lodger franchise across United Kingdom, though personal rates payment still retained for Scotland.

Ratio enfranchised: circa 6 adult males in 10. Electorate increased by 75 per cent in England; 88 per cent in Wales; 91 per cent in Scotland and 222 per cent in Ireland.

Redistribution very roughly according to population ; single member constituencies in most locations. Large towns subdivided, creating constituencies partly based on social homogeneity. Minority clause repealed.

Boundary Commission established for future redistributions.

1888 Local Government Act   Establishes elected county councils in place of county magistrates. Allows larger boroughs to become county boroughs.

1889   Directly elected London County Council replaces indirectly elected Metropolitan Board of Works.

1889   Courts declare only men can stand as municipal candidates.

1894 Local Government Act   Establishes elected urban and rural district councils; abolishes property-weighted voting in Poor Law elections; removes medical relief from disenfranchisement attached to pauperism.

1899 London vestries replaced by borough councils. Parish meetings in small parishes now the only remaining element of institutionalised direct democracy.

1907 Women allowed to stand as municipal candidates.

1911 Payment of MPs.

1911 Parliament Act House of Lords precluded from rejecting money Bills; ability to delay other Bills limited to two years.

1918 Representation of the People Act Establishes adult suffrage for men over 21 (and temporarily for returning servicemen over 18); women over 30 enfranchised provided they are either ratepayers or their wives. Residence requirements reduced to six months. Poor relief removed from franchise. University seats increased to 7, but maximum votes per elector reduced to 2. Electorate increased to 21 400,000 (180 per cent since 1910), 39.6 per cent of which is female. Compiling electoral register becomes purely bureaucratic and party influence removed. Major reallocation of seats and boundaries in line with demographic change, and aiming at 70 000 voters per constituency. All voting to take place on the same day, not over several weeks as before.

1919 Nancy Astor elected as first woman MP.

1922 Irish Partition In Ulster, municipal franchise restricted to homeowning ratepayers. Business plural voting increased.

1928 Equalisation of the Franchise Act Women enfranchised on the same basis as men for both parliamentary and municipal purposes. Living-in servants enfranchised. Adds 5 300 000 voters; female proportion 52.2 per cent.

1948 Representation of the People Act One person one vote finally established. Abolishes university and business votes; six-month residential qualification (around 5 per cent previously disenfranchised by this provision); and remaining two-seat constituencies. Seats and boundaries reallocated in line with demographic change.

1949 Parliament Act   Lord's veto reduced to one year.

1958   Life peers allowed to enter Lords. Women hereditary peers allowed into Lords.

1969   Vote extended to 18-year-olds.

1999   Hereditary basis of Lords abolished.

2001   Enfranchisement of homeless people.

Introduction

Democratisation has been intermittently under way for two centuries, and has a long history. There is nothing unique, or even uniquely inspired, about Britain, though it has been one of the more fortunate and closely-managed experiences. Internationally speaking, democratisation has occurred in several phases. Britain is one of several polities that can be retrospectively located in the first and most extended phase, beginning in the nineteenth century and 'completing' in the twentieth. It shared essentially evolutionary experiences, presided over by pre-existing elites, with countries in north-west Europe, North America, Australia and, less securely, parts of Southern Europe. Thus far, these have been followed by four equally distinctive and more rapid phases. The first was a largely uncontrolled phase in the inter-war years, particularly amongst autocracies defeated in the First World War and successor-states emerging from the Versailles Settlement. The second occurred immediately after 1945, and comprised right-wing dictatorships defeated in the Second World War, particularly Italy, Germany, Austria and Japan, whose transition was closely supervised by the Western liberal-democratic victors. In the 1970s, there was a third phase in Spain and Portugal, again succeeding right-wing dictatorships. Fourth, and most recently, democratisation has emerged in largely uncontrolled form amongst states surviving or emerging from Communist collapse in Russia and East-Central Europe after 1989. Outside Europe, there have also been recent bouts of democratisation in Africa and Latin America, either from one-party states or from military dictatorships.

As the result of these most recent phases, democratisation, real or pretended, has become normative amongst polities. What J.K. Galbraith noted in 1966 is even truer at the turn of the twenty-first century as least as an official target: 'Like the family and truth and sunshine and Florence Nightingale, democracy stands above doubt'.[1] Consequently, democratisation has become fashionable as a topic of academic study. In fact, Britain's enfranchisement story, like other first-phase examples, has rarely attracted the democratising label, either from historians, or participating contemporaries. In offering it now, I do not imply a consciously-conducted process. Indeed, one characteristic, and good fortune, of democratising polities in this phase was the absence of democratically-directed intention amongst those in charge, at least in the early decades. However, using the label will, I hope, be helpful to both political scientists and historians, and interesting to students and general readers. For historians, it may throw new light on the characteristics and underpinnings of an oft-told story, enabling Britain's experience to be seen in broader perspective. For political scientists, exploring the democratisation of a polity in the first phase may provide useful comparison, and particularly contrast, with experience amongst those in later phases. This is particularly relevant because so many leaders of post-Communist systems take first-phase Western polities, particularly Britain and the United States, as their desired model, rather than countries in any of the later phases.[2]

As used here, the notion of democratisation implies three characteristics about the end-product. First, the system has regular and free elections, with accountable governments, coming and going according to the results. Second, all adults have the opportunity of influencing the political process, even if they do not necessarily choose to exercise it, or succeed if they do. Third, the end-product is *liberal* democracy, where liberal freedoms of speech, association, press, and so on are securely safeguarded. Whilst some regimes, notably in the Far-East, would claim to be democratic whilst restricting these freedoms, most Western observers regard such values not just as good in themselves, but essential to the maintenance of democracy in the two senses outlined above. Defined even in these fairly minimal ways, democratisation may still have some way to go even in first-phase countries: terminating matters around 1950 does not imply Britain's story is complete; still less that it has resulted in 'complete democracy'.

The book has two central and inter-linked intentions. First, particularly in Chapters 2 and 8, it will explore the process whereby successive social groups were formally inducted into Britain's political system, whilst also learning to behave in democratically appropriate ways. Second, inter-connectedly, and in all eight chapters, it will try to explain why democratisation was relatively successful – in the sense that large numbers were given significant opportunity for influence over the political process, and the system remained stable while this was happening.

I will argue that, partly because of the nature of the process, partly due to its context, and probably like others in this first phase, Britain's democratisation happened in particularly benign circumstances. If pre-requisites are important, and some would question this,[3] these were generously in place before commencement, whilst democratisation was ongoing, and after completion. As Chapter 1 will suggest, pre-existing politics, whilst undoubtedly oligarchic, were not wholly closed to public access and pressure, even from relatively lowly people. Even if grudg-ingly granted, liberal freedoms commanded widespread consensus and were reasonably secure before the process started, particularly when supplemented by the limited resources and efficiency of the forces of repression, law and order. Thus demands for political entry and other satisfactions could be articulated and significantly responded to. Unlike the instant democratisations occurring since 1918, Britain's took place in extended stages. As Chapters 1 and 2 suggest, even the political entry of individual social groups was long-continuing. The electorate was sub-stantially composed of the middling orders before 1832, and the last middle-class males were admitted in 1918. Working-class men were significantly present amongst electors before 1832 and 1867; they could also legitimately pressurise the system from outside. Their formal inclusion was extended between the Acts of 1867, 1884/5 and 1918, as well as being subject to the effects of socio-economic and demographic change, and party competition. Some women were admitted as local government electors in 1869 and could participate in pressure politics throughout the period, whilst their formal parliamentary admission was extended over 1918 and 1928. Thus no group was unfamiliar with political participation before formal entry. The staging of admission, however haphazardly, also enabled each group and its most urgent demands to be at least partially absorbed and incorporated before entry by the next became irresistible or politically advantageous. As Chapters 4–7 argue, the staging of admission also coincided with the acquisition of political fitness and appropriate values, whether defined by political elites or more detached criteria. Finally, the democratisation of political behaviour, the emergence of opinion-politics, could build on substantial bases of conditional deference, financially reinforced parti-sanship and increasingly benign economic circumstances.

The book's structure, analysis and explanations partly rest upon arguments in the recent literature of democratisation, particularly about two variable factors often seen as rival explanations of success or failure: the relative roles of political elites and civil society. In the

British context, I will argue that both were important and benign in effect. Elites have often been seen as crucial in managing democratisation. Their skill or otherwise determine how the difficult transition from previous autocracy to democracy is negotiated, how forces with interests in the dying system are neutralised, new ones introduced and absorbed, and crucial economic transitions to market-economics overseen. Some have even implied that, given skilful elites, the absence of other pre-requisites supposedly essential for successful democratisation can be circumvented.[4] Against this, political elites have been seen as essentially prisoners of circumstances created by other more important contextual factors. At best, politicians take advantage of opportunities presented by the decline or collapse of the old regime, the fortunate alignment of new circumstances, or, more fundamentally still, by the dynamics of a vibrant civil society.[5]

Chapter 3 will argue that, due to a mixture of political skill, good fortune, and the functional effect of policies pursued for other reasons, British political elites were highly important in shaping and successfully managing Britain's democratisation. Aristocratic domination of Parliament, of large swathes of electoral politics and rural society ensured them significant autonomy. Consequently, their agenda, albeit often pursued for primarily self-preserving or party-political reasons, heavily influenced the extended character of the process, and the timing and content of particular episodes. The often highly political instincts of national and local elites substantially affected how democratisation was managed, and the resulting demands responded to. Partly deliberately, partly for unconnected reasons, national politicians also significantly facilitated, even helped shape, the emergence of civil society. The survival and evolutionary democratisation of the central elite, and its significant supplementation by similar local elites, also ensured that, unlike post-1918 Germany and many East-Central European countries in the same period, or post-1989 Russia, there was no displaced and disgruntled group of formerly privileged persons waiting to turn the clock back if the democratised regime faltered.

Finally, the role played by traditional elites had significant costs. It helped ensure that the eventual democracy was one of the less demanding, less participatory, and more elite-centred versions on offer, either theoretically or in practice. Thus, there was no PR, no recourse to referenda and recall; only a limited sense that MPs or councillors were delegates rather than more autonomous representatives. Moreover, just as British democracy was underpinned by democratic practices within civil society, so its restricted character mirrored and probably influenced increasing autonomy for the popularly-legitim-ised leadership of civil organisations. Amongst some, particularly middle-class dominated associations, as evident in Chapter 4, these habits appeared early. Amongst others, particularly working-class groups, they emerged much later – as organisations grew larger and less localised, as more pleasurable pursuits increasingly rivalled participatory joys, and as the need for leaders able to operate as flexible and relatively autonomous negotiators emerged from Britain's relatively open political and eco-nomic bargaining processes.

This points to the second variable often highlighted as responsible for democratising success or failure, and explored in Chapters 4–7: civil society. Britain's aristocratic politicians were probably fortunate in being mostly unable to foresee the mismatch between their intention only to admit the fit and unthreatening on the one hand, and where things were ultimately headed on the other. They therefore had no particular reason to hesitate over what turned out to be the initiating steps. The fact that democracy nevertheless was the end-product, and entrant-groups were able to handle the democratic demands made upon them, had much to do with the spread of a vibrant civil society. This term has been intermit-tently current for around 250 years, and has had various meanings. Now, it most commonly implies two interconnected characteristics considered essential to successful democratisation. First, and dependent on the second, it implies civility, civilised and mutually-forbearing ways of conducting social, political and economic relations.[6] Second and more commonly, the term refers to how the space between the state and the family is associationally occupied. A healthy and widely-spread network of voluntary organisations supposedly has several highly func-tional effects for emergent liberal democracies, interconnectedly ser-vicing both their liberal and democratic characteristics. Polities are rendered more securely *liberal* by myriad associations, independent of the state and capable of protecting individuals against its incursions by collective action and by providing them with alternative identities and interests. Voluntary organisations also encourage self-help and inde-pendence, and discourage over-reliance on state provision. Political organisations provide alternative venues for generating ideas and pre-scriptions. The overall liberal (and democratic) effect is to enhance individual autonomy. Polities are rendered more securely *democratic* because civil associations are voluntary and thus self-governing. To ensure accountability, they must formulate elaborate rules about elections,

annual general meetings and annual reportage. This reinforces democratic values and expectations in the wider polity, rendering them
normative. Participation trains participants in using democratic procedures, and equips them with skills and self-confidence in getting things
done. Thus voluntary associations can also train political leaders, equip-
ping them with skills suitable for elective office. Finally, political organisations in particular provide channels for defining, defending and
advancing individual and group interests.

With significant reservations, Chapters 4–7 endorse these views for
successive entrants to Britain's political system. Middle-class and
working-class males, and women, all showed substantial attachments
to civil association before enfranchisement. Their organisations were
rising while it took place, and their growth continued accelerating
thereafter, partly responding to aspirations created by inclusion. This
helped generate a generalised liberal consensus, a passionate desire for
full citizenship, an ability to articulate it, and advance interests after,
even before, admission. Equally important, and particularly relevant
amongst economically-deprived groups after 1867, the vibrant and
satisfying network of civil association reinforced low expectations of
the state, and thus about what would follow after inclusion. For a still-
developing capitalist economy, whatever one's opinions about current
issues of state-welfare, the minimal economic burdens thus created were
democratically functional. So too was the elite's own only part-intended
contribution: the creation of a state at once encouraging to civil associations and deeply baleful to those seeking its aid. This state eventually
expanded, but more in response to what elites thought 'good for'
deprived groups than to demands clearly articulated by them. Only
with rising expectations before 1914 and, more importantly, women's
political admission after 1918, did the situation significantly change.
Finally, as Chapter 8 will suggest, civil association also partly underpinned the emergence of democratised political behaviour, and the
retreat of deference- and market politics. In the British context, civil
society was less important in enhancing autonomy from a minimally
ambitious state than from landowning and employing elites.

The primary reservations about the democratically-functional impact
of civil association in Britain are twofold. First, partly for reasons
connected with the separation of spheres, and domesticity's late renais-
sance amongst working men and their wives, associational life was least
vibrant amongst working-class women. Second, and more important,
given associational multiplication amongst most groups, one might

expect more desire for political participation than was evident in the twentieth century. The apparent mismatch is partly due to the emergence of pleasures rivalling associational ones, and the inevitable bureaucratisation and professionalisation of organisations in response to their increasing size and expanding roles. It is also ascribable to the elite-influenced character of democratisation already outlined, and how this interacted with the operation of civil society. The relatively circumscribed and highly representational emphases of British democracy, coupled with politicians' willingness to incorporate key political and economic groups into policy-making, probably impacted upon the internal processes of civil associations, producing increasing needs to mirror the wider polity. Faced with the necessity to negotiate, civil-associational leaders, quite aside from their own ambitions, often sought forms of internal democracy enhancing their detachment from their followers, and marginalising the more strident ones.[7]

A fig-leaf of modesty is appropriate at this point. This book is intended as a first rather than definitive word. Besides insights hopefully arising from my own work, I have extensively mined research produced by others. Much of the latter has been directed at purposes rather different from mine. Few historians, till very recently, have thought about associational activity in civil-society terms, and most, whether using the idea or not, have been interested in how civil organisations presented themselves to the world, their conflicts with others, or their impact, rather than in how they ran themselves. Using such work to think about the underpinnings of democracy may well cause difficulties; if so the faults are entirely mine. Given the research mountain created in history as in other disciplines in recent years, there will undoubtedly be much work that I have not had time to consult: to the many inadvertently ignored, I apologise. Finally, besides the factors focused upon in this book, there are undoubtedly others. Some will be noted as we proceed; others will be picked up in the conclusion. However, whatever its inadequacies, I hope what follows will stimulate debate.

Before moving on, it may be helpful to outline some basic concepts, particularly some of those around which the debates about what eventually became democratisation were conducted. These ideas became the bases from which people pressed for, resisted, or assessed the process; some remain important to the debate about what is perceived to be the need to further democratise politics in the present-day. Sometimes their meanings have changed in response to democratisation. Our main focus will be on Britain's legislative and consultative institutions, national and local. However, due to the arguments this book explores about the importance of civil society, and because civil organisations too were affected by many of the same influences, attention will also extend to this area. Readers familiar with these ideas may wish to skip to Chapter 1. On the other hand, the discussion may help reinforce and clarify some of the themes informing this book.

From a national standpoint, it is obvious but nevertheless important that the debate was always about the popularisation or democratisation of *representative government*. That is to say, it always concerned who and how many should participate in choosing persons to act as agents in the taking of governmental decisions; also from what social pool those agents should be drawn. The debate was never seriously about who should participate in some popular legislative assembly of citizens: *direct democracy* was never on the national agenda. This was so for both historical and practical reasons: Parliament from its thirteenth-century beginnings consisted of representative knights elected in county courts, and summoned by the King, to give the nation's consent to taxation necessary to his government. However, as even Rousseau implicitly understood, once any society grew beyond a few thousand adult inhabitants living in reasonable proximity to one another, Athenian styles of democracy became increasingly impracticable. Furthermore, the aristocratic and strongly top-down character of British (compared, say, to French or American) democratisation meant that even elements of direct democracy practised in other highly industrialised and urbanised polities, would be only minimally utilised. Successive French Republics and Empires might regularly consult (and manipulate) their citizens in referenda; citizens in western American states might regularly initiate polls on major policy-issues. Yet Britain's politicians have permitted a mere scattering of such exercises; always initiated by themselves and partly as a means of resolving their own internal divisions. These have most recently occurred in Northern Ireland in 1972 and 1998; in Scotland and Wales on devolution in 1978/9 and 1997; and about the Common Market in 1975.

Local representative government has also been a primary focus of democratising attention. Admittedly, vestries, ratepayers meetings and polls, as we shall see, were traditional and sometimes central parts of local decision-making into the early-nineteenth century. Indeed, this was one of several areas where change in representative directions might well involve decreases in popular input into local decision-making: replacing vestries by property-weighted elections to Boards of Guardians for example. Nevertheless, it was representative government that emerged as the main focus for popularising pressures: police commissions, boards of trustees, municipal councils, boards of guardians and unelected county magistrates. Quite aside from elite desires to control policy-making, this was necessarily so as urban society became ever more complex.

Civil organisations, being smaller in scale, and for a long time highly localised, were understandably far more attached to direct democracy, and able to resist pressures of the representative sort for far longer. This was one reason why, as argued later, they were crucial social underpinnings of the successful democratisation of the broader political system. Yet, in the longer run, indeed amongst the middle class in the far shorter term, civil society also succumbed to representativeness; doing so again under pressures of ever-growing size and complexity, and the perceived need to centralise.

We should also note that the concept of representation itself has had unstable, contested and changing meanings.[8] Some of the debates about democratisation centred upon *what* was being represented, *how*, and what the representative's *duties to the represented* should be. Versions of representativeness became bases from which democratisation could be resisted; others became the means through which it could be advanced on an ever-wider front. Some were also linked to broader disagreements, particularly within the political elite, about Parliament's proper role in relation to monarchy and government.

One thing that most aristocratic politicians agreed about, particularly in the early decades of what eventually became democratisation, was that MPs should represent '*communities*'. By this, they mostly meant identifiable, geographically-defined gatherings of residential people, normally with a simply definable economic interest, clear and legitimised hierarchies, and natural leaders. These might be parliamentary boroughs with clear social and economic leaders, or counties presided over by networks of landowners. Such considerations heavily influenced which boroughs were representationally retained, reduced or ejected during the debates over the 1832 Reform Act; they also helped determine which previously-unrepresented towns were selected or rejected for inclusion in both 1832 and 1867. They became the bases from which to resist claims from locations that, however populous or otherwise important, did not seem to possess clearly communal, and thus safely controllable and predictable, characteristics. Only in 1885, and in face of increasingly dramatic urban and suburban development, were such ideas formally and substantially abandoned, and shifted into the representation of individuals and even classes. Meanwhile, community also helped provide some indication of who should vote: those with some sort of 'stake' in the collectivity. For the most part, this meant property.

Community in turn was linked to a broader notion available to both Whigs and Tories: that of *virtual representation*. In fact it had several meanings, but in this context indicated that an MP, elected by, say, an agricultural constituency or a port, represented not just that constituency but all similar areas and interests across the country. This supposedly gave him clout within Parliament quite independent of the numbers of MPs from similar locations. It became the intellectual basis from which to resist both constituency-boundary reallocation on the basis of either population or economic importance, and any major franchise extension. On this argument, so long as some ports or industrial towns had constituencies, there was no need for all such places to be similarly fortunate. Furthermore, apparently under-represented industrial areas were argued to be politically strengthened by the ability of major industrialists to buy their way into the representation of some county constituencies. Meanwhile, the vast unenfranchised population amongst the urban and rural lower orders were alleged to be 'virtually represented' by MPs from constituencies where the franchise was relatively open, in particular by the scattering of 'pot-walloper', 'scot- and-lot', even some freemen seats. On the other hand, although primarily useful to those wishing to resist further popular inclusions, and when allied to perceptions of economic importance, virtual representation could also permit extending parliamentary representation to embrace some new interests created by industrial expansion: more representation for Lancashire cotton interests, for example, besides Preston and South Lancashire.

Notions that interest and community should be the primary bases for constituency formation gave virtual representation a second meaning, also resting upon a selective franchise, though available for radical as well as conservative exploitation. This was the idea that electors were themselves representative of those not possessing the vote: they were casting votes for wives and families; also for other male non-electors. This was a major justification for open voting: it should be public so that non-voters, who were part, if not yet full, citizens of the same community, should know what had been done partly on their behalf; and under what persuasive pressures. Obviously, this rendered voters susceptible to influences emanating from the top of the local hierarchy, whether of the deferential, intimidating, or financial and alcoholic sort. This was one reason why conservative Whigs and Tories became doubly resistant to the ballot once the removal of rotten and nomination boroughs had supposedly expunged the grosser forms of corruption from the otherwise acceptable 'politics of influence'. However, as we shall see, open voting was also a major factor rendering pre- and indeed post-1832 politics more open than immediately appeared the case. Notions of representational voting partly legitimised pressures emanating from below: allowing non-voters to express opinions about what should be done, by persuasive pressure on husbands, or rougher forms of inducement like 'exclusive dealing' with or against shopkeeping electors. Even the scattering of voters in corporation boroughs before 1832 probably felt obliged to cast their votes in representative ways, more particularly with eyes on the patronage sitting MPs were directing into the communities they supposedly governed.[9] This was why radicals felt decidedly ambivalent about the secret ballot in the absence of manhood suffrage: its effect might be to close the system to lower-class pressures of the sort attempted by the Chartists and others in the 1830s and 1840s. Even John Stuart Mill in 1861 could resist the ballot on the grounds that the vote was a trust to be 'exercised in the interest of the public', and that it provided opportunities for non-voters to train themselves politically by deliberating about what their voters should do.[10]

Nevertheless, if politics were to be reliably and legitimately opened to popular pressures, and before democratisation could become a conscious destination for those engaged in its management, the notion of what could justifiably be represented had to move beyond community and interest into that of individuals and thereby to manhood or universal suffrage. For radicals, two forms of justification were available: one deriving from notions of 'natural rights'; the other from individual self-interest.

For working-class radicals, and those who might be persuaded to follow them even at some danger to themselves (and later for many feminists), rights were necessarily more persuasive. Customary rights to succour had been a central part of the old paternalism; notions about just rewards for one's labour were important in the newly-emerging world of negotiation and contract. Rights were also more capable of arousing indignation about political exclusion, particularly when allied

to emerging ideas about labour standing at the base of wealth-produc-
tion. It was in this general context that Thomas Paine's *Rights of Man* had
so dramatic an effect on working-class perceptions, becoming in Edward
Thompson's words, 'the foundation-text of the English working-class
movement'.[11] This was as evident when agitation culminated in Chartism as it had been at the start. Central to the petition accompanying the
People's Charter to Parliament in 1838 was the claim that

> the universal political right of every human being is superior and
> stands apart from all customs forms or ancient usage: a fundamental
> right not in the power of man to confer or justly to deprive him
> of... to take away this right... is a wilful perversion of justice and
> common sense...[12]

Whatever their other disagreements, all Chartists agreed about this.
Unsurprisingly militants were determined 'to obtain our rights, peacefully if we can, forcibly if we must... by the pistol, the bullet, the pike
and the bayonet'.[13] Yet moderates like William Lovett, who believed
that moral improvement was the key to successful working-class political
inclusion, did so partly from indignation that 'a man should be deprived
of his rights on the plea of ignorance' whilst 'the knowledge requisite to
make a man acquainted with his rights and duties should be purposively
withheld from him'.[14]

Radicals somewhat closer to the political inside-track, particularly the
early utilitarians, ostensibly rejected notions of natural rights. For them,
and their primarily middle-class followers, the crucial facts were that
people were primarily motivated by self-interest, and that each adult
was likely to be the most accurate judge of that interest. In fact, even
utilitarian arguments for democracy could embrace, indeed might be
unable wholly to dispense with, ideas about rights since they held that
each individual's self-interest was equally worthy of consideration. What
justified legislation, aside from cheapness and efficiency, was its ability to
induce the greatest happiness for the greatest number of people. Given
all this, for many utilitarian radicals, the only way of ensuring that
legislators promoted general happiness, whilst ensuring their own, was
to elect and threaten to reject them by universal manhood suffrage. To
make doubly certain, Parliament should be subject to frequent election,
and the Commons rendered the only real point of decision-making.

Later utilitarians, notably John Stuart Mill, were more uncertain that
people were invariably expert judges of their own interests, more doubt-

ful about the equal worth of individual self-interest, and more persuadable that there might be public interests somewhat beyond the mere sum of perceived individual interests. Yet this brought them to a further argument for democracy, or at least for steadily widening democratisation. Democratic participation itself was educational and improving; if people could not fully or immediately judge where their interests lay, participation in choosing representatives could make them so. Indeed, it could maximise not just human happiness, but also the underlying well-being in terms of intellectual, practical and moral excellence.[15]

As these arguments became more dominant, and as individuals consequently acquired equal access at least to electoral politics by virtue of simple adulthood, the various versions of virtual representation became increasingly untenable. If individuals were politically equal, whether by natural right or respectability of self-interest, notions of proportionality had to inform how their numbers, if not their opinions, were represented. As was recognised in 1885, and confirmed in 1918, this meant granting the originally Chartist demand for equal electoral districts.

If community eventually succumbed to individuals as the primary basis of what should be represented, and if proportionality took over from virtuality as the dominant notion about how this should be done, the need to represent, or at least recognise, the *interests* those individuals saw themselves as having remained important in Britain as in other democratising polities. Defenders of the old system always accepted the need to represent broad, 'natural' interests, like agriculture, trade and industry, but were hostile to those conceived as specially organised and 'artificial'. Democratisation, along with accelerating socio-economic change, rendered such reservations practically and theoretically untenable. Indeed, the interests and causes demanding recognition became ever more complex. Franchise extension and changing attitudes by elected representatives could only partially accommodate such demands. Government itself had to expand the channels for more direct and less formal forms of representational access, thereby raising questions about the elected representative system.

Amongst the foregoing ideas, only the radical ones gave representatives, whether MPs, councillors, guardians, or civil-society officials, much indication about how to behave in relation to their 'constituencies'. In fact, there were at least two versions of the relationship, each having somewhat ambiguous connections with democratisation: they are broadly summarisable as *trusteeship*, and *delegation* or *spokesperson-*

ship. According to the first, MPs were selected and elected for their intelligence, judgement and experience and sent into the legislative chamber to exercise them on their constituents' or indeed nation's or town's behalf. Though voters might attempt to persuade, they had no right to demand that representatives vote accordingly if their judgements suggested otherwise. Edmund Burke's elegant disquisition to his presumably grateful Bristol constituents in 1774 seems the most appropriate description of the ideal:

> it ought to be the happiness and glory of the representative to live in the strictest union...with his constituents. Their wishes ought to have great weight with him; their opinion high respect.... It is his duty to sacrifice his repose...his satisfactions to theirs...But his unbiased opinion, his mature judgement, his enlightened conscience, he ought not to sacrifice to...any man living.

Burke was the pre-eminent Whig theorist of his age, and this view of the representational role was central to his party's view of the world, more particularly of Parliament, and its relationship with king and government. In this, Parliament, rather than the monarch, was the centre of power and authority: its role was to deliberate, and authoritatively decide upon the legislation laid before it. It did so on behalf of 'the nation' rather than any parochial part of it. In Whig eyes, Parliament was 'a deliberative assembly of one nation, with one interest, that of the whole'.[16] Members of such an august chamber could hardly be expected to take instructions from outside. However, though primarily Whig-originated, and continuingly persuasive to Whig governments into the early 1860s,[17] the role of representative as man of principle was (and continues to be) available to any MP wishing to justify departure from what the majority, or the most vociferous minority, within his constituency, or indeed his party, wished him to do. It was particularly attractive at any point, and in any legislative context, parliamentary or municipal, where party lines were hazy. Furthermore, though originally set within the context of a narrow franchise, and mostly hostile to outside pressure, it did not wholly exclude popular responsiveness since parliamentarians, or indeed civil organisational leaders, might well claim to be acting in the best interests of their constituents, even if the latter did not currently see things that way.

The polar opposite of trusteeship was delegation: representatives purveyed and acted in accordance with the opinions of their constituents, quite irrespective of their own views upon a given issue. This would seem to provide the basis for behaviour far more sympathetic to democratic conceptions of politics. However, spokesmanship was actually available for legitimisation in relation to at least two very different ideas about the political system, who was entitled to participate in it, and how much. Tories, who broadly accepted the governing and initiating role of monarchs and their governments, could see themselves as petitioners for the redress of hardship or grievance on their constituents' behalf: kings and/or governments made policy, MPs respectfully told them about the resultant pain. In so far as they required reasons beyond self-preservation, this role helped significant numbers of Tory MPs to respond to popular constituency anger at the Wellington Government's intransigence over franchise reform in 1830–1.

Though the original deferential view of Parliament's role has faded, and been replaced by theoretically more forthright conceptions of how MPs should behave in relation to government, spokesmanship has provided subsequent justification for many members over the decades. Certainly, it has assisted Conservative MPs and candidates keen to exploit grievances about immigration, whether produced by Irishmen in mid-Victorian decades, East European Jews between 1880 and 1914, Commonwealth blacks and browns since 1945, or suspect political refugees from everywhere in the 1990s.

Meanwhile, radicals of all kinds, in Britain and beyond, have posed as delegates for various versions of 'the people'. As this suggests, this version of spokesmanship arose within very different and more clearly democratic beliefs from those underpinning the Tory version: convictions that the people were sovereign, and representatives their agents. From this perspective, radical–Liberal MPs in the 1830s and 1840s held annual meetings with their electors and non-electors to account for their parliamentary behaviour over the past year; Lib–Lab members in the 1870s and 1880s did the same; numerous socialist and Labour aspirants for Parliament and council, particularly before 1914, claimed they 'would look upon themselves as delegates' or 'would go as a delegate not a dictator'.[18] Not merely were these sensible ways of exploiting the aspirations of previously excluded social groups; they also reflected the habits of working-class civil society. As we shall see, trade-union activists have regularly expected elected representatives to annual conferences to act as delegates of the districts sending them. This was a natural response to, indeed a *quid pro quo* for, the abandonment of direct democracy within such organisations.

If spokespersonship could increasingly only be accommodated within the context of a polity that was at least becoming democratic, one where people had a right to have their voices heard, this was even more clearly true of two other associated versions of representation. These also presupposed the importance for representative purposes of certain sorts of social identity. They may most appropriately be labelled *direct* and *symbolic representation*. Notions of direct representation became bases from which to argue that social groups, particularly those recently politically admitted, or who felt themselves somehow socially excluded, had a right to a level of legislative representation roughly commensurate with their numbers in the population and the electorate. Admittedly, the extended failure of middle-class males to enter Parliament in large numbers after 1832, whilst puzzling to later historians, did not seem to greatly exercise a predominantly middle-class electorate, aside from a scattering of radicals. This was due to a mix of political expense, deference, massive representation on municipal councils, and the coincidence of aristocratic and middle-class interests over economic policy. Working-class activists, on the other hand, were more troubled, at least up to 1918. The right to 'direct working-class representation', the notion that only working men could truly understand and communicate the interests of their social kind, became a central factor fuelling the rise of 'Lib–Labs' in Parliament and municipal councils after 1870, and the Labour Party after 1900. It also informed pressure for the emergence of 'working-men's committees' as part of the policy-making apparatus of local charitable hospitals around the same period. Similarly, and more recently, feminists have measured women's democratic success, especially since 1918, by their representation in parliament, councils, trade unions, and amongst the upper echelons of the civil service and business. Similar expectations have emerged amongst Afro-Caribbean and Asian activists since 1945. As we shall see, symbolic representation links into notions of full citizenship, since it has been taken as a mark of recognised incorporation into the community.

Notions of direct representation merge seamlessly into those about symbolism. The demand is not for representation proportionate to numbers, nor really even about power and the ability to defend or advance groups' interests; rather it is for recognition of status and importance within the broader community. A society and its institutions is deemed to democratise to the extent to which this is granted. One of the implications of later chapters is that this sort of claim, at least in Britain, has been just as important to groups seeking entry as has access to power. Claims for the vote, whether by middle- or working-class men or by women, have been partly claims for recognition. Claims for 'direct representation', whether in political or civil bodies, concerned status as well as interest. Representation on municipal councils, particularly given the mass visibility available to social and political leaders in nineteenth-century towns, was capable of satisfying both. More obviously, claims for symbolic representation have focused upon ceremony and ritual: the presence of representatives of a social group, or its civil organisations, at royal garden parties and in civic processions. Moreover, as we shall also see, some of the most intense claims have focused upon the mayoralty itself – its ceremonial occasions, and even more whether representatives of a group or party (particularly the Labour Party) are allowed to occupy the mayoral chair, thereby 'establishing its (and its followers) prestige in the public life of the borough'.[19] One factor underpinning the success of British democratisation, it is argued, has been the ability of the system at all levels both to elevate and satisfy such symbolic representational claims.

At this point, ideas about representation connect with those about another concept that I argue is highly important at least to the British version of democratisation: that of *citizenship*. Implied in claims for the vote by all social groups were demands for their formal recognition as full members of the community. Like the other ideas under review here, the expected content of citizenship has changed over time, and the idea has been used to make various claims to share in communal resources. However, the implication of much that follows in later chapters is that this content was for a long time heavily circumscribed. Indeed, this was an important potential reason for the success of British democratisation, or at least for the relative ease with which it was undertaken and its consequences adjusted to.

We can most conveniently explore this area by drawing on the ideas of T.H. Marshall, perhaps the most influential post-war writer on citizenship. Writing, or rather lecturing, in 1949, in the midst of a socially-reforming Labour government, Marshall's arguments started from two premises. The first was that there was potential incompatibility between citizenship and class inequality. There was always the possibility that social deprivation might come to be perceived as rendering impossible the effective performance of citizens' duties and the enjoyment of their rights. The second was that, as a result, citizenship was likely to be an evolving concept whose content changed according to evolving social and economic conditions.

These ideas flowed naturally from the way Marshall defined citizenship:

> a status bestowed on those who are full members of a community. All
> who possess the status are equal with respect to the rights and duties
> with which the status is endowed. There is no universal principle that
> determines what those rights and duties shall be, but societies in
> which citizenship is a developing institution create an image of an
> ideal citizenship against which achievement can be measured and
> towards which aspiration can be directed.[20]

It consisted of individual rights and duties in civil, political and social
areas. In pre-industrial, pre-capitalist societies, these were combined
indivisibly. People existed in hierarchical communities wherein the
rights and duties of the rich to the poor, and vice versa, were defined,
accepted and reciprocal. However, capitalisation and industrialisation
caused these strands to separate and, though Marshall does not explicitly say so, the radical curtailment of the social strand as the hierarchy
underpinning social obligation eroded. The notion of mutual social
obligation received its death-blow with the emergence of the New
Poor Law in 1834, and the consequent destruction of mutuality's final
expression in the form of the 1794 Speenhamland System. Thereafter,
the three strands evolved at different rates. In Britain, the seventeenth
and eighteenth centuries saw the establishment of universally available
civil rights, starting with Habeas Corpus and extending to equality
before the law and liberal freedoms in the decades around the late-
eighteenth, early-nineteenth century. The main business of the latter
century, however, was the extension of the political rights of citizenship.
This happened initially via the replacement of voting qualifications
resting upon inheritance and/or conferment (freemen and scot- and-
lot qualifications for example) with purely economic criteria which could
be acquired by anyone able to efficiently exercise their newly-acquired
civil rights. This started with the £10 householder qualification in 1832
which was then lowered to simple householder status in 1867 and 1884.
   The problem, according to Marshall, was that class inequality could
render the effective exercise of civil rights impossible. Moreover, the
New Poor Law, if resorted to, could threaten even these. Only slowly did
the state begin to reinvigorate social rights. This started indirectly with
the 1870 Education Act and the safeguarding of trade-union rights in
1871 and 1875. These latter Acts reinforced the viability of working-

class civil rights by enabling their collective use to achieve economic ends, and thereby a measure of social improvement. Then, from 1906, and following revelations from the Booth reports about the extent of social deprivation and the impossibility of alleviating this through individual civil effort, government began involving itself directly in the expansion of social rights. Thereby, citizenship began shifting to a set of material expectations, and the demand that at least some of its social aspects should be guaranteed by the state.

Marshall's ideas are one way of seeing democratisation. They also have clear links with arguments about its character and success that will be set down in later chapters. They provide another vantage-point on the view that democratisation is a multifaceted phenomenon; as much social as political. More importantly, they enable us to reinforce our assertions about the democratic functionality of low mass-expectations while democratisation was taking place. To put our argument in Marshall's language, in Britain, the reconnection of the social with the civil and political strands of citizenship occurred remarkably slowly in the popular mind. Citizenship was central to demands from all groups claiming inclusion, but for most of the democratising period it remained civil and political. Social class and citizenship did not come to be widely seen as incompatible until after 1918, at least by those most visited by the contradiction. This left managing the remedy in the hands of the elite, spurred on by the likes of New Liberalism and social democracy. Perhaps only as the Welfare State began creating its own client-groups did assertions of entitlement to the social rights of citizenship begin welling up from below.

Yet Marshall also misses what was most important about the role citizenship played in the claims made by those seeking entry to the political system. What they demanded was certainly partly social, but less for its content in terms of rights and duties, more for its importance as a status category. Male suffrage organisations, and for a long time those of women also, sought recognition as full members of the community, for its own sake, rather than because it gave access to channels for the making of demands for social rights.

1 The Old System

We start at the beginning by exploring the most obvious features of the undemocratised system – its closed and oligarchic characteristics, reinforced by an apparently undemanding political culture. We will then examine the implications of more recent research, suggesting a more popular and responsive side to both system and culture. Though massively advantaging the topmost socio-economic ranks, particularly if elevation rested upon landed property and heredity, the pre-1832 system contained points where other groups, even lowly ones, could achieve access and gain recognition for their needs and feelings. This is doubly evident if less formal channels of transmission, those involving 'the moral economy', are considered; still more if allowance is made for the crucial local governmental sector. These aspects are important to understanding why the old system was so extendedly tolerated in spite of accelerating socio-economic change; how demands for its popularisation eventually found effective expression; and how a degree of popularisation became supportable – both in terms of elite responsiveness and popular capacity for participation.

1. A Closed System?

The old system was in many respects closed and, from the end of the Civil War until the late-eighteenth century, there were few who thought it should be otherwise. Indeed, in some ways, the eighteenth century saw its further closure – due partly to deliberately engineered legislative change; and partly to the stability of electoral boundaries and qualifications in face of accelerating economic and demographic transformation.

The facts are well-known. Borough electoral qualifications were admittedly intensely varied and sometimes 'open' to the point of embracing most adult males, as in the scot-and-lot, potwalloper and some freemen constituencies for example. However, they were mostly narrowly drawn – sometimes embracing no more than self-elected corporations, or certain types of property-owner. Consequently, the electorate was small and, though increasing, its ratio to rapidly rising population was worsening. In 1754, England and Wales had an estimated 282 000 voters, constituting 1 in 23 of the population, 1 in 10 males, and 1 in 6 male adults, ratios that were already worsening. By 1831, while the electorate had risen by approximately 20 per cent and has been calculated at 366 000, the population had doubled to render enfranchised only 1 in 38 of the total, 1 in 18.5 males and approximately 1 in 8.5 male adults.[1] Voters were lonelier still in Ireland: Catholics were permitted to vote under the 1801 Act of Union, just as before, but in no great numbers. Furthermore, removing the forty-shilling freehold qualification in order to counter-weight Catholic Emancipation in 1829 had decimated voters in some counties. It had also reduced the overall electorate to less than 1 per cent (c60 000) of the population.[2] Scotland's population was still worse represented: even by the mid-eighteenth century, against England's 1 in 10, Scottish voters represented only 1 in 100 of the male population; by 1831, this had fallen to around 1 in 250. One reason was the narrow character of most Scottish constituencies: Edinburgh's 162 000 people were represented by just thirty-three corporate voters electing one MP.

Representation was also spectacularly out of kilter with the geographical spread of population and to a somewhat lesser extent wealth. In 1700, most substantial towns had constituencies;[3] by 1800, many did not. Whilst England's population was shifting northwards and towards larger towns, most parliamentary seats were concentrated amongst small southern communities. Many substantial industrial towns, including Leeds, Birmingham, Manchester and most Lancashire cotton towns, were represented only through their respective counties. Irish constituencies and constituency boundaries had been deliberately designed in 1801 politically to neutralise the Catholic majority. To use American terminology, parliamentary representation was massively malapportioned. In 1801, Cornwall and Lancashire both contained around 192 000 people, but were represented by 44 and just 14 MPs respectively. In the same year, the six southernmost counties possessed one-third of English borough and county MPs but just 15 per cent of the population. The system's defenders pointed to notions of 'virtual representation' to justify this situation, arguing that most interests, whatever their size or economic importance, were represented in some way. Yet, even in these terms, small primarily rural communities did far better than large industrial ones: Lancashire's textile interests and towns were virtually represented only by Preston and the two county MPs. In Scotland, obscure centres like Inverury, Kintore and Rothesay each sent one MP, whilst Greenock, Leith, Paisley and Port Glasgow had no separate representation. All these mismatches, moreover, were rapidly intensifying under pressure from industrialisation and urbanisation. By 1831, Cornwall's 44 MPs represented 301 000 people whilst Lancashire's 14 provided political expression for 1 337 000.

A fundamental problem was that most constituency boundaries had remained unchanged for centuries. There were facilities for representational inclusion and exclusion, but they were cumbersome and used rarely. Of the 202 English boroughs, 125 had been established under Edward 1. Virtually nowhere had been added, in spite of accelerating demographic change, since Newark and Durham in the 1670s. Many borough constituencies were consequently tiny, even though still possessing two MPs; some had 'rotted' to the point of becoming wholly population-liberated, either by demographic change or coastal erosion.

These boroughs were merely extreme examples of a much more general phenomenon – the many that were effectively in the 'pocket' and thus the gift of one or more wealthy men, or occasionally women. Most forms of borough franchise advantaged property, particularly the landed sort. The results were intensified by the fact that many boroughs were themselves effectively species of property – to be bought, sold, and especially enjoyed, by proprietors able to determine who was nominated and, in the absence of contest, thereby elected. This was evident not merely in reality (around 270 MPs represented such constituencies) but also in perception. The latter helps explain the determination of some parliamentary opposition to the Reform Bill, and indeed the shape the Act ultimately took: both deriving partly from the need to negotiate with borough-owners, genuinely outraged at the prospective uncompensated loss of property.

As already suggested, this phenomenon rested partly upon the smallness of many borough electorates. This was evident everywhere, though particularly in Ireland, and even more in Scotland where the average constituency, closed though rarely rotten, boasted just 100 mostly amenable electors. However, some proprietary seats were quite large; amongst the counties, decidedly so. This is particularly evident if we include seats shared, and sometimes squabbled over, by several patrons.

In fact, few constituencies, large or small, were wholly immune from influence of some sort. This betokens the further fact that the predominant force at play amongst unreformed voters, in many places and for long periods, was not political opinion at all, at least not in the first instance. Across the country, but again particularly in Scotland and Ireland, many electors did not see their votes as expressions of opinion about issues. Rather they were vehicles for expressing deference to local landowners upon whom they depended in various ways, or market commodities for which, like any other, reasonable returns could be expected in money, inebriation or other largesse. In fact, as we shall see, what are often called the 'politics of influence' and 'market' were not polar opposites; nor wholly separable from the 'politics of opinion'; rather they constituted a graduated continuum. Nevertheless, what we now see as corruption, though contemporaries only sometimes did, was immensely widespread. It rested upon voting's open character, the absence of effective preventative legislation, and the lack of desire to produce any. Underlying all this, as argued in Chapter 8, was the whole character of British state and society at almost all levels well into the nineteenth century. The system might be insulated from popular opinion, but its underpinnings were not without widespread popular consent.

Politics was further insulated by another, and connected, feature: the fact that at every election, many borough and county constituencies were uncontested; indeed could remain so for decades. Patrons decided who should be nominated, and were sufficiently influential to ensure no one else was. Alternatively, rival patrons and/or parties agreed to divide representation amongst themselves – continuing to do so during successive elections – such that voters, whether few or many, were never called to exercise choice. In 1761, only four English counties and 42 boroughs were actually contested.

Given all this, it is unsurprising that Parliament's traditional hostility towards pressure from 'artificial' special interests remained intense. These were regarded as illegitimate interferences with its proper deliberative functions, functions that were 'representative' in the narrow, if important, sense that MPs were elected to exercise on their constituents' behalf their independent judgements about the issues of the day. Parliament might be the nation's 'cockpit', but this rarely permitted susceptibility to organised pressure from groups of like-minded people. Such attitudes reinforced parliamentary resistance to reform agitation. Not all pressure was suspect. 'Naturally-occurring' interests were regarded more benevolently, but the category was restrictive (to those of Anglicanism, land, trade and eventually manufacturing), and mostly enhanced the agenda, and other, control already enjoyed by substantial property.

Overall, Britain's pre-Reform electoral and legislative politics often seemed remarkably torpid, providing enormous in-built advantages to men, and occasionally women, of wealth. In particular, these advantages accrued to the ruling landed oligarchy, around whose interests the system had been snugly fitted since 1688, and upon whose estates, wealth and command of patronage and dependency so much of it rested. The system also provided considerable advantage to government. Not merely were there several naval and military constituencies under its effective control, but also rather more whose patrons had sufficient access to government patronage to lend it dependable loyalty. Most of Scotland's 45 MPs, for example, had seats of this kind.

Furthermore, during the century up to 1832, the system seemed to be closing still further. Party division, the only real contest-generator, was declining from the 1730s until at least the 1780s, for many commentators until at least the 1810s. Partly in consequence, numbers of uncontested seats appeared to be increasing: more and more of the system apparently operated quite autonomously of the electorate. For example, Cheshire, having been contested in 8 of 10 elections between 1701 and 1734, thereafter remained torpid until 1832. Nottinghamshire's forty-shilling freeholders slept peacefully for 110 years from 1722; Gloucestershire's were woken just once after 1734; 65 per cent of county constituencies were contested in 1705; just 7.5 per cent in 1747. In the 1826 election, just 500 of the 25 000 Welsh electors were given an airing, and none in Scotland.[4] Primarily impelled by a Whig majority bent on self-perpetuation, Parliament itself enhanced the oligarchic and wealth-advantaging trend by insisting on property-qualifications for MPs in 1711, and by increasing the maximum interval between elections from three to seven years in the 1716 Septennial Act. It had also opened voting to even more pressure by facilitating the publication of ballot books in 1688.

2. The Entry Points

However, to portray the world of power and politics as wholly insulated from the surrounding society would be inaccurate. The traditional politically-enclosed picture has been seriously challenged by several historians.[5] Furthermore, to fully understand the exercise of power and influence in any society, particularly one wherein government, especially central government, had so limited a role, we must venture beyond the conventionally political. We have to examine the local as well as the national picture, and the world of moral as well as political economy. What emerges is not remotely democratic or even popular; nor were power and advantage other than extremely unequal. Yet, it is clear that Britain's social, economic and political elites, even before 1832, could never wholly insulate themselves from the needs, problems and emotions of the surrounding society. Nor, by many contemporary standards, did they seriously try. There were entry points, of both a political and non-political sort, even for lowly economic groups. Indeed, this was one reason why change was possible in 1832.

One important conditioning fact is that, for all its venality, Britain's was a constitutional and political system wherein state and central government's actions were heavily circumscribed. Both were limited by liberal traditions enshrined by the Glorious Revolution and later by *laissez faire*. After 1688, the 1689 Bill of Rights and subsequently emerging political practices, citizens were generally guaranteed legal equality and freedom from at least the cruder forms of arbitrary arrest. Government and taxation mostly rested upon some form of consent, doubly so because Parliament sat annually and elections, however manipulated, were held regularly (at least triennially after 1694 and at least septennially after 1716). Although their civil rights remained truncated until 1828, Protestant dissenters could worship freely. Even before 1829, Catholics were not actively prevented from church-attendance. Though government and law looked more authoritarian the further down the social scale one was located, even there, the system never lost a certain basic liberalism. Even at the post-Napoleonic height of repression, the application of the Six Acts and anti-Combination Laws lacked efficiency, resources and consistency. In spite of authoritarianism from police and judiciary, many working-class radicals benefited from the obstinacy and liberalism of juries. Careful hand-picking was required if they were to convict political dissenters for blasphemous libel or high treason. Judges might be deeply conservative, but never quite forgot the obligation of due process. The Whigs believed they derived ideological legitimacy from liberal freedoms. Tory governments might produce special justifications for 'suspending' them – by virtue of national danger or threat to what passed for the constitution. However, particularly after the 'Six Acts' were repealed, there was widespread agreement that circumstances had to be very special indeed.

Ultimately, the state had neither the determination, ambition nor effectiveness to suppress even working-class civil organisations. Indeed, in important respects as we shall see, it was increasingly eager to encourage them. Nor, its spy network notwithstanding, was government sufficiently repressive or troublesome to propel such organisations into authoritarian behaviour, attitudes, or even modes of self-governance.[6] Effective authoritarian and totalitarian regimes may be unable wholly to suppress civil society. However, they tend to push what they cannot suppress into attitudes and aspirations very similar to their own, if only from self-defence, and this necessarily affects the alternatives that are possible when those regimes fall.

As the foregoing jury behaviour suggests, all this was underpinned by the fact that liberal values commanded extensive and increasing consent amongst most people. This might not stop them periodically thumping Catholics. Nevertheless most would have assented to the bundle of values associated with notions about the 'free-born Englishman', either actively as part of broad-ranging popular radicalism, or as more passive and inarticulate opposition to governmental invasions of perceived interest. This was reinforced as such ideas increasingly came to be associated with national identity, and Britons' sense of superiority over most foreigners. Overall, what became British democracy was preceded and facilitated by a system that was limited, and fairly rapidly becoming liberal.

We should also note that, contrary to radical propaganda in 1830–1, electoral and parliamentary politics before 1832 did not exclude the middle classes, even urban ones. Ironically, given the propaganda, wealthy merchants and occasional manufacturers could enter parliament by purchasing closed boroughs. Middling-order males were the dominant segments amongst most constituency electorates. Taken overall, the pre-1832 electorate has been estimated to comprise 13.6 per cent gentry and professionals; 5.8 per cent merchants and manufacturers; 20.5 per cent retailers; 39.5 per cent skilled craftsmen; 14.2 per cent semi-skilled workers, and 6.4 per cent in agricultural occupations.[7] Indeed, it was revolt by these groups that thrust Reform to the centre of the 1830 and 1832 general elections in many constituencies, thus persuasively alarming many within the traditional elite.

Even the electorate's apparent decline proportionate to rising population may be misleading. Frank O'Gorman has argued persuasively that most estimates of the pre-1832 electorate in England and Wales have been based upon turnout rather than numbers on the electoral rolls, and that the real figures should be increased by around 20 per cent: for example, to 439 200 in 1832 rather than 366 000. Indeed, the pre-Reform electorate was expanding rapidly and kept pace with rising population at least as well as its post-1832 counterpart. He also suggests the electorate's composition reflected economic and industrial change: the coming and going of different occupational groups were registered, as were 'most of the important social and economic realities of the (eighteenth-century) period'. This included a large rurally-based elite, many professionals, large numbers of craftsmen and artisans, and a large retail sector.[8] The electorate also reached well down the social structure, even if not to the bottom, or proportionate to numbers in the population. Indeed, the interests of manual workers emerged strongly in open boroughs like Preston, Westminster and Bristol. They could also pressurise or terrorise more restricted electorates elsewhere when so minded. The argument for the 'virtual representation' of such groups was not unpersuasive.

Britain's was a very mixed representative system. Whilst containing many small boroughs, apparently closed and representing little, there were also significant numbers where scot-and-lot, potwalloper or even freeman franchises involved virtual manhood suffrage, even if not necessarily rendering them democratic or open. Seven English boroughs had over 5000 voters in 1830; 36 had electorates of 1–5000. Admittedly, these voters were often dedicatedly venal. Yet, they also provided channels for lower-class discontent – as radical candidates demonstrated at Westminster in 1807 and Preston in 1831.

Furthermore, the forty-shilling freeholder franchise in the counties, because of declining money values since its inception in 1430, embraced a wide social range. It could include many modest shopkeepers, artisans and small farmers, along with more elevated male persons. County electorates could thus also be very large. Admittedly, this hardly rendered them democratic in any normal sense: many small freeholders were fairly docile dependants of landholding interests. Electorate size was also manipulable. Often being attached to very small property, forty-shilling freeholds could easily be created by buying land and parcelling it into 'faggot' freeholds with obedient nominal owners. Yet even this dubious facility, unchanged in 1832, was a potential access-point for interest representation, as the Anti-Corn Law League later discovered. Furthermore, many entirely unmanipulated freeholders were urban dwellers, thus providing input into some county electorates for otherwise under-represented urban-industrial interests. This fact was dramatically demonstrated in Yorkshire's 1830 election where manufacturing interests led by Edward Baines elected Henry Brougham against the established Whig squirearchy. Overall, county electorates were too large to be easily controllable.

These more open constituencies were a minority. However, their clout was somewhat reinforced by the notion of 'virtual representation'. This widely-used term had varied meanings, but three implications are particularly relevant: first, voters, whether numerous or few, voted not just for themselves but on behalf of those not qualified; second, MPs represented the whole of their communities, not just the immediate electorate; third, any given constituency was representative of others of the same type – ports, industrial towns and so on. As already noted, the notion was often used to resist calls for electoral reapportionment or expanded enfranchisement, and was thus partly a useful myth for protecting over-represented vested interests. Nevertheless, it had some impact on how MPs behaved, and the influence those from popular constituencies could have on those from narrower ones. This was heightened somewhat by weak party discipline before 1832, and the opportunities thus presented for independent behaviour. Virtual representation also legitimised the various pressures non-voters could levy upon voters.

In fact, the pre-Reform system could deliver significant satisfactions and outlets to quite large numbers, and wide varieties, of people – to some degree via legislation, perhaps even more through less formal if still political channels. In legislative terms, much of the *laissez faire* state – the demolition of Elizabethan regulations over labour mobility, apprenticeship, internal trade and so on – was delivered by Parliament to the middle class before rather than after 1832. This was partly because commercial, industrial and landed interests coincided over substantial policy areas – after all, many substantial and titled landowners were, and remained, substantial capitalists, albeit often of a rather passive, *rentier* kind. However, it also rested upon the 'virtual' aspects of representation outlined above. Similar factors also facilitated parliamentary and governmental responses to popular pressure to abolish the African slave trade between 1787 and 1807. According to J.R.Oldfield, this was a tribute to 'the increasingly powerful role of the middle classes in influencing Parliamentary politics from outside ... Westminster'.[9] Government also responded to later agitation to partially abolish Nonconformist and Catholic civil disabilities in 1828–9.

This points to a more general feature of pre-1832 politics – the fact that, for all its insistence upon independence, there were legitimised ways whereby Parliament could be externally pressurised. Nick Rogers has argued that 'instructions' from constituencies to MPs about current issues of local and national concern were quite frequently issued in the century before Reform. There was some quite widespread sense that members were bound at least to listen to these, and electors entitled to issue them. Moreover, though sometimes acting at borough patrons' behest, electors were also quite often free agents, instructions most frequently emerging from constituencies with large popular electorates. Such pressures often related to local grievances. They also focused upon broader issues like foreign policy or political reform, with complaints about electoral and parliamentary corruption, or pressures to remove government placemen from the Commons, or repeal the Septennial Act.[10]

Unsurprisingly, manual workers did least well here. They were after all the victims of the demolition of state-regulated paternalism, and this greatly contributed to their discontent in 1830–1. Yet it is indicative of the limited but significant representativeness of the system that, in the decades up to 1832, various manual occupational groups felt it worth petitioning Parliament for the preservation or reinstatement of particular sorts of regulation. It is also significant that parliamentarians were prepared to receive and extensively debate such petitions, even if rejection was predetermined. Refusal produced anger, but the willingness to formally entertain probably helped retain popular legitimacy for the system, ensuring Parliament's continuing role as the ultimate target for working-class radical aspiration.

The point should not be over-emphasised. There were very significant limits to the outside pressure the system could entertain. Two facilities were crucially absent. First, the ability to prevent unpopular measures being passed by incumbent governments. Administrations would occasionally change course, but only – as with the 1732 Excise Crisis – after what Rogers has called 'incredible popular pressure'.[11] Second, and underpinning this first constraint, unpopular governments could rarely be unseated via elections. Ministerial, parliamentary and electoral patronage was generally too strong, and there were too many seats wherein narrow franchises or influence-based political culture rendered public opinion irrelevant. Only system-threatening crises of the sort evident during 1830–1 could enable dissatisfaction to break through to this extent.

However, the system was also responsive in other ways. Many satisfactions available from politics before, and long-continuingly after, 1832 were of a less formal, non-legislative sort. Two points are important here. First, long before 1832, elections were undoubtedly popular. They were occasions of much intensely enjoyable public ritual: the ceremonial entry of the candidates to the constituency, the hustings, 'chairing' the victor round the town at the end. They often embraced, no matter how narrow the constituency, much of the population: non-electors equally with electors; men as well as women; and drawing on a mix of official culture generated from above and vibrant folk culture generated from below. This was a culture wherein, significantly for the democratic future, all apparently thought they had rights to participate.[12] Second, contrary to what earlier historians have sometimes assumed,[13] there was no clear division between politics based upon deference and those resting on bribery or opinion. Rather the three forms of political behaviour, and the responses required from elites, were deeply intermingled. The satisfactions also arguably rested upon an uncertain dividing-line between political and non-political life – in that they were often delivered through philanthropic, non-political or at least non-governmental means.

For a start, as Frank O'Gorman argues, the widespread deference upon which so much pre-1832 politics depended was never unconditional, but always in varying degrees 'negotiated'. The relationship between patron and voters, still more non-voters, was admittedly unequal. However, it was normally reciprocal: honour and deference being given in return for support and aid. This was one reason why politics, even in uncontested seats, and even in narrow constituencies, was so expensive, a game only for rich men. Only these could afford the largesse electors, even non-electors, expected. Crucially, these anticipations related not just to elections where patronage could easily slither into outright bribery, but the long periods in between. Thus they could embrace not just money and drink, but also charitable donations, government jobs for the genteel poor, public works and civic buildings. This was a key reason why few boroughs, even closed ones, were owned with total security. Voters, however few, might always take their deferential favours elsewhere.

For O'Gorman, it was unimportant that pre-1832 electorates were often tiny, or seats uncontested, sometimes for decades. Corporations, in boroughs where they were the only voters, even where they were self-perpetuating rather than elected, saw themselves as negotiating with patrons for largesse on their town's behalf. Moreover, in these, as in other sorts of constituency, non-contest signified satisfaction with the terms of deference. Threatened contests, particularly in counties, indicated dissatisfaction. Unhappiness could be resolved either by successful renegotiation with existing patrons and consequent withdrawal of threatened opposition, or by pushing into electoral contest and possible transfer to some rival patron offering better terms. Elections therefore became periodic means of checking sufficient paternalism was being delivered in return for deference and pocket-behaviour.[14] In a world where government did little, and was rarely expected to do more, some satisfactions now available through government aid were often delivered through private channels, even if still negotiated through electoral politics. This was evident not just on the mainland, but also in Ireland. The Dukes of Devonshire's political influence over the five southern Irish boroughs where they were dominant landowners was never secure even when actively attempted. This was in spite of extensive and long-continuing expenditure on urban improvement.[15]

The system was capable of even less formal, and less political, responses during crisis. Several historians have argued that the conditionality of deference was evident most of the way down the social structure. Since George Rudé's work in the 1960s, riots are widely accepted as regular features of social life before 1800, drawing upon the unruly services of women as well as men. Rudé was primarily interested in those interpretable in 'proto-radical' terms, most notably food riots. More recent research has revealed or confirmed that many were jingoistic, directed against out-groups like Catholics or Dissenters, strongly ritualistic, or just paid-for. Nevertheless, protest was clearly one theme underpinning social disturbance – particularly about food prices and threats to 'customary wages'. This was linked to popular attachments to 'moral economy', the notion that there existed basic rights to sustenance, or at least subsistence, which elites were obliged to recognise. Furthermore, authority-responses, expressed by local magistrates, showed elites at least partially accepted these obligations. Faced by disturbance, justices often intervened to reimpose 'just' prices or customary wages. To suggest this amounted to 'collective bargaining by riot' may be anachronistic since such judicial actions rested not just on fear, but also consensus about the terms of social hierarchy. And the rewards were as likely to be ritualistic as material. None the less, the terms were clearly somewhat negotiable.[16]

If such arguments have validity, it suggests that what emerged as democratisation got under way was not so much negotiation *per se*, as its formalisation, institutionalisation and, much more tardily, its linkage to governmental, rather than patron-supplied, aid. What also shifted was the framework within which negotiation took place: a shift from paternalism to something more egalitarian and certainly contractual.

If there was no clear boundary between the politics of influence and those of private inducement, borderlines between the latter and opinion-politics also seem hazy in the light of recent research. Many historians have seen bribery as resting upon a distinctive political culture where opinions about issues were irrelevant. For venal electors, votes were simply saleable commodities. Tom Nossiter, writing about post-Reform politics but with equal relevance to the pre-1832 period, saw widespread bribery as characteristic of small-town communities wherein money-making opportunities were limited.[17] More recent research suggests that, at least in the early nineteenth century, many electors saw money and alcohol as inducements to turn out and vote for candidates towards whom conviction already inclined them. John Phillips uncovered widespread and consistent party voting in popular constituencies at elections from at least 1818, sometimes greatly intensifying in the post-Reform years. He also found quite extensive discussion of issues. Yet this co-existed with widespread corruption, suggesting few minds were actually changed by such inducement.[18]

In fact, political opinion, laced by bribery or not, had a substantial history. Whilst Namierite historians of the eighteenth century emphasised the patronage-based, non-ideological and elite-dominated character of politics, it has become evident that, inter-laced amongst these undoubted features, were substantial elements of opinion-based behaviour. During the eighteenth century, as already implied by the constituency instructions to MPs mentioned earlier, events and policies intermittently emerged capable of arousing intense expressions of popular opinion from a wide social spectrum including tradesmen and artisans. These particularly focused on the elective and representative institutions of the City of London, the Common Hall and Council. They also sometimes extended to other cities like Bristol, Norwich, Coventry, Edinburgh and York. They were particularly potent when exploited by Tory sections of the political elite in opposition to the ruling Whigs. Thus the 1720s financial scandals, the successful campaign against the Excise in 1732, the Spanish Convention in 1739, the events leading to Walpole's resignation in February 1742, and the 1756 Minorca crisis all attracted significant popular agitation capable of influencing events. Important also as commentary upon and reinforcer of popular political culture was the way Whig governments attempted to deal with the attacks upon them produced by these crises – 'playing the liberty card', and posing as the only available bulwark of English freedoms against Jacobite restoration.[19]

There is evidence that party voting particularly, and opinion-based political behaviour generally, were intensifying in the decades before

1832. Underpinning this was significant social 'modernisation' – evident partly in spreading communications networks, particularly newspapers; partly in the emergent middle classes who formed the primary market for such communications; partly in the developing civil society reviewed in later chapters; and partly in accelerating social change. In particular, substantial population movement occurring at most social levels, throughout the eighteenth century, was destabilising traditional social ties. Most probably moved in search of better prospects, thus suggesting more calculative, less fatalistic views of life. Transposed into politics, this might imply more conditional attitudes to authority, particularly because migration inevitably involved breaking traditional ties and networks. Even more was this so because migration was associated with expanding urbanisation and industrialisation. This entailed increasing complexities of economic, political and social interest and identity.

Important here was class. Admittedly, it rarely affected how people voted. This was unsurprising since the two party elites were indistinguishable in social terms, and deeply bound to the *status quo,* and voters were predominantly middling-class. Even though individual politicians might eventually try to exploit social grievances, party leaders were primarily concerned to neutralise social class if only from self-preservation. Nevertheless, emergent class-division, whether disguised and tempered by inclusive populism or not, undoubtedly helped erode deference. It also became an important focus for the development of civil organisations of economic, social and political kinds, most relevantly around the issue of Reform. Equally significant in fuelling independent political behaviour, and giving content to opinion, was religion. Contemporaries certainly thought so, widely testifying to links between Dissent and Whig electoral support. This is rarely quantitatively testable due to problems of identifying voters' religious allegiances. However, where information is available, the link at least between Nonconformity and Whiggism seems strong.[20]

As already implied, Reform itself intensified trends towards opinion both amongst voters, and those angry about their political exclusion. It re-emerged as an extra-parliamentary issue for the first time since the Civil War in the 1768 election, with John Wilkes' return for Middlesex, and the agitation surrounding his subsequent removal. Subsequently, Reform made intermittent progress. It re-emerged in 1774, again during the 1780s, achieving a working-class edge in the 1790s. During the Napoleonic wars, the issue faded, but then re-emerged in 1815. Thereafter, it enjoyed a fairly direct if inverse relationship with the economic cycle. As a result, magnates found it steadily harder to control their electorates in the decade before 1832. Reform was significant in the 1830 Election when most established borough interests became insecure, even more in that of 1831.[21] The issue even penetrated the inebriated haze of very venal constituencies, and otherwise hostile MPs found reformist discretion the better part of valour. It was crucial even in popular constituencies like Bristol whose voters could gain nothing, and even lose something, from extended enfranchisement.[22]

Thus far, we have concentrated primarily upon constituencies. However, local governments, at least in urban areas, clearly also provided focuses for opinion-politics, and channels for their effective expression. As already evident with the City of London, this was partly because local governments were important points where opinions about parliamentary politics could be articulated and transmitted, and were to remain so throughout the century. However, equally relevant was the fact that, in a world where the centre's role was decidedly limited, local government was the focus of considerable decisional power. It was thus a point where interests of many sorts could develop and be expressed. Here, of course, the key date was not 1832 but 1835. However, the Municipal Corporations Act produced immediate change only in towns with existing charters of incorporation; even there, change was partial and often slow-moving. Moreover, in many towns, local government reform had actually commenced around the turn of the century through local acts of Parliament, and the adoption of various sorts of commissioners or trustees.

By the 1830s, local government was extremely variegated. Some parts were undoubtedly closed and oligarchic. Centrally-appointed county magistrates had significant governmental powers. Indeed, in most rural areas, they were the only effective authorities – a fact effectively delivering power into the hands of local landowners, where these were resident. In urban as well as rural parishes, magistrates also had authority to appoint the key officials of the old Poor Law, the overseers. Policing functions in many towns were presided over by a boroughreeve and constables, themselves appointed by local court leets, whose members were selected rather mysteriously by local lords of the manor. Many pre-1835 corporations were self-selecting. Even some governing authorities established by local act of Parliament either shared this characteristic or were selected by processes heavily advantaging property. One of Bolton's two Boards of Trustees was self-selecting, while Rochdale's Police Commission until 1844 consisted of any willing ratepayer of £35 annual value.

Nevertheless, other local institutions, particularly in urban areas, were altogether more accessible. In the decades before 1835, or whenever incorporation under the Municipal Corporations Act occurred, these were often multiplying. Parish and township meetings could elect churchwardens (who often had Poor-Law as well as church-adminis-trative functions) and assistant overseers. They could nominate over-seers, which some magistrates chose to confirm as effective appointees. Such meetings were legally open to all ratepayers, often effectively to anyone pretending to be such, not difficult in the crowded and tumultu-ous conditions often prevailing. As James Vernon has noted, partici-pants included not just men at many social levels but also, given appropriate issues and circumstances, women.[23] Meanwhile, court leets might well permit town-meetings, open in the same sort of unregu-lated way, effectively to appoint the police authorities. Given sympa-thetic local traditions, and intense party competition, these meetings also became ultimate points of decision about major issues, particularly those involving applications for local improvement acts. Meanwhile, although many corporations were self-nominating and apparently closed, some charters, like those in Maidstone and Norwich, established altogether more popular bodies, elected in wards by the ratepayers. In Norwich, from the fifteenth century, the sixty Common Councilmen and twenty-four Aldermen were annually elected by freemen who by 1730 constituted around one-third (admittedly declining to 22 per cent by 1800) of adult males and extended well down the social scale. Even the mayoralty was effectively elective. Again, the system's popular char-acter was intensified by fervent partisanship. Finally, around 1800, these older institutions were increasingly supplemented by other elective governmental institutions like police and improvement commissioners, as the result of improvement legislation.

Admittedly, elective proceedings to these various bodies were often heavily laced with corruption and patronage. Nevertheless, like the more open parliamentary boroughs, they provided access-points for opinion about local politics whenever it emerged. This was often en-couraged by intense partisan divisions within local elites. There resulted perpetual temptations for the two sides to appeal downwards in their battles for control – temptations rendered more urgent by the sheer multiplicity and consequent uncontrollability of the institutions concerned. At points where the population was already aroused, this behaviour might contrive to render parts of the local political system significantly open to popular pressure.[24]

Taken overall, British politics before the start of democratisation are still most usefully described as oligarchic. They were presided over by a traditional landed elite whose possession of advantage was emphatic, whose legitimacy was scarcely threatened, and which controlled most of the governmental and non-governmental areas it aspired to. Yet its ambition and remit were limited, and quite a lot of what it did control was significantly negotiated, or at least conditional upon satisfactory delivery of patronage, support, subsistence or simple inebriation. Partly, this resulted from its own internal rivalry, and from the way this interacted with the access-points available through constituency and local politics. As the result of the 1688 Revolution, libertarian values were quite widespread. Notions that one could have opinions about what national and local government did, and that political attachments could rest upon more than just dependency and deference, were at least intermittently present amongst significant segments of the adult population, and increasingly so. As we shall see, these conditional and participatory aspects of power were being reinforced by a developing civil society, spreading wider and more deeply than for example in Germany. Even in 1820, Peel believed public opinion was 'growing too large for the channels that it has been accustomed to run through'.[25]

The foregoing may help explain the ultimate success of British democratisation. Even before formal commencement, this was a system capable of providing significant segments of its population, at many levels, with experiences of political participation. These were experiences they found meaningful, important and sometimes effective. This was partly due to the emergence of organisational points of political access, partly to people's growing readiness to exploit them. Helping underpin this in turn was the fact that the system was significantly liberal, a fact sharply contrasting with many twentieth-century democratising polities. Important also were elites that, in spite and even because of their possession of great economic advantage, were well-used to various sorts of political and non-political negotiation in order to maintain their legitimacy.

However, to take explanatory matters further, we must examine the character of British political elites, and the developing civil attachments of the population that was about to be politically included. Before that, we need to understand the democratisation process itself.

2   The Process of Inclusion

In this chapter, we will explore the character of British democratisation: how Britain became a liberal democracy, a polity where liberal freedoms are guaranteed, elections free, fair and regular, and adults participate as a matter of equal right, irrespective of race, creed, class or gender. In practice, the notion probably also implies the opportunity for some degree of *effective* participation, and thus popular empowerment. The central concentration will be upon enfranchisement and redistribution, although it should be remembered that, on the foregoing definition, several other contemporary policy themes had democratising effects, notably the removal of Nonconformist and Catholic civil disabilities.

Before starting, several introductory points are relevant. First, quite aside from the fact that the term was rarely used before the twentieth century, few contemporary participants identified what they were doing as democratisation; partly because, as we shall see, local and particularly national elites played important parts in managing the process. For most Whigs, the 1832 Reform Act was a 'final' settlement, or at least a very extended stopping-place, rather than a step on the way to something more popular. It was 'the means of separating the respectable part of the community from those who thought they could never demand enough'.[1] Moreover, the Act was to reinforce a constitution based upon property rather than to create one based on individual rights. Tories like Peel took less terminated views, but deployed them only as dark predictive arguments against the Bill. Until beyond 1885, most parliamentarians believed they were including groups as and when they became 'politically fit' – possessing sufficient rationality to exercise political choice, and values and virtues sufficient to ensure their inclusion would neither disrupt the political system nor damage the interests of those already on the inside-track. These latter characteristics supposedly included self-help, respectability, industry, sobriety and thrift, along with clear evidence (via some sort of property-relationship) of attachment to and stake in the existing socio-economic system. They also included independence, combined until a fairly late stage with varying degrees of

37

deference. As we shall see in Chapter 3, these considerations influenced the selection of the £10 householder in 1832, and the exclusion of the old open-borough voters. By 1867, urban working men were perceived to be safely fit, as were their rural counterparts by 1884. The coming of universal male suffrage in 1918 admittedly signalled the termination of these management-criteria for men, even those previously designated as 'the residuum'. However, the selection only of women over thirty for inclusion in the same year expressed not just male fears of female majority, but also about the 'giddy-headedness' of women in their twenties. In all this, politicians were often rather optimistic about fitness,[2] even perhaps persuaded by Millite arguments that political participation itself could render people fit. However, this was more from faith in the free market, and the absence of reliable socio-economic data, than conceptions of democratic rights.

Furthermore, until at least 1885, inclusive acts were steadily counter-weighted by others designed to preserve the political position of land-owners, and of property and quality more generally. This inspired the famous Chandos clause in 1832, along with the insistence on voters being direct rather than 'compounded' ratepayers, and the complicated registration provisions conditioning the electoral process until 1918. It partly motivated the minority clause in 1867; attempted separations of rural and urban areas in terms both of voting qualifications until 1884/5; and the determined advantaging of rural and small-town interests in framing constituency boundaries until the same date. Even in 1885, the splitting of some county constituencies was an attempt to preserve the remains of squirearchical influence. Similar concerns about property (at least the scattered sort) and quality underpinned the long-continued preservation of multiple voting in parliamentary elections (and in those to local boards of guardians), in one respect (university seats) until 1948. Equally important until 1885 was the other criterion besides population determining the inclusion of particular urban locations: the notion that, to qualify as constituencies, towns should represent definable 'interests' (for example manufacturing) and be 'communities', safely attached to identifiable elites. Thus, in 1832, many Lancashire cotton towns were granted two MPs, whilst Salford, with more population than any of them (Manchester and Liverpool aside) was begrudged just one because 'it was a mere suburb of Manchester, separated by a filthy stream and inhabited by people of the . . . lowest description'.[3] Partly for the same reason, London remained under-represented, even by urban standards, until 1885. Meanwhile, as evidenced in Chapter 3, even if parliamentarians desired to popularise the political system, competitive party and factional considerations partly explained who was enfranchised at any given time, how constituency boundaries were drawn, and which MP voted for what. This was so even if calculations were less indecently unclothed than they often were in say France or the USA.

Yet, there clearly were other motivations closer to what we would now call democratisation. Many radicals preached at least manhood suffrage, and democratic ideas had been part of radical currency intermittently since the Civil War. Meanwhile, many elite figures felt politics should at least be popularised. Even in 1820, and though eventually hostile to the first Reform Bill, Peel concluded public opinion had overgrown 'the channels... it has been accustomed to run through'.[4] Preparing that Bill, and admittedly seeking to frustrate anything more democratic, the Whigs also felt the representative system needed adjusting to reflect social change. They wished to enhance popular consent, and were responding to mass agitation seeming to imply its withdrawal. This informed not just the £10 householder's enfranchisement, but also seats-redistribution, and the division of some very populous counties into two, each with two MPs. By 1864, Gladstone was ruminating hazily about moral if not individual rights: 'any man... not presumably incapacitated by some consideration of personal unfitness or political danger is morally entitled to come within the pale of the constitution'.[5] The 1872 Ballot Act, by removing the transparency necessary if voters were to be conceived as representing non-voters, also at least implied franchise was some sort of right.

Second, as noted in Chapter 1 and unlike most polities democratising since 1918, Britain was substantially liberal, or at least liberalised, before democratisation began. This conditioned the context wherein the process occurred. Liberal freedoms of speech, press, association, belief and freedom from arbitrary arrest commanded widespread consensus amongst the public, the courts, even the elite. Significantly, the Crimean War, just two decades after the start of political inclusion, and for all the jingoism it induced, failed to produce justification for their suspension, in spite of producing considerable domestic opposition. Nor did campaigns for enfranchisement after 1830. In 1832, admittedly, the 'knowledge taxes' remained in place. Yet rising popular radicalism notwithstanding, or perhaps because of it (system-supportive publications being unable to compete with 'the unstamped'), the stamp duty was reduced from 4d to 1d in 1836 and removed altogether in 1855. The advertising duty suffered a similar fate in 1833 and 1853.

Third, like north-west Europe and North America, but unlike most post-1918 democratisations, Britain's was a staged process. This is the primary concern of the current chapter. However, I will not supply the traditional blow-by-blow story of enfranchisement, seat re-allocations and the like (see **Democratisation and Liberalisation Diary** in appendix). This has been done many times, from our standpoint fairly unrevealingly. Rather, the focus is on political inclusion by class and gender. We examine first the process whereby adult middle-class males, especially urban ones, were included and empowered; second, that whereby working men were included; third, women's political inclusion. Treating British democratisation in this way has two advantages: first, it highlights a key way in which contemporaries viewed and worried about what they were doing both in formal and informal, incorporative terms. Contemporaries clearly perceived middle-class enfranchisement as the central issue up to 1832. This was so even if the frequency of this language varied over time, even if the term's meaning varied somewhat according to time and person, and owed as much to political necessities as to social realities.[6] It was what the Whigs said they had primarily done, and the middle class became a primary target-group for politicians after 1832.[7] Similarly, all recognised it was working men who had been included for better or worse in 1867 and 1884. Second, the approach enables us, here and in later chapters, to focus on certain characteristics and problems of the process, and some of the reasons for its relative success.

Yet proceeding in this way also raises problems. The process was about more than just political and symbolic inclusion by class and gender. It also involved attempts to adjust the political system to increasingly rapid social, economic and demographic change. A representative system that had got badly out of kilter with such change, and continued to trail behind it until at least 1885, was adjusted by periodic redrawals of constituency boundaries – first by Parliament, after 1885 by Boundary Commissions. This reinforced inclusions by class and gender, but was also justified on its own terms. Notions of virtual representation also gave way steadily to the popular representation of numbers. Meanwhile, the idea of gendered inclusion was not totally meaningful to contemporaries before the late-nineteenth century. Admittedly, when the issue was posed, elites would specifically admit that it was categories of men who were being deemed fit for inclusion. Most would then have declared women politically unfit. However, by including men in 1832, 1867 and 1885, politicians also assumed they were permitting entry to particular socio-economic groups, whether men or women. Notions of virtual representation retained sufficient force to presuppose that men represented their dependent womenfolk.

Nevertheless, the approach will reveal several important features of Britain's democratisation, some obvious, some less so. First, notwithstanding the undoubted advantage the system, and its surrounding society, gave wealth, property and manhood, especially the landed sort, it becomes clear that no group was wholly excluded before its formal inclusion. Representative government had long been an important feature of that system. This was partly what enabled claims for inclusion to be advanced. Alongside civil society, it also permitted all groups a degree of 'political training' prior to formal admission.

Second, and partly in consequence, inclusion was not just staged and somewhat managed; it was also long-continuing and mostly peaceful. Groups were inducted into an existing political and electoral system, rather than forcing violent entry: they might threaten violence, like the middle classes and their working-class allies in 1830–1. However, this date possibly aside, they saw no serious need to use it. Furthermore, though distinguished by landmarks, each group's political inclusion was extended and complex. The overall result was that the political system retained legitimacy, and thus the stability that many commentators see as essential for successful democratisation. Also, in a mix of accident and design, each entrant could be substantially absorbed before the next group gained entry. Meanwhile, staged inclusion meant that groups included at any given stage influenced the speed and terms under which subsequent entrants gained admission. All this gives meaning to an otherwise self-admiring British cliché: the process was evolutionary.

Third, evolution also characterised British democratisation because it involved not just legal enfranchisement, but other formal enactments, in women's case probably including legal equality. Furthermore, democratisation entailed political responses from national and local elites of the sort reviewed in Chapter 3. It depended for its effect upon social, economic and demographic changes. Finally, democratisation also entailed various sorts of incorporation. In turn, this meant that it involved ceding symbolism and status as well as influence.

Fourth, and supplementing the picture of something far beyond mere enfranchisement, democratisation was as much local as national. Britain's central government was unambitious. Local developments therefore deepened the democratisation taking place. They also made the demands released by inclusion easier to handle. Fifth, though democratisation moved predominantly forward, it also involved short- or medium-term reverses for particular groups.

Given these characteristics, only part of the process will be fully covered here. Some will receive main attention in later chapters.

1. Middle-Class Male Political Inclusion

Although the key date for middle-class male inclusion, particularly the expanding urban segment, was 1832, the process also involved other more long-continuing changes, and in some respects was incomplete before 1918. These were partly legal, partly political and partly socio-economic. Furthermore, although the Reform Act was crucial, middle-class males were highly salient before 1832.

As Chapter 1 suggested, most of Britain's pre-Reform electorate was middle- or middling-class, allowing some anti-Reformers to argue that it was already fully represented.[8] It was this, alongside the alliance with working-class radicals, that enabled its leaders crucially to influence the 1830–1 Reform crisis, particularly via the 1831 election. Middling groups were also active and legitimate participants in pressure-group politics from at least the late-eighteenth century, on behalf of both economic and moral causes. Furthermore, they participated eagerly in the widely-conducted politics of conditional deference, whereby borough patrons distributed various sorts of largesse in return for polling obedience, and periodically had to negotiate about the content.

Middle-class influence was further underpinned by notions of virtual representation. This legitimised participation by some groups under the guise of broad 'interests' – manufacturing, trading, ports and the like. These interests supposedly encompassed all so engaged, however humble; in practice, it primarily entailed representation of middling interests by middle-class leaders. This was enhanced by the fact that the pre-reformed system permitted a few manufacturers to enter Parliament via industrialising counties, large or small boroughs.

Reinforcing such influence, in a highly uncentralised polity, was the role of middle-class men in the serried structures of pre-1835 local governance. Here, whether in small or larger towns, middling males normally dominated local officialdom, whether elected or appointed. They were themselves often subject to heavy influence by others, particularly local ground-landlords, and sometimes the unpropertied ranks below. They might be unrepresentative of the religious or party predilections of most of the local population. Nevertheless, their personnel, and probably their primary economic interests, were in the middle segments of the population.

Yet, as the system-threatening agitation of 1830–1 indicated, there were serious problems. Most important was the severe under-representation of the expanding urban-industrial middle class, compared particularly with the landed interest, and the small-town middle class, who were often anyway dependants and clients of the landed order. This was partly because urban-industrial males frequently could not vote even in industrialising towns possessing parliamentary representatives, the electors being self-perpetuating corporations or burgage-holders. Meanwhile, in open boroughs like Preston or Westminster, lower-class voters were sufficiently numerous to swamp the local middle class. It was also because representative boundaries had not shifted in tune with demographic and economic change, thus rendering many industrial middle-class locations wholly unrepresented except via the counties of which they were part. The same mismatch also left urbanising and industrialising areas severely under-represented. Adding to general dissatisfaction was the disproportionate influence often exercised by local landowners in urban local governance, their role as ground-landlords and/or lords of the manor often giving them considerable appointing powers through county magistrates and court leets. This, in turn, often reinforced Tory, Anglican and mercantile control over local institutions to the outrage of newer manufacturing, Dissenting and Liberal interests. All this was pronounced in England, but far worse in Scotland where only 4500 of 565 000 adult males were enfranchised.

The Act effectively neutralised the agitation by removing middle-class support. This was not exactly because it increased the middle-class proportions of the electorate, though most contemporaries probably believed it did. Shopkeepers and artisans constituted an estimated 60 per cent of electors after 1832 just as they had before.[9] Nevertheless, outside Ireland, the increased electorate meant the vote was extended to most middle-class men. Equally important, this symbolically granted them the status of full citizenship. The £10 householder's universal enfranchisement was primarily responsible for an immediate 64 per cent increase in the overall United Kingdom electorate, from around 492 700[10] to 806 000. In England and Wales, the rise was 49 per cent, with approximately 1 in 5 adult males enfranchised. The 4500 voters in Scotland's 'vast rotten borough' were engulfed by 59 500 more, even if the country's slower economic growth outside the central belt still generated only 1 elector for every 8 grown men.[11] Electoral registration, energised by heightened party competition, rapidly increased these figures. Within nine years, England's electorate expanded by 167 000 (27 per cent); that in Wales by 13 000 (31 per cent); while Scottish voters were augmented by 20 000 (31 per cent).

Even Ireland saw some redress of the very restricted franchise created in 1829 to counterbalance the 'democratising' effects of Catholic Emancipation. More important than the £10-household borough qualification, whose impact was limited due to the stagnancy of Irish town life, was the new £10-leasehold county franchise. In consequence, Irish electors rose from 49 000 in 1831 to 90 000 in 1832. However, compared to population, and partly due to the eccentricities of Ireland's registration system, they were still far below the English and Welsh ratio. In 1833, there was still only one elector for every 20 male adults. In fact, the main increase occurred in 1850 when a new occupation-based rather than ownership-based franchise, and revised registration procedures, increased the post-Famine electorate from 45 000 to 163 000. In the longer term, the clarity of the new qualifications and procedures rendered the electorate more clearly middling class: first by eliminating many dependent marginal men whom landlords had slipped in under the old system; second, by admitting increasing numbers of relatively secure post-Famine small farmers.[12] In important respects, 1850 also made Irish electors more representative of the population than the Mainland's: non-industrial voters in a non-industrial society.

Outside Ireland, urban middle-class influence upon the system was enhanced by including as boroughs substantial numbers of locations where this social group was common, and excluding rotten boroughs where, along with most other inhabitants, they were absent. Many towns and cities, particularly industrial ones, were represented for the first time, while others, already armed with MPs, increased their representation. Meanwhile, the 1832 Act also permitted the enfranchisement, via the continuing 40-shilling freeholder qualification in the counties, of urban shopkeepers and artisans unable to qualify as £10 householders in the boroughs. This expanded the middle-class vote, and, in heavily urbanised counties, diluted the deferential voters introduced by the Chandos clause.

However, the events around 1832 also 'democratised' politics in other ways. The withholding of full voting rights had seemed to represent an outrageous denial of citizenship to many urban middle-class men. This appeared the more galling because they felt themselves the primary generators of economic growth and progress. In many urban-industrial areas, and in others far beyond, this produced not just mass indignation, but surges of opinion-politics, breaking the constraints of deference and material inducement.[13] Thus, the 1832 Reform Act did not just widen the electorate: the agitation producing it also helped democratise political behaviour at least in the short to medium term. Even if deference and bribery subsequently reasserted themselves, there remained an enhanced tendency for such pressures to coincide with conviction. This in turn was encouraged by intensified party competition in the 1830s: caused partly by arguments over Reform; partly by emerging issues like religious equality and anti-slavery; and partly by the need to work the new registration system and test comparative strengths in newly created constituencies. The agitation, and Parliament's response, also helped legitimise pressure-group politics. The way was opened for other agitations – over church rates, free trade, disestablishment and civil-service reform. Each made the next seem more normal – enhancing both popular support and the likelihood of parliamentary sympathy, even though the originators were clearly no longer just traditionally legitimate general interests. Those able to take most immediate advantage of this widening avenue were middle-class males.

Nevertheless, as many historians have noted,[14] Reform's impact was limited. Long after 1832, both Parliamentary Houses remained predominantly landed. In the terms outlined in the introduction, parliamentarians were in no sense *directly* representative of the electorate. There was little increase in numbers of manufacturers, or salaried professionals, amongst MPs. Equally lacking was much acceptance of such Members when they appeared; they remained outside the 'exclusive circles'. Indeed, until John Bright and Joseph Chamberlaine entered Gladstone's first and second cabinets respectively, none were appointed to key government posts. This modest impact was partly due to the Act itself. Notwithstanding significant redistribution, urban-industrial areas, where the newer middle classes were strongest, remained decidedly under-represented, continuing thus until 1885. This was in spite of constituency boundaries being generously drawn around industrial locations to allow for expansion. Quite deliberately, whilst removing rotten boroughs, the Act's mentors had permitted, even reinforced, the representative importance of small non-industrial boroughs, a significance they broadly retained until 1885. Along with counties (whose representation was also strengthened in 1832, and whose electorate was rendered somewhat more compliant by Chandos' inclusion of £50 tenants-at-will),[15] these were locations where landed persons could command at least conditional deference through the traditional politics of influence and corruption. So too could they even amongst many males of the newer middle class, once full citizenship had been at least symbolically granted. Indeed, in areas like north-east England, where economic partnership in coal mining made relations with local landowners particularly close, landed influence even in industrial constituencies remained strong.[16] Furthermore, the impact of the £10-householder qualification was intentionally uneven even amongst the middling class. In rapidly growing industrial areas, it enfranchised men in large and immediate numbers. In locations, even industrial ones, where growth-rates were slower, the immediate effect, even amongst the shopocracy, was far less generous.

Nor did the Act exactly create popular government, middle-class or otherwise. Political parties, although more vibrant and disciplined than before 1832, were still sufficiently fluid to preclude much idea of governments acquiring popular mandates from general elections. Contemporary supporters of post-1832 politics saw parties as ideally suited not to popular but to parliamentary government – sufficiently disciplined to sustain administrations and circumscribe monarchical influence, but sufficiently indisciplined to prevent Parliament becoming a house of elected delegates. Of nine governments formed between 1835 and 1868, eight were terminated by adverse Parliamentary votes, and one by prime-ministerial death. All six Parliaments elected between 1841 and 1865 felled at least one ministry before dissolution.[17] Electors might make governments – a fact sufficient to enhance politicians' electoral sensitivities – but they did not break them.

For these reasons, other enactments besides the 1832 Reform Act, and other sorts of change, were important to complete the political inclusion and empowerment of middle-class men. We have already noted the effect of the 1850 Irish Franchise Act. On the Mainland, the 1867 Reform Act, though primarily enfranchising urban working men, also extended the county franchise to £5 lease and copyholders, and more importantly £12 occupiers. This produced 250 000 new electors in England and Wales alone (the Irish county electorate remained unchanged). It entailed the inclusion of small farmers, some shopkeepers and artisans. If these are counted within a rural middle class (albeit a frequently dependent one, with limited commonality with its urban counterparts), then 1867 has some importance for our current concerns. Some seats were transferred to manufacturing towns like Burnley, Darlington and Middlesbrough where the urban middle class were powerful. The Act probably had greatest, though least measurable, significance by increasing the political influence of industrial middle-class elites. The 1832 Act had arguably primarily extended the enfranchisement of non-industrial middling groups like shopkeepers and artisans. In 1867, the most important group of enfranchised working men were industrial workers often loyal to substantial employers. This was one reason why enfranchisement was supported by manufacturers in both parties. They could see their clout within the system, whether for class, religious, party, or urban-community purposes, being greatly enhanced if it rested on amenable mass electorates.[18]

More important, however, were the 1884/5 franchise and redistribution Acts. It can be noted in passing that standardising county qualifications across the United Kingdom enfranchised many small Irish farmers, thereby enlarging the representative channels for the emerging alliance of rural radicalism and Irish nationalism.[19] From the more relevant standpoint of the Mainland urban middle classes, redistribution was important in two senses. First, it established the principle that representation should be allotted primarily according to population. As such, it strengthened the position of urban middle-class men, just as it did that of their working-class counterparts. Second, it eroded the notion that towns, irrespective of size, were 'communities', permitting larger ones to be sub-divided for constituency purposes. One key criterion for boundary-drawing was social homogeneity. As suggested later, this was crucial for working men. However, it also produced many constituencies heavily influenced by middle-class suburbanites. At a time when class was reasserting itself as an underpinning for political behaviour, this was crucially important to their empowerment. This was clearly understood by Salisbury's Conservatives in their insistence that redistribution accompany rural working-class enfranchisement. The Conservative-dominated coalition which passed the 1918 Representation of the People Act, whose redistribution clauses further enhanced suburban representation, was to have similarly calculative prescience. From the 1880s, the urban middle class increasingly replaced the rapidly weakening and dividing landed orders as the primary Tory target group. Along with other changes reviewed later, this surely helps explain why proportions of professional and industrial-commercial middle-class MPs now rose rapidly – from 24 to 32 per cent and 24 to 38 per cent respectively between 1874 and 1885.[20]

However, even now, some middle-class groups remained electorally under-represented. The 1832 Reform Act's residential requirements, in tandem with the complexities of the registration timetable, effectively entailed that most otherwise qualified individuals had to reside within a constituency for at least two years before achieving exercisable voting-rights. The intention was to increase the elector's political 'safety' by cementing his relationship to property, interest and community. These requirements were retained in the 1867 and 1885 Acts, and even strengthened for lodgers. The purpose was to exclude working men whose poverty and/or occupations rendered them geographically un-stable and thus politically unsafe. However, these provisions also unin-tentionally disenfranchised many professionals and other white-collar workers whose upward mobility entailed regular residential transfer; tendencies probably increasing due to the emergence of nationally recognised professional qualifications, and of industrial, banking and retail firms whose operations extended far beyond particular towns and even regions. For these highly important middle-class segments, it took the relaxation of residential requirements in the 1918 Act to produce full political inclusion.[21] This probably helped usher in the 'rise of profes-sional society'[22] in political life.

However, middle-class inclusion and empowerment also occurred at another equally important level – the urban locality. Indeed, alongside the all-embracing impact of *laissez faire*, this was one reason why the middle class remained apparently unperturbed by their relative exclusion from Parliament. Here, the key enactment was the 1835 Municipal Corporations Act. Some 178 elected borough councils were thereby created through the automatic transformation of existing unelected cor-porations. In subsequent decades, many others followed as urban local-ities successfully applied for incorporation under the Act. Initial results were mixed. Many places chose not to apply. There were also severe problems amongst those who did, or who were incorporated automatic-ally. Though doomed in the long run, older institutions of local govern-ment like court leets, boroughreeves and constables, town-meetings, county magistrates benches and Improvement Commissioners, were not obliged to disappear, or concede power to new corporations. They often became vantage-points which parties and factions, defeated in struggles to control new councils, could exploit to hamstring their rivals. The result was frequently short-term governmental paralysis.[23]

Nevertheless, in the medium-to-long term, the Act produced several important inclusive results. First, in the early decades, and in fast-growing locations, incorporation often shifted power from older Tory pre-industrial, mercantile and primarily Anglican middle-class elites and their followers to newer Liberal, industrial, primarily Dissenting elites and theirs.[24] The Act thereby gave local control to those middle-class sections feeling most excluded by the system as it existed nationally before (and for radicals, after) 1832, and locally before 1835. This was not always so, since there were places like Liverpool where the older forces successfully controlled the new system as they had the old. Nevertheless, at least the contest was now reasonably open to whichever side possessed a majority amongst the ratepayers, give or take some cheerful gerrymandering. For this reason, 1835 was important in confirming the political attachment of those groups (working-class as well as middle-class) who felt most passionately about the 1832 Reform Act.

Secondly, relatedly, and in the longer term, municipal government provided middle-class elites and their followers with political and social bases from which to express and exploit their invigorated sense of citizenship. They were bases that, if they desired, they could secure from incursions by local or national landed elites. This could be achieved through the supercession of county by municipally-nominated borough magistrates, and via the disappearance of manorial bodies like court leets. Things were not wholly secure even then: sending improvement bills to Parliament was risky. Landed-dominated private bill committees of Parliament were liable to take crippling swings at anything they disliked, particularly if it involved interference with local landowning rights. Nevertheless, local autonomy, backed increasingly by civic pride, was far more complete than ever before. Furthermore, rather than landed interference, what local improvement processes mainly involved were the arbitration by private bill committees of unresolved disputes between middle-class groups within the relevant town – for example over regulation of house-building, river-pollution, or other attempted interferences with property rights.

Meanwhile, and here we see how the political inclusion of one group could condition political access for others, incorporation also enabled local elites to secure themselves against unpredictable interventions from below. Whereas radical and chartist groups had been able to gain access to local policy-making via guerrilla incursions at town and vestry meetings, or gaining election as police or improvement commissioners, municipal elective and decision-making processes were easier to control. There were fewer points of popular or elective access, and fewer institutions to have access to. As evident later, other interests, including working-class ones, still required appeasement. Nevertheless, the agenda of negotiation was now under greater control.

The overall result was that middle-class municipal elites and their followers now controlled most matters fundamentally affecting their lives and interests, even if they profoundly disagreed over their management. This included public health, smoke and river pollution, licensing, roads, increasingly public utilities and the most important form of direct taxation, the rates. Though the Poor Law Amendment Act produced significant centralisation in theory, in practice poor relief also remained substantially under local control via elected boards of guardians, as eventually did education provision. Meanwhile, local charities, also middle-class controlled, occupied substantial chunks of a policy-making field that would now be termed social welfare. Some areas, of course, remained centrally controlled, particularly industrial regulation and the terms of external trade. Nevertheless, the autonomy of local governance, particularly when set alongside central government attachment to *laissez faire*, virtually removed the need for resentment about the apparently puny national results of middle-class male political inclusion.

Doubly was this so because autonomous urban localities also provided focuses for civic pride, and arenas within which middle-class elites, and many below them, could realise desires for recognition, esteem and thus citizenship. This was secure from the more elevated, unnerving and critical standards prevailing at national level, where even major local employers 'found themselves very little boys...(having) to deal with men such as Lord Redesdale'.[25] Compared to a world wherein local newspapers guaranteed extended and respectful coverage of one's progress from birth, coming-of-age, marriage, charitable and municipal endeavours, and participation in frequent ceremonial display, all splendidly terminated by a well-attended funeral and admiring obituary, the national arena often seemed uninviting, even after the property qualification for MPs was abolished in 1859. Nineteenth-century urban life provided numerous locations where middle-class males (and eventually females) could celebrate their sense of arrival, citizenship and economic importance. It was also the primary focus for most middle-class civil activity. It thus became an important means whereby their civil organisations became civically oriented, thereby committed to the system, and doubly functional to a polity undergoing democratisation. Local political and social life consequently set the terms upon which many middle-class people became attached to, and incorporated within, national political life. These were terms largely set by themselves, requiring little negotiation or consent from the aristocratically-dominated centre. Where consent was required, as with disputed improvement legislation, negotiations were often headed by local mayors, increasingly splendid figures representing the pinnacle of middle-class civic and social ambition. Finally, although for many people locally-derived satisfactions obviated the need for national participation,[26] municipal life also provided valuable political experience for those choosing to take the parliamentary plunge.

One final way whereby the impact of urban middle-class males upon the political system was enhanced was through accelerating socio-economic change. The £10-householder qualification had enfranchised rather unevenly, according to local economic conditions, house-size and rating-policy. However, the continuing rise in urban population, industrialisation and increasing real incomes over the decades further popularised politics in many places. By 1866, the borough electorate in England and Wales had increased by 82 per cent since 1832.

All these factors ensured the impact of middle-class males upon politics and society after 1832 was far greater than formal institutional analysis might imply. So too did the competitive political instincts of rival national politicians, and the broad consensus about minimum government. This impact ensured middle-class predilections would have considerable influence upon the terms on which working men were considered for inclusion. It probably shifted the meanings attached to political fitness so as to align them more closely to industrial entrepreneurial preferences, and placing even greater emphasis upon virtues like thrift and self-help. It may also have been this latter group's enhanced feelings of security about their employees' loyalties after the Cotton Famine that convinced aristocratic politicians, particularly those with industrial links like the Earl of Derby, that it was safe to make a generous 'leap in the dark'.

2. Working-class Male Political Inclusion

Many points already made about middle-class males are equally relevant to working men's political inclusion. The key dates of 1867, 1884 and 1918 highlight the fact that inclusion, even in terms of formal enfranchisement, was long drawn out. Indeed, in many respects, and viewed retrospectively, it was under way substantially before 1867. However, inclusion also involved other even more elongated developments, both legislative and non-legislative. It involved not just the parliamentary vote – the key issue both for recipients and those granting it – but also at least five other interlinked processes. First, a decidedly complex process involving inclusion within the local political system. Second, a broader legal one: eroding residence requirements for voters; the secret ballot; reapportioning constituency boundaries; restricting the extent and purposes of election spending; removing legislative property qualifications, and paying MPs. Third, and partly covered elsewhere, there were broader political processes, involving the acceptance and competitive exploitation of working-class participation by competing national and local elites and the erosion of deference and dependency. Fourth, inclusion partly resulted from broader economic and demographic changes producing rising real wages, residential stabilisation and steadily blurring rural–urban distinctions. The first two enabled working men to qualify under existing qualifications, whilst the last strengthened the case for extending the householder franchise to rural areas. Finally, for working men, as for other groups, democratisation was a social process involving various forms of incorporation, and underpinned by the democratic and otherwise functional character of working-class civil organisation. Given all this, what is said here will overlap with later chapters.

If we are to understand the character and ultimate success of this phase of political inclusion, we should realise that working men had never been fully excluded from national, still less local, politics. Though far less significant than their middle-class counterparts, they participated legitimately in pre-1832 politics. As noted in Chapter 1, they dominated the scattering of open boroughs. However venal their motives, many voted: sometimes drunkenly and at the behest of others; sometimes, as in Westminster, Preston and Middlesex, in more radical if still sometimes inebriated directions. As non-voters in less open constituencies, they could pressurise electors – behaviour also legitimised by notions of virtual representation. Working men were also legitimate parliamentary petitioners, and periodic interveners in local politics. All this helps explain their presence in the 1830–1 franchise agitation, sometimes allied to middle-class radicals, sometimes independently. Meanwhile, within the traditional moral–economic framework, working men (and women) rioted semi-legitimately. Indeed, mutual acceptance of moral economy, by the poor, and to some degree by local elites, had always lent implicit conditionality to acquiescence in hierarchy by those at its base, mutually-accepted limits to the deprivations 'the crowd' could be expected to suffer. This helps explain why some elite politicians were already prepared to contemplate the poor in political ways.

In important respects, the 1832 Reform Act constituted a serious representational reverse for working men. The development of market-based relationships had already undermined non-political areas of conditionality and influence before 1800. The Act made no concessions to the working-class radicals providing the persuasive mass-base for Reform agitation. Still more bitterly disappointing, no further franchise expansion followed of the sort radicals felt promised by their middle-class allies. Indeed, as the Whigs hoped, the Act provided a 35-year resting-place. Furthermore, by standardising the £10 householder borough franchise, Reform seriously eroded at least one political avenue for the relatively poor – their position in the open boroughs. Although existing electors survived, their votes disappeared when they died, or moved to other constituencies. Partly in consequence, partly due to the exclusionary policies of local middle-class elites, Preston's electorate declined from 6325 (and adult male suffrage) in 1832, to 2834 (and 1 adult male in 5) in 1862.[27] Here, as elsewhere, the Whigs proved remarkably successful at creating an electorate drawn from the 'class above want'.[28]

Nor did the working-class politicisation, aroused by the 1830–1 agitation and subsequent disappointments, produce any other obvious democratic benefits. It enhanced political interest and eroded deference in the short term, but hardly increased working-class political fitness in the eyes of the elite or even their erstwhile middle-class allies. Moreover, the Poor Law Amendment Act (whatever its inadvertent contribution to working-class civil society) suggested the enfranchised classes perceived working men more as suitable cases for treatment than political appeasement.

However, 1832 left some significant political avenues in place, and others open to the effects of economic change. Formally excluded or not, working men retained legitimate roles as parliamentary petitioners. Furthermore, the surviving 'open voters', taken together with affluent manual workers enfranchised as £10 householders, meant that approximately 20 per cent of the immediate post-1832 electorate were classifiable as working-class. In spite of the steady demise of 'open voters', rising real incomes, particularly from the 1860s, increased this to around 25 per cent by 1866. In older largely pre-industrial boroughs, this could reach as high as 50 per cent. Admittedly and significantly, working-class electors were always most sparsely distributed in new and potentially radical industrial towns. Nevertheless, even where not qualified, working men's semi-legal ability to influence and sometimes terrorise

voters continued. In locations like Manchester, Dewsbury and Oldham
in the 1830s, or Stoke-on-Trent in 1852, shopkeepers might be sufficiently dependent on working-class custom to be open to threats of
'exclusive dealing' if voting in unacceptable ways, particularly if these
were underpinned by mouthed imprecations at the hustings and some
untraceable vandalism later.[29]

All this meant that, the Poor Law notwithstanding, working men
retained political salience, even influence, prior to 1867. This was
particularly evident in those industrialised boroughs where class or
ethnic tension provided strong temptations to intensely competing political parties, or where radicals gained access to nomination processes.
As evident in Chapter 3, in the conflictual 1830s and 1840s, parliamentary candidates in Lancashire and other industrial locations vied to
consult 'meetings of the non-electors', where their nominations received
popular legitimation, and where in return they made pledges over issues
like the Poor Law and Factory Reform. Local politicians sometimes
appeared on Chartist and other agitational platforms, making speeches
sailing close to the sympathetic wind. In parts of Lancashire during the
1850s and 1860s, Tory politicians tuned into English working-class
hostility to Irish immigration[30] – they could hardly take sympathy
further because Irishmen were supposedly British and not therefore
legally excludable in the way of more recent migrants.

Also underpinning such behaviour, besides non-electors' potential for
mild terrorism, were working men's roles in many local political systems
prior to whenever towns were incorporated under the 1835 Municipal
Corporations Act, and whenever older institutions could be prevailed
upon to disappear. Until then, and even subsequently in more controlled
ways, working men possessed considerable capacities for significant
intervention – through open town-, township- and parish-meetings via
the often uncontrollable nomination processes for representative bodies
like police commissioners. Furthermore, although incorporation might
well narrow the local franchise due to the Act's two-and-a-half-year
ratepaying requirements, this was often re-expanded by municipalities
deciding to adopt the 1850 Small Tenements Act, enfranchising compounded ratepayers. More generally, interventions were facilitated by
mass politicisation like that created by anti-Poor Law hostility or Chartism, and by the many points of popular entry that often existed, effectively immunising local politics against closure by local elites. The party-
political competitiveness of such elites often precluded attempts in this
direction anyway; instead heightening temptations to exploit those

entry-points, thereby keeping them open. Furthermore, although parties ostensibly battled to control local politics, the real prize was often access to constituency electoral registers through control of obscure but crucial offices like overseers and assistant overseers of the poor. These officials, due to their role in rates-collection, were also involved in composing the register. Thus the party controlling them could also influence its composition. Though appointed by magistrates, local custom often dictated overseers being nominated, and effectively appointed by town-meetings. Incentives to competitively appease potential participants at these meetings, either by rhetorical gesture or more tangible benefits, were thus strong. Openings like this, given appropriate circumstances of intense party competition, could allow working men significant influence in local government policy areas like Poor Law administration, local rates-levels, even the provision of gas and water, where these services were municipalised.[31]

Competitive appeasement of parliamentary non-electors, as of poor electors, also edged into non-governmental sectors. This was most obviously expressed in bribery and politically-induced inebriation. However, there were also more salubrious forms of non-political appeasement, with more enduring results for the recipients. In a society wedded to *laissez faire*, where poverty and insecurity were central facts of life, support for those wishing to retain respectability could only be provided by philanthropy or self-help. Before as well as after 1867, this opened tempting opportunities for wealthy local leaders. They responded in multiple ways. Most obviously tangible were the Conservative Working Men's Friendly and Burial Societies, appearing across Northern England during the 1830s and 1840s. In return for modest subscriptions and canvassing activity, politically co-operative working men received immunity from the Poor Law and subsidised support in sickness and death. They also might be assisted into £10-householder status.[32] For non-electors as for electors, particularly urban ones, and in political as well as non-political areas, deference tended to be conditional and implicitly negotiated.

Such political salience was partly a commentary upon the fact that local elites, perhaps more clearly than national ones, could imagine parliamentary non-electors eventually becoming enfranchised, just as some already were in local government. In these circumstances, some constituency parties, Conservative as well as Liberal, began incorporating organised working men into their ranks.[33] Some MPs, mainly but not exclusively radicals, regarded themselves as wholly or partly working-class spokesmen. Amongst these were William Cobbett, MP for Oldham 1832–5, John Fielden (Oldham 1832–47), Joseph Brotherton (Salford 1832–57), Edward Miall and T. B. Potter, successive MPs for Rochdale up to 1857 and 1867. In fact, in the disturbed 1830s and 1840s, most parliamentarians from industrial constituencies were prepared at least to pretend some spokesmanship and sympathy for those beyond the electoral pale. This helped produce local Poor Law administrations more generous than the centre desired. Such MPs were generally the channels for working-class petitioning after 1832. Provided manual organisations could accept agendas set by a property-dominated Parliament, provided demands coincided with parliamentary conceptions of what was good for them, and granted respectable intermediaries like the Christian Socialists, they could achieve influence even before 1867. Partly in response to Ten Hours Movement pressure, Parliament enacted factory regulations protecting women and children. On the same basis, from the 1830s, friendly societies, building societies and co-ops were permitted to influence legislation protecting and framing their existence.

These various forms of political access probably raised working men's expectations of more formal inclusion. Nevertheless, the influence available, after as well as before 1832, was peripheral. Under virtual representation, working-class access, even more than urban middle-class access, was confined to deliberately limited numbers of constituencies. Furthermore, in some respects, 1832 worsened the working-class representational situation by increasing the domination of the electorate by a middle class comprising around 15 per cent of the population. Working-class petitioning, meanwhile, was sympathetically received provided Parliament already had its own reasons for feeling positive: if, for example, demands fitted the legislative framework for the free market it was minded to create. Though local politics provided important points of influence before and after municipal incorporation, the inbuilt advantages intentionally given those higher up the social scale were formidable. From 1818, the Sturges-Bourne Acts were always available to limit who could legitimately attend vestry meetings, and (where limitation failed) vote in subsequent polls. Here, as in boards of guardians elections from 1834, propertied ratepayers were permitted up to six votes. Council candidates had to own real or personal property to the value of £1000 (£500 in small boroughs) or occupy property of £30 rateable value. After incorporation, elites frequently made deliberate and successful attempts to exclude humble inhabitants from local politics by institutional arrangements, including incorporation itself, narrowing and formalising the access-points.[34] Perhaps also they began employing language designed to exclude.[35] As will be evident with women, Britain's democratisation was not wholly uni-directional. However, what crucially fuelled working-class indignation was the denial of respectable citizenship symbolised by the parliamentary vote; this was what made formal inclusion so important.

Working men's enfranchisement resulted from interactions between deliberate management and other less controllable and controlling factors. It was also a compromise between processes designed to safely manage the inclusion of the politically fit, and others aimed at exploiting its political possibilities. At very important legal levels, inclusion was mostly controlled, staged and managed. In parliamentary terms, it occurred in two stages embodying three steps. The first stage involved enfranchising working men with some direct, stable and safety-inducing relationship to residential property – male householders of twelve months formal standing. This substantially extended trends established in 1832 by the inclusion of 'ten pounders'. Householders were enfranchised in boroughs in 1867 and in counties in 1884. This was admission subject to carefully-inserted if somewhat random counterweights. These eroded the political effects of apparent generosity, and tried to exclude the 'residuum' – a vaguely defined and somewhat imaginary group hitherto residing on the edges of legitimised participation along with other non-electors. Second, 1918 saw the enfranchisement of all adult working men as of right (along with women over thirty).

This attempted control was undermined by other non-legal factors: party competition within and outside Parliament; politicisation born of pressure for enfranchisement itself; and by the broader context of ever-accelerating socio-economic change that helped create the original demand. This, together with the way legal inclusion was framed, gave working men's inclusion a self-generating momentum. 1832 led only distantly to 1867, but 1867, aided by social and demographic change, inexorably produced 1884. Furthermore, the 1867 Reform Act, as will be evident in Chapter 8, created equally irresistible compulsions towards the 1872 Ballot, and the 1883 Corrupt and Illegal Practices, Acts. This was partly because of the enhanced potential for corruptibility and intimidation it created; partly because the substantially enlarged electorate made electioneering immensely expensive, producing demands from within the elite itself to curb campaign expenditure. Partly also householder enfranchisement removed lingering radical sympathy for the plausible argument that, without greatly widened enfranchisement, the ballot would narrow effective participation by removing non-electors' abilities to influence voters.

We will examine each stage in turn, exploring first the openings created for legitimised participation by working men, and their subsequent widening by non-legal factors. We will then explore the substantial counterweights to inclusion and their political effects, both those inserted by parliamentarians anxious to ensure 'political fitness', and those created by competing machine-politicians. As with other aspects of British democratisation, and as elsewhere, inclusion was rarely a passive, bureaucratic process; rather it expressed the needs of initiating politicians motivated both by calculations of advantage and system-preservation.

Including Male Householders

Although retrospectively part of broader legal, political and social processes, and perhaps sanctioned by parliamentarians beset by competitively-induced absent-mindedness,[36] the theoretically universal inclusion of male householders, effectively uninhibited by any need for direct rates-payment, was seen as highly important by contemporaries. This was evident in the 1866–7 parliamentary debates and in the press. Local elites too often felt they were standing uncertainly at the start of crucial assimilative processes, with potentially dangerous consequences if they got their responses wrong. For some, what was at stake was even preventing 'the lower classes combining with the rough class, and governing those above'.[37]

For many, however, the territory was less unfamiliar. Partly this was due to experience of previous more open local electorates. Sometimes parliamentary enfranchisement had been municipally anticipated by the early adoption of the permissive Small Tenements Act of 1850, thereby allowing compounded ratepayers municipal votes. Sometimes even this had been anticipated because towns fixed the rateable value at which compounding began at low levels. Overall, in such locations, the 1867 Reform Act greatly increased the parliamentary electorate. However, the 1869 Municipal Franchise Act, bringing local electors more or less into line, had less dramatic effects on the municipal electorate, though it did add some women. Thus whilst Birmingham's municipal voters shot from 3 to 18 per cent of the population between 1861 and 1871, those of Leeds were already 9 per cent in 1851, and 13 per cent in 1861, and rose to just 18 per cent in 1871.[38]

None the less, most urban elites had some sense of unfamiliar territory, a sense underpinning the transformation of party organisation and ambition occurring after 1867. This was understandable. In boroughs, the link between parliamentary voting and property was substantially eroded. Any male householder of sufficient residential standing, plus a scattering of lodgers, could now register. This inclusion increased the United Kingdom electorate by 82.5 per cent from 1 357 519 in 1866 to 2 476 745 in 1868. Only in Ireland, with its primarily rural and non-industrial population, did the Act have little effect. Its electorate increased by just 9.9 per cent between 1865 and 1868, and remained wholly unaffected by the registration fever that increased the Mainland electorate by around 10 per cent between 1868 and 1874.

The increase in borough voters after 1867 varied greatly from place to place, according to demographic and economic circumstances. However, it rose overall by 138 per cent. Even county electors, boosted by modestly including £12 householders, increased by some 38 per cent. Not unexpectedly, the greatest rises occurred in industrial towns where working-class householders were most numerous – Birmingham and Leeds tripled their electorates; Lancashire towns quintupled theirs; Merthyr Tydfil's increased tenfold. Overall, although the lodger franchise did little to increase the representation even of tramping artisans (for whom it was primarily intended), the 1867 householder clauses created a clear working-class majority in the boroughs, massively so in most industrial ones. Furthermore, as implied above, many incorporated towns had not adopted the Small Tenements Act. Here, the municipal vote also rose substantially in 1869.

The medium-term effect of the 1867 Reform Act was enhanced by supplementary legislation and the decisions of revising barristers in the late 1860s and early 1870s. These establish the electoral rights of those like miners living in rent-free accommodation, and householders moving around inside the same constituency. The householder vote was also increased by legislation in 1869 giving compounders the same rights as direct ratepayers, thus removing problems arising because some municipal boroughs found it administratively impossible to abolish compounding.

As with 1832, the 1867 Act's longer-term democratising effect was heightened by local party competition and socio-economic change. Party competition, as Chapter 3 shows, had ambiguous effects upon democratisation. However, it could enhance it in at least three ways. First, contested elections greatly increased after enfranchisement, and, unlike the aftermath of 1832, did so permanently. In England, the average proportion of contested seats between 1832 and 1865 was 61 per cent; between 1868 and 1910, it was 84 per cent, with a low (in 1900) of 67 per cent. In Wales, the equivalent proportions were 25 per cent and 76 per cent (a low of 58 per cent); in Scotland 38 per cent and 86 per cent (low 55 per cent). Only in Ireland, with its different franchise history and more polarised society, and therefore fewer seats worth competing over, was there little change: 51 per cent against 56 per cent (low 20 per cent in 1906). Even after the far more decisive 1884 Act, Irish contests declined to 45 per cent.[39] On the Mainland, not merely were far more working men politically included after 1867, but their very presence enhanced opportunities for electoral choice and the need for electoral appeasement. Second, party involvement in voter registration in highly competitive urban locations meant that there was strong motivation to increase the registration at least of supporters up to the edge of what was legally allowable. Alongside the changed electoral status of compounders, this was crucial to explaining why many urban electorates expanded substantially between 1868 and 1874. Third, parties after 1867 were not merely more competitive; they were also more disciplined within and outside Parliament, especially from the late 1870s. National politicians tentatively also began making electoral pledges; more uncertainly, offering programmes. Local politicians did so even more, not with always mutually compatible results. Overall, governments began receiving electoral mandates, albeit within fairly circumscribed limits. They also came under less direct electoral pressure from electoral pledges offered by local MPs. More certainly, the electorate now became not just the maker but also the breaker of governments. Between 1868 and 1918, only three resigned after Commons defeats; the rest allowed 'the country' to decide their fates.[40]

Equally important were the effects of socio-economic change. Particularly significant here were two things. First, continued industrialisation was tending to enhance residential stability. The 1867 Act (like the 1835 Municipal Corporations Act) heavily rewarded this characteristic, and penalised its opposite, particularly where movement occurred across constituency boundaries. One reason why electorates between 1866 and 1868 increased so spectacularly in industrial towns like those in Lancashire, South Wales and north-east England was that these were areas of permanent employment. By contrast, increases were far less significant in London (just two-thirds), Liverpool (90 per cent) and some other large cities. This was partly because their predominant consumer and other trades were heavily seasonal and casual, and tended to encourage the opposite.[41] However, the long-run trend, even here, was towards factory-based and more permanent employment, perhaps one reason why party registration drives so successfully increased London's electorate in the late 1870s.

Second was the rapid expansion, numerically and geographically, of the urban population. This obviously increased numbers of borough voters. Far more important, it reinforced tendencies, already evident in the householder clauses of the 1867 Act, for democratisation to become self-sustaining. In England particularly, urban and suburban expansion was dissolving the meaningfulness of the distinction between urban and rural, and borough and county, constituencies. Thereby, it undermined the rationale for distinct franchise arrangements, if not for separating such areas in boundary terms. Even in 1867, franchise distinctions were heavily questionable because of the presence of many miners and other industrial workers in county constituencies. By 1885, with landed power eroding rapidly, separate franchises seemed indefensible.

In this regard, outward population movement was important in three ways. First, it could affect the political status of urban working men. Working-class families, bettering themselves (and presumably enhancing their political fitness) by moving to nicer houses on the outskirts of industrial towns, paradoxically found they had surrendered the head-of-household's vote by moving into the county. They thereby joined many manual inhabitants of industrial villages and townlets, whose exclusion from full citizenship seemed equally indefensible. The second way relates to the links between working-class and middle-class inclusion. One reason why Conservatives in 1884/5 could consider dissolving the distinction between borough and county, by permitting the enfranchisement of male householders in the latter locations, was that they could see rich pickings for themselves. In return for consenting to rural working-class inclusion, Tory leaders insisted upon radically redistributing constituency boundaries, thereby enhancing, amongst other things, middle-class suburban representation. This allied them with radicals in Gladstone's Liberal Cabinet wanting to equalise, and thus democratise, representation on the basis of population.[42] The potency of this alliance was in turn increased, by the way population movement was rapidly undermining the lingering legitimacy of virtual representation by increasing the already massive mismatch between the locations of seats and voters.

Third, industrialisation, urbanisation and suburbanisation were steadily eroding the autonomy of rural social, economic and political relationships. So too was the stuttering but significant growth of rural trade unionism and the Agricultural Depression. In many counties, not merely were landowner–tenant relations being disrupted, but also those between tenant and labourer. Even Liberals found it ever harder to think that agricultural workers were politically unfit by virtue of supposed economic dependency and social deference. Rural labourers had long felt the pull of urban wages, particularly if they were unskilled and pushed by agricultural modernisation, the state of rural housing and local boards of guardians. Their children had long been excited by prospects of urban sociability.[43] Now, agricultural decline eroded the sense of worth and loyalty even of skilled rural workers, and their sense of separation was reinforced in good times by rural unionism. Meanwhile, in many counties, urban-industrial sprawl, ever-extending urban tramways, and the advertising columns of expanding local newspapers, rendered the delights of urban life steadily more available, adjacent and inviting.

These various factors help explain why franchise reform in 1884 occasioned so little parliamentary debate. In fact, although making no explicit new admissions of principle, and merely universalising the householder franchise (along with that for £10 householders and lodgers), the 1884 franchise expansion was in many respects more important than that of 1867. This was particularly so when allied to a redistribution that made the key admission that representation should roughly relate to population, the creation of Boundary Commissions to supervise future redistributions, and the further effects of suburbanisation, residential stabilisation and party competition. The electorate between 1880 and 1885 was massively increased – in England by 75 per cent; Wales by 88 per cent; Scotland 91 per cent; and Ireland by 222 per cent. As this suggests, the impact varied according to the rurality of local economies: county-division voters rose threefold. With around 60 per cent of adult males now enfranchised, there was a clear working-class majority amongst the electorate. Furthermore, its potential political impact was greatly enhanced by a redistribution that not merely allied representation roughly to population but did so in such a way as to open the system to class identities and thus to class issues as never before. The near-universal shift to single-member constituencies, and the consequent widespread abandonment of community representation, changed the representational basis upon which the political agenda was composed and substantially controlled. Moreover, it did this at almost precisely the point when class identity, for the middle as much as for the working class, was reasserting itself, whilst other identities like those of community and religion were eroding. The Acts also included Scottish crofters at their point of radicalisation. Beyond this, the 1884–5 Acts also greatly widened channels for the political expression of national identity – an opportunity with huge implications for Ireland's future.

Equally important, this period saw the further democratisation of local government, and the re-multiplication of institutions offering popular access-points. Though often narrower after municipal incorporation than before, the ratepayer franchise was always more generous than the £10 householder qualification because it set no minimum rateable value at which payers could be enfranchised. This was particularly evident after whenever municipalities chose to adopt the 1850 Small Tenements Act enfranchising compounded ratepayers. The 1867 Reform Act briefly changed this situation in favour of parliamentary voters, only to see it rapidly restored by the 1869 Municipal Franchise Act. This unified parliamentary and municipal qualifications, by uniformly enfranchising compounders, but also lowered the qualification period from two-and-a-half years to one year, and allowed the vote to unmarried female heads of household. The overall result may be indicated by the number of cellar-dwellers on urban municipal registers. For example, around 1870, there were 442 in Salford, 683 in Manchester, 154 in Rochdale and 125 in Stockport. The residuum had invaded the municipal citadel.[44]

Meanwhile, continued local government reform further democratised this sector, even if also increasing its chaos. In 1870, many ratepayers, already possessing two voting opportunities (municipal and Poor Law), acquired a third if their areas were deemed insufficiently endowed with voluntary elementary schools to warrant creating Education Boards. Amongst other things, this opened local politics to waves of working-class anger about compulsory school attendance for otherwise useful wage-earning children; this entry point being rendered doubly viable by the provision (intended for religious minorities) that each elector had as many votes as there were posts to be filled and was permitted to 'plump' all of them for one candidate. The 1875 Public Health Act created a complete network of elected local sanitary authorities in areas not already municipalised. In 1882, the councillor's property qualification was abolished. The 1888 Act did for county government what the 1884 Franchise Reform Act had done for the county franchise, only more dramatically. It replaced Elizabethan quarter sessions with elected county and county-borough councils. In 1889, the London County Council replaced the indirectly-elected Metropolitan Board of Works. In 1894, the Liberals fulfilled long-standing commitments to complete the elective network by creating urban and rural district councils, parish councils and, in small parishes, parish meetings. The same Act abolished weighted voting in Poor Law elections. From 1892, the Liberals also began appointing working men as local magistrates. One further modernising, if not democratising, act remained: the replacement of the London vestries by metropolitan borough councils in 1899. This was a step, like many of its predecessors, partly born of party-political calculation, an attempt to Conservatively counter-balance the LCC's Liberal-leaning inclinations.

However, the popularisations of the political system enacted between 1867 and 1899 were significantly limited in their impact both on the size and composition of the electorate, and the political agenda. Viewed overall, outside Ireland, urban and rural working-class political inclusion prior to 1918 was absorbed with remarkably little serious strain. For all the fears of the rich, taxation as a proportion of gross national product did not start rising until 1891. Existing institutions, particularly the Liberal Party, clearly experienced problems, particularly as growing class identity produced some radicalisation of working-class political demands. However, for all the massive argument amongst historians about its fortunes, even the stresses within Liberalism were not demonstrably terminal, not clearly worse than what is normal for a major party in a popular political system, presiding over a complex society. More important, outside Ireland again, the system itself was never seriously endangered.

As Chapter 3 shows, this was partly because of the populistic skills of national and local politicians. It was also because householder- and ratepayer-enfranchisement, bouts of unemployment notwithstanding, was followed by steadily rising real wages. More important were the character and attitudes of the male population included in 1867 and 1884. Those most liable for inclusion were also most closely linked to working-class civil society, and thus were those with greatest reason for attachment to minimum government.[45] However, this cannot be divorced from the deliberate character of these enfranchisements and the way this could interact with calculations by competing party machines. Although various proposals for 'fancy franchises', giving additional votes to those with more education or property, were mostly abandoned, the system remained weighted against those whose fitness, for all the optimism of reformers, was regarded as contestable.

The legal constraints were partly short-, partly longer-term. Up to 1884, only urban, and not rural, householders were enfranchised. Furthermore, the representative system, in spite of some reallocation of seats towards urban areas in 1867, remained heavily weighted not just against towns, but particularly against those urban-industrial areas where manual workers were most numerous, and might be expected to be most self-conscious. The same demographic change that enhanced working-class enfranchisement after 1867 also rendered this maldistribution more serious. The effect of these restrictions was reinforced, admittedly rather precariously, by the 1867 Act's continued insistence on community representation. Industrial towns and cities might be granted several MPs, but outside London, they remained undivided before 1885. Furthermore, in larger cities, the so-called 'minority clause' decreed that, in any three-seat borough, any elector only possessed two votes. This was partly a deliberate attempt by the framers of the 1867 Act to safeguard, in our terms over-represent, the interests of the more extensively propertied. Admittedly, parties circumvented the clause: 'plumping' ensured the majority in any constituency took all the seats. Nevertheless, the intention to counter-balance majority influence was clear. Admittedly, the minority identity might be religious, partisan or even ethnic, and the clause was anyway defensible on liberal grounds as a defence against majority 'tyranny',[46] but class and property certainly bulked large in the minds of those originating this clause.

These constraints upon the majority were substantially eroded in 1884–5. Nevertheless, very significant and agenda-influencing counterbalances remained. These were intended to discriminate against dependency and residential instability. They also excluded those whose needs, even if not demands, were most urgent. Indeed, they tended to exclude people at the precise point when those needs *became* urgent, and were thus a means of safeguarding the system against the potentially radicalising effects of economic crisis. Obviously, even after 1884, only male householders, along with a few relatively affluent (£10), stable, determined and fortunate lodgers, possessed parliamentary votes. Quite aside from its gendered character, this automatically excluded many adult males without the supposedly fitness-inducing relationship with property and independence. Amongst these were all adult male occupants other than householders (municipally, all adults other than the ratepayer), notably their sons and, for working men, their lodgers. Also excluded were male living-in servants. These were thought too dependent for democratic participation. So too, for both parliamentary and municipal purposes, were those on poor relief. If hardship drove men to the Guardians, electoral regulations deliberately removed them from the political loop, though this was somewhat compensated for, first by removing medical relief from the categories of disenfranchisement, and second by extending the lodger franchise to Poor Law elections in 1894. The latter opened poor relief to influence from a few of those probably most likely to fall under its sway, even if it still disenfranchised them when they actually fell.

Equally important were regulations on residence and registration. Basically, the system advantaged residential stability and political commitment, and penalised their opposites. To qualify for their parliamentary votes, householders had to reside in a constituency for a minimum of twelve months. Given the timing of register-compilation, this normally involved a minimum of eighteen months, and an average of over two years – partly because any movement out of the constituency, or for lodgers even next-door, involved recommencing the qualification process. In urban worlds of constant movement, this penalised many sorts of people. Around 20–30 per cent of potential borough electors allegedly moved across borough boundaries even in 1900, by which time, as we have seen, urban populations were stabilising. Not all of those thus penalised were poor. Working-class movement tended to occur within small areas, often just a moonlight-flit ahead of the landlord. Middle-class families, particularly those of upwardly mobile professionals, were more likely to move across constituency and town boundaries. However, several mobile groups were clearly working-class. The skilled unemployed were apt to travel long distances in search of work. Increasing numbers of people were displaced, but rarely satisfactorily rehoused, by street and slum clearance. Many city dwellers undertook a rhythmic migration between urban and rural locations – spending the spring, summer and autumn in agricultural pursuits, and returning to urban areas in winter when these contracted. Again the system displayed a tendency, albeit somewhat randomly directed, to politically neutralise at points of maximum suffering and perhaps radicalisation.

As noted, different disadvantage was inherent in the way the register was compiled, and in the central role given to local party agents in objecting to known voters for the other side and inserting their own supporters. Parties are often cited as important democratising agencies.

In many respects, this is accurate in Britain as elsewhere. They provide electoral competition and organisation, information and choice for the voter. However, they perform these functions incidentally to pursuing their own interests. These interests are framed by the character of the system wherein parties operate. In some circumstances this may lead them to operate in ways dysfunctional to popular politics. In nineteenth-century Britain, much of what parties did was entirely functional. They were important in all the respects already outlined. Indeed, as evident in Chapter 3, party rivalry could lead even the most prestigious local elites into competitively appeasing, and thus significantly empowering, lowly social groups. On the other hand, parties' role in parliamentary and municipal registration processes was altogether more ambivalent. After draft electoral registers were published, interest dictated that agents should make claims for including as many of their own supporters as possible, and objecting to the presence of multiple supporters of their opponents. This was decided by Registration Courts. Where competition was high, and both party machines equally efficient, electoral registers were likely to be significantly democratised. In such circumstances, even Tories probably had little interest in low working-class registration, whatever the party high command might think.[47] However, where party strength and efficiency were less evenly matched, the weaker side's supporters tended to find their names expunged, often arbitrarily. This was a system likely to disadvantage the less partisan, and those on the weaker side. It also particularly disadvantaged working men, the nature of whose education and daytime work commitments (registration courts invariably met during working hours) made re-inclusion without help from party machines very difficult.

Electoral registration also produced another problem from a democratic viewpoint. Although parties provided electoral competition and choice, considerations of interest might well lead them to do the opposite. Admittedly, contests and thus choice rose in the wake of enfranchisement. However, it might also be in party interests to avoid contests in parliamentary, even more municipal, elections. Some constituencies, and more municipal wards, went uncontested for many years as parties came to 'arrangements to avoid...expense and tumult'. Aside from satisfaction about the terms of deference in some constituencies (declining rapidly after 1880), what primarily underpinned this behaviour were understandings by both sides about the state of post-registration electoral rolls. Effectively, the real contest had already occurred without voters being consulted.

The foregoing inertia was not visited particularly upon working-class voters. Indeed, small-town constituencies were the most frequent targets of such arrangements. Far more clearly disadvantageous to the poor was multiple voting. Though electors could only cast one vote per constituency, owners or occupiers of property elsewhere might well have others. Many businessmen, particularly as the century progressed and ownership separated increasingly from management, had at least two votes: from business-premises in one constituency and a house elsewhere. Many had far more. Although not consistently advantaging large property (scattered property was more useful), working men were never so empowered.

Taken overall, the 1867 and 1884 inclusions, whilst extensive, were also limited. While many were included, some overlapping groups of males were also rather haphazardly excluded – the politically uncommitted, the geographically mobile or unstable, certain sorts of dependants and the acutely suffering. This was partly underpinned by party calculation. Equally important was a consensus amongst most of those included – respectable working men contemplating the abyss below as much as elites and middle-class reformers concerned about political demand and rationality – that one group, the 'residuum' must be excluded. Few would have disagreed with Bright, popular tribune as he was, that they should exclude 'the excessively poor . . . in a condition of dependence such as to give no reasonable expectation . . . they would be able to resist the many temptations rich and unscrupulous men would offer them'.[48] Certainly not the working-class Reform League with their belief that manhood suffrage excluded 'half-adult' men like paupers and criminals, unable to vote rationally and independently.[49] The residuum was amorphous, and as the First World War demonstrated, rather mythical. Nevertheless, even sophisticated observers believed it existed and was potentially dangerous or at least infective. Consequently, the negative impact of such perceptions upon further democratisation was significant and enduring.

Indeed, political demarcations drawn in 1884 lasted until 1918. They produced consensus amongst politicians and policy-makers about whose needs and demands were permissible and whose illegitimate. After 1867, attempts to reach out to male non-electors, through meetings or attempts to address their concerns, ceased. So too did attempts to use them to influence electors, a closure reinforced by the 1872 Ballot Act. Politicians happily competed to satisfy the legitimate desires of working-class electors – for trade-union legal immunity; further legal protection for co-ops and friendly societies; extended factory regulation; limited direct representation; even eventually for certain sorts of social welfare. Local politicians competed to 'improve' and entertain working men, and grant their organisations local ceremonial status. However, the supposed residuum were largely excluded from political concern, except in so far as they provided additional reasons for appeasing and eventually protecting the respectable working class – to avoid them becoming radicalised or morally contaminated by contact.[50] If anything, respectable working-class enfranchisement coincided with hardening attitudes towards those below – expressed through reinvigorating the Poor Law from 1871, measures of slum clearance, and discussions of 'labour colonies' up to 1914.

Universal Male Suffrage

Of all the franchise reforms, that of 1918 was the first to explicitly exhibit democratic, as distinct from merely increasingly popular, intentions. Admittedly, business and university voters remained significant qualifications to the principle of one-vote-one-value (indeed university seats were increased from 2 to 7), and were justified on traditional grounds of quality and interest.[51] There were still clear signs both of traditional notions that full citizenship was an earned privilege, and partisan calculation. Massive wartime participation and sacrifice by men (and women) had greatly enhanced the governing elite's belief in their political safety, loyalty and therefore fitness. This partly underpinned its willingness to enfranchise existing 18–20 year-old servicemen, legitimised even by Gladstone's conception of 'moral fitness'. Fears of the 'residuum' somewhat receded from political discussion, even though reviving for some in the 1930s.[52] Meanwhile, all politicians, particularly Conservatives, could draw comfort from the knowledge, steadily emerging in recent years, that new male citizens included not merely many residentially unstable working men but also numerous commercial travellers, and upwardly and thus geographically mobile professionals. Conservatives could also contemplate the business and university votes with agreeable anticipation.

Yet such rationalisations rang hollow. Few within the Coalition Government felt they had much choice about including men. Agitation played no more part in 1918 than in 1884/5. However, most assumed that, if the system was to survive and 'contentment and stability prevail', universal citizenship could not be denied men, perceived to have suffered so much and to have noticed Russia's Revolution. Politicians therefore surrendered most of the controls they had hitherto maintained over the democratisation process, even though eugenics was fuelling lingering fears about the residuum. This explains why pauperism and most other forms of dependency were so easily removed from the disqualifications, for women as well as men. It also explains why most remaining links between voting and property disappeared: residence requirements were reduced to six months and restrictions on lodgers heavily reduced; even possessors of chaotically scattered property, along with university graduates, were allowed just two votes (eventually losing them altogether in 1948). This surrender of control, along with women's enfranchisement, and the coming-of-age of many men since 1910, explains why the Act coincided with the largest numerical and percentage increase ever in the electorate. In 1910, there were some 7.7 million voters; in 1918, this rose by 180 per cent to 21.4 million. The male electorate alone rose by 67 per cent to 12.9 million. For men, voting became an individual rather than 'moral right'.

The same managerial retreat was expressed in two further highly significant steps. First, electoral registration became bureaucratic rather than party-political and legal. The highly politicised, haphazard and lawyer-friendly system, operating since 1832, was thereby terminated. With qualifications simplified and disqualifications few, the needs originally spawning it had largely disappeared. Second, 1918 witnessed another substantial seats-redistribution in line with accelerating demographic change. With social homogeneity still the primary criterion for boundary-change, channels were kept open for expressing working-class, along with middle-class, feelings. Reallocation did not actually happen again until 1948, but it was assumed that population was the only criterion for seat-allocation.

This surrender of control, and the consequent granting of citizenship by virtue of male adulthood alone, is finally evident in the abandonment of another key-stone of political fitness. Politicians, with little explicit protest, conceded all this without assurance that new voters would be decently self-reliant. Indeed, they conceded in spite of the fact that, even because, they believed working men and women (existing voters or not) had become radicalised by wartime experience – thereby wanting more than just citizenship. Along with women's enfranchisement, this also helps explain why this bout of democratisation, unlike 1832, 1867 and 1884/5, coincided so closely with the accelerated emergence of state welfare on to the political, and more significantly the electoral, agenda: why unemployment insurance was so rapidly universalised, in spite of the hostility working people had shown it in 1911; why 'homes fit for heroes' figured so prominently in the 1918 election; and why house-provision and rent-control remained central to governmental activity in subsequent decades.

Inclusion and Incorporation

However, as with the other groups under consideration, though enfranchisement ultimately symbolised working men's political inclusion, other aspects were also significant. Most important was direct representation. Like the franchise, this was facilitated by legal enactment. Yet, as with urban middle-class males after 1832, representative inclusion proceeded slowly. Furthermore, slow parliamentary entry was not greatly compensated for by rapid municipal inclusion.

The first working-class MPs emerged in 1874. By 1905, 38 years after 1867, there were just 12. Only after the growth of the Labour Party, itself initially a reaction to the paucity of working-men candidates produced by the two main parties, did working-class parliamentary representation significantly rise. Of Labour's 42 MPs in December 1910, nearly all were from manual backgrounds. Indeed, the inter-war years saw manual representation at its height, particularly within Labour cabinets where it topped 50 per cent.

Similar patterns were evident locally. In the 1890s, around 7 per cent of Birmingham councillors were manual workers or union officials. In the same decade, 1.5 per cent of Leeds councillors could be so classified, as could 6 per cent of Wolverhampton's, 2.4 per cent of Blackburn's, 0.6 per cent of Bolton's. Salford, one of Britain's most proletarian cities, elected none. By around 1914, these had risen to 7.5 per cent in Birmingham, 10 per cent in Leeds, 10 per cent in Wolverhampton, 6.9 per cent in Blackburn, 7.9 per cent in Bolton, 2.7 per cent in Salford. The numbers increase somewhat if we add insurance agents, an occupation having the cardinal qualification for municipal service, that of flexible time. They are also more impressive on urban district and parish councils where demands on time were less. However, only in inter-war and post-1945 Britain, with Labour's rise, are there substantial increases in manual municipal representation. In Birmingham, the 1920s saw manual/trade union representation running at between 13.4 and 15.8 per cent, though this fell with Labour's national collapse in the 1930s, and rose little after 1945. Manual workers reached 16–17 per cent of Wolverhampton's inter-war council. In Blackburn, they attained 20.8 per cent by 1926–30, and 27.6 by 1931–35, though again it rose little after 1945. In Bolton, working men reached 16.4 per cent in 1926–30 and 23.5 in 1946–50. In Salford, they attained 21.4 per cent of council membership in 1926–30, and in the one-party-state conditions after 1945 ranged between 30.6 (1946–50) to 41.8 per cent (1961–5).[53]

This pattern is significant both for its increase and its limitation, compared to the proportions of manual workers amongst the population and the electorate, and compared to middle-class representation, even in Labour ranks. Both require explanation.

Substantially increased manual representation after 1918 was facilitated by legal changes. The parliamentary property qualification, abolished in 1859, had never been relevant. However, election expense emphatically was. This explains the importance for labour representation of limiting campaign expenses via the 1883 Corrupt and Illegal Practices, and even more the 1918 Representation of the People, Acts.[54] Equally significant were the £400 salary granted to MPs in 1911, and allowing councillors expenses in lieu of wages lost through municipal work in 1948. Yet, like other aspects of political inclusion, social development was also involved. Most important, even more than for middle-class males, was the growth and vibrancy of working men's civil society. It was no accident that early Lib–Lab MPs were nominated and elected in constituencies where unions were strong, normally where one was dominant. Union membership had increased steadily from around 1850, but greatly accelerated in the early-twentieth century, particularly just before and after the First World War. Moreover, at a less general level, the Labour Party, itself an expression of working-class civil society, varied in strength and ability to elect MPs in direct proportion to local union vitality both before and after 1914–18.[55] Unions did not just provide unwitting political training for early working-class MPs; they also funded their election expenses, provided canvassers and legions of loyal voters and, until 1911, allowed them some sort of parliamentary salary. This was why the 1908 Osbourne Judgment preventing unions from using their funds for party-political purposes, and the 1913 Trade Union Act reversing this decision, were so important both to Labour and more generally to direct representation.

Yet there were clear limitations to working-class representation. Before 1914, this was partly due to resistance from those already on the inside political track. Just as the aristocratically-dominated political system proved resistant to the emergence and acceptance of urban professional and manufacturing MPs, so middle-class-dominated constituency associations after 1867 (and ward associations after 1882) were less than welcoming to working-men candidates. One cause was social prejudice, easy to enforce in caucuses where democratic control was counter-balanced by deference and powers of co-option.[56] Similar feelings underpinned non-Labour resistance in many towns to Labour's mayoral aspirations in inter-war councils. Yet, other factors were also involved. Before 1914, one was democratisation itself. The developing mass electorate greatly accelerated the already substantial cost of elections. Constituency parties had to operate in increasingly expensive worlds, ones moreover where poverty often precluded membership subscriptions. The only means of creating mass organisations was therefore to make membership a simple matter of declared agreement with party principles. This meant local parties had little money of their own. Consequently, the only viable candidates were those who could substantially contribute to campaign expenses, as well as funding themselves once elected. Further factors were manual jobs and wages – essentially inflexible except for shift-workers and union officials (and insurance agents), and permitting insufficient surplus income to permit the assumption of what councillors before 1914 saw as gentlemanly status. Political expense was important for parliamentary recruitment until MPs were paid in 1911, and remained permanently disadvantageous for councillors. Even trends towards evening council meetings only partly alleviated the problems, since there necessarily remained increasing hosts of day-time committee meetings, themselves produced by expanding council functions in the wake of democratisation.

Yet choice was also involved. In the last resort, union interest in legislative involvement, whilst substantial, was also limited. Though 'pure and simple' unionism was redundant, there was still a strong and understandable tendency to regard economic negotiation as the main priority – a tendency increased by the shift towards corporatism after 1918. Furthermore, the inclusion desired was as much symbolic as actual. As Chapter 3 will argue, existing elites proved reasonably adept at satisfying inclusive aspirations of this sort. Certainly, the mere fact of having *some* working-class MPs or councillors was sufficient for many. This was the logical extension of a concentration upon access to Parliament evident from the commencement of working-class, as of middle-class, radicalism. From at least the Chartist 'six points', the vote was as much about citizenship as power and policy: 'a vote for a man because he was a man'.[57] Similar pre-occupations can be read further down the system: from celebrations of council entry, embannered union processions greeting the first working-class mayors, even more from the insensate fury produced amongst inter-war Labour councillors across the country when the party was denied access to this office by anti-Socialist majorities in the inter-war years.

3. Women's Political Inclusion

Women's inclusion, like men's, possessed clear landmarks: 1869, 1918 and 1928. For these and other reasons, it was long-continuing. It was also as much local as national; as much socio-economic as legal; and as much incorporative and symbolic as power-related. However, it was different from the inclusion of men in that, at least by the time women achieved the parliamentary franchise in 1918 and 1928, most other legal inhibitions on free and representative democracy had disappeared – open voting, malapportionment, unpaid MPs, and more uncertainly unlimited election spending. Furthermore, women's parliamentary enfranchisement coincided with, and helped finally dissolve, links between voting and property. It also coincided with the final near-severance of the relationship between party interest and constituency boundary redrawal. This said, just as with middle- and working-class men, there was a considerable time-lag between enfranchisement and significant direct entry into Parliament. Indeed, like manual workers, women have never to date been legislatively represented proportionate to their population numbers. Moreover, though far more women became local councillors, those doing so were long drawn predominantly from the solid middle, upper middle, or upper class. This was primarily due to civil society's relatively undeveloped character amongst working-class women, and their apparently cheerful re-embracing of home-life after 1918. As with other groups, political inclusion, and indeed the desire for it, was related to broader changes in women's social and economic position.

Though more marginal than middle- or working-class men, women were not wholly absent from politics before 1869, nor entirely without influence. There is some evidence of them participating in parish meetings and other open institutions of local governance.[58] Unmarried female householders also had voting-rights in more formal local elective processes until 1835. In this sense, as in some others, the 1832 Reform and 1835 Municipal Corporation Acts represented democratic steps backwards since they formally declared voting a male prerogative, a situation confirmed by the courts in 1869. However, women's interests might also find expression through notions of virtual representation:

men casting their votes on their wives' and daughters' behalf as well as their own, a persuasive opportunity for strong-minded women until at least 1872.

In turn, this gave some legitimacy to women's participation in pressure-group politics, particularly those related to moral reform, and thus to their sanctioned role as moral carriers for the family. As we shall see, they became important and influential participants in campaigns ranging from anti-slavery and prison reform to temperance and Contagious Diseases Acts agitation. This was further legitimised by roles elsewhere. In a world heavily influenced by attachments to minimum government, considerable power was likely to reside in the social sector. Here, at least middle-class women enjoyed significant scope for influential activity, particularly in the vast network of organised charity. They became increasingly crucial, first as volunteers and then committee participants. This gave them potential influence, both through direct contact with the recipients of largesse and over policy making in what would now be seen as the welfare field. Meanwhile, at the top of the social pyramid, some older women were powerful gatekeepers of aristocratic society.[59]

Finally, women's lack of formal access did not prevent Parliament taking their assumed interests into account. Indeed, their perceived special vulnerability within the public world, and crucial maternal and educative roles, rendered protective action almost essential. Thus, along with children, they were primary targets for ever-expanding factory and mines regulation. This eventually displeased equal rights feminists, and represented a very male-centred perception of women's interests. However, it is also significant that women achieved, or at least were granted, significant amounts of legal equality in the decades before 1918. Their rights in relation to child custody improved in 1886, as did access to divorce from 1857 and legal separation in 1878. After 1870 and 1882, they were no longer perceived to have surrendered all property rights and wealth upon marriage. Even prostitutes were guaranteed against compulsory hospital confinement in 1886.

Nevertheless, women's political access was more marginal and informal prior to formal inclusion than any other group of political entrants. Inclusion occurred in two basic stages – the first local, the second national. The former emphasises how important the local political scene was to women's political inclusion, as it had been to that of middle- and working-class males. Due to its continuing relative autonomy from the centre, locality provided an alternative focus for real influence, where women could be elected, and sometimes inadvertently trained for ultimate national entry, and where their slow acceptance as full citizens could be celebrated.

It was a mark of the influence of separated spheres that local inclusion preceded the national sort far more clearly than for either group of men. Local government, with its concern with various sorts of service-regulation and provision – education, poor relief, gas and water, housing, public health – was far more easily legitimisable as an arena for women's participation than its national counterpart. Particularly was this so because the way had already been shown by women's role in organised charity – a field which even many men saw as closely akin to local government, in that service in either was part of 'the duties and burdens' of the comfortably-off. Contemporaries therefore perceived little incongruity in the 1867 Reform Act being immediately succeeded by two apparently contradictory actions: the one, a court decision that the householder franchise was specifically male; the other, the 1869 Local Government Act, permitting unmarried female ratepayers to vote in local elections. The result was that, by 1900, over a million women were registered on municipal, Poor Law, education board and county electoral rolls, representing around 20 per cent of the electorate. This was one reason why social welfare issues like the provision of baths, wash-houses, lodging-houses and nurseries, the care of pauper children, and girls' education began emerging on to local political agendas. It was also why local politicians began perceiving the electoral need, irrespective of sanitary risk, to 'kiss dirty little slum children in order to propitiate their slatternly mothers'.[60]

Women were also explicitly permitted to stand as Poor Law guardians and education board members, even if a legal decision in 1889 specifically excluded them from becoming councillors until 1907. This permitted first a trickle, then more steady flows of women on to these bodies. By 1895, there were 800 female guardians, and by 1902 370 education board members. In this respect, women probably kept approximate pace with working men. This was primarily because, as a group, women spanned the entire social spectrum. Their ranks therefore included many educated, self-confident and articulate people, with surplus energy and time derived from separated spheres and servanthood. For many, charitable participation had provided at least as much local visibility and political training as trade unions and the like had for working men. Most women representatives were drawn from these sources, their selection and election often resting upon local celebrity flowing from their families' economic and social leadership. The same factors ensured them forcefulness and expertise, providing influence out of proportion to their numbers, and reinforcing the tendency for women's issues to emerge on to the local legislative agenda. Those who stayed elected could also achieve rapid political elevation. By 1914, just seven years after they were permitted to become councillors, 50 had done so, and one had become mayor of Oldham.[61]

However, unless one assumes class to be wholly irrelevant, this was only a partial form of direct representation, particularly given that the vast majority of those who came within the purview, at least of boards of guardians and education, were working class. The socially elevated character of women's local representation perhaps mattered little in relation to educational or municipal services. Realising the poor needed baths and wash-houses did not necessarily depend on class background (though it helped), even if perceptions of appropriate treatment of school children sometimes did. However, greater problems arose over the Poor Law. This was particularly because women guardians emerged at the precise point when central government was leading a determined return to the 'principles of 1834'. Many also emerged from charitable backgrounds at a time when charities were being influenced by related ideas purveyed by the Charity Organisation Society. Though women guardians undoubtedly helped humanise the treatment of workhouse and Poor Law hospital inmates, they were constrained even here by their attachment to 'less eligibility'. More important was their belief in the virtues of indoor relief at a time when the Local Government Board's campaign was reinvigorating working-class hatred of the workhouse.

All this points to the fact that working women were even more constrained from legislative participation at least up to 1914 than working men. This was not just by education and economic circumstances. Many also faced the 'double-shift' imposed by family responsibilities alongside paid work. As we shall see in Chapter 7, working women also had only limited access to civil organisations where political training might be available. Operative here were the same factors that, outside Lancashire, rendered them so indifferent to suffrage agitation before 1914.

Nevertheless, this local phase of political inclusion was highly important. In some respects, it paved the way for national inclusion: training some women for future parliamentary participation, giving rather more a sense that women were capable of filling elective political roles and could do so legitimately. Men too probably had their horizons similarly expanded – both as legislative colleagues and voters. This is particularly plausible at a time when urban locality could still command considerable mass attention, an ability greatly facilitated by intensely serious local newspapers now in their expansive prime. It also again highlights the importance of local government and the local scene generally to the political inclusion of all the groups reviewed in this book. Until 1914, localities were focuses of substantial, autonomous, if now declining, power. Local government thus gave access to policy-making, in areas important to women, as to both middle- and working-class men. Along with civil society, of which some observers see it as part, local government gave access to politically-relevant training. Local-government participation could also provide considerable honour and esteem, thus becoming a powerful means of marking a group's arrival in social and political life. By 1914, women notables were becoming aldermen and mayors – a development given considerable attention by local newspapers, and important symbolic attention by those involved. Partly as result, they also began eroding the hitherto male-exclusive preserve of local obituaries. In these senses, for women as for men, the local arena provided the means of marking important degrees of citizenship.

For some, women's local-government participation probably helped legitimise broader national inclusion. Certainly, along with charitable endeavour, it fuelled many feminists' indignation at women's continued non-possession of the parliamentary vote, particularly when it had so long been granted to what seemed so many less-deserving men. Beyond this, matters are more uncertain. Separated spheres could be stretched to permit women's participation in local government, as in organised charity. They could also sanction certain sorts of socially-conscious pressure-group activity like prison reform, temperance, social purity and prostitution. Entry to Parliament, however, with its preoccupation with imperial and national financial affairs, was far harder to legitimise. Indeed, participation there, even as voters, required separation to be explicitly eroded if not rejected. This was hard even for some philanthropically and locally active women, and was one reason why the anti-suffragists picked up considerable pre-war support from this quarter just before the war. It was equally hard for many politicians, reliant as they often were upon wifely accomplishments as hostesses, creators of peaceful domestic refuges from the conflicts of public life, and purveyors of witty but essentially diverting conversation.[62] It was difficult for many middle-class males, whose business and professional success probably still rested upon domesticated but well-connected wives. It may have been equally problematic for working men in a period when real wage rises, allied to spreading by-law housing, were permitting working-class families to embrace domesticity more enthusiastically than ever before. (Notions of 'family wages' earned by men remained resilient.) Alongside long-nurtured resentment about bossy charitable women, this may have rendered the Suffragettes' full-frontal challenge to separation sufficiently outrageous to legitimise violence against them in working-class areas just before the First World War.

This highlights another feature of Britain's pattern of staged democratisation: the way the predilections of those already included, and politicians' calculations about them, helped set the timing and terms for admitting those still outside. It seems clear that, although the House of Commons had voted in favour of enfranchisement since 1897, things were moving against suffrage-supporters just before 1914. As argued already, this was partly due to Suffragette behaviour interacting with male prejudices – something evident to George Lansbury when he resigned to unsuccessfully fight a by-election in Bow and Bromley in 1912 on the enfranchisement issue. It was also because of calculations by politicians of all parties about the electoral consequences of votes for women. These determined that enfranchisement of the sort desired by most prominent suffragists – on the same basis as existing male qualifications – was politically impossible. To Liberal and Labour MPs alike, whatever their suffrage sympathies, votes restricted to female householders seemed likely to upset the existing balance of male social forces, creating a permanent Conservative majority from which that party would have no incentive to escape via further enfranchisement. Yet, for many politicians, and probably many voters of all classes, universal suffrage, with its apparent inclusion of the 'residuum', seemed equally threatening. In this sense the First World War was highly important: women's role in the wartime economy reinforced their claims to full citizenship; it familiarised many with the idea that women could move far beyond the domestic sphere, and do so without threatening male jobs (particularly if they could be safely ejected afterwards); and it both established the loyalties and strengthened the claims to full citizenship even of the casual poor. Meanwhile the Russian Revolution seemed to show the dangers of refusing these claims. Yet, even in 1917, the Speaker's Conference avoided recommending enfranchising women under thirty primarily for fear of overturning male domination of the electorate.

This brings us to the final acts of inclusion. As with men, the 1918 Representation of the People Act produced a major change in principle. The effective enfranchisement of almost all women over thirty (votes being given to female ratepayers and wives of ratepayers) meant they acquired votes as rights, rather than privileges earned through demonstrating appropriate virtues. In this sense, this was the first act of explicit democratisation, doubly so because, like men, they only had to possess their qualifications for six months prior to registration, rather than the previous twelve. As a result, around 8.4 million women became voters, representing some 39.6 per cent of the total. By 1924, this had risen to around 9.3 million (42.8 per cent).[63] Of equal benefit to women, as to men, were other changes wrought by the 1918 Act: reducing plural voters to under 2 per cent of the electorate and the further redistribution of seats on the basis of population. With voting almost a right, the Act also bureaucratised the registration process, thereby removing party agents and thus the greatest informal impediment to enfranchisement.

However, as Chapter 3 shows, older concerns were still evident for women if not men. Women under 30 were considered too 'giddy headed' and too unmarried to be capable of exercising safely rational democratic choice.[64] Furthermore, like working men in 1867, women could be safely enfranchised precisely because they had abandoned extreme franchise agitation of the sort pursued by the Chartists and Suffragettes respectively. Still excluded at any age, partly on grounds of dependence though mainly because their inclusion would have increased female proportions amongst the electorate, were daughters living in parental homes, female lodgers and living-in servants.

Nevertheless, the Representation of the People Act finally killed off these concerns, by setting going the second of the self-sustaining phases of democratisation. Just as 1867 had led almost inexorably to 1884, so the 1928 Equalisation of the Franchise Act emerged inevitably from anomalies created in 1918. There was little popular pressure for enfranchisement, and (unlike 1918) little fear of any. However, just as by the 1880s there no longer seemed any good reason to exclude agricultural male householders, so now there was little real justification beyond male fears of female majority for excluding the remaining adult women – those between 21 and 30 and those over 30 (around 1.8 million[65]) who were neither ratepayers nor their wives. The result in 1928 was 5.3 million extra voters, bringing the parliamentary electorate to 28 854 748, of which 52.2 per cent were women. 1928 also saw the sexes equally enfranchised for municipal purposes. Finally, and without qualification, the vote thus became a right possessed through simple adulthood. Even if one-vote-one-value still remained to be fully established, notions of unfitness remained only in relation to prisoners and (by virtue of dependency) serving soldiers. Even living-in servants were now declared fit.

However, as with working- and middle-class males, there was considerable delay between enfranchisement and other forms of political inclusion such as election to Parliament. Women's representational numbers undoubtedly increased in the inter-war years. However these have never matched their proportions within either population or electorate. This is evident in Parliament. Though the first woman MP arrived in 1919, there were never more than 15 before 1945. By 1964, there were just 28. Only since 1987 have numbers begun substantially accelerating. The 1997 election increased women MPs from 62 to 119. Municipal patterns are similar, though here matters were modified by the fact that some women were enfranchised from 1869, and eligible for service as guardians and education-board members from the same date, and as councillors from 1907. Nevertheless, although their numbers increased, they hardly invaded the municipal scene in the inter-war years or even after 1945. Salford's primarily working-class population elected no women at all before the Second World War; by 1949, 8 of its 64 council members were of a female persuasion; the same number were present in 1979; by 2000, there were 15 out of 60. Next door in Manchester, there were 2 (out of 136) in 1919, 10 (of 144) in 1939, 18 (of 152) in 1959, 18 out of 98 in 1979, and 22 out of 99 in 2000. Matters were not markedly more representative in socially far more salubrious Canterbury. In 1929, 2 of the 24 council members were women; 3 in 1939; 3 in 1958; 6 (of 49) in 1979, and 12 in 1999. If these figures are representative, most councils seem to have reached a stage where 25 per cent of their membership is female.

Underpinning this are several factors. One has obviously been, as with the franchise, and as with previous included groups, the predilections of those already on the political inside track. Admittedly, women became increasingly significant, indeed essential, participants in mass politics from the 1880s. The electioneering role of the Primrose League, Women's Liberal Federation and later, Women's Labour League increased steadily and impressively. However, outside these bodies, male domination of office-holding in all three party organisations hardly created sympathetic atmospheres or cultures for women's political recruitment. Class tended to reinforce these tendencies. Indeed, it is one reason why working-class representation as a whole never matched electoral or demographic numbers, even at municipal level. Working men emerged in increasingly significant representational numbers, but were scarcely followed by their wives and daughters. Underpinning this has been the fact that male-dominated working-class civil organisations have been even more resistant to women's representative claims than their middle-class counterparts. As Chapter 7 suggests, working-class women's access to civil society was significant, increasing and better than many other European countries. Nevertheless, women only slowly became office-holders in unions, friendly societies and, the Women's Co-operative Guild notwithstanding, the co-operative movement. Given these have been primary agencies of political training and recruitment, working-class women's slow representational inclusion is unsurprising. This is doubly so because, as evident later, at the precise point when middle-class women and their families began abandoning separated spheres, their working-class counterparts embraced them with increasing enthusiasm, spurred on by rising real wages and improving housing standards. Thus working men's continuing preferences for domesticated wives were matched, particularly in the inter-war years, by women's own preference for home-making, given that houses became increasingly comfortable, whilst paid work remained as boring as ever.

The Most Recent Steps

Though from 1928, the principle that voting was a right of simple adulthood (defined as 21 in 1918 and 18 in 1969) was broadly established and accepted, there still remained significant qualifications to the ideal of equal electoral access. On the Mainland, after the 1918 redistribution, the disproportion between population and representation was allowed to grow very significantly until 1948. Certain sorts of fitness still received additional reward by virtue of the business and university votes. Indeed, so persuaded were politicians by these traditional notions of quality that graduates were actually granted five further seats in 1918. In the early 1920s business voters numbered around 200 000 (217 000 by 1945) and graduate-electors 60 000. Property and education were thereby rewarded with up to two votes (additional to that gained by simple residence). Effectively, it also rewarded manhood and Conservatism (the business vote alone is believed to have swung constituencies rightwards on 18 occasions between 1922 and 1945, quite aside from the two seats regularly bequeathed by the City of London). Only in 1948 were these remaining qualifications to a fully democratic franchise finally expunged, along with the six-months residency qualification and two-seat constituencies. In 1969, adulthood was redefined from 21 to 18. 2001 witnessed the enfranchisement of the homeless.

After Partition in 1922, Ulster actually retreated very significantly from full democracy. Parliamentary seats and boundaries were selected and arranged on the same basis as the Mainland, though a simple majority system and religious polarisation ensured relatively few were contested before 1945. However, municipal electors were restricted to homeowning ratepayers. Gender aside, this rendered them more restricted than before 1869, producing just 600 000 voters compared with 900 000 of the parliamentary sort. Generously-propertied businessmen could garner up to six votes. Most important, initial provisions for PR for both Stormont and municipal councils had by 1929 been abandoned in favour of first-past-the-post. This, together with careful ward-gerrymandering, Unionist unity and the low level of Catholic business activity and home-ownership, ensured that a Protestant majority of 66 per cent captured 85 per cent of Ulster's municipalities. This orientation towards Protestantism, property and male gender continued until Stormont was terminated in 1972.

The process of inclusion clearly tells us something about why British democratisation was successful in the sense that formal inclusion was accomplished without significant threats to the resulting system. It was slow and thus digestible. Elites changed sufficiently gradually never to perceive themselves as threatened before becoming resigned to disappearance. Groups could achieve satisfaction at more than one level. The national and local institutions targeted for democratisation were themselves sufficiently prestigious to become powerfully self-legitimising, such that democratisation itself became an agency of incorporation. Beyond this is the ambivalent fact that even the Mainland liberal democracy rounded off in 1948 and 1969 is outwardly one of the less ambitious models on offer. It has little tradition or provision for referenda and recall, little interest in anything beyond first-past-the-post voting-systems, and a parliamentary upper house whose links with democracy still defy rational imagination. However, to fully understand both the character and success of democratisation, it is clear even from this chapter that we must take things further. We must examine the interactions between this process and Britain's elites; and between it and the civil character of those being included.

3 The Role of British Political Elites

In the literature attempting to explain democratisation's success or failure, there has been considerable argument about the importance of elites compared to other, more contextual, factors – economic forces, the impact of international events, mass social and political attitudes, and civil society. Elite-centred explanations emphasise the importance of choices made by key political figures during democratic transitions: leaders might be constrained by the national and international context, but they still possess considerable freedom to make decisions and adopt policies deeply influential for success or failure.[1] Opponents have argued that elites are prisoners of context. At most, leaders display skill in seizing opportunities created by this context, or sensitivity to changes in public mood. In many democratising polities, they fail to understand what is happening – traditional elites through being out of touch with social and political change; new elites by being insulated from the hard compromises of ordinary politics until suddenly required to confront them as old exclusive political patterns give way to more open ones.[2]

Much of this argument derives from contemplating twentieth-century democratisations, particularly post-1945 – at times and in polities therefore where transitions have been rapid. However, in the much longer transitions characterising many polities in the first, nineteenth-century, phase of democratisation in North-West Europe and North America, political leadership probably had more chance of crucial impact. This appears particularly likely because the international context, though significant, impinged on internal politics far less than today: mass communications were far slower, economies more self-contained, and the IMF non-existent.

In one sense, elites are always important, and this will flavour much of the following argument. Democratisation is never just a passive process presided over by bureaucrats, or by democratic ideologues concerned only to design perfect systems. Rather, it is intensely political, and undertaken by leaders, groups or parties who – whatever their concerns about the system, and their wish to popularise it – also have interests to protect and serve. This has long been a truism in writings about reforms to existing democracies – for example, changes in French electoral systems or American legislative-district reapportionment. The point is less often made about broader acts of democratisation. Yet, political calculation is important, and certainly affected Britain's progress until at least 1918.

None of this implies Britain's leaders were the only factor underpinning success, nor that, from Edward I's time onwards, they were somehow uniquely far-sighted, though after 1688 they were certainly flexible. I am also not offering wholesale support for historical advocates of 'high politics'. They presuppose political processes insulated from the outside world. In fact, the competitiveness of British elites connected them directly with that world through calculations about the loyalties and grievances of groups within and beyond the political pale. The approach here is eclectic. We have already noted democratisation's fortunate coincidence with sustained economic growth; later chapters will explore the importance of civil society. There is also evidence of incomprehension, mishandling and stupidity by elements amongst British elites, also of policies deeply constrained by irresistible outside pressure. Peterloo, and Tory diehard attitudes to the 1830–1 Reform crisis stand testimony to the first three. So too does the House of Lords' decision to 'die in the dark' over the 1909 Budget. Running through the nineteenth century were also widely-shared demographic and terminological uncertainties about the extent of political fitness, and about how many people particular qualifications might allow into the electorate.

At more enlightened but nevertheless responsive levels, the Whigs' decision to embrace Reform in 1830 grew from broader agreement across much of the elite that political change was obligatory if system-threatening disturbance was to be avoided. The wave of popular acclaim greeting the perceived radicalism of their solution, and the fury at its rejection by the Lords, meant there could be no turning back – whatever some ministers might desire. A high-political picture of the 1867 Reform Act may be more plausible. However, there seems little doubt that, once extra-parliamentary agitation had got underway after Lowe's famous insult to the unenfranchised, the incoming Derby–Disraeli Administration felt compelled to take up the issue and adopt provisions with at least approximately apparent effects to those Gladstone and Russell had envisaged. By 1918, few politicians felt they had much choice about enfranchising the remaining 40 per cent of adult males, even existing servicemen under 21, if they were to avoid serious disturbance. Meanwhile, there was a logic to the democratisation process alongside simple responsiveness. De Tocqueville was perhaps overstating the case in 1848 in predicting:

> Once a people begin to interfere with the voting qualification, one can be sure ... sooner or later it will abolish it altogether ... after each ... concession, the forces of democracy are strengthened ... the ambition of those below the qualifying limit increases in proportion to the number of those above it ... there is no halting-place until universal suffrage has been attained.[3]

Nevertheless, politicians like Peel felt the same way, and the nineteenth-century progress of democratisation in North-West European and North American polities possessed a retrospective inevitability that is hard to deny. Certainly in Britain, some steps were partly produced by simple logic. 1832 did not exactly produce 1867, but the household suffrage principle, once granted to boroughs in 1867, could not long be denied to counties, even in the absence of major agitation. Moreover, the new electorate's perceived corruptibility pointed logically to the ballot in 1872, and to effective control over bribery in 1883.

However, there is much about British politics and society suggesting that leaders – local and national – were likely to play a more significant and autonomous role in democratisation, as in other policy areas. British, particularly English, society was highly susceptible to elite influence. In 1800, it was strongly hierarchical and deferential. Over the long term, urbanisation, industrialisation and, as we shall argue, civil organisation eroded these characteristics, but in the short-to-medium term, hierarchy remained significant. The rise of industrial business enterprise notwithstanding, the landed classes dominated the national governmental, parliamentary and administrative elite until at least the 1880s. In conjunction with wealthy business families with whom they were merging to produce 'a generalised upper class', they remained centrally important until at least 1914.[4] The elite's role was underpinned by the fact that landowners remained the wealthiest social group until at least the Agricultural Depression.[5] They retained significant patronage powers. Land dominated the exclusive London Circle, and subsidiary county circles, until the 1880s.[6] In those numerous rural localities where landholdings were large and owners resident, they dominated local administrative, social, political and economic life – commanding dependency, deference, patronage and social admission. Titled land-owners also influenced urban life – especially in small towns (still in many respects the dominant urban unit until late in the century), and in larger ones where the character of local industry – mining for example – encouraged economic and thus social partnership between landed and industrial capital.[7] The overall result was a national elite with immense if diminishing power by virtue of combining political, social and economic leadership, doing so not just nationally but also in many rural localities. Legitimacy was reinforced by the deference the elite commanded even amongst some radicals and their working-class followers. Both the factory-reform and Chartist movements exhibited significant nostalgia for a rural and aristocratically-dominated past, as the charisma of Richard Oastler and Feargus O'Connor both amply testify.

In many urban-industrial places, aristocratic and gentlemanly influence was admittedly minimal. Yet here, the very personal character of industrial leadership, before the coming of purpose-created limited companies, and the in-turned character of nineteenth-century local life, often meant domination by a sort of urban squirearchy – also combining political (municipal and party) with social (philanthropic and sociable) and economic leadership. Its power was admittedly circumscribed due to the pluralistic and conflictual character of urban life and its fractured local political systems. Nevertheless, local elites' ability to win in situations of political conflict, and influence the political agenda in more discreet ways, was considerable. And in urban, as in rural, places, due to vibrant local autonomy, there was much power to be had.

Also contributing to elite importance was the fact that national and local politics were for a long time partly insulated against popular opinion, and opinion was only part of what influenced people. After as well as before 1832, much in the continuing character of electoral behaviour, the political culture amongst some of those enfranchised, the distribution of seats, and the murky borderline between political parties between 1846 and 1867, contributed to this situation. Parliamentary culture also gave elites considerable autonomy of outside pressure. However responsive to his constituents the MP might be in practice, convention powerfully insisted he was their trustee not their delegate. Until at least the 1850s, Parliament's view of its proper functions also decreed that pressure groups were illegitimate, indeed artificial, originated by unrepresentative agitators. 'Naturally arising interests' like land and trade were the only legitimate exceptions.

All nineteenth-century elites, moreover, whether national or local, rural or urban, tended to possess not just elevated views of their political role, but were also highly ambitious about shaping social attitudes. Far more than leading groups after 1914, they had high opinions of the values they felt they represented, and strongly desired to spread them downwards. They were social as well as political leaders, taking their 'improving' responsibilities very seriously. Such attitudes underpinned most charitable and educational effort. Such ambitions also informed much legislative reform – housing and factory regulation, as well as more obvious moral-reform areas like licensing, prisons and prostitution. Most important from our current standpoint, as evident later, they underlay legislative action on poverty relief. Even political inclusion itself, quite aside from efforts to cleanse and 'dry out' elections, was thought morally cleansing by some.

Finally, attitudes of most leading governmental figures indicated substantial predispositions towards autonomous decision-making. Whilst sometimes from only marginally landed backgrounds, they were nevertheless strongly attached to the aristocratic elite, philosophically, maritally, socially and by acquired property. This was particularly evident between 1846 and 1867 when Conservative decay produced Whig hegemony, and reinforced tendencies for ministers to see themselves as administrators rather than politicians, and ones uniquely fitted to govern.[8] Moreover, Gladstone, the most central figure in the democratisation process and a highly successful popular tribune, viewed politics as a high calling, throughout his career showing a strong desire to relate political action to a Christian moral code about which he thought extensively and wrote much.[9]

None of this implies politicians ignored outside pressure or opinion. Indeed, this chapter has a central contention that British elites, national and local, had strongly developed political sensitivities. What is argued is that, contrary to theories minimising the role of elites in democratic transitions, these leaders often possessed very considerable choices – about popularising the political system; about responding or not to popular pressures. Furthermore, to understand the extent and character of the various stages of British democratisation, one must understand the character and preoccupations of British political elites. In the rest of this chapter, we shall argue that they influenced first, the timing and character of democratisation; second, the context wherein it occurred and thus potentially the political agenda that followed; third, elites deeply affected how the consequences were handled.

1. Timing and Character

Britain's progress towards democracy, in the most obvious sense of enfranchisement, happened in stages. Whilst sometimes responding to outside pressures, national politicians also had their own more autonomous agendas, influencing the timing and character of these stages. Three intertwined and not always compatible motivations were continuously in play. First, they desired to adjust the political system to socioeconomic change, and, as already noted, enhance its legitimacy by including social groups when they became 'politically fit' – as close as most politicians got to democratising aspirations, before 1918 at least. For many Liberals (and most radicals), this entailed rationality and independence. For rather more, it included a decently direct relationship with property. Associatedly, it also entailed possessing values compatible with the relevant group's untroubled absorption into the existing socio-economic and thus political system. These included industry, sobriety, thrift, self-help, independence, loyalty – and for many politicians, implicitly or explicitly, respectable amounts of deference. For a long time, fitness was also associated with masculinity.

These opinions about the constituents of fitness were admittedly shared by many beyond the elites. This probably included most of those enfranchised before 1914, though this was partly consequent upon the elite's ability to influence the agenda of political aspiration. Whatever the reason, citizenship was central to what entrants wanted up to and beyond 1914. However, what distinguished politicians' versions was their linkage with the second, equally strong system-shaping concern: they desired to preserve and legitimise the power and privileges of the class to which most parliamentarians, especially before 1880, belonged. The third, not always compatible, aspiration, determining whom they included and on what terms, was to maximise the competitive advantages, within Parliament and outside, of their own party or faction. Leading politicians also wished to enhance their own position within it.

These concerns influenced political inclusion throughout. The first and second, allied to the intermittent character of popular pressure, determined that it was staged. This had the functional, if only halfforeseen, result that, unlike most twentieth-century democratisations, each new group could be included and absorbed before the next had to be coped with. The same elite preoccupations deeply affected the terms of inclusion at each stage. The intention in 1832 to attach the urban middle class to the system, and keep their hopefully dependent working class in order, is clear. Nevertheless, the characteristic landed versions of political fitness, the concern to ensure continued landed domination, and the results of negotiations within the landed interest about the terms of that domination, all infused the Act. As Cannon has noted, the £10 householder was selected not just because his inclusion would satisfy middle-class demands. It was also because he seemingly combined just the right degree of independence (by virtue of his relation to property) with deference to his betters (by virtue of the modesty of that property).[10] Meanwhile, the Act enfranchised many previously unrepresented industrial towns, yet these were selected partly for their 'virtual' representation of new 'interests' – especially manufacturing ones. They were also chosen by virtue of being 'communities', whose respectful population could be securely attached to the constitution as part of localised hierarchies, presided over by identifiable social, economic and political leaderships.

Such concerns were connected with determination to preserve landed power and privilege. This partly underpinned the Whig decision to opt for what most perceived as a radical solution – to 'settle' the matter sufficiently to neutralise middle-class resentment while leaving underlying landed control intact. Grey was only moderately hyperbolic in labelling it 'the most aristocratic measure...ever...proposed in Parliament'.[11] The notion of settlement informed the selection of the £10 householder, amputating the 'rotten' boroughs, even reallocating seats towards industrial areas. By removing the worst abuses, respectable landed 'influence' could be re-legitimised, even reinforced: by enfranchising deferential voters in English counties (£50 tenants at will); by dividing larger counties into smaller units, more easily controllable by landed magnates; by increasing the separation of urban from rural voters thereby partially confining urban freeholders to the boroughs; and especially by ensuring the persistence, even proliferation, of small boroughs, often enlarged to include surrounding rural areas. Small-town voters' 'political fitness' effectively amounted to uninhibited venality, and dependence on neighbouring landed interests for custom and patronage.

Admittedly, these clauses were not necessarily produced by a united landed interest, single-mindedly pursuing its interests. Nor were they all equally desired by Whig ministers – who, whilst preserving underlying landed hegemony, also desired some respectable degree of balance against other interests. Nevertheless, there was consensus about the need for extensive reform evident across the Whig establishment in the decades before 1832, including crucially the great landed families.[12] The final shape of the key clauses resulted from implicit and explicit negotiation between primarily Whig titled landowners and frequently Tory country gentlemen. Moreover, few historians would go as far as D.C. Moore[13] in seeing the 1832 Act as some sort of Whig confidence-trick. Gash's picture[14] of post-1832 politics remaining undisturbed has also been modified by evidence about developing opinion-politics. Nevertheless, the impact of elite concerns upon the shape and conse-quences of the Act is clear. Most historians would agree the Whigs succeeded in their central aim of re-establishing middle-class consent for the system, detaching this group from its working-class allies, whilst preserving the essentials of aristocratic control. This was so even if, as we shall see, middle-class interests impinged upon policy more than before.

Given this strategy's success in maintaining a pre-eminently landed Parliament, it is unsurprising that similar concerns re-emerged to sig-nificantly shape working-class inclusion in 1866–7. They were rendered the more autonomous because, until Lowe insulted working-class polit-ical fitness in 1866, there was little need to respond to popular pressure. Indeed, it is a mark of politicians' initiating importance that Palmer-ston's opposition should so long rule inclusion off the effective parlia-mentary agenda, and his death should allow its re-emergence. What was different from 1830–1 was that, because external threats were relatively absent, competition within the elite more clearly accompanied the other concerns about fitness and self-perpetuation.

Indeed, for one historian, party and faction were the only operative factors, with their interplay wholly insulated from extra-parliamentary opinion. In 1866, Parliament was highly factional, with no party or party-fragment commanding an enduring majority. The one constant variable was Disraeli's tactical skill – first in opposition to the Glad-stone–Russell Bill, and then in government with Derby, in charge of something he claimed as his own. Disraeli cared little about the details of reform, but, after twenty years in the political wilderness, was passionate about defeating Gladstone and then staying on top. Proposals and amendments were adopted or rejected according to their Tory or Liberal origin, and capacity to embarrass the Liberal front bench and detach Whig, even radical, dissidents. Thus 'fancy franchises' curbing the effect of working-class inclusion in the boroughs were first proposed, then allowed to disappear; so too were rating, rental, and direct-payment restrictions upon householder-electors. Even lodgers were

thinly admitted. The result was an Act more radical than anyone
expected, or most wanted.[15] It was supported even by Tory country
gentlemen because it entailed staying in government.

Such concerns and manœuvres, though influenced by external as well
as internal calculations, undoubtedly shaped many clauses. Also relevant were rival prognostications about the likely allegiances of particular
groups of prospective voters. Liberals saw respectable artisans as their
natural constituency, whilst many Tories believed theirs lurked 'below
the combining class' or 'very low in suffrage' where 'rank and position
made' people like themselves 'irresistible'.[16] Such calculations also
informed many exchanges about boundary redrawal, and what to do
about borough dwellers qualifying for county votes. Both sides saw them
as potentially Liberal: the Tories wanted them excluded from their rural
strongholds, whilst Liberals saw them as essential additions to limited
county strength.[17] This explains why Gladstone's 1866 Bill included
them in county constituencies whilst Disraeli's in 1867 excluded them.
Central to manœuvres on both sides were also the insecure positions of
the two party leaderships amidst intense factionalism – and Gladstone's
and Disraeli's need to prove to their supporters their abilities to lead,
govern and outmanœuvre the other side. The impact on perceptions of
enfranchisement is revealed in Derby's famous message to Disraeli: 'Of
all the possible hares to start, I do not know a better than the extension
to household suffrage, coupled to plurality of voting'. Equally indicative
was Disraeli's later invitation to Stanley, after rejecting a lodger
franchise as coming from Gladstone: 'I wish...you would get up an
anti-lodger speech or a speech either way...our debates want a little
variety....'.[18]

This interpretation does not exactly presuppose an elite in charge of
its destiny. Nevertheless, if we are to understand the 1867 Act we must
understand these characteristic preoccupations.

Meanwhile other, more controlling, concerns also helped shape the
clauses. Both front benches desired to preserve the landed interest,
though conceptions of the 'upper classes' were now somewhat more
likely to include middle-class elites. In all Russell's abortive Bills from
1852, it was expressed in various fancy franchises designed to advantage
quality, thus counter-balancing the limited working-class inclusion being
proposed. Gladstone, for all his apparent subsequent radicalism, did not
dissent from the consensus. Unsurprisingly, Disraeli and his Conservative colleagues were even more persuaded of the landed elite's enduring
worth – particularly of its large gentlemanly tail, underpinning the

apparatus of local government, and thus social and political stability.[19] Tories too were attached to borough fancy franchises, and more enduringly to county qualifications drawing on landed deference networks.

Calculations of competitive party advantage, as already evident, somewhat modified the effects of these aspirations – though they also reinforced them: Disraeli valued country gentlemen for their estates *and* influential Toryism. Party rivalry eventually removed most constraints upon male-householder enfranchisement. However, this was rendered permissible to an elite attached to landed conservation by two factors. First, because the Act only marginally re-allocated parliamentary seats still massively weighted towards rural and small-town constituencies where working men were few and landed dependants and deferentials numerous. Second was Disraeli's conviction that many working men were both Tory and enduringly respectful of their betters. As this implies, estimations of political fitness remained as central to parliamentary debates about working-class inclusion in the 1850s and 1860s as to those about the middle class before 1832. These considerations had partly underpinned the contemptuous rejection of Chartist demands. They were central to parliamentary debates from 1852. What made Parliament increasingly sympathetic owed nothing to outside pressure. Rather it was increasing perceptions that many working men were rendering themselves acceptable by their willingness to pass through an agenda-fixing gateway of political fitness: by abandoning Chartism; rioting rather rarely; and by embracing rationality, self-improvement, self-help and thrift through participation in savings banks, retail co-ops and friendly societies. Equally persuasively, the Northern working-class's mute suffering during the Cotton Famine suggested male breadwinners possessed a near-totality of proper values: 'self-command, self-control, respect for order, patience under suffering, confidence in the law, regard for superiors'.[20] Though Gladstone was sufficiently persuaded by such behaviour, and by working-class saving, and thus retrenchment,[21] to concede moral entitlement to the vote,[22] this was still a privilege to be earned, not a right to be demanded. Here at least, Gladstone and Disraeli agreed, after as before 1867: voting was 'a popular privilege', and what had been created was not democracy.[23]

This assumption prompted initial preferences for rated or rental limitation – many politicians believed in a working-class aristocracy even if historians no longer do. Parliamentarians were eventually persuaded to abandon these restrictions by competing party opportunism, demographic uncertainty about where unfitness started, and probably optimism about the beneficial effects of the economic cycle. None the less, enfranchisement was still dominated by fundamental elite attachments to the 'tradition of a limited polity of independent freemen'.[24] This still decreed household rather than manhood suffrage, formidable residence requirements for householders, virtually impossible ones for lodgers and continued prohibition upon most forms of pauperism, up to 1918.

Preoccupations about preserving the landed interest's and the party's political base continued to rule at least Conservative actions through the 1870s and early 1880s – effectively inhibiting extending household suffrage into the counties.[25] However, by the 1880s, Britain's political elite was changing. The aristocratic and gentlemanly element, though still important, was weakening, as connectedly was its hold upon the countryside – due to the direct and indirect effects of the Agricultural Depression, rural migration, and suburbanisation. To a degree, the elite itself was democratising as more of the wealthy middle class entered Parliament, and, more modestly, Government. The Commons even contained a few working men. These changes somewhat altered the considerations in play, even though they all remained highly relevant – particularly because, the fleeting effects of agricultural trade unionism aside, there was little public pressure for enhanced democratisation.

Thus concerns about political fitness, and convictions that it stopped with male householders, remained firmly in place, except that politicians concluded that householder-fitness could endure life even in industrial or rural villages. Some wanted to enfranchise female householders, but none the hazily-defined but nevertheless unsober, feckless and dependent residuum. Indeed, increased middle-class input into the elite may even have elevated independence as a constituent of fitness. Furthermore, the enhanced position given to mere numbers by universalising householder enfranchisement, and by constituency realignment, was still counterbalanced by the multiple votes given the possessors of certain sorts of political fitness, particularly those connected with scattered property and university education.

As this implies, considerations of elite self-preservation also remained important. Though the 10 Bills of 1884/5 represented very substantial surrenders of landed power, few politicians wanted to dispense with landed political service altogether. Desires to preserve it still helped shape what was done. The Ballot and Corrupt and Illegal Practices Acts, socio-economic change, and landed impoverishment, all severely constrained influence-politics. Vastly increased numbers of voters would do so even more, as well as adding to expense and effort. County constituencies were carefully subdivided to perpetuate remaining territorial influence in a world where landowners' political impact was increasingly confined to areas immediately adjacent to estates.

Party considerations also powerfully influenced the 1884/5 legislation. Admittedly, results roughly coincided with what was democratically defensible, and produced significant surrenders of party control for the future. Thus the vote was spread to rural labourers, and industrial workers outside the boroughs, and constituency boundaries were radically redrawn to broadly coincide with population. The latter process was removed from parliamentary politicians' control, and consigned to four Boundary Commissions for England, Wales, Scotland and Ireland, who were to conduct impartial local enquiries. Local party considerations of advantage and disadvantage were relevant to their deliberations, but so too were population and the social character of the areas concerned.

However, this overall situation resulted from extended and immensely detailed inter-party negotiations, resting upon fundamental shifts in Conservative thinking about overall advantage. The Liberals, partly because they saw agricultural and non-urban industrial workers as natural supporters, were committed to universalising household enfranchisement in the 1880 General Election. This produced intense Conservative fears that, if done using anything like existing constituency boundaries, it would swamp their natural sources of rural support, rendered precarious anyway by the Agricultural Depression. Since at least 1874, some Conservatives increasingly and accurately perceived middle-class suburbanites as capable of replacing the land as their natural bedrock constituency. In 1884, the Front Bench refused House of Lords sanction for universalising the householder qualification without wholesale boundary redrawal. Previously, Conservatives had been suspicious of its popular overtones, inclined to use it as a means of counterbalancing the effects of enfranchisement. Now they came to see redrawal as a means of gaining advantage from enfranchisement. In particular, they perceived single-member constituencies (especially homogeneous ones) as a means of maximising Conservative advantage in the suburbs and in rural areas adjacent to towns where naturally Tory rural voters could be separated from urban Liberal ones. Furthermore, 'from the strongest instincts of self-preservation', they believed such constituencies would minimise the automatic majorities they felt expanded enfranchisement would bring the Liberals.[26] This put them into odd alliance with Cabinet radicals wanting to equalise seat distribution on the basis of population, and strongly tempted by single-member constituencies for the advantages they seemingly offered in working-class areas. There resulted a set of complex negotiations, most centrally between Dilke, Gladstone, Hartington and Salisbury (for the radicals, Liberals, Whigs and Conservatives respectively). These involved calculations of party and factional advantage in England, Wales, Scotland and Ireland; in rural and urban and suburban areas; and in small and large towns. The result was arguably the most radical democratisation thus far. It produced major shifts in principle: population, area and occupation (effectively class) replaced interest and community as bases for representation. Representation was thus shifted to accord with social and demographic reality. However, the settlement was also one from which every party and faction, except the Whigs, gained substantial advantage: Liberals and radicals from the new voters, continued Irish over- representation, and the new predominantly working-class constituencies; Conservatives from landed influence in newly sub-divided counties, and middle-class suburban constituencies.[27]

In subsequent decades, land faded steadily from deliberations about inclusion, as from the composition of the Commons and new recruitment to the Lords.[28] However, considerations of political fitness and party advantage remained important. Reluctance to politically penetrate the residuum explains why householder enfranchisement provided a fifty-year resting-place even for men. The unfitness of this spectral group helped indirectly to block women's enfranchisement up to 1914. For many politicians, of course, politics' public character, and the dependence assumed under the separation of spheres, rendered women politically unfit anyway – perceptions probably reinforced by Suffragette activities. However, the residuum created further problems. Women's suffrage groups deliberately demanded enfranchisement on the basis of the existing male franchise, partly on grounds of equality, but also partly to avoid getting enmeshed in the acute difficulties raised by this group. However, this produced problems for many left-wing politicians because female householders were fewer, and assumed to be wealthier and thus more Conservative than their male counterparts. Yet few, apart from Labour and some radicals, wanted to go beyond householder enfranchisement. This partly helped Asquith before the War to outmanœuvre the Suffragettes by opting for universal suffrage as an alternative to female-householder enfranchisement – at once disguising his own opposition to women's suffrage, courting the radicals and ruling the demand off-limits for most moderates and right-wingers. An added ingredient here was party competition. For many radicals, female householder enfranchisement would create a built-in Conservative electoral majority. Similar considerations led Unionist leaders to insist on something even more propertied as a condition of support.[29]

With the 1918 Act, the elite finally surrendered considerable control over inclusion. The desire to preserve the landed element within the elite also had little impact. The franchise was conceded as a right of adult manhood, rather than a privilege deriving from worthy attitudes and behaviour, clear and stable relationships to property, or from independence of poor relief. Moreover, this was granted because politicians felt they had little choice if they wished to avoid system-endangering protest resulting from perceived mass-radicalisation following wartime suffering and the Russian Revolution. For similar reasons, the Coalition extended the vote to 19–20 year-olds serving at the front. Party considerations also had less impact than in 1884–5. The Act was framed by a Coalition. The Boundary Commission took charge of constituency re-allocation. The old party-infested process of electoral registration was also abandoned.

Nevertheless, the elite's traditional agenda remained important. Male enfranchisement was universalised partly because wartime participation had removed the darkest fears about the population's bottom-end. Since it appeared so ready, where physically able, to die for its country, its loyalty was no longer questionable. Furthermore, politicians were increasingly aware that those disenfranchised by residential restrictions included not just supposedly feckless working men but also upwardly-mobile professionals. Multiple votes from property and education were greatly reduced but not wholly abandoned, and Conservatives continued defending them on grounds of superior fitness until 1948.[30] Until 1928, similar considerations restricted women's enfranchisement to those over 30, who were ratepayers in their own right, or ratepayers' wives. This emphasis on maturity, property and marriage was a very different reward for war-service from that accorded men – since the 21 to 29 year-olds excluded were most likely to have taken paid war-work, as well as being dangerously unattached to men. Both considerations rendered their fitness suspect in terms of a separated-spheres doctrine actually reinforced by the perceived need to get women back into the home to replace the lost generation.

Party calculation also contributed to democratisation's final stages. The Conservative-dominated Coalition in 1918 was unlikely to hesitate long about enfranchising upwardly mobile professionals. With long Primrose League experience, it also probably occurred to some that older women, especially if safely married with children, were most likely to have sympathetic affinities. Meanwhile, further boundary redrawal, based on social homogeneity as well as population, could be reckoned to create more constituencies of the temptingly suburban sort. Only in 1948, with the final abandonment of extra votes for property and university graduation did politicians finally surrender control. However, elites were also important in other, more subtle, ways – affecting not just the character but also the likely consequences of democratisation.

2.   The Context of Democratisation

As argued in later chapters, democratisation derives considerable bene-fit from low mass expectations about its economic consequences, and from the presence of thriving civil organisations amongst groups being included. Both were evident in Britain, and both were partly generated from below. Nevertheless, the state and its elites also played active and influential parts – sometimes deliberately, sometimes because of actions taken for other reasons. Central to much of the influence attempted is an apparent paradox: creating the conditions wherein *laissez faire* and the market economy could operate required a degree of active state intervention. Sometimes, as in Ireland, this could be admitted as well as simply enacted. Even Gladstone, and even on the Mainland, admitted the state might intervene in three situations:

> the highest form [the first] ... positive regulations requiring this or that thing to be done in the course of private commercial arrange-ments, for the sake of obviating social, moral or political evils ... the second ... has been interference by sheer naked prohibition ... the third and mildest is ... [where] you offer ... members of the commu-nity ... certain facilities for ... self-help.[31]

In taking such actions, the state helped create a social context highly functional for successful democratisation. We shall argue this was ac-complished in two ways: first, because the state was rendered baleful to those seeking its aid; second, because it also tried to assist those wishful of self-help. Politicians, though outwardly sanguine about the fitness of those being admitted, were often deeply pessimistic about the long-term consequences for the incomes of supposed wealth-producers.[32] The indications are that, partly due to their own actions, they need not have been.

(a) The Baleful State

For many working people throughout the century up to 1914, the state probably seemed an enemy. Its hostile image was partly deliberate, partly semi-accidental, and probably appeared more malign the further down the manual scale one was located, and the greater one's need. For many, it constituted a series of interferences with the informal means of survival. The state was the nosy policeman. It was the sanitary official banning pigs from backyards, closing cellar-dwellings and other slum accommodation without providing affordable housing in return and forcing relatives into isolation hospitals. It was the horrifying agent of forcible vaccination;[33] the licensing magistrate; the education inspector who prevented children contributing to family incomes by forcing them into school. Even factory inspectors were ambivalent figures – supported by unions, as safety enforcers and preventers of overwork by wives and children, but also further agents of interference with the means of subsistence.

Thus far, the state's balefulness was only partly intentional. However, in the crucial area of poverty relief, its hostility was coldly deliberate and significantly effective. In some respects, there was nothing new about the New Poor Law. Its Elizabethan predecessor was never exactly friendly, and even though Speenhamland and associated laxities widely limited its ferocity, less eligible principles were creeping into many parishes in the years before 1834. However, the Poor Law Amendment Act was far more ambitious, systematic and dramatically publicised than anything before. Its principles are too well-known to require detailed reiteration. The key thing from our current viewpoint is that this was vigorous state intervention in quest of *laissez faire*. The central aim was to reinvigorate the free market, in uniform and centralised ways, by lending all relief a strongly deterrent quality. The able-bodied pauper's lot was to be rendered harsher than that of the worse-paid 'free' labourer. The respectable poor were to be deterred from applying altogether, whilst the pauper was preferably to be remoralised, or at least prevented from 'infecting' the respectables, through disciplined and uncomfortable confinement within purpose-built workhouses. More generally, paupers were to be rendered a disreputable race apart.

As is also well-known, the New Poor Law did not work as intended. The workhouse could never accommodate all able-bodied applicants, particularly during economic down-turns. Due partly to short-term popular protest, and partly to British society's longer-term heterogeneity, centralised and uniform administration emerged only slowly. It continually had to confront the vibrant force of local community, and the tendency for relief to become the result of implicit face-to-face negotiation between authority and recipient. There are good grounds for thinking that application levels remained high, intended deterrence notwithstanding.[34] In the early years, many Poor Law Unions ignored the Act's central principles altogether, and some, like those in north-east England, continued operating in decidedly gentler ways for many decades. Particularly in rural areas, workhouses retained their traditional roles as shelters for the sick, orphaned and elderly.[35] Out-relief remained normative for most applicants. Amongst many, too desperate or demoralised to care, poor relief long remained one of multiple means of getting by. In Scotland, the Law did not apply, perhaps helping explain the country's lesser wariness of state-aid. From the mid-1850s, even central attempts to enforce deterrence slackened somewhat, partly in the apparent belief that sufficient unpleasant medicine had been administered.[36] The Law's framers had anyway never intended to inflict the same deterrence upon the deserving poor they directed against the undeserving able-bodied. This underpinned their concern, expressed in the new workhouses, to physically separate facilities with different sorts of relief-recipients.

Yet, in various ways, some only half-intended, the New Poor Law was an ultimately successful exercise in social engineering, effective in breaking whatever link there once had been between the state and working-class moral economy. Though impossible to enact in material terms without recourse to concentration camps (the low-paid condition being so awful), less eligibility operated very effectively through shame – easy to inflict in in-turned nineteenth-century urban environments. The enquiries connected with out-relief were always intrusive, and rarely less than demeaning, their characteristics often reinforced by Guardians' responsiveness to local desires for low rates. In many Unions, increasing resort to the 'labour test', with unpleasant labour often performed in uniform alongside disreputables who really had given up on respectability, rendered out-relief publicly degrading, whether in workhouse yards or outside. Model workhouses were eventually built, with their message about the shaming consequences of pauperism publicly proclaimed on the main thoroughfares where they were often situated. Some recipients found their way inside more or less automatically. Sufficient others were 'offered the house' to create a threat looming over all. The threat was enhanced by the likelihood of association with such automatic entrants as vagrants, the Irish and unmarried mothers: 'to the reputable and clean-minded ... the bitterest and most humiliating experience of life'.[37] At the end, in an age setting great store by the rituals of death, there was the unmitigated shame of unceremonious burial in unmarked pauper graves.

Around the time of working-class enfranchisement, two factors crucially enhanced the balefulness of state-aid. First, the 1867 Act retained the provision first enacted in 1832 whereby any sort of poor relief involved automatic local and parliamentary disenfranchisement. This neatly removed people from the political loop at their point of greatest need. It also greatly increased the shame attached to relief by removing this long-sought and much-celebrated symbol of respectable citizenship – in introspective working-class terraces where voting was almost obligatory, doing so very publicly. This perhaps had little impact upon 'the willing parasite' (probably not registered anyway), but it emphatically 'deterred the good and self-respecting'.[38] Thus enfranchisement itself was co-opted into the machinery of balefulness. Second, from 1871, the new Local Government Board commenced a determined and fairly successful fifteen-year campaign to persuade Unions to return to 1834 principles. It reinvigorated suspicion about the deservingness of claimants, and renewed insistence upon workhouse-relief, discipline and enquiry into circumstances. This significantly harshened the whole spirit of poor relief across the country. It coincided with a substantial downturn in relief-application, and, to judge by very widespread testimony, seems to have rendered horror of the system almost universal amongst those even remotely threatened by its ministrations.

Overall, the Poor Law had two results important for democratisation. First, it greatly reinforced the state's baleful image – especially for those in need, a condition likely for almost anyone at some point in their life-cycle. State-aid came to be associated with harshness, intrusion, discipline, tyrannous officialdom, and especially shame and threatened respectability. The 1909 Minority Royal Commission Report on the Poor Laws, 42 years after working-class enfranchisement began, discovered that virtually every branch of the Poor Law, no matter how deserving its recipients, was widely regarded with horror by 'the refined poor', who would go to almost any lengths to avoid its ministrations. Broad national figures confirmed that, at a time when up to a third of the urban population was in poverty, just 3 per cent were on poor relief.[39]

Second, the Poor Law, though not initiating working-class self-help, undoubtedly accelerated it, probably continuing to do so many years after 1834, even more after 1871. Some, like the frequent resort in hard times to pawning and other credit, were hardly what the framers had in mind. Other sorts emphatically were. The friendly-society movement long pre-dated 1834, but grew massively in the subsequent decade, and was actively encouraged by Guardians under instruction from the centre. Poor-Law officials' testimony to less eligibility's role in society-formation is obviously suspect, though frequently given and allegedly supported by much testimony from society officials. However, figures suggest the same conclusion: the Manchester Unity of Oddfellows, one of the nationwide Affiliated Orders, acquired 1470 new lodges between 1835 and 1845, a threefold increase over 1825–35. It is hard to imagine another explanation for this – certainly not the acute depression starting in 1837 in precisely those Northern areas where societies were strongest. This acceleration rate was not maintained in later decades. However, membership increase remained rapid, and accelerated again in the decade following the Local Government Board campaign from 1871. Moreover, in these later years, officials constantly congratulated their societies upon keeping members clear of parish relief, thus 'raising them from groveling depths to cheerfulness, manliness and self-esteem'.[40] Such proclamations were always greeted with enthusiasm, suggesting such liberation was regarded as positive respectable virtue rather than just negative good fortune. This was unsurprising since the Poor Law thereby became deeply intertwined with the cardinal working-class virtue of respectability.

This impinges upon civil organisation which, as argued later, had great impact upon popular political fitness – generating both functional virtues and appropriate political training. What is argued here is that the state, and thus its national and local elites, played an important negative part in creating civil society. As we shall now see, it also had an important positive role, actively encouraging organisations and attitudes functional to minimum government, and, as it turned out, democratic training.

(b)   The Enabling State

The state actively developed legal infra-structures favourable to developing a market economy. As is well-known, this included regulating banking, encouraging internal and external trade, and actively co-operating with private individuals and companies in building roads and railways. More important from our current standpoint is its developing willingness to provide legal frameworks guaranteeing and encouraging middle-class charity, and working-class self-help – savings banks, friendly societies, retail and industrial co-ops, and eventually even trade unions. Effectively, in this 'gentlest' of Gladstone's delineations of legitimate state activity, it acted as guarantor to civil organisation.

The *laissez-faire* state always assumed active middle-class charitable effort, even if it provided no special legal framework for its operation. (The 1819 Charitable Trusts Act did not extend to charities based on voluntary contributions.)[41] Initially, Parliament was less encouraging to working-class civil organisations since they were perceived as seditious. Indeed, intermittently, it actively sought their repression – most dramatically expressed in the Anti-Combination Laws. However, it increasingly began seeing legalisation as a means of ensuring oversight and thus safety. Legislation affecting friendly societies, always the most securely respectable of working-class civil organisations, began as early as 1793. This first Act aimed to prevent sedition through registration, and to 'diminish public burthens' by encouraging self-helping behaviour. It and subsequent legislation in 1817, 1819, 1829, 1834, 1845, 1855 and 1875 gave societies steadily increasing financial security – through the right to invest, sue and be sued, and protection against defaulting officials. Legislation also encouraged sound financial management. The range of legitimate activities was progressively widened. The Affiliated Orders were legally recognised; then (with more democratically ambivalent results), encouraged to become increasingly centralised. All this was available in return for registration, first with local magistrates and later with a Friendly Societies Registrar who came to be seen as 'Minister for self-help for the whole of the industrious classes', a source of expertise and advice, some of it even wanted by the recipients.

Co-ops also gained legal recognition, and consequent ability to protect their funds through registration under friendly-society legislation – first in 1834, then more usefully under the 'frugal investment clause' of the 1846 Act. From the 1856 Industrial and Provident Societies Act, societies acquired nearly all the privileges of friendly societies, a framework greatly facilitating further growth. In 1862, limited-liability status became available, immensely useful for the increasingly numerous large societies. Cross-investment between societies was permitted. They could also federate – thereby clearing a wide legal pathway for the

Co-operative Wholesale Society and its subsequent Scottish counter-part.[42] This framework was expanded by legislation in 1876 and 1893. Co-ops were not given friendly societies' fiscal privileges, but, to the fury of shopkeepers' organisations, their dividends remained exempt from income tax into the inter-war years.

Elite attitudes towards unions were more ambivalent. The sort of self-help they represented was more suspect; some saw them as conspiracies against the free market rather than just part of it, not surprisingly because many urban leaders were themselves employers. In the early decades, parliamentarians also perceived unions as seditious. These attitudes produced the 1797 Illegal Oaths Act and the 1799 Combination Laws – whereby unions and their activities became effectively illegal. Furthermore, whatever expanding toleration politicians ultimately granted these working-class civil organisations tended to be steadily, if inconsistently, eroded by decisions from the judicial elite into the early twentieth century.

Nevertheless, even unions gained grudging tolerance. Indeed, as the competing sections of the national elite, particularly the Conservatives, began contemplating working-class voters as well as apparent union attachment to political economy, they became prepared to grant unions legal security, even significant privileges as free-market players. The Combination Laws were repealed in 1824, with significant consent from employers appearing before the Select Committee, even if some of the advantages were clawed back by partially restoring the law of conspiracy in 1825. This provided stable, if uneasy, ground-rules for union growth and patchily developing collective bargaining until the 1870s. Peaceful picketing was tolerated, and then (partly responding to union pressure) insecurely legalised in 1859, and more certainly in 1875. Unions gained formal legal status and thus financial security against corrupt officials in 1869 and 1871. Strikes were granted growing immunity from breach-of-contract proceedings in 1867, and more significantly in 1875. When this was eroded by legal decisions culminating in the 1901 Taff Vale Judgment, the Liberals restored the situation in 1906. Meanwhile, arbitration and conciliation processes were legally facilitated in 1867, 1872 and 1896. Most union political activity was never endangered, though the Liberals rescued the right to create political funds from the 1909 Osbourne Judgment in return for continued co-operation from the nascent Labour Party. As this begins to suggest, politicians' efforts to shape the context of democratisation shade into efforts to influence the consequences.

(c)   Handling the Consequences

Whilst often optimistic about the political fitness of those being included, politicians were also fearful about the consequences of democratisation. In 1832, most Conservatives, and some Whigs, shared Peel's view that, inevitable or not, a door had been opened which could not be closed – and were troubled about what might come through. In 1867, Derby's anxieties about his 'leap in the dark' were embellished by George Glyn, the Liberal Chief Whip: 'All is new and changed and large and . . . in some respects *dark*.'[43] Some feared chaos and threats to legitimacy. Many more believed enfranchisement would lead inevitably to increasing taxation, even confiscation, as the newly-included demanded shares in the good life.

In fact, national and local political elites played important parts in handling the consequences of inclusion, and determinedly tried to minimise the disruptions they feared. They attempted first to educate the emerging democracy, influence its political agenda and maintain their own legitimacy. Second, they aimed to incorporate the organisations of the enfranchised. Third, within limits largely endorsed by the enfranchised, politicians tried to appease, respond to, and anticipate their demands. These efforts had some effect, particularly when taken together with other factors: the impact of civil society which politicians, as we have noted, sought to encourage; elites' own social and economic power; and the space granted by the staged character of democratisation.

(i)   Educating Democracy. De Tocqueville believed 'the first duty imposed on those who now direct society is to educate democracy; . . . put . . . new life into its beliefs; . . . purify its mores; . . . control its actions; gradually to substitute understanding of statecraft for present inexperience and knowledge of its true interests for blind instincts'.[44] In Britain, this educative task, as de Tocqueville clearly believed appropriate, was interpreted broadly to include not just transmitting information but also system-preserving values. Groups were included because they were believed to be politically fit in the widest sense; following inclusion, elites made considerable efforts to ensure the accuracy of this prognostication.

Admittedly, there is little evidence of such efforts being directed at middle-class males. Politicians had touching faith in their rationality, independence, political morality and respect for authority. Certainly, there seems little debate or concern about their state of mind. Judging by the dedicated venality of the many small boroughs created in 1832, this faith was somewhat misplaced – many £10 householders were wholly innocent of three of the above attributes of fitness, and assessed authority by the depth of its pocket. This occasioned little apparent disquiet, probably because, corruptible though middle-class men often were, their appetites were affordable and hardly endangered the system.

There was far more worry about working men – partly because corrupting them was expensive, partly because deprivation potentially opened them to the sin of envy. Concerns about their fitness surfaced both nationally and locally, and were part of much broader efforts at moral improvement by governmental and voluntary agencies throughout the century.

At national level, working men's enfranchisement, and politicians' contemplation of its apparently distasteful and expensive results during the often inebriated 1868 election, produced the secret ballot in 1872 and, more tardily, effective curbs upon corruption in 1883. Meanwhile, one cardinal intention behind the 1870 Education Act was to educate the emerging democracy – not just making it more literate, but also reinforcing values amongst the newly-included likely to enhance attachment to the *status quo*. The methods chosen for inculcating desirable skills and virtue – rote-learning and collective recitation of the results – hardly encouraged the making of intelligent democratic choices, or indeed anything beyond mental passivity. Nevertheless the intentions were clear. The Conservative government 1874–80 had narrower but still controlling agendas as it contemplated educational compulsion in 1875; to ensure sufficient income for rural voluntary schools to prevent the emergence of Education Boards. These would only provide 'platforms for the Dissenting preacher and . . . agitator' and 'by means of their triennial elections and Board meetings exactly the training in political agitation . . . which will be mischievous to the state' and undermine the Tory heartland.[45] In respects like these, state education and indeed its avoidance merely embraced value-transferring intentions long-evident in elite-sponsored voluntary education: mechanics institutes, workingmen's clubs and the like.

As this suggests, similar ambitions were evident amongst local urban elites, expressed most directly through political parties. In working-class areas, these had often long been much more than purely political organisations – as Operative Conservative Friendly and Burial Society activities in the 1830s and 1840s widely demonstrated. By helping suitably committed working men escape the dreaded Poor Law in sickness and in death, Conservative elites tried to heighten not just their own legitimacy, but that of authority in general. They worried about 'the breaking up of the old framework of society...the poverty and discontent...the facility... presented to every political agitator', and urged the operative Conservative 'to encourage his poorer neighbour to become a member...attend our reading room, and thereby learn to be content in that station of life which providence has pleased to call him'.[46] Given such early concerns, it is unsurprising that they persisted and intensified after 1867. Local parties became not just electoral, propaganda and registration organisations, but also vehicles for political instruction and value-transmission. Liberal clubs particularly mounted regular programmes of lectures and debates on current issues, and more general historical topics, to promote 'a due appreciation of the principles of good government'.[47] They also provided 'admirable newspapers' which members were urged to read 'not carelessly but critically especially in those concerning the welfare of themselves and their neighbours'.[48] Parties also conducted vigorous social activities – partly to entertain and reward activists, but also to promote improvement and 'orderly habits'. This was to be achieved through the mingling of classes, the provision of 'rational recreation', preferably (mainly a Liberal concern) 'away from the contaminating influence of the public house', and by elevating 'the moral and social conditions of young men'.[49] As noted, some even sought to separate respectable working men from 'the rough class', preventing both contamination and 'governing those above'. The provision of all this came quite naturally to local employers and social leaders, who often accurately saw local parties as extensions of dependency networks centring upon their factories and works, and programmed to perceive contact points between the classes as value-transmission-belts.

How far such educative and improving efforts were successful is obviously uncertain and ultimately unproveable. Democratic education, as noted, was part of much broader efforts at 'improvement'. Notions of social control have had a bad historical press: understandably because of the inflated explanatory claims sometimes made for them, yet also unfairly because of assumptions that, if 'control' is implausible, then 'influence' can also be ejected. Given the resources behind such efforts, and the strong elements of hierarchy in British society, this seems unwise. What can be admitted is that modified versions of these elevated values were also being generated from below. The argument available from later chapters is that, if elite-sponsored efforts at political improvement had any effect, it was partly because they had some commonality with versions of fitness being produced by civil society. Anyway, their success can only be asessed alongside associated and somewhat more testable attempts at incorporation, to ensure the enfranchised became and felt themselves part of the political community, and accepted its broad outlines.

(ii)   Incorporating Democracy. Incorporation is hard to separate from democratisation, since the vote was itself incorporative: it said much about respectable citizenship, and was seen as such by those seeking it. However, so far as separation is possible, like democratic education, it had both national and local dimensions. Nationally, it focused particularly upon the monarchy, upon Parliament, later upon entry to the elite itself, and later still upon efforts at corporatism. Locally, it centred on municipal councils, mayors, charitable organisations and political parties. Incorporation was at once a source of legitimacy and stability for the expanding polity, another effort at agenda-control, and itself an important symbolic aspect of democratisation.

Over the years after 1832, the monarchy adapted its style to the assumed values of those within the political pale. In Victoria's early decades, under Albert's influence, its public demeanour became modest, respectable, family-centred and middle-class. After his death, the monarchy for a while became withdrawn and unpopular. However, from the 1870s, aided by rapidly expanding and nationalising mass media, influenced by key politicians and courtiers, and latterly, increasing public demand, Victoria permitted herself to be reinvented. She became more popularly available, and a vehicle for emphasising inclusion and shared national sympathies. Royal ceremonies were more frequent, more theatrical, better organised, more public, better publicised and more welcoming to those wishing to watch, as vast numbers increasingly did. Royals themselves became more visible, visiting more places outside London, meeting more civic leaders, and showing themselves in more varied locations – suburbs and slums as well as country houses and city centres. From Edward VII onwards, recently-deceased monarchs obligingly reclined in Westminster Hall, available to the many thousands wishing to pay homage, and, for those wishful but unable, permitting press photographs of the 'People's Lying-in-State'. All this was associated with growing political impotence, and increasing consequent possibilities, particularly evident from George V onwards, of incumbents being viewed as impartial sources of consensus, calm and stability in an increasingly troubled world. Amongst these troubles was class conflict (and clashing national identities in Ireland), a phenomenon given increasing political salience by democratisation, especially after the 1885 boundary reallocations.[50] In all this, monarchy was being limitedly democratised, whilst also being utilised to maintain the polity's stability (normally perceived as crucial to successful democratisation) and the legitimacy of its elites. These changes were part of broader international trends, as heads of state and politicians adapted their styles to cope with situations wherein common people were increasingly important, as at least formal participants.

Aided by monarchy's role as the fount of all social honour, royal ceremony was also utilised to legitimise the arrival as citizens of new groups – working men, women and eventually racial minorities. Knighthoods, eventually peerages, and the multiple categories of Britain's complex honours system were all increasingly used for these purposes. So too were royal entertainments like garden parties. Equally important, though less noticed by historians, were numerous, resplendent local celebrations of royal anniversaries. For example, Victoria's coronation, just five years after the first bout of enfranchisement, was marked by elongated and spectacularly decorated processions in many Northern towns and cities. So too were her successive jubilees. Amongst other functions, these enabled representatives and civil organisations of groups already included to celebrate arrival, whilst the more approval-worthy of those still outside could mark their social, if not political, membership of local communities – all shared with vast crowds. In the 1838 Coronation processions, all carefully organised and marshalled by local elites, there walked all segments of the respectable local male community – civic authorities, charities, masons, 'gentlemen of the town four abreast', 'the trades' generously embannered, and, similarly decorated, the local friendly societies. By Victoria's Diamond Jubilee in 1897, these were joined by many other groups and organisations, including local co-ops and trade unions. These celebrations of national events were highly important, due to the in-turned character of local communities and the consequent attention they commanded from watching crowds and prolix local newspapers. Not merely were they key locations for celebrating local inclusion, but, where required, also important occasions for implicit negotiation about the terms of co-existence between national aristocratic and local values. In 1838, Bolton watchers were offered, amongst others, a flag inscribed 'Success to the Union Foundry' and on the other side 'the town and trade of Bolton'; the figure of Vulcan, and the arms of Bolton; Victoria and the Queen for ever; a locomotive and portable engine; VR and Crown.[51]

Like other rituals, particularly at times of social cleavage, these were as much exercises in persuasion as announcements of reality. Nevertheless, given the attention they commanded, they were probably influential.

In Britain, Parliament too was a powerful incorporative agency, one whose entry-points were long-policed by national and local elites . It was the focus of all demands for political inclusion. Gaining membership of course was about access to power. However, it was also a symbolic form of representation. It dramatically indicated acceptance and arrival for the groups thus included – whether businessmen, working men, women or racial minorities – and was celebrated as such. Thus the later-nineteenth century arrival and consolidation of cohorts of Jewish MPs received extended self-congratulatory attention in publications like the *Jewish Chronicle*. This was invariably seen as indicating that community's growing integration, particularly once they were demonstrably the result of Tory as well as Liberal nomination. Meanwhile, notwithstanding the contempt heaped upon them by contemporary socialists and some later historians, the early Lib–Lab MPs were centres of massive pride, at least amongst their own communities.[52] Miliband's argument that Parliament was a crucial part of capitalism's defence structures, moderating Labour radicalism, is doubtful: working people accepted capitalism long before Labour emerged; most Labour MPs embraced gradualism well before arrival. Nevertheless, he produces more convincing evidence of Parliament's mesmerising effect upon early Labour MPs, its ceremonies, traditions, and the associated prospects of mixing with the great and graceful. It is not unreasonable to think this reinforced the system's acceptability, for those directly affected, and for the class from which they were drawn, by symbolically marking arrival.

Until well into the twentieth century, the local urban arena, with its ability to command popular attention, and greater social accessibility, was home to equally potent means of marking arrival and inclusion. Britain's powerful tradition of local autonomy had great importance in facilitating peaceful democratisation, enabling groups who might other-wise have proved incompatible to co-exist, and achieve satisfaction for their political and social aspirations without coming into serious conflict. The very existence of powerful, visible and respected local elites says much about where the urban middle class found the satisfactions and marks of inclusion they expected from enfranchisement, probably helping explain their acquiescence at continued landed domination of Parliament long after 1832.[53] Consequently, the 1835 Municipal Corporations Act was probably the most important single fruit granted the urban middle class following enfranchisement. However, because of the local arena's ability to command mass attention, local elites and institutions themselves became crucial agencies for satisfying the aspirations, and marking the arrival, of other groups within and beyond the middle class.

Central here were municipal councils. They provided far more widely-available access to office, status and marks of acceptance than Parliament ever could. This explains the absolute obligation on council aspirants never apparently to seek nomination, only indicating acceptance after receiving socially resplendent deputations, or 'numerously and respectably signed petitions'. Particularly important was the mayoralty. This highly visible office was crucial to symbolic representation and incorporation in two ways. First, the office was itself an increasing source of aspiration – initially for middle-class groups, then for working-class leaders, later still for women, and at various points religious and racial minorities. To an extent that national positions never could, mayors came to symbolise the notion that, in an allegedly mobile society, office was open to all. The increasingly visible and congratulatory tone of mayor-making ceremonies makes one instantly aware of this. The social elevation of the manufacturers, professionals or shopkeepers concerned were often carefully highlighted by those proposing and accepting. Working men's later elevation to mayoral incumbency was given even greater attention for the recognition it bestowed upon all manual workers – by elite figures who proposed, manual figures who accepted, and working-class organisations who subsequently celebrated by participation in ever-lengthening mayoral processions. By the 1920s, in industrial towns, denial of occupancy by traditional council majority-parties produced incandescent fury amongst Labour councillors, generating not rejection but heightened determination to force entry. In Salford, as many other towns, activists demanded:

> Are we again to see the flouting of the claims of. . . Labour members to recognition. The party is well-established in local and national politics. . .much as the old-stagers would like to ignore it, and means to fight for its prestige in the public life of the borough.[54]

Second, the mayoralty was an expanding centre of inclusive ceremony, again one very much controlled by existing local elites. Monarchy's reinvention in the 1870s was paralleled by a contemporaneous
vamping-up of mayoralty, probably for similar reasons. Processions to
church on Mayoral Sundays had always been indicators of which
groups were currently on the inside-track. From the 1870s, these were
glitteringly supplemented by other well-publicised ceremonies – mayoral 'at homes', soirees, garden parties, inaugurations, attendances.
Mayors delivered congratulatory words at associational meetings of all
kinds. Increasingly, local co-operative and union leaders began finding
themselves on mayoral guest-lists, along with groups of 'old folk', war
veterans, teachers, 'poor children', women's charitable groups and so
on. Underpinning this was the same mix of competitive party and
system-reinforcing calculation noted before, along now with civic
pride. Just how powerful could be the effect of such inclusion in fixing
loyalty, particularly when undertaken by prestigious social leaders, is
evident from the prognostications of the *Rochdale Labour News* about a
wealthy cotton spinner's mayoral festivities in 1896. Though viewing
monarchy as 'a relic of barbarism', this socialist publication was bowled
over by mayoralty:

> The mayor did a handsome thing by inviting the 'Day School
> Teachers of the borough' to a reception and ball at the town
> hall...The weary humdrum life of an elementary teacher makes
> an event of this kind particularly acceptable. The teachers turned
> up in full force, and the affair was both brilliant and refined.[55]

Mayoral festivities were part of much wider local ceremonial scenes.
Town-hall openings, civic anniversaries, hospital inaugurations and the
like all required processions and guests, attracted vast crowds – and
could thus be used to visibly mark acceptance. So too could local charity
committees.[56]

Local parties were another incorporative agency – drawing in groups
before as well as after their formal inclusion. In urban areas after 1867,
they mounted increasingly impressive exercises in the highly competitive
politics of sociability – conveying hundreds and thousands of supporters
to seaside resorts, country houses, often in specially chartered trains.
Nearer home, networks of clubs were annually supplemented by fetes
and fairs. By the 1880s, such offensives embraced not just working men,
but also many women – the Primrose League's myriad habitations being

the most spectacular examples. In fact, Lancashire Tories had anticipated this as far back as 1836 when the regional agent incited conservative working men to 'Make the women of Preston your allies in this
glorious fight'.[57] Two years later, Salford's Operative Conservatives
'held a tea party and ball, at which more than 3000 persons attended,
nine-tenths of them ladies'.[58]

The version of incorporation implied here assumes elites were influential in persuading incoming groups to accept the system in return for
rewards they deemed valuable. Elite actions were part-intended, part-
byproducts of simple competitiveness. Thus far, these actions have been
primarily social and concerned with status. Others, however, were
political – and here we move even more directly towards notions of
appeasement.

(iii) Appeasing Democracy. Within important limits, the competing
sections of Britain's national and local elites responded flexibly, opportunistically and politically to enfranchisement. Some scholars would
deny this. They emphasise how much mass pressure and intimidation
was required to pass the 1832 Reform Act, and the essential adminis-
tration-mindedness of Whig governments in mid-century. They highlight the importance of conviction rather than opportunism in
producing apparent responsiveness and the way party fluidity after
1832 produced parliamentary rather than popular government. Such
historians also emphasise the suspicion, confusion, timidity, even hostility of many Tories facing a working-class electorate after 1867, reinforced by a political system wherein working-class dominated
constituencies were a minority. They would also point to alleged Liberal
inflexibility faced by working-class radicalisation after around 1890.
More generally, they would emphasise the 'high-political' character of
much governmental deliberation over the period.[59]

All this rightly emphasises that elite responsiveness had clear limits.
However, we have already noted how the timing and character of
democratising stages was influenced by elite calculations of electoral
advantage. It would be surprising if similar motivations did not influence
how they responded to the results. Parliament, after all, always felt it
legitimate to mediate amongst competing interests, even if it was wary of
subordinating itself to them. There are also expectational questions.
Should we be more impressed by elite tardiness in face of democracy,
or the fast political footwork of leaders whose socio-economic background and reliance upon deference politics should have rendered

them ill-equipped to comprehend opinion of any sort? Should we notice inflexibility, or traditional parties' ability to survive until 1914; then to be disrupted (partially) only by total war?

In general, the latter judgement in each of the alternatives offered above seems most appropriate. As Biagini has argued for the Liberal part of the elite, 'What is really remarkable in the British case is not the liberalism of the subaltern classes but the populism of their elite'.[60] Some quotations can serve as starting-points. The first is John Fowden Hindle, a Lancashire squire hopefully positioning himself for parliamentary nomination for Blackburn's new constituency in 1832, just after the passing of the Reform Act which many of his kind had fervently opposed:

> I shall always be found among the advocates of every constitutional reform, having for its object the happiness of the community... In particular I shall be a zealous advocate of the Abolition of the Slave Trade... a careful revision of the Corn Laws... the charter of the Bank of England... the East India Monopoly, and every other exclusive privilege which cramps the energies and depresses the manufacturing industry of the country.[61]

Hindle was echoing behaviour already evident amongst gentlemanly MPs in the 1831 Election as they contemplated their rapidly, if temporarily, radicalising constituencies. Four years later, Peel, who had led Tory opposition to reform, publicly proclaimed his whole party's passionate friendship with the new voters, both in the Tamworth Manifesto and in his speech to the Merchant Tailors: 'We deny we are separated by any line or... separate interest from the middle classes. Why, who are we if we are not the middle classes... our interests and theirs are united'.[62] Following Corn Law Repeal, Lord Francis Egerton, South Lancashire's late MP, and still its leading Tory politician, contemplated the League with realistic distaste: 'I cannot acknowledge the right of that body to dictate to the county, though I in common with others must submit if necessary to the... lever they have organised'.[63]

Peel himself had already privately unsheathed equally sensitive political antennae, announcing his belief that 'the vast mass of mankind... the highest as well as the lowest... cannot be disregarded in politics'.[64] This underlay his appointment of Frances Bonham as party agent, and the latter's subsequent creation of a viable party organisation.

Thirty years on, John Gorst could be found considering Tory relations with the Nine Hours Movement:

> The election in Lancashire hinged upon the nine hours bill and the demands of trade unionists (for legal protection)...every candidate for a borough...has had to promise compliance...Sir Thomas Bazley having to explain away his votes and speeches last session ...[our] idea was to ask Mr Disraeli...to propose 56 hours and enable him to say he had...the agreement of the factory workers to say this would be accepted. Thus Mr Mundella would have been virtually put aside and the chief of Her Majesty's Opposition [Disraeli]...recognised as the channel through which our people express their wishes...[65]

Here, just seven years after working-class enfranchisement, and from the Conservatives' long-serving National Agent, is the essence of the politician's craft – opportunism and complex political calculation reinforced by party competition. Gorst often despaired of the blunted political sensitivities of Tory leaders. Yet they too knew about balancing one group against another in competitive party situations, even if their sums did not always agree with his. Disraeli contemplated the year 1875 and noted its ability to 'greatly content the mass of the people', enabling working men to perceive 'that the object of all the measures of the present Ministry is...to elevate their condition'.[66] In 1892, considering a union delegation on the eight-hour day, Salisbury's private secretary told his master:

> Middleton...thinks...the best party manœuvre would be for Y[our] L[ordship] to receive the Deputation and...demolish their arguments. He holds that if this were done firmly but judiciously it w[oul]d help us with the Employers and would not injure the Government in the estimation of the working classes; while it would put Mr Gladstone in an awkward position.[67]

Salisbury too, democratic pessimist though he was, could do his sums, and was already treating the employers' liability issue

> as a function of electoral arithmetic...you would lose more by the wrath of the employers than you would gain by the gratitude of the men. If both...parties were...in an impartial frame of mind

towards us – the favour of the workmen might be the best investment... But the favour of the employers if we do not adopt Gorst's
suggestion (in favour of employers' liability) is much more to be
counted on than the favour of the men if we do.[68]

As noted, elite flexibility can be exaggerated: many on both sides had far
less taste and talent for political opportunism; both parties contained
powerful elements for whom populism was anathema. Particularly in a
religious age, politicians were swayed by conviction as much as opportunism, particularly in dealing with religious groups. Nevertheless, the
prominence and rapid emergence of electoral sensitivities are surely
remarkable. So too were abilities to harness conviction to popular
causes. Indeed, electoral skills had a long, if intermittent, eighteenth-
century history. Nick Rogers, for example, has noted Tory prepared-
ness, in London and elsewhere, to attempt exploitation of artisan
and small-business resentments against the rich and ruling Whig oligarchy.[69]

Such skills originated partly from the character of British elites themselves, partly from the political context wherein they operated. We have
already noted the negotiated character now claimed for many aristocratically-dominated constituencies before as well as after 1832, and
arguments for a continuum between influence- and market-politics. For
such men, a degree of political appeasement hardly seemed strange.
Flexibility was thus an early feature of the system. The elite was also
enduringly split by party; both parties possessed ideological baggage
permitting appeals to those below: the Tories through paternalism, the
Liberals by developing notions of freedom in positive as well as negative
directions. Both parties therefore, as William Greenleaf has argued,[70]
contained both collectivist and individualist strands.

However, party competition and sensitivity was contextually reinforced by a decentralised, multi-layered, and interlocking political
and governmental system. As noted, this permitted social groups significant input before formal inclusion in 1832, 1867 and 1918. Both parties
thus needed to appeal in different ways to different audiences at different levels, for interlinking local governmental and constituency purposes. This enabled satisfactions, incapable of delivery at national
level, to be offered locally. In the 1830s and 1840s, for example, they
could be found competing for working-class radical support. Local Tory
candidates waved energetic sympathy at factory reform.[71] Local
Tory elites, for all the support their national leadership had given the

Poor Law Amendment Act, cheerfully exploited working-class anger about its enforcement: denouncing it from local platforms; administering it with well-advertised liberality when gaining control of local boards of guardians; and through their network of Operative Conservative Friendly and Burial Societies, protecting their manual followers from the Law's attentions in sickness and death. With local sensitivities evident before inclusion, it is unsurprising they should be even more evident afterwards: in the 1890s for example, from Tory parliamentary candidates advertising sympathy with Old Age Pensions, restrictions on alien immigration, employers' accident liability and 'freedom from grandmotherly legislation' over drink.[72]

Also contextually functional perhaps was early industrialism, and the extension into politics of the associated 'revolution in organisation'. Thus political sensitivities were reinforced and expressed in parties' willingness and ability to create viable electoral organisations following the enfranchisements of 1832 and 1867, capable of assessing opinion where it existed and mobilising support. Ireland provided another inspiration: in many respects, the real model for mass parties came not from industry but the Nationalists operating in Ireland's entirely rural environment.

Whatever the cause, British political leaders had strong political sensitivities from early on. Sure indicators are relationships with newspapers. Leading national and local politicians realised their importance from at least 1800, and determinedly tried influencing them – through bribery; discreet subsidy; granting or withholding government and municipal advertising; offering privileged information about forthcoming events; anonymously-written articles; wining and dining proprietors, editors and journalists; and vigorous attempts to persuade wealthy London and provincial businessmen to start or rescue party-supporting newspapers. This is a central theme in Stephen Koss' *The Rise and Fall of the Political Press*. So too, especially in volume 1, is the success of this enterprise.[73] Even Palmerston, traditional titled-landowner though he was, and with 'only a carriage knowledge of mankind',[74] understood the need to persuade the press and, through it, the public.

Equally interesting is how quickly national and local politicians acquired platform-skills. Admittedly, many national figures, unsurprisingly given their landed backgrounds, remained unskilful and unconvinced of the need. Equally unstartling is the prevalence of such attitudes prior to 1832 and during the twenty-year Whig hegemony after 1846. Lord John Russell made many attempts at franchise expansion, yet as prime

minister shared his wife's astonishment when crowds met him in Sheffield in 1857 – 'so little had we expected *any* reception...I could not
think what was the matter'.[75] Many colleagues experienced equal sur-
prise and alarm at the requirements of the platform. Even Gladstone,
observing his transformation from pocket-borough incumbent to popular tribune in the 1860s, was troubled.[76]

Yet, given newspapers' ability and willingness, partly under elite-
influence, to act as verbatim extended platforms, the reticence of some
aristocratic politicians hardly mattered. Meanwhile, others experienced
less disquiet. Even Gladstone did not permit his aristocratic ties to
inhibit his developing abilities to captivate and mobilise vast crowds,
far removed from him in economic and cultural experience,[77] nor from
acting as mediator between the elite and the urban middle and working
classes. Furthermore, national figures' ability to behave populistically
was crucially underpinned, in a localised society, by many others
amongst parochial elites. Urban businessmen were frequently genuinely
reticent about parliamentary honours, and pretended to be about municipal ones.[78] Yet, for reasons connected with the deference and dependency they often commanded, the self-made character they often
claimed ('one of yourselves'), and the skills they developed as visible and
personal figures in the factories they owned and managed, many
became highly adept platform performers, regularly commanding
crowds of hundreds, even thousands.

Loud voices, in a world before microphones, greatly assisted. So too
did abilities to tune into popular values and emotions. This might
require little legislative action: the health of democratising and fully
democratic polities partly rests upon politicians' ability to address feelings; causing people to believe popular emotions are sympathetically
recognised. Both parties into the 1860s, and particularly the Tories
thereafter, exploited popular nationalism. From the 1860s, local Tories
successfully appealed to the anti-Catholicism of many working people in
areas like Lancashire, beset as they saw it by Irish immigrant competition.[79] Equally successful were Tory appeals to working men's pleasures,
supposedly beset by Liberal puritanism and temperance attachments,
in the 1830s, 1840s, and after 1867.[80] Meanwhile, from at least the
late 1850s, and assisted by middle-class radicals, Liberal rhetoric
skilfully addressed traditional radical working-class attachments to
independence, liberty, retrenchment, free trade and popular control.[81]
This probably helped draw many former Chartists within the political
fold.

Some grievances required more concrete remedy, even when, as argued later, *laissez faire* possessed widespread popular consent. It was thus crucial that political sensitivity should produce legislative action, capable of appeasing groups within the expanding electorate and beyond. Even before 1832, Wellington's Tory ministry responded to widespread Dissenting and Catholic pressures by repealing legal disabilities in 1828 and 1829 respectively. Unsurprisingly, since they accurately perceived Dissenters as a client-group, doubly so following agitation during the 1835 General Election, the Whigs offered up the Dissenters Marriages Act, state-registration of births marriages and deaths, a tithe commutation Act, and a royal charter for the new non-confessional London University in 1836. They made less successful attempts to address grievances over church rates and education. More widely-directed political calculations about the middle classes produced the popularisation of urban corporate government in Scotland (1833), England and Wales (1835) and Ireland (1840). Equally significant, influenced by Peel's calculations about the new electorate, and though deriving great advantage from the old closed corporations, the Tories consented.

Similar competitive appeasement emerged after 1867. Indeed, for working men, this began substantially beforehand – partly born of opportunism, partly from desires to pacify dangerous agitation. It is evidenced by local Tory willingness to administer the Poor Law more generously than the Poor Law Commission. It is revealed in advancing factory and friendly-society legislation, the extension of companies legislation to embrace co-ops in privileged ways, and indeed the content of the 1867 Reform Act itself. In 1871, the Liberal Government further enhanced co-ops' legal position, and partially satisfied union demands about theirs. The subsequent Conservatives were inhibited in what they could offer working men by their landed base; also by their emerging ambition, opportunistically significant in itself, to become the main repository for the fears and discontents of middle-class electors, alarmed by the radical and apparently expensive implications of a mass manual electorate. Nevertheless, under pressure from candidates and MPs in industrial areas, driven by initiatives from individual ministers, and influenced by his own admittedly shrinking 'One Nation' emotions, Disraeli permitted his administration to substantially satisfy union demands over factory hours in 1874, and their legal position in 1875. The Government also passed comprehensive friendly-society legislation in the same year and further strengthened the Co-op's position in 1876.

Similar motivations partly underpinned legislation on artisans' dwell-
ings, food and drug regulation, public health and ship safety – even if
these were clumsily executed, or based upon less accurate prognostications about what pleased manual workers. Meanwhile, politicians
were aware of the electoral benefits available from exploiting manual
identities other than class – from educational provisions advantaging
Nonconformists, Catholics or Anglicans, for example.

As already implied, there were clear limits to flexibility and opportunism. These were imposed by the elevated backgrounds particularly of
nineteenth-century national politicians; the wide consensus amongst
them about political economy, and thus the limits of what government
could or should do. Also relevant were the limits to party competition
and the consequent habit of not contesting parliamentary and municipal
seats. Furthermore, class, religious and other social tensions ensured that
appeals to one group might hamper what could be offered to another.
Post-modernists have pointed out that one aspect of the politician's art
was to persuade people to construct their identities in less, rather than
more, troublesome ways – as part of 'the people' and 'the nation' rather
than as members of a class. Furthermore, drawing groups into politics,
even more into policy-making, had a significant tariff. In tempting
business-groups and the TUC into increasingly continuous consultation
about policy from 1918, governments expected them to control their
members. Governments were also attempting to marginalise 'rogue'-
groups to the political left and right of the centre.[82] In all such attempts
at agenda-control, British elites also proved immensely skilled.

Total flexibility would anyway have been dysfunctional, given the
limits to what a developing industrial economy could be expected to
bear in terms of taxation and other burdens. However, this was not what
Britain's democratising society required. Gladstone and Bright could
hold thousands of working men in thrall with disquisitions about Retrenchment, bloated aristocratic government[83] and exciting stories
about persecutions abroad.[84] Tories could command wild enthusiasm
amongst similar audiences with speeches against 'grandmotherly government' destroying their rightful pleasures.[85] These abilities to derive
popularity from the minimum state were partly due to the control elites
exercised over who was politically included. As we shall now see, it was
also rooted in the limited expectations that newly-included groups,
partly through elite influence and partly for their own good reasons,
had about what government would and should do for them.

4 The Political Fitness of Middle-Class Males

Having examined how democratisation occurred, we now turn to the character of the groups thus politically admitted. How far were they politically fit in the varied senses understood by contemporaries and making sense to us, and how far does this help explain the apparent success and painlessness of the democratisation process? This implies three interlinked questions. First, how far were these groups fit in terms of independence, rationality, political training and commitment to the values of the slowly emerging liberal democratic system? Second, how far did they possess values and virtues likely to render them and their political demands absorbable? Third, how far were they capable of becoming effective citizens, able to achieve their ends by political means? We start where democratisation started – with middle-class males.

This is appropriate since the middle class is often seen as crucial to liberal–democratic success or failure. Its members are perceived to be important to success as a supposed reservoir of commitment to liberal values like free speech and toleration. They are a repository of intelligence and reflection, while the more energetic are essential to the growth of a healthy capitalist economy, which is itself perceived as essential underpinning of stable liberal democracy. On the other hand, a discontented, frustrated, frightened or oppressed middle class has been believed capable of supplying ready support and sympathy for right-wing authoritarian solutions seeming to promise order and safety.[1] In later chapters, we may find reason to doubt that the middle class , when happy, were unique in their attachment to liberal values. Given how they ran their civil organisations, and the causes they supported, the attachment of working men may seem even more intense and unconditional. Nevertheless, the middle class are clearly highly important to liberal–democratic health. Thus we must examine their attitudes and values.

In fact, as we shall see, the situation was rather ambiguous, at least in the short-to-medium term. On the one hand, many middle-class males seem rather unfit. Certainly, the seats of many parliamentarians, who testified so optimistically to the independence and moral probity of £10 householders when debating their political admission, depended on more venal characteristics when it came to defending them, particularly in the many small-town constituencies created by the 1832 Reform Act. This in turn partly rested upon the somewhat uneven spread of civil society, and the fact that middle-class organisations did not always assume the same fervent membership participation that their working-class counterparts expected, however unrealistically. Furthermore, the substantial and rising levels of political fitness, particularly amongst more urbanised middle-class males, rested upon a life-style likely to be rather unfriendly to the fitness of their wives, adult daughters and servants. Moreover, if we adjudge fitness to be partly produced by participation in civil society, then the patronising relationship some middle-class organisations had with working people, whose perceived needs they sought to service, whose passive gratitude they often expected, and whose minds they sought to influence, might also be deemed ambivalent in liberal–democratic terms. This may not have been wholly destructive of liberal–democratic virtue, still less of com-mitments to the capitalist economy upon which the emerging liberal–democratic polity rested, but nevertheless the relationship was some-what problematic.

On the other hand, long-term trends, emerging well before formal political inclusion, and accelerating steadily thereafter, were sufficient to ensure widespread fitness at the point of formal enfranchisement, and ever-broadening fitness thereafter. After all, most middle-class males could read competently, and judging by assumptions amongst Victorian newspaper editors, were prepared extensively and seriously to do so. There were also ample and expanding means of education and self-education for those seeking to take matters further – libraries, Sunday Schools, mechanics institutes and so on. Moreover, their presence and the eagerness with which they were utilised, was symptomatic of an increasing powerful ideology emphasising 'self-instruction, self-command and self-acting energy'[2] and equating independence with manhood. Middle-class incomes and profits, particularly in expanding urban-industrial areas, were becoming sufficient to render their recipients independent of what we would now call clientelist relationships with the landed elite. In the same areas, more flexible types of property, like land-rents and mortgages, and new forms of economic organisation like the joint-stock company, were emerging to permit increasing independence from the landed elite.[3] Middle-class male occupations were also pushing in similar directions, particularly for profit-making industrial entrepreneurs and expanding numbers of expertise-embracing professionals (around 20 per cent of middle-class males in 1851).[4] This may also have been true of many relatively comfortable shopkeepers, used to dealing on equal terms with customers both above and below them, and consequently claimed by Tom Nossiter as key initiators of opinion-based political behaviour.[5] Finally, and most important, middle-class males were deeply and richly linked into ever-broadening networks of civil organisation, wherein democratic procedures, rituals and modes of operation were very evident. They were thereby initiators and participants in activity likely to produce, or reinforce liberal and at least conditionally democratic commitments in the broader polity. In what follows, we will in turn explore the context within which middle-class male organisations had their being; their extent, including that of the press; their internal procedures, and their effectiveness.

1. The Context

As will subsequently be argued for working men, though in rather different ways, the context wherein middle-class males increasingly had their being was highly favourable to developing civil organisation. Central to much of this were the forces of industrialisation and urbanisation. They produced major expansions amongst all segments of the middle class. They rendered most of them increasingly affluent – such that even the lower-middle class, in precipitous decline as many commentators have claimed, could fuel large numbers of clerkly suburbs and an emerging mass-circulation press in the late nineteenth century. Urbanisation was friendly to associational life. Along with industrialisation it also helped divide the middle classes, thus proliferating the interests, in the broadest sense, requiring representation. In the urban-industrial context, action of any sort required organisation, and was a key reason why the informal, pub-based culture of the early eighteenth century and before gave way to one distinguished by formal association. This in turn posed immediate questions about how such organisation, whether political, cultural, religious or charitable, was to be governed and rendered accountable. The almost universal and culturally significant answer was the annual general meeting, the elected committee, the annual report, and the society rule-book.

These forces also had a further relevant effect. Whilst, alongside expanding communications, they increased economic, social and political inter-dependence, thus undermining the long-term bases of locality, in the short-to-medium term they served to enhance local identity. This was partly due to the character of industrial capital, which remained substantially localised until at least the 1880s. It was also caused by continuing aristocratic domination of the national arena, rendering participation there, even for wealthy middle-class males, uninviting, expensive and unavailable. Those venturing to London were apt to find themselves 'very little boys...[having] to deal with such men as Lord Redesdale'.[6] Partly as a result, industrial towns came to symbolise middle-class notions of progress against backward and aristocratic rural areas. Hence the town halls, even of relatively un-industrial locations like Reading, could become 'a picture and a type of the best form of present civilisation', one moreover 'every humble townsman can feel belongs to himself'.[7] Particularly in the context of a governmental system that, whilst unitary, was nevertheless deeply decentralised, towns and cities were also repositories of very considerable social, economic and political power. Once all this was linked to the influence of religion and middle-class self-esteem, there emerged notions of community, as a palpable, self-contained, internally inter-dependent and visible entity. Thus, for middle-class men, even more than for working men, urban localities became hugely important focuses for self-identity, attention and interest, ambition and loyalty.

All this was highly important in a polity that, however unconsciously, was democratising. Industrial towns provided arenas, sufficiently small to be comprehensible yet sufficiently large to have significance in terms of decision-making effort and commitment; ones moreover independent of the aristocratically-dominated centre, with its closed and unattainable status system. They offered middle-class men, and even working men, relatively open access-points for intense political involvement and commitment, of civic as well as civil kinds. Equally crucial, they were locations where the aspirations, disputes and demands of the middle classes, between them and the working class, and the demands released by ongoing democratisation, could be negotiated. They could be negotiated moreover without coming into irresolvable conflict with those of the landed interest dominant at the centre. Towns, with their autonomy enhanced by municipal reform, one of the key fruits of middle-class political inclusion, and with their sense of worth constantly reinforced by increasingly luxuriant civic ritual, also came to provide channels through which many people, working-class as well as middle-class, could be attached, at least conditionally to the broader polity. Furthermore, satisfactions obtainable in these arenas, became one of several factors determining that what most people desired from democratisation was not any specific set of state actions or benefits, but the simple recognition of citizenship. For all these reasons, and because they were increasingly complex socially, towns and cities became the main focuses for the development of civil association.

A further feature of the context within which middle-class male political inclusion occurred, and civil association developed, was the state itself. As already noted for working men, it became an important negative reason for the development of middle-class civil organisation. There were three closely-associated factors here. One was *laissez faire*; the second was the New Poor Law; and the third, active state enlistment of charitable partnership. Taken together with Christian concern and fears about violent discontent, they produced perceived needs to assist the 'deserving poor', those who, through no fault of their own, proved incapable of effective self-help. They also induced the desire to undertake what was, in complex urban environments, the immensely difficult task of distinguishing such worthy persons from 'sturdy beggars'. The overall result was one of the most characteristic forms of middle-class association, the charitable organisation. As with working men, civil organisation in Britain was less the means whereby citizens resisted the state, more their response to its indifference and lack of ambition.

There were also three cultural facts about the urban middle class that were important to producing civil organisation and political fitness. First, male middle-class attachments to self-help, independence, education and work were friendly to creating voluntary organisation even if the entrepreneur's competitive individualism was arguably less functional. So too, secondly, was the obligatory character of religious observance in middle-class life-styles and self-perception.[8] Middle-class religiosity was often evangelical in inspiration, and predominantly Protestant. Admittedly, this might produce withdrawal from the corrupting world, particularly from its scruffier political bits. For most, however, it induced participation in civil as well as business life. For many, the world was an interdependent place, distinguished by mutuality of fortune and duty. Here, 'a man must act, whether to earn his living, or, even if not, he must act'.[9] Personal salvation required good works, often through collective effort, whether to save souls, succour the weak and helpless, or improve the town. In the Protestant world, moreover, there were many alternative and conflicting roads to salvation; sectarianism produced a multiplicity of associational activity – aimed both at worshipping God and pursuing His ends in the secular world.

Linked to religion, and important in a third way to middle-class associational life, was the family. Like the State and by definition, this was not part of civil society. However, the middle-class man's participation in civil society, like his dedicated pursuit of business, rested upon its support. His ability to devote his energies to a vibrant public life was underpinned, at least in the medium-term, by the abilities of his wife, adult daughters and mainly female servants to provide a resting-place from its toils.

We can now turn to civil society itself, starting first with the segment that also provides part of the context for the rest.

2. The Press

Newspapers are often seen as a democratically-functional segment of civil society, in that they form part of a network of voluntary activity capable of producing and reinforcing desirable liberal–democratic virtues like independence of the state, attachment to liberal freedoms, political participation and debate. Beyond this, they are crucial communication-carriers between elites and the masses, conveying persuasion and information downwards, demands and desires upwards. Newspapers are also the people's watchdog, drawing attention to governmental abuses and problems within society.

There is much to be said for this view. Most newspapers, after all, were owned by and aimed at the middle classes. They became established in the eighteenth century well before formal enfranchisement began. Even when burdened by stamp duties, they still managed to reach a yearly circulation of well over 10 000 000 by the mid-1750s, and 25 000 000 by 1826 – leaving aside the unstamped, and mainly working-class, press. This suggests a weekly circulation for legitimate and mainly middle-class newspapers of around 500 000. Titles and circulations amongst London and provincial dailies, and local weeklies expanded rapidly after the lowering and subsequent abolition of stamp and paper duties in 1837 and the mid-1850s. Thus newspapers were rendered more commercially viable, more able to invest in new technology, and to lower their cover-price. This brought them within the pocket-range of most middle-class males. All circulations rose substantially after 1837, even more after 1855.

Together with emerging news agencies like Reuters, this also provided the middle-class press with at least qualified independence of the governing elite in terms of finance and access to news. Like other more obvious voluntary organisations, newspapers also enhanced the independence and political self-confidence of their readers, helping them articulate and generalise a set of distinctive middle-class values and views of the world. These included not just faith in progress and work, but also the more obviously functional values, for citizens in an emerging liberal–democratic polity, of individualism and seriousness. This last was particularly crucial given the tight-packed greyness of the Victorian press.

Newspapers' very existence, with the access they could increasingly provide to commercial, political and social information, also probably enhanced middle-class attachment to liberal freedoms. Even though the emergence of a turbulently radical press after the Napoleonic Wars might have qualified the attachments of some, the campaign against the Taxes on Knowledge, led as it was by middle- as well working-class spokesmen, probably reinforced them again. This was particularly likely, given tempting arguments that abolition would destroy the price-advantage of the unstamped press, thereby opening working men to the improving blandishments of respectable publications.

Like other branches of civil society, the partisan character of most newspapers, and the very approximate balance between the two sides their proliferating numbers permitted, helped set the terms of political debate. So too did party factionalism which in turn enabled yet more newspapers to survive. Editorials provided readers with competing opinions about current issues, even if the same partisanship only permitted most middle-class males access to their own side's views. Newspapers' increasing coverage of national and international events also made them the principal means whereby middle-class males learnt about the world around them – doing so if they wished at immense length, and, as news-gathering and printing technology improved in the mid-nineteenth century, with increasing speed.

However, even more than in the late twentieth century, nineteenth-century newspapers also had a special function for middle-class males, just as they did for working men, and later for women. The press was not just a branch of civil society. Greatly aided by its increasing circulation and readership, and by its journalists' growing numbers and professionalism, it provided a crucial informational matrix within which the rest of that society could have its being. As such, it was also an important part of the machinery of accountability so far as civil organisations were concerned.

Most important here is the vast reportage Victorian newspapers provided about the activities of religious, charitable, economic and political organisations. Most significant were the local weeklies – primarily because so much of civil society, like the rest of contemporary life, was localised. Indeed, most space not occupied by adverts, parliamentary reports and local government activity, was absorbed by the verbose and verbatimly-reported proceedings and debates, annual reports, and financial statements of manifold local societies. Given the increasing size and verbal content of the local press, this was coverage indeed. This became particularly evident as the focus of such newspapers became increasingly localised after their various duties' final repeal in the mid-1850s. They could make civil-organisational participation seem normative. However, newspapers also provided extended platforms, whereby proceedings became available to those unable to attend, or who could, but in the absence of microphones could not hear. Moreover, here could be found not just the proceedings of middle-class civil society, but, also at some length, particularly during alarming unrest, those of its working-class counterpart – albeit often viewed through jaundiced eyes.

Also important, but in more specialised ways, was the professional and religious press. Both were burgeoning in the nineteenth century. Each religious sect supported at least one newspaper, quite aside from thousands of parish magazines. Professional publications were similarly healthy. For doctors, these had been emerging since around 1750; by the 1880s, gas engineers alone could choose between the monthly editions of four separate journals. In them, these necessarily solitary men (there was rarely more than one per town) could discover news of their 'brethren' elsewhere and extended reportage of the deliberations and often impassioned debates of their local, regional and national associations. Since they were an internationally-oriented profession, they could also discover much about 'fraternal' counterparts abroad. All this, along with learned-paper and article publication, enhanced gas engineers' sense of *esprit*, possession of expertise and consequent independence of their private or municipal employers. Religious newspapers also carried extended coverage of co-religionists all over the country, and of the deliberations of the relevant representative assemblies. They also reported extensively upon relevant agitations. The Nonconformist press, for example, was central to creating and co-ordinating the various campaigns punctuating nineteenth-century political life. Overall, if independence, group-solidarity and self-confidence are important in an emerging liberal democracy, as they probably are if people are to operate as politically effective and responsible citizens, then these specialised publications were active agents in promoting such qualities.

All this said, the middle-class press arguably left something to be desired in the way it serviced the democratic requirements of this segment of the polity. There is reason to doubt the extent of its debate-inducing abilities. This is partly because of its presentational style. The grey and tight-packed columns, the paucity of headlines and the absence of synthesis, all persisting unrelievedly until late-century, render Victorian newspapers fairly unapproachable, at least to us. The daily and weekly arrival of these novel-length publications must have placed high premiums on the famed seriousness of their readers. More important problems arose from the passionate partisanship of most daily and many weekly papers, rendering them far more effective at covering the words and actions of those with whom readers could be expected to agree than the less comforting ones from the other side.

The same factors helped limit newspapers' ability to induce accountability at least in the political field. If the watchdog role is central to press functions in liberal democratic societies, then most papers performed it partially: far better at covering the misdeeds of political opponents, whether in central or municipal government, than their own side's. There also seems evidence that daily newspapers in particular were less than efficient in highlighting other sorts of abuse. Coverage of contentious social issues and problems tended to follow relevant parliamentary debates rather than forcing these issues to legislative notice.

This was partly because of the relative absence of muck-raking traditions amongst British newspapers as compared say to their American counterparts.[10] It was also due to many daily (and probably local-weekly) newspapers' limited independence of governing elites. For all the increasing possibilities of autonomy deriving from their growing advertising revenue, profitability and reporting-resources, there is much evidence to suggest newspaper editors remained dependent upon leading politicians and their acolytes for insider information, argument and even indirect subsidy. What saved their ability to ensure governmental accountability was perhaps less their own determined independence, than the intense partisanship and competing cliquishness of various sections of the elite. Politicians could also be unpredictable, making discipleship problematic for even very slavish editors.[11]

3. Access to Civil Organisation

There is much contemporary (indeed subsequent historical) testimony to the centrality of civil organisation to nineteenth-century life. What Alexis de Tocqueville said about civil society in the USA – 'there is no end which the human will despairs of attaining by the free action of the collective power of individuals'[12] – would have found frequent echoes in Britain. 'The present is pre-eminently an age of societies', observed the *Church of England Temperance Chronicle* in 1887, suggesting future historians would be preoccupied with tracing 'the rise and progress of the associated movements which have so largely developed... in the past fifty years'.[13] Thirty-five years earlier, Edward Baines junior could still look back over two generations and discover 'many institutions and associations... for the dispensing of every kind of good... which have flourished most in the industrial towns and villages'.[14] Robert Vaughan referred to 'the voluntary combinations... which hold so conspicuous a place in our social history'.[15]

As this suggests, the wealth of voluntary organisation was a source of pride for many middle-class observers – pride in national, civic and class terms; testifying to and probably enhancing the health of voluntarist culture amongst this group. During the eighteenth, even more the nineteenth, century, it was expressed in growing numbers of resplendent buildings. The meeting-rooms of athenaeums, mechanics institutes, larger charities, chambers of commerce, engineering institutes, party headquarters, and gentleman's clubs, increasingly replaced the pub as venues for middle-class male public life, in larger towns, and by late-century, even smaller ones.

As this implies, civil organisation was widespread throughout the urban parts of the country, and not confined to the metropolis, as is sometimes the case in late-twentieth-century democratising societies. Indeed, it was a force marking and reinforcing urban as well as middle-class identity. Significantly, it was also increasingly evident throughout middle-class public life substantially before the onset of formal political inclusion, indeed was probably accelerating from the 1790s.[16] It continued to expand rapidly throughout the enfranchisement period. This is important to explaining the success of the process for two reasons. First, as we have seen, full inclusion arguably took a long time even for middle-class males. Second, a vibrant middle class is assumed important for the health of a polity that is including other groups besides just its middle class.

All this is clearly evident in the case of religion. Active observance, after all, was obligatory for both middle-class men and women. There is ample testimony to this central cultural fact from many contemporary observers, as well as from official and unofficial censuses Whatever the variations in local working-class traditions of religiosity, the more middle-class the town or area, the more observant it was likely to be. For most, this implied at least one weekly attendance at church or chapel, and thus some regular contact with, if not proven participation in, this very central segment of civil society. What is also important is just how much of this contact involved the various branches of Nonconformity, and thus that part of organised religion placing greatest emphasis upon localised self-governance, having greatest expectations of its lay adherents. Given the large numbers of lower-middle-class people drawn into Nonconformity, religion may have compensated for the paucity of occupational organisation distinguishing this group. Certainly, by the late eighteenth century, old and new Dissent were growing much faster than Anglicanism, both in numbers and places of worship. For example, Anglican churches and chapels grew from 11 379 in 1801 to 11 883 by 1831 – rising by just 4.4 per cent at a time when the population rose by 56.3 per cent. Over roughly the same period, Baptist chapels approximately doubled, and Wesleyan Methodists increased their membership by 167 per cent. By 1851, Anglicanism was fighting back quite formidably. Nevertheless, its attendances on Census Sunday in 1851 barely exceeded those of Dissent (3.8 as against 3.5 million), and there were grounds for thinking it was actually lagging behind in terms of active members. Meanwhile, the associational potential of religious life is enhanced still further if one considers the impact of 'the associational ideal':[17] particularly from the 1870s, Christian commitment was expressed and sustained not just through church-attendance but also by working in the burgeoning ancillary sector. Every church and chapel, even Catholic ones, increasingly generated Sunday Schools, guilds, sporting clubs, youth sections, men's societies, brotherhoods and so on. All required some degree of administration, policy-decision, selection of voluntary personnel, and thus normally processes of election and accountability. As we shall see, this was highly likely to involve working men. However, as the most obligatory participants in organised religion, the middle class were sucked into this branch of civil society in very large numbers.

Religion also underpinned another branch, organised charity. Philanthropy has a long British tradition and has often been seen as a central cultural fact. What is important from our current standpoint is the fact that, from the early eighteenth century, long before formal political inclusion began, the size and complexity of urban problems was demanding more collective and flexible means of handling human need than the traditional endowment-based charity administered by trustees. Charity was thus forced to become more organised; also more specialised, a tendency further enhanced by the fissiparous character of nineteenth-century religion and the localised character of urban life. The overall result was a vast and increasing array of charitable organisations. Many found cause for patriotic celebration in their sheer numbers; even foreign observers sometimes listed them in 'swarms':

> for saving ... life, for the conversion of Jews ... the propagation of the Bible, the advancement of science ... the protection of animals ... the suppression of vice ... the abolition of tithes ... building good houses for the working class ... savings banks ... emigration ... the propagation ... of knowledge, for Sabbath-day observance, against drunkenness, for founding schools, etc, etc.[18]

Taine was writing in the 1860s. Already by 1850, an attempt to list *The Charities of London* discovered around 600 and ran into six volumes. By 1860, 144 new agencies had emerged.[19] By 1870, these included over 35 Jewish charities, a number that immediately began rising sharply as the community grappled with East-European immigration.[20] However, organised philanthropy spread far beyond the Metropolis. It was clearly visible in most significant towns. In Manchester, 49 agencies were established between 1752 and 1850; 69 between 1851 and 1914.[21] Though most charities were primarily local until at least the 1860s, national organisations with branches were emerging from the 1820s – for example, the RNLI and RSPCA in 1824. By the early twentieth century, the charitable sphere was shrinking somewhat, or at least becoming less autonomous, as the nascent Welfare State began emerging. Nevertheless, this did not stop some 20 000 new charities being created during the First World War; unlike their counterparts in Germany, all were created independently of state initiative.[22]

Contemporaries often claimed charities pauperised their clientele. Historians have sometimes accused them of misapplied, inadequate, patronising and duplicated effort.[23] However, if civil organisation is deemed democratically functional, then even charities' multiplying character may be seen to have prima facie utility so far as middle-class men (and women) were concerned, even if their impact upon recipients was less incontestably healthy. Furthermore, though disproportionately led by middle-class elites, there seems evidence that participation and even leadership embraced the entire middling social spectrum.[24] Meanwhile, in larger towns and cities, charities were joined by many other self-educative organisations, such as statistical, literary and philosophical, and social science societies.

If charity posed difficulties for *laissez faire*, collective economic and occupational action might seem even more problematic. Indeed, historians have sometimes seen this as an area wherein individualistically-inclined middle-class men were necessarily deficient, perhaps needing to be little else in a system so market-driven. Even contemporaries doubted whether 'gentlemen...having different commercial interests...(could) meet and act for a common object'.[25] The isolated character of so many professional jobs also seemed associationally unfriendly. Most towns could boast just one gas engineer, and only a scattering of solicitors, for example. However, for all these undoubted obstacles, and in spite of undoubted reluctance to organise for political purposes, it is now clear that 'gentlemen' were rather good at this sector of civil association too.

Professionals were emphatically the most associationally talented. Though having neither need nor inclination for class-wide organisation,[26] individual professions organised very readily, often doing so before or very approximately to 1832. The Royal College of Physicians was established in 1800; civil engineers commenced association in 1771, and continuously from 1818; the Law Society emerged in 1825; architects in 1837, pharmacists in 1841 and mechanical engineers in 1847. These were national organisations. However, partly because of perennial fears of 'centralisation', and partly due to continuing problems of long-distance travel, professionals also established many local and regional associations. Indeed, in clear demonstration of these organisations' voluntary character, they often preceded and initiated the national dimension.

For all their undoubted inhibitions, businessmen too managed considerable collective feats, again starting significantly before 1832. In his study of the cotton industry, Anthony Howe uncovered a multiplicity of organisation, classifiable into at least four different types: 1) early-nineteenth-century combinations aimed at trade unions which, from the mid-1850s, began moving into more negotiational stances; 2) associations to co-ordinate opposition to factory legislation, and later to negotiate its more comfortable application; 3) commercial associations concerned about the industry's future, raw-material supplies, government

commercial and fiscal policies; 4) specialised pressure groups like the
Anti-Corn Law League and the Public School Association. Amongst all
these were not merely regional but also numerous local organisations,
including temporary *ad hoc* combinations aimed at particular segments
of municipal improvement bills. Furthermore, some regional associations, like those aimed at factory regulation, also drew support from
masters' organisations in Yorkshire, Derbyshire, Cumberland, Ireland
and Scotland. Overall, it seems safe to assent to Howe's conclusion that,
'these associations reveal the Lancashire textile capitalist, not as the
heroic individual who *par exception* subscribed to the Anti-Corn Law
League, but as a member of a defined occupational interest, integrated
into a network of temporary and permanent associations for the defence
of economic and class interest.'[27] Other industries were probably less
well articulated; nevertheless, the trend is clear.

As this implies, economic and occupational civil organisation was
patchy amongst the middle class just as amongst working men. Partly
because of enduring attachments to individualism, it was most thinly
spread amongst lower-middle-class males[28] – a fact which, along with
economic marginality, may help explain the continuing corruptibility of
so many £10 householders. White-collar unions have had a tenuous
history until recent decades. Organisations of the propertied lower-
middle class were more prone than those of any other middling segment
to under-recruitment and apathy. They were therefore more tenuous, as
any review of the chimerical history of ratepayers and small-property
associations rapidly shows. Nevertheless, if they kept disappearing, it is
arguably testimony to the strength of associational habits even here that
they also constantly reappeared. Some white-collar unions were fairly
resilient: teachers for example. While general shopkeepers organisations
came and went, more specialised groups, like Butchers' Guardians
Associations and grocers' organisations were more resilient. Meanwhile,
in the 1880s, tenant-farmers' organisations emerged in Scotland and
several parts of England,[29] thereby expressing and reinforcing a growing
and democratically functional independence of landlords, and starting
to match what, under the additional stimulus of nationalism, had long
been the pattern in Ireland.

Middle-class religious, charitable and economic organisations were all
capable of becoming political. This trend, as we shall see, increased over
the decades – either interspersed with more self-regulatory concerns (for
example, business groups that intermittently became political) or, as
specialised pressure groups, often stimulated by mobilisation from op-

ponents. On the religious side, or deriving from Christian, particularly Nonconformist, commitment, these produced multiplying hosts of moral reform and causal associations drawing middle-class male (and female) energies in large and passionate numbers. Like many others, these emerged substantially before formal enfranchisement: formidable campaigns against slavery started in 1788 and 1792,[30] joined in the next century by those against spirits-drinking, religious disabilities, and in favour of enfranchisement itself. Middle-class politicking continued accelerating thereafter, into agitations about temperance and prohibition, administrative reform, church rates, disestablishment, working-class education, peace, contagious diseases legislation, persecutions abroad, gambling, social purity and franchise reform. They proliferated further in the 1870s as the Nonconformist conscience took off.[31] None were obviously class causes, since they passionately divided middle-class people, often reflected deeper religious divisions amongst them, and frequently involved alliances with working-class and women's organisations. Nevertheless, the recurring, multiple, even the moralised, character of such agitations expressed something important about middle-class culture, just as those about say nuclear weapons and the environment do today, something manifestly functional in a democratising polity.

We have shown that civil participation by middle-class males was extensive, often impassioned, and embraced many sectors of public life – the political, economic and social. Probably, many individuals, particularly in the interlinking host of 'faddist' organisations around Nonconformity and Liberalism, had multiple attachments. However, to fully establish democratic functionality in terms of reinforcing democratic values and producing popular influence, we must explore how these organisations ran themselves, and how effective they were.

4. Self-Governance and Political Training

To what extent were middle-class civil organisations popularly self-governing, and how far did they provide training suitable to operation in the broader democratising polity? Several important points can be made at the outset. First, with significant exceptions, but commencing substantially before formal inclusion, most civil organisations wherein British middle-class males participated followed certain key rituals of internal democracy, or at least accountability. They were founded by open public meeting. Using an invariable process of proposed, seconded, debated, perhaps amended, and ratified motions, this defined aims and elected a provisional committee to produce rules for the emerging organisation. A subsequent gathering ratified or revised these rules, and elected a permanent committee. Thereafter, proceedings were legitimised by Annual General Meetings of the membership, its title always dignified by capital letters, and its advent normally advertised in the press. Here committee-reports on work over the year, along with statements of account, were received and committee-members were formally elected. Where necessary, decisions were taken on policy and rule-changes. This ritual is now so generalised we take it for granted. What is interesting is that, from at least the early eighteenth century, middling-class males (and all other sections of the mobilised population) did likewise. There are other imaginable ways of running organisations: leaders might 'emerge', decide policy and not feel, or be, obliged to seek broader consent, or render accounts. Of itself, the ritual did not guarantee popular governance. However, it provided a permanently available popular access-point to even the most oligarchic organisation. Furthermore, the normativeness of the democratic culture was such that the procedure became obligatory, indeed reflexive, long before the democratisation of the broader polity began, or was seriously considered. The culture was also rhythmically reinforced by the fact that, in any reasonable-sized town, there were increasing numbers of organisations undertaking this ritual in any given year.

Second, this was symptomatic of the fact that these were voluntary organisations, depending for sustenance on supporters' and/or subscribers' good will. It was also important that, with some significant exceptions, they were formed from below, at least in the sense of being created by those who subscribed. Moreover, however federated they might later become, they were initially locally created, that is to say from the bottom up.

Third, and however unwittingly, middle-class male participation in civil society had several consequences highly functional in democratic terms. Even non-political associations, as we shall argue, trained people for participation, even leadership, in the broader polity, and enhanced their political self-confidence.[32] Sometimes, they provided forums for debate about new ideas. Furthermore, civil organisations often expressed and reinforced what is most appropriately termed strong civic consciousness. No matter how unrealistic their social diagnoses and prescriptions, charities and moral-reform groups expressed widespread social concern. So too did many pressure groups. Many very consciously attached themselves to their urban location, participating eagerly in civic-processional ritual. These norms, allied to the modesty of entrepreneurial numbers, also dictated that even businessmen's groups often had to address their aspirations in public-interest terms.

Fourth, however, there are significant qualifications to the foregoing. They arise from the obvious fact that middle-class civil organisation existed in a particular historical and social dimension, wherein inequality and hierarchy were central. Thus, as we shall see, whatever the democratic functionality of Nonconformist chapels, the Anglican Church, linked as it was to the State and landed elite, was less certain in this respect. Charities are increasingly seen as channels through which local elites assuaged the effects of party conflict. Such conflict was often interspersed with long periods of municipal electoral torpor, as 'gentlemen' avoided the 'expense and tumult of a contest'. In so far as charity was responsible, it was probably dysfunctional to popular participation by virtue of robbing the electors of choice. There were, anyway, strong elements of hierarchy in much middle-class civil organisation; they seem to have been more tolerant of oligarchy and 'vice-presidential models'[33] of civil organisation than their working-class counterparts – though in the longer run, the 'democratic deficit' became evident in both. Such characteristics determined that some participants were more powerful than others. In chapel, charity, pressure-group and party constitutions, men were more powerful than women, however much informal influence the latter might exercise in reality. Synagogues were even more male-centred. Chapel 'elders' had more claims to power than the young and immature, however much the latter might assert 'their claim to equal rights upon every occasion in a vehement and contentious manner'.[34] Within Wesleyan Methodism, there was steady and effective pressure for centralisation and institutionalisation. In charities, large subscribers were often given more powers than small ones. Subscribing members of parties and chapels were more influential than mere declaratory ones or mere chapel 'hearers'.

This edges into the further point that, wherever middle-class organisation touched the working classes, the intended relationship tended to become deference-inducing, controlling, didactic, or, where working people threatened to move beyond control, sometimes excluding. In Chapter 3, we noted how common was the didactic tone amongst local party organisations from 1867, even long before. Charities too expected some change of recipient-conduct, in return for their aid, in the direction of industry, sobriety and thrift. Educational institutions were simi-

larly ambitious. The Leeds Popular Instruction Society in 1840 noted
the 'ignorance . . . vice . . . improvidence, drunkenness' of 'our vast population', observed how their 'erroneous' knowledge 'induces . . . a sense of
wrong' which 'excites in them a sullen and reckless discontent', and set
out to counteract it.[35]

Furthermore, in some sectors of religious life, self-governance was
hardly vibrant. Hierarchy and centralisation were obviously particularly
evident in the Catholic Church. Indeed, it seems fairly evident that a
strong Roman Church, with its extra-national allegiances, strongly-
articulated hierarchy, priestly authority and deep conservatism posed
major problems for many actual or emergent liberal-democratic polities
until the Second World War. The histories of France, Germany, Italy,
Spain, and Latin America seem to point strongly in this direction.[36] In
this sense, Britain was probably fortunate in its determined Protestantism.

Anglicanism too hardly courted popular consent. It was deeply hierarchical, particularly at its High Church end. Parliament and government's major role in appointments and institutional change, Anglican
mistrust of lay-participation in decision-making until at least the mid-
nineteenth century, particularly at national level, all rendered it an
unlikely instrument for internal democracy, and an improbable vehicle
for spreading democratic values in the wider world. So too did the fact
that there was no formal concept of church membership to provide
consultative rights, aside from baptism and Confirmation. Equally
problematic was its close association with the landed interest, expressed
both in its appointive policies and the partnership between parson and
squire in the governance and local judiciary of many rural areas.

However, even here, popular self-governance was significant and
increasing. Although 'Established', Anglicanism had lost its monopol-
istic position as a prescribed church with the 1689 Toleration Act. As
A.D. Gilbert has pointed out, from this point it was ultimately a
voluntary organisation like any other, competing in an increasingly
pluralistic religious market-place.[37] In the long run, this inevitably
produced growing reliance upon lay support, and a need to encourage
and reward its presence. This meant ministers had to pay considerable
attention to the tolerances of their parishioners in deciding how doctrinally 'high' or 'low' to pitch their message and ritual: in the last resort,
worshippers could always go elsewhere. It also probably helped enhance
the role of annual vestry meetings. Open all to male occupiers (effectively most household heads), they provided potentially important access-

points for widely-embracing lay participation. This was particularly significant given their powers to levy (and, by implication, refuse) the rate, elect churchwardens and sidesmen, even consider issues related to rebuilding their churches.[38] In many urban places as a result, the vestry became a focus for growing tensions between the local minister and his lay activists. There were even some places where vestries elected their ministers.[39] It was also the primary vehicle through which Nonconformists, by packing the meeting with crowds of their supporters, waged their campaign against compulsory church rates.

The need to recruit adherents in a competitive market, along with the desire to reach the working class, enhanced lay influence in two other ways. First, it produced a growing panoply of ancillary organisations just as it did amongst Nonconformists and Catholics. These emerged quite early and accelerated from the 1880s. Churches became gathering-points for ever-multiplying missionary groups, social and sporting clubs, debating societies and so on. Apart from the civic concern that particularly the first of these symbolised, their main importance from our current standpoint is that they required to be run by somebody. This entailed increasing lay-participation, accompanied by annual general meetings, elected committees and the other paraphernalia of accountability. Second, the foregoing forces, alongside Anglicanism's perceived need to defend itself politically against organised Nonconformity, produced two important associational developments. First, the Church Defence Institution was founded in 1859, and began breeding a network of local Associations devoted to the same end. Second and more important, from 1860, there emerged the Anglican Congress and from 1920, the Church Assembly – though here the democratic record is ambivalent: one of the Assembly's three colleges was lay, chosen from baptised Anglicans, but this college was for some long time dominated by the decidedly unbourgeois Cecil family.

Anglicanism rendered one other unwitting service to emerging liberal democracy, this time in no sense just confined to its middle-class segment. In an age when religion was central to so much political conflict, it supplied the stabilising medium for the right-wing of the two-party system that was clearly emerging from at least the 1830s. Whilst never totally polarised, Anglicanism and Nonconformity throughout the century represent the single most useful variable explaining why Victorians and their adjacent predecessors[40] voted as they did, and why parties adopted some of their more central policies. They were also central to generating alternative social and political cultures for the middle class, arguably into the inter-war years.[41] In this sense, Anglicanism combined with its competitors in Britain's intensely heterogeneous religious environment to provide the emerging electorate with political choices, choices moreover combining stability with greater margins of consensus than the clerical versus anti-clerical conflict which sometimes proved capable of eroding the legitimacy of political systems in France and Southern Europe.

If Anglicanism possessed significant liberal-democratic functionality, the various branches of Dissent did so even more. Here, what can be claimed for the middle class, as evident later, is in many respects equally applicable to the religiously-inclined working men forming the majority of most Nonconformist, like most Anglican, memberships. For both, internal democracy was inherent from the start. The initial splits from the Church, even more subsequent break-aways from Wesleyanism, along with schisms in individual chapels, often centred at least partly on issues of self-governance, with dissidents reacting against centralisation, or seeking enhanced democratic control. Moreover, decisions to found new sects or chapels presented near-models of autonomous and voluntary action. So too did individual decisions to join a chapel. Particularly in the early decades, both involved rejections of existing hierarchies in favour of 'an alternative community, the gathered church of believers'.[42] Given this central point, and what follows, it becomes important that Dissent as a whole was growing much faster than Anglicanism until the 1850s. Furthermore, the most rapidly expanding dissenting sects included those most attached to popular control. From more specifically middle-class viewpoints, it is significant that fission mostly occurred before 1832.

Certainly, although the intensity of commitment varied, with Wesleyan Methodists most obviously tolerant of centralising tendencies, lay-participation and self-governance were central to dissenting chapel life. Many chapels were founded by their first generation of members – often breakaways from existing congregations. Monthly meetings of members controlled much of what happened thereafter, taking decisions about admission and exclusion, allocating money, and participating in choosing pastors and electing officers; this in return for leading visibly Christian lives and playing their part in chapel affairs. Citing rival biblical authority, they could also argue furiously about the rights and privileges of rich members as against poorer but harder-working ones, the powers of their pastor, and the voting-rights of women.

Lay participation was further enhanced by the extensive use of lay preachers.

It was further increased as Nonconformity, like Anglicanism, Judaism and indeed Catholicism, succumbed to the multiple charms of ancillary organisations, with their elected hosts of office-holders and rhythmic annual meetings. All this might become rather oligarchic and hierarchical. Here, deference by lower to higher parts of the middle class, the increasing numbers of non-participatory 'hearers' as compared to full members, and machinations by power-holders all undoubtedly contributed. However satisfaction about performances of existing office-holders was also likely to be involved. Anyway, chapel life's ever-increasing demands, along with democratic communal norms, were likely to produce formidable pressure to share the 'burdens of office', just as they did amongst working-class chapel members. The sheer numbers of chapels is also relevant here. If we grant chapels a degree of popular decision-making, and that this was at least reinforcive for democracy within the wider polity, then this was being generated from many points. This is so both country-wide and within many towns, even rural areas. In the decade of enfranchisement in 1831–40, and excluding Wesleyanism, there were some 4540 temporary and 2784 permanent dissenting chapels in England and Wales alone.[43]

Admittedly Wesleyans, and to a lesser extent other dissenting sects, experienced increasingly effective pressures towards regionalisation and centralisation. Here, particularly amongst Wesleyans, the record is ambivalent. Admittedly, there was an increasingly complex machinery of consultation, but here there was again resistance to lay participation. Until the 1870s, the Wesleyan Annual Conference was composed exclusively of ordained ministers. The 1877 Constitution formalised increasing lay-representation, though ministers played a considerable part in its choosing. However, as the decades went by, the lay sessions became increasingly influential and assertive. As in the broader polity, representative democracy was becoming increasingly normative, distinguished both from oligarchy and direct democracy.

Many of these trends were evident within Judaism. On the one hand, Jewish communal life was imbued with considerable internal democracy, at least so far as its men were concerned. All aspects of synagogue-life, whether Orthodox or Reform, were run by a lay management committee, elected by the paying male membership ('the free members'). The Rabbi, elected by this committee, was regarded as their servant, even in religious matters. The constant need to secure

communities, particularly the Jewish poor, against the twin threats of
anti-Semitism and assimilation, as well as the need to preserve Jewish
ritual law, produced ever more spectacular arrays of voluntary organisations of both charitable and self-helping kinds, designed to cover every
aspect of Jewish life. All were run by committees, elected and held
accountable via civil rituals very similar to those in gentile voluntary
organisations. The community also had its own parliament, the Jewish
Board of Deputies, elected originally from synagogues across the country, more recently from lay organisations as well. From 1919, there was
also a growing network of local Representative Councils, starting in
Manchester and Liverpool, and then spreading across the country.
Their members were elected or appointed by local synagogues and
other communal organisations.

As this suggests, community democracy was subject to the same
trends evident elsewhere in civil society, and indeed within the broader
polity. On the one hand, it became representative from an early stage,
and in some sectors increasingly bureaucratic. Many organisations were
substantially hierarchical, greatly influenced by prestigious and often
wealthy local figures. On the other hand, there was regularly renewed
conflict between old-established and newly-arrived (normally immigrant) elements. Anglo-Jewish elites found themselves and their privileges under similar pressures to those focused upon the broader national
political elite. In many communities, in the 1830s and 1840s, and again
from the 1890s, tensions found outlet in pressures from synagogue seat-
holders for admission to the politically privileged category of membership. Here, these democratising pressures seemed to mesh with those
evident in the broader polity. In Liverpool in 1837, a spokesman for
disaffected seat-holders proclaimed:

> The day we live in – the things that have passed around us for the
> past ten years – the constitution of the country – the municipal
> government of this town – the nature of every public and private
> society, show that the power of the few over the many is passing
> away, and that every man with a stake in society is . . . entitled to a
> stake in its management.[44]

It is also evident that, amongst the range of civil organisation in
nineteenth-century Britain, religion was particularly good at propelling
many middle-, as well as working-class, people into other civil sectors:
charitable activity, moral reform and, most important from our current

viewpoint, local and national politics. Admittedly, this seems increasingly untrue of rank-and-file religious ministers, whose work pressures often limited political involvement.[45] However, lay-Dissenters, Catholics, Anglo-Jews and more tardily Anglicans were propelled into politics throughout the century, in quest of removing religious disabilities, controlling working-class education, attacking and defending Established religion, and over the role of Irish and Jewish immigrants. Less conflictually, and more indirectly, middle- as well as working-class Christians and occasionally Anglo-Jews, entered the political lists to defend persecuted co-religionists abroad, defend or imprison ladies-of-the-street, dry out or otherwise moralise the idle and drink-sodden residuum, and later, 'on a tide of pity', to improve welfare provision for respectable workers. All these reasons meant religious organisations were primary initiators of that archetypical nineteenth-century expression of 'pressure from without': popular petitioning. Furthermore, we see here a cardinal example of the way civil organisation, once started, becomes self-sustaining. Organised Nonconformity and its kindred political associations generated defensive organisation on the other side: the Liberation Society bred Church-Defence; temperance helped politicise the drink interest. Overall, religion was as powerful an initiator of mass-politics as was class.

Religious commitment also helped train middle-class men for, and push them into, political leadership. It was not the only inspiration. Business life was widely and plausibly believed to produce reliable political training: men of property, through managerial and financial experience, and the skills thereby acquired, were thought naturally suited to elective, particularly municipal, office. Economic interest might also create the motivation. However, religion was highly important. Lay-preaching could provide otherwise inarticulate and reticent businessmen with bases of political self-confidence – for council, even parliamentary, life. For rather more, the same services might be available through ancillary organisations, more particularly church or chapel debating societies and mock-parliaments, these being widely in place by the 1830s. These bodies also provided sounding-boards for new political ideas. More formidable here was 'the culminating glory of the sermon'.[46] This was an institutionalised occasion where Anglican or Dissenting pastors could come to resemble official consciences, free to raise issues of central theological, moral or political importance, prompting their listeners into discussion and sometimes action – whether to agitate for co-religionists abroad, secular or religious education, worry about the residuum, or simply enter local councils in quest of social reform. This last points to the way notions of Christian brotherhood, inter-dependence and thus 'community' could reinforce middle-class men's civic consciousness, their willingness to 'take on the duties and burdens of municipal office'.[47] Finally, as the century progressed, churches were joined by other generating agencies for moral ideas and political action, notably secular and ethical societies.

As already evident, our survey of religious decision-making inevitably edges into the internal processes of organised charity, if only because so much of the latter was religiously-inspired. This was one reason why charities occurred in such large and democratically-functional numbers. However, unlike churches and chapels, the insistence upon subscription confined membership and thus participation to the middle class. Only with emerging 'Hospital Saturdays', and other forms of working-class financial contribution in late-century, did recipients' representatives begin emerging on local hospital committees, their incidence probably varying with local trade-union strength. However, for those who did subscribe, charities provided open decision-making forums, doing so as soon as they began appearing in the early eighteenth century. For example, the Westminster Charitable Society was founded in 1719, and even small subscribers were classified as governors, entitled to vote at board meetings.

In a world of pronounced hierarchy, however, oligarchy was always an option, and occasioned less resistance than in working-class organisations where exhaustion and scarce resources produced strong expectations of circulating office. Charitable office could become almost proprietorial. There is evidence that, while charities multiplied, activists spread themselves rather thinly.[48] Charities might also give more power to large than small subscribers – the Westminster Charity's egalitarian democracy caused a secession by wealthy members to form St George's Hospital where only five-guinea subscribers could become governors.[49] Large subscribers also found themselves on honorary committees more often and more permanently. Amongst Anglican-inspired charities, local aristocrats glittered in presidential positions more resiliently than was really decent for middle-class creations.[50] Nevertheless, sheer numbers of organisations in any given location, the elective character of charitable governance, the rhythm of annual accountability, and the ever-growing need for myriad small subscriptions and voluntary effort, constrained oligarchy.

Thus, whilst AGMs and elections torpidly passed, barely marking collective consciousness, and whilst nominations were often pre-arranged, contested-elections seeming rather vulgar, these occasions sometimes became crowded forums for passionate debate about purposes and policies. In Manchester, Henshaw's Blind Asylum from 1854 became an arena for long-running conflict between Anglicanism and Dissent. In 1902, Manchester Infirmary's elections became bitterly embattled over whether the hospital should move to a more southerly site. Jewish charities, like much else in communal life, were riven with passionate argument. Another mark of inbuilt resistance to oligarchy was the widespread and long-persisting use, amongst Jewish and gentile charities, of subscribers' ballots to decide on charitable recipients. In microcosms of the qualified patterns of popular politics evident nationally, subscribers had votes in proportion to the size of donations, and rivals canvassed in deeply 'vulgar' ways. Elite figures were often hostile to 'the best method of electing the least eligible',[51] yet these 'voting charities' mostly persisted up to 1914.

Charity performed another service for politics – this time not so much propelling men into civic life, or training them for it, as providing legitimisation. Partly because municipal participation was seen by many almost as a branch of philanthropy, charitable action was often a pre-requisite for successful office-seeking. Certainly, it bulked large in many municipal, and even parliamentary, election addresses. It established credentials of civic concern (and from our standpoint, was one of many marks of middle-class civil society's civic character), provided reservoirs of electorally useful dependency, and in in-turned nineteenth-century towns, lent dignified visibility to candidates. To some degree, it also rendered local political leadership more open. Whilst philanthropic often accompanied economic leadership as a basis for political participation, it was not inseparable from it. Successful charity required work just as much as large subscriptions. In consequence, even economically modest middle-class figures could establish legitimate claims to social and thus political respect.[52]

Economic and occupational associations were similarly functional in political terms. Representative business organisations were run on customary bases of Annual General Meetings with annual reports from elected committees. Where purely local, there were often additional meetings open to all members, where matters of common concern were discussed. Such associations might be passive for long periods, tolerating considerable oligarchy. Yet this was mainly produced by members' satisfaction. Sometimes office was widely spread, as with the Manchester Chamber of Commerce and Commercial Association.[53] Meanwhile, equally important for the sort of polity that was slowly emerging, was the fact that, although often formed to destroy trade unions, employers' organisations by the 1860s were coming to accept them, even becoming 'quite friendly to the deliberations which ought , and quite frequently did, occur between employers and the employed'.[54] By the start of formal working-class inclusion, some employers were starting to accept their role in an emerging negotiational culture.

Professional associations too were determinedly self-governing. Though their annual conferences were primarily about exchanging expertise along with sociability, they were also arenas for passionately-conducted debate about common concerns, particularly the policing of professional borders, the role of 'touts' and other legal 'marginals', the character of training, and what constituted proper professional conduct. Gas engineers discussed 'commissions' on contracts, the role of traders and trading-engineers, and whether they should be admitted and allowed conference votes. Extending from these arguments, elections were periodically fiercely contested. All this was repeated regionally and locally, where associational meetings were quarterly as well as annual, where professionals often felt more at home, and from where they defended themselves against dangerous tendencies towards 'centralisation' emanating from national headquarters.

In the long run, the democratic legacy of professional organisations has been ambivalent. The expertise they generated rendered members increasingly independent of employers and gave them leverage. Here as elsewhere, declining dependence (characteristically in Britain, of elites rather than the state) was democratically functional. Like unions, professional associations also facilitated negotiation with employers. Yet the latter were often elected public authorities, and professional autonomy was one of many forces moving policy-making beyond elective control.

Similar, if still qualified, patterns of self-government were also evident amongst causal and political associations. They exhibited customary rituals of AGMs, elections and annual reports. Because of their frequent claims to popular representativeness, movements like those against slavery, drink, and the Corn Laws showed strong attachment to exercises in popular legitimisation via 'numerously attended public meetings', with proposed, seconded and enthusiastically proclaimed resolutions. In popular constituencies, political parties, before as after

1867, showed similar attachments, particularly in nominating parliamentary and municipal candidates. From the late 1860s, both parties, particularly the Liberals, middle-class dominated though they remained, became attached to the rituals of mass politics – committees elected by mass meetings where party-membership rested on self-proclamation rather than subscription, candidates similarly selected, and discussion of policy at annual conferences. Local party machines became vehicles for quite lowly middle-class figures to acquire political influence and achieve at least municipal position. Parties might be dominated by elites, national and local, but managing the local political machine was irksome and time-consuming for men of property and standing. Consequently, little men discovered space to render themselves indispensable.[55]

However, against this popular side we must set more ambivalent behaviour from large subscribers and traditional 'wire-pullers'. Parliamentary leaders, particularly Conservative ones, were often deeply mistrustful of mass parties, seeking to neutralise and bypass their pressures, even while utilising their electoral services. At all levels, even of the National Liberal Federation, popularly elected committees and delegates were carefully counterweighted by nominated ones. However extensive the participation in the formal processes of candidate selection for Parliament or municipality, the real decisions were taken by much smaller committees. Though emphasising popular representativeness, cause-groups were perfectly prepared to exploit less savoury forms of traditional politics, like the creation of 'faggot votes' in county elections, if it suited their purposes. To judge by the Anti-Corn Law League at least,[56] they also gave great power to their largest subscribers, and, amongst these, to those regularly attending their meetings. Whilst underpinning the broader democracy, here as elsewhere, civil society also showed, and sometimes reflected, some of its more oligarchic and bureaucratic characteristics.

5. The Articulation of Interest

The final aspect of political fitness we must consider is how far middle-class males were rendered capable, by their civil organisations, of advancing and defending their perceived political interests – either in broad class terms, or the multiple causes for which they (and increasingly middle-class women) characteristically if not monopolistically campaigned. If they were politically effective, what impact did the recognition of their aspirations have upon the role of the state? Both questions are important if we are to understand how political inclusion impacted upon the political system wherein it occurred.

An important initial point is that the interests of many middle-class groups required little governmental action or political activity. For most economic interest groups at least, whether business, white-collar or professional, their concerns were most effectively served, or perceived to be served, within the framework of *laissez faire*. Indeed, the very existence of a minimally-ambitious state partly resulted from political sensitivity to their needs, or perhaps the assumed generalisability of those needs to the rest of British society.[57] Interests were thus protected through influence upon political agendas rather than mobilisation. Even where activity was required, middle-class interests might best be served by action within non-political sectors of life – by business self-regulation, professional self-governance, or attempts directly to moralise the surrounding society.

This had important consequences. Many interests and identities articulated by middle-class people were relatively easy to satisfy. They required either little action, or action to procure negative rather than positive freedoms, or indeed actual state withdrawal from spheres previously occupied. This rendered most £10 householders politically fit in senses also understood by those enfranchising them: potential voters accepted the broad outlines of the free market whose regulatory context their leaders had helped shape even before 1832. In its first phase, as more surprisingly in later ones, democratisation thus produced few direct burdens for the emerging industrial capitalist economy. The most central middle-class male demand, one substantially satisfied by enfranchisement itself, and by actions like removing religious disabilities, was for full citizenship, the granting of full political rights for their own sake.

Let us explore this argument in more detail. Charities were arguably the most central and representative sectors of middle-class civil society. They drew much of their existence and justification from the state's absence or withdrawal from most forms of social protection. They also operated within the authoritarian context set by the Poor Law, aimed at procuring conditions facilitating the State's ultimate withdrawal. Furthermore, if charities served middle-class interests, and it is not unreasonable to think they partly did,[58] this was best achieved by trying to act directly upon the recipients: 'moralising' them in ways friendly to the free market, in return for aid; pacifying the 'deserving' whilst leaving the 'undeserving' to the Poor Law's harsh ministrations. Charities served those interests also by realising middle-class aspirations to enhanced status and citizenship within vibrant local communities. In so far as state action was required, and this barely seems to have been the case, it was simply to provide a legally secure framework wherein to operate.

What was true of charities was also partly evident amongst religious and moral reform organisations. Nonconformists, not of course exclusively middle class, but certainly heavily empowered by the 1832 Act, were often mobilised to achieve political ends. However, what they primarily sought was largely negative state action to remove religious disability. In this, their actions coincided with high levels of success, in a process beginning in 1828, and terminating in 1898.[59] Moral reform organisations were also at best only intermittently concerned with the state, and again in primarily negative directions. Whether for class or spiritual ends, their preferred mode was to moralise the lower orders by direct persuasion. After the decline of the anti-spirits campaign, temperance for example turned directly to 'suasion' in the form of teetotalism. Only after that failed did it return to state regulation expressed in prohibition (a quest in which it achieved only minimal success partly because of counter-mobilisation by the drink interest). Even then, pledge-taking remained important in local temperance strategy, and prohibition was seen as a necessary preliminary to the free market once more rational, less drink-sodden, behaviour had been established.

Meanwhile, more obviously middle-class organisations – business, professional and white-collar organisations – also saw many of their functions in non-political terms. Business associations perceived their role substantially as attempting the self-policing of business practice and minimum standards. They also sought to co-ordinate action, first against unions, and later to negotiate with them. Professional organisations were mostly concerned to police occupational entry-points, with or without formal state sanction; to advance professional status; and enhance their possession of expertise by facilitating its exchange amongst members. These areas were the focuses of passionate debate, even amongst lawyers who were necessarily more concerned with the law and thus the state. Small-business organisations – aspirant organisers of the largest groups enfranchised in 1832 – were also partly concerned with regulating standards of goods and services. The shopocracy, and emerging white-collar workers, were deeply attached to the free market, unlike their counterparts in mainland Europe and arguably therefore against their own best interests, eschewing state protection notwithstanding the combines emerging in late-century.[60] Almost their only appeal (unsuccessful until 1933) was for governments to terminate the co-operative movement's tax-exempt status.[61]

Business organisations also sought to curb state regulation of factories and mines, river and smoke pollution, house-building and public health. In this quest, they were quite effective for many decades. This was partly because they were also able to control the political agenda in various ways: for example, associating 'muck with brass' in the public mind; or appearing so powerful that potential reformers did not think agitation likely to be cost-effective. Success was also due to businessmen's domination of elected municipal life and thus of regulatory committees after, even more than before, 1832 and 1835.

Particularly in the long-run, there was not of course a total consensus about the role of the state amongst middle-class groups. That business interests, organised or otherwise, could ultimately do no more than delay and modify regulation was partly because of pressure in contrary directions from other middling groups. Admittedly effective agitation for factory regulation came partly from trade unions. However, equally important in regulatory expansion was pressure from groups like sanitary organisations, and even more the self-generating momentum articulated by the growing army of professional servants of central and municipal government.[62]

6. Conclusion

With significant short-term exceptions, middle-class males were either reasonably fit politically by the point of formal political inclusion in 1832, or likely to become so by virtue of their attachments to civil society. Civil organisations generated by middling groups were broadly programmed to develop and reinforce liberal-democratic values amongst their members, encourage them into politics, effectively articulate demands, and train sufficient supplies of leadership. This was so, even if, like voluntary organisations at other social levels, they also showed some of the same bureaucratic and oligarchic tendencies as the polity they underpinned. Their organised interests and identities were also highly influential, but created few demands upon the state other than for its withdrawal from areas previously occupied. Due to the high economic consensus between land and business, and the liberal inclinations of predominant segments of the central political elite, these were mostly easy to satisfy. Later, some middle-class groups, impelled by evangelical, humanitarian, professional or self-preserving concerns, began generating pressure for state expansion on behalf of what they perceived as the interests of the suffering lower orders. Indeed, they arguably became the primary initiators of the expanding state. In this they received only qualified support from working-class organisations. One purpose of the next two chapters is to investigate why this was so.

5 Working Men and Political Fitness: Access to Civil Society

The next two chapters have the same purpose as Chapter 4. They will investigate the political fitness, absorbability and impact of the working men, enfranchised in 1867, 1884 and 1918, in the varying terms understood by contemporaries and present-day analysts. We will contend that, through their organisations of self-help, self-defence, worship and enjoyment, and through the vibrant working-class press, many manual workers were being attached (or at least having existing attachments strongly reinforced) not just to democratic, but liberal-democratic, values and aspirations. It is centrally important that this was substantially happening in the decades before formal inclusion began, as well as acceleratingly thereafter. We shall also argue that, at least to the extent required by the expanding polity and its elites, this rendered many working men politically fit: some received training in leadership, rather more in the skills and advantages of organisation; many more probably gained a sense that consultation about matters intimately affecting them was a matter of right, duty, habit, even enjoyment. Working-class connections to civil society also reinforced 'fitness' by strengthening attachments to liberal values. This was true both generally, and in the important specific sense that the newly-included citizens were enduringly unlikely to make expensive demands through the political system on the developing industrial and capitalist economy that it might be unable to bear. Finally, and partly underpinning this, civil organisation also became the means whereby working men were not just politically included, but also incorporated into the status-giving and negotiational structures of the expanding polity.

This chapter first examines the working-class press, arguably a special aspect of civil society, providing the informational matrix within which the rest existed. The main part then focuses upon the extent of civil organisation, examining how widely and deeply it spread amongst working men, and how this related to the progress of enfranchisement. Chapter 6 explores how working men's organisations conducted themselves, and what democratically functional services they were capable of rendering their numerous members.

Let us begin with some general points about working-class political fitness. For a start, the picture that follows will not show evenly distributed participatory enthusiasm. There will be evidence of apathy even in associationally well-endowed parts of the working class, and certainly the presence of motivations for civil participation besides just desires for consultation. Yet working-class civil organisation was more vibrant than its late-twentieth-century counterpart. Furthermore, we should remember the point emphasised earlier – that, to judge by the twentieth century, liberal democracy does not require, and may be unable to absorb, constantly high levels of political excitement and participation. Some observers have even argued that extended intense political involvement may precede the collapse of democratic systems.[1]

It will also become evident that civil organisation, although vibrant, was not evenly spread amongst working men. Civil participation was intense and multi-faceted amongst the most secure and proudly-skilled: for artisans indeed, it was central to their culture. In all its manifestations, it was also more evident in expanding northern and midland industrial towns, and indeed contributed to their strong sense of community, than in cities, southern areas and rural locations. On the other hand, civil organisation emerged early, and was spreading steadily amongst respectable working men from at least mid-century. By late-century, aside from the most residual and economically desperate levels, there were few locations where it was completely absent.

We should also reiterate the point made earlier: the relationship between working-class civil organisation and the state was rather different from that envisaged by proponents of the virtues of civil society who learnt their trade in the totalitarian twentieth century. Admittedly some working-class agitation saw itself as opposing a repressive state, and few saw it as exactly friendly. Early nineteenth-century unions and radical newspapers became important means of resisting state-induced oppression. Anti-Poor-Law agitation was strongly anti-statist in some respects, as even more was the 'defence of working-class bodies' passionately mounted by the Anti-Vaccination movement from 1853 to 1907.[2] However, for the most part, once the authoritarian and fearful decades surrounding the French Wars had passed, *laissez faire* ensured Britain's liberal state remained profoundly and realistically unambitious so far as civil control was concerned. Apart from maintaining law and order, the national state's only real ambition, an important one, was to encourage amongst the working class the associational means of self-help. This it did, as noted in Chapter 3, partly by the draconian Poor Law, and partly through legislation providing legal security for working-class organisations as they became seen as safely respectable. Thus working-class civil society became less the means of resisting state encroachment than partly the product of the minimal state – encouraged by its legal framework, and designed to fill gaps in personal security it refused to occupy. In so far as working-class organisations could procure democratically-functional autonomy for their members, as they increasingly could, this was required less against the state than against elites, normally local ones, upon whom working men and their families depended.

In many places, and for several decades, locally-induced paternalism represented a powerful countervailing influence to that released by civil organisation.[3] As with the small-town middle class, this was one reason why democratising working-class electoral behaviour sometimes took longer than democratising the electoral system. Indeed, in some areas (some factory towns and many rural areas with residential landowners), paternalism could partially incorporate working-class civil organisations into the network of dependency – at least in the short-to-medium term. However, particularly in urban areas, this incorporation was never more than partial; deference was always conditional; and in the medium-to-long term the impact of working-class associational life was towards increasing the independence of participants.

In considering working-class civil organisation, we should remember that at no point in the nineteenth century do we see any sort of meritocratic society. Unless one makes the probably unwarranted assumption that everyone, given equal access to educational and other advantages, will prove equally talented, an important point probably follows. It seems reasonable to think the reservoir of untapped working-class talent for leadership, organisation and even participation was substantial; probably more than in the late-twentieth century when education, social mobility and technological change have substantially thinned the ranks of manual workers.

1. The Context

Before examining working men's civil organisations, we should consider the environment conditioning their existence. In some respects, this was admittedly inhibiting. Massive and constant influxes into urban areas from the countryside, even more divisively from Ireland, hardly encouraged solidaristic behaviour, particularly early on. Even more apparently discouraging was the way urban areas became locations of constant movement even for those who arrived. Industrial towns eventually provided sufficient permanent employment to promote residential stability. Cities, on the other hand, with their strong predilection for low-paid, sweated, casual and seasonal trades induced the opposite. They were scenes of continual relocation – out of and back into town according to the seasonal pulsations of the unskilled agricultural job market; or around inside the urban slum. Such constant movement provided poor soil for organisation, especially for those at the bottom of the working-class hierarchy where residential mobility was reinforced by constant needs to seek cheaper accommodation or to escape landlords wanting rent-arrears.[4]

Economic marginality had other, equally associationally discouraging, effects. Many contemporary observers testified to the existence of what we should now call a culture of poverty at the base of the working class. This was a world where there was little time, energy or inclination for anything beyond basic survival, a situation reinforced by minimal education. This culture was indifferent, often hostile, to any form of voluntary organisation. Contemporary middle-class observers noticed it primarily as resistance to religious observance. Yet, what churches experienced was no more than what confronted unions, political and other organisations.[5] Amongst the most desperate layers of working-class life, very thick in some city areas, contact with civil society was minimal and passive, largely restricted to receiving handouts from the local church and visits from the collector of the large funeral society.

On balance, however, industrialisation and urbanisation encouraged civil organisation for working-class, as for middle-class, men. Certainly, friendly-society lodges were most thickly distributed in areas of dynamic industrial and urban growth;[6] so too were co-ops and trade unions. These forces concentrated people geographically, facilitating association and the contemplation of social contrast and mutual interest, doubly so because rural migrants often sought security by establishing themselves close to family or friends from the same locations. This points to the general fact that, though urbanisation posed severe problems for human relationships of all kinds, it also dictated these problems could only be grappled with in organised ways; and facilitated the means of so doing. Furthermore, though urban dwellers moved often, they rarely moved far. Extended families and neighbourhoods thus remained capable of providing informal support-networks for wives and more organised forms of protection and sociability for their husbands. Friendly-society lodges appeared to rest heavily upon such localised contexts;[7] so too did more political forms of civil association, including the Anti-Vaccination Movement and eventually Labour Party branches.[8] Even in rural areas, urban migration, and the pull it exerted on those left behind, may well have facilitated resistance and independence of local elites. Meanwhile, although industrialisation spread across the country in rather slow and varied ways, the resulting work situation was frequently and increasingly such as to encourage organised occupational solidarity. Certainly trade unionism, however intense employer-opposition might be, found fertile ground for its operations in the many permanent jobs available in factories, mines and the engineering works of Central Scotland, South Wales and Northern England. This greatly enhanced longer-term pre-dilections for union organisation created by skilled artisan traditions, in spite, indeed because of, constant 'tramping'.

A further and more universal encouragement to association, at least for men and until the very late-nineteenth century,[9] was the state of working-class housing. The internally cramped, close-packed, rather segregated[10] and uniformly dismal state of these habitations was such as not merely to provide solidarity, but to push working men into locations that encouraged informal association and formal organisation. It may also be that the steady switch from court to more open forms of terraced housing, a change eagerly encouraged by many local authority elites anxious about sedition and incest,[11] encouraged wider and more integrated forms of solidarity than those available in the more insular former housing world.

Nevertheless, there was little, even in terraced houses, to encourage lingering by working-class patriarchs and their grown-up sons. Foremost amongst the places where they fled, in rural as in urban places, were the beerhouse and pub. Beerhouses particularly were situated in epidemic numbers[12] in working-class areas. Admittedly, for many, these were simply warm, brightly-lit places where they could forget their dismal homes, their burgeoning families, and their often dire financial circum-stances. Indeed, the remarkable and rising level of working-class inbi-bulation did not just horrify middle-class observers. It also drove many working-class radicals, both early and late in the century, into either despair or the temperance movement.[13] They were appalled by the escapism, apathy, irrationality and sheer lumpenness alcohol apparently induced, or at least betokened. The exasperation was understandable: amongst several other things, pubs and beerhouses provided fertile locations where many more than just working men could enjoy being politically corrupted by social superiors. With some justice, the 1868 election, immediately after the first substantial bout of working-class enfranchisement, was seen as the most drink-sodden to date.

Yet, pubs also facilitated more democratically-functional associational life. They were places where newspapers could be jointly purchased, read by the literate, read out to the illiterate, and maybe discussed. Their upper rooms provided locations for more formal associational life. Very often, pubs were the only places available – as even temperance societies discovered, and sometimes sheepishly accepted.[14] More enthusiastic patronage came from union branches and friendly societies. Of the thirty-five society lodges of various sorts in Chorley in 1890, all but one were dedicatedly bibulous; in Blackburn in 1907, just one lodge of the Manchester Unity was temperate and lonely. Indeed most lodges everywhere drew their names from the hostelry where they met, sometimes making the landlord treasurer. Hardly surprisingly, this fact of working-class associational life could detract from the gravity of business. Meetings of Blackburn's Philanthropic and Burial Society were regularly foreshortened by the thought of 'the eighteen-gallon barrels to come after'.[15] Sometimes they were disrupted by the already-inebriated, including in 1866 the President himself. He was suspended after having 'been drunk at the committee meeting and refused to be called to order'. Nor was he saved by the helpful friend who pointed out he had 'not been drunk at every meeting'.[16] Nevertheless, pubs greatly added to the attractions of associational life[17] and were important factors ensuring its inner democracy. Political corruption aside, they mostly also enhanced its autonomy from Victorian elites.

2. Access to the Media

We can now examine the working-class civil association emerging in this environment. We start by looking at the press, arguably a special aspect of civil society. In one sense, newspapers were simply a crucial part of civil society, perhaps particularly for working men. They were important points of articulation located between the state and the family. As such, and more clearly than their middle-class counterparts, with their susceptibility to influence from politicians, radical papers constituted very significant resistance-points to the state and its government, particularly in the first half of the century when repression was being intermittently attempted. They also themselves became important focuses of defensive organisation during the extended battle over the 'taxes on knowledge'. As such, most historians believed they enhanced working-class articulation over a range of issues, and, as we shall see, undoubtedly strengthened attachments to liberal as well as democratic values. Yet, as noted in Chapter 4, newspapers were also different from the rest of civil society, providing an informational matrix within which the other elements existed. In the absence of other forms of mass communications, they were crucial to both the formation and articulation of civil organisation. They were particularly important for those at the bottom of the social scale for two reasons. First, given the state and character of working-class education, few other means of gaining access to information, argument and ideas were actually available. Second, even more than other agitation, working-class action up to around 1850 had constantly to confront the fact that political organisations, possessing branches with whom they formally communicated, were actually illegal.

It is highly important for our present concerns that a thriving popular political press, aimed primarily at working men, and demanding their political inclusion, emerged long before inclusion substantially began. It is also important that working-class newspapers continued thriving whilst the process was taking place.

It will illustrate the point, if this development is briefly painted in. The radical working-class press emerged in a series of phases, not all entirely progressive for some historians.[18] Around 1800, and particularly from the end of the Napoleonic Wars, several papers and periodicals were published subsisting on the legal edge of the 'taxes on Knowledge', the stamp and paper duties. This they did either by paying the fourpenny stamp and hoping their once-weekly appearance would make communal purchase viable and attractive, or by pretending to be 'periodicals', thereby avoiding duty altogether. The most famous of the first sort was *The Black Dwarf*, and of the second, Cobbett's *Political Register*. Most disappeared – either directly suppressed by the relevant parts of the Six Acts of 1819, or forced beyond financial viability when the definition of a newspaper was extended to include periodicals in 1830. They were succeeded from the late 1820s by a thriving set of 'unstamped' and thus illegal newspapers, for whom risks involved in evading the law were rendered worthwhile by their consequent cheapness and competitive advantage over their middle-class-inspired rivals. Of these, the most famous or notorious was the *Poor Man's Guardian*. Their brief but vibrant golden age lasted until their market advantage was destroyed by stamp-duty reduction to one penny in 1836. Their successors in the medium-term were several radical, primarily Chartist, and almost exclusively political, newspapers. The most significant and successful of these was Feargus O'Connor's *Northern Star*. There were also several union papers, particularly *The Beehive*. However, starting around the same time as the likes of the *Northern Star*, were much longer-term inheritors of this mantle, the working-class Sunday press[19] – most famously *Lloyd's Weekly*, *Reynold's News* and *The News of the World* – far more commercially-minded, more moderate, less political but still respectably radical.

Significantly all these substantially predated the 1867 and 1884 Reform Acts. Then, from the late 1880s, working-class Sundays were earnestly joined by a rash of purely political journals in the form of socialist and labour weeklies. A few were London-based and at least semi-national, like Robert Blatchford's *Clarion*, Henry Hyndman's *Justice* and Keir Hardy's *Labour Leader*. Most were perpetually shifting local titles.[20] Finally, the decade before the First World War witnessed the emergence of the first working-class daily, the *Daily Herald*, financed from 1929 by Odhams Press and the TUC.

If the radical press, as we shall argue, connected working men to civil society before, whilst and after they were being embraced by democratisation, it was doing so for substantial numbers. This was doubly so because of the habit of communal reading, evident throughout the century,[21] but particularly until the 1850s.[22] At its height in 1816–17, the *Political Register* sold 40–60 000 copies each week. Amongst the swelling ranks of the unstamped, the *Voice of the People* was selling 30 000 weekly, and the *Poor Man's Guardian* 16 000. Pat Hollis has argued that actual readers and listeners multiplied these figures by as much as twenty.[23] Meanwhile, the *Northern Star* had a stamped circulation of 50 000 in July 1839, considerably more than the contemporary *Times* or *Manchester Guardian*. Eight months earlier, the *Star* claimed a readership of 400 000 – perhaps not unreasonably, if Hollis' suppositions are anything like correct: the paper was designed to be read aloud, and regularly was in pubs, coffee-houses, workshops and homes. It seems justifiable to use the term 'mass circulation' to describe this almost wholly political publication. The term is even more appropriate for the working-class Sunday press. *Reynolds News* and *Lloyds Weekly* were selling 300 000 and 600 000 respectively by the 1880s, and the former reached one million in 1896, the year the *Daily Mail* began.

Such figures are important because, particularly up to around 1850, when working-class access to transport was so limited, these publications provided crucial connections between otherwise unconnected individuals and groups. Newspapers carried extensive information about problems and grievances, and the activities of unions, co-ops, Chartist and other radical organisations. They co-joined otherwise isolated agitations, enabling participants to feel and become part of broader movements. They became focuses of organisation and political culture in their own right: Chartist meetings often started with readings from *The Northern Star*.[24] They did all this far more cheaply, economically, and thus more availably and effectively, than the postal service, for all the Corresponding Societies' determination and ingenuity in the 1790s. Without this press, and corresponding social change, it is hard to see how the 'pre-industrial crowd', with its semi-spontaneous outbreaks of bread-rioting spreading by word of mouth and foot-passage along the lines of the road system, could have become transformed into more political, more articulate, more organised and more co-ordinated forms of protest. Certainly, it is hard to see how this transformation could have spread beyond the ranks of isolated groups of artisans. Even more than the middle classes, and for all sorts of reasons, manual workers lived in intensely localised worlds.[25] The tendency was enhanced by the partial and varied impact of industrialisation. As a result, socio-economic structures varied greatly from region to region, even from town to town within regions – and long continued to do so. Without the 'pauper press', the factory reform or Poor Law agitations would not have become even regionally articulated. Nor, without *The Northern Star*, could the pressures for political reform culminating in Chartism have achieved national co-ordination. Only the existence of the *Star* made the National Charter Association, with its widespread branch-network, conceivable, even for its two-year existence. Even with a working-class press, the Plug Strikes still managed to move from town to town in oddly pre-industrial ways – with decisions about where next to go in quest of boiler-plugs sometimes taken on the hoof, at night and in the hills above the location concerned.

By mid-century, working-class access to railways had improved significantly – witness the many Northern excursions to the 1851 Great Exhibition. Nevertheless, British society, even its urban sectors, remained remarkably localised – partly because of the continuingly heterogeneous character of its socio-economic structures; partly because, even for the middle class, the medium-term impact of industrialisation and urbanisation was to reinforce urban identities as much as to create interdependence between urban places. In this situation, the copious labour coverage of *Reynolds News* and *Lloyds Weekly* was surely crucial to the regional and national articulation of trade unionism and the mid-1860s political-reform movement. Equally, the foundation of the *Co-operative Union News*, with its determined encouragement to local co-operative societies to achieve at least some national orientation, was important to solidifying the Co-operative Union, and to the movement's longer-term ability to articulate and defend its interests against plans to subject its dividends to tax. Even in late century, the likes of the *Labour Leader, Clarion* and *Justice* – with their constant coverage of local socialist activity – were surely crucial to the national articulation of the ILP and SDF. The localising pressures, caused by enduringly distinctive industrial conditions and labour relations across trades and regions, remained formidable.[26]

However, newspapers do not just carry news of activity and organisation. In a developing, as well as a mature, liberal-democratic system, at least some need to purvey ideas and debate.[27] In editorials, even more in massively covering political meetings, newspapers carried popular radical arguments around the country. The oratorical powers of Hunt, Cobbett, Harney and O'Connor were undoubtedly formidable. But, in a world where few at open-air rallies could hear what was being said, the verbatim coverage of radical speeches turned newspapers into the equivalent of delayed loudspeakers. This role probably became even more effective due to a journalistic sense of professionalism that impelled its practitioners to turn even broken-backed rhetoric into decently coherent prose.[28] Furthermore, the extended platform papers like the *Northern Star* provided for Chartist leaders was supplied, even more integratively, by the working-class Sundays for more elevated populist leaders like Gladstone and Bright.

It is also important that, in the 1820s and 1830s, popular radical newspapers themselves became major issues and points of agitation. Thus they not merely enhanced and shaped working-class civil organisation, and its desire and ability to resist state pressure; oddly, they also helped integrate that organisation into the broader polity by reinforcing attachment to values that were liberal as well as democratic. This was so partly because the struggle helped shape the liberal state itself.

There is neither room nor need, to explore this extended running-battle in detail. It continued intermittently for around twenty years, occurring in two phases, each focusing upon moderately determined attempts by the state, and its not very united elite, to legally suppress the owners, editors and purveyors of the radical press. The first lasted from

1817 to around 1823, focusing upon numerous, very visible and often unsuccessful attempts by the authorities to prosecute radical publishers and newspaper-sellers for blasphemous or seditious libel. The effect was to render these laws effectively inoperable for suppressive purposes. The authorities then increasingly turned to the stamp duties, particularly after raising them to 4d in 1830. There ensued the campaign by the 'unstamped', their printers, newsagents, and street-sellers, to evade these duties – producing another extended series of prosecutions. In both phases, particularly the second, considerable ingenuity and organisational flair were exhibited in ensuring the circulation of papers that were not merely illegal but also unable, by virtue of being stampless, to use the normal postal methods of long-range distribution. Considerable organisation was also required to raise money and petition for the defence and support of the many editors, journalists, news-sellers and volunteer martyrs being prosecuted. All this reinforced the artisan intellectual culture underpinning attachment to the idea of a free press. It also created broader mass-solidarity – and this probably transferred over to later issues like the Poor Law, Factory Reform and Chartism, leaving a residue of organisation and leadership for these causes. Edward Thompson has argued for the existence of 'a Radical nucleus...in every county, in the smallest market-towns and even in the larger rural villages...in nearly every case based on the local artisans'.[29]

As is well-known, this later campaign against the taxes on knowledge was supported, and in Government eyes greatly legitimised, by parallel efforts led by middle-class radicals like Richard Cobden. Their motives were decidedly mixed – partly in decent pursuit of liberal freedoms, partly hoping to undermine plebeian radical newspapers by opening the market to competition from more respectable, more moderate and now cheaper middle-class dominated publications.[30] Nevertheless, or perhaps partly because of the long-term success of such aspirations, the effect was to attach working-class radicals and their publications even more firmly to liberal society and its increasingly reticent state. This reinforced long-existing and widely evident traditions about 'the freeborn Englishman'. Furthermore, and partly in consequence, the battle to establish this key liberal freedom in Britain always focused upon working-class, rather than middle-class, radical publications. As Thompson has observed with only mild hyperbole, 'There is perhaps no country in the world in which the contest for the rights of the press was so sharp, so emphatically victorious, and so peculiarly identified with the cause of the artisans and labourers.'[31]

Moreover, one result was to strengthen, at least for the medium term, what many have seen as another democratically positive consequence of the creation of organisations between family and state: conditional and sceptical attitudes towards authority. Radical papers were immensely hostile to the aristocratic elite. What was being prosecuted, and thus widely publicised and popularised by the plaintiffs, was the strong radical taste for mockery: as for example when the publication of William Hone's splendidly irreverent version of the Lord's Prayer helped push the Government into yet another unwise prosecution for blasphemous libel:

> Our Lord who art in the Treasury, whatsoever be thy name, thy power be prolonged, thy will be done throughout the empire, as it is in each session. Give us our usual sops, and forgive us our occasional absences on divisions; as we promise not to forgive those that divide against thee. Turn us not out of our places; but keep us in the House of Commons, the Land of Pensions and Plenty; and deliver us from the People. Amen.[32]

However, there were other less functional segments of the working-class press throughout the century, perhaps particularly from mid-century, which tied into less functional parts of working-class culture. Though arguably often having radical, even anti-elitist, roots,[33] much of it was not political, not serious and sometimes primarily pornographic. There is anyway a plausible argument that the commercialisation of the working-class press, following stamp-duty removal in the 1850s, began inevitable trends towards trivialisation and depoliticisation, helping moreover narrow the range of debate being let through to its audience by this crucial gatekeeper. This is argued to have flowed from the policies of editors, mindful of their circulations and the assumed predilections of their advertisers for uncontroversial content. Thus control over the working-class political agenda began, consciously or unconsciously, to be surrendered to others higher up the social hierarchy.[34]

There is much evidence seemingly supporting this view. Working-class Sundays probably were less radical and certainly less militant than their weekly predecessors. They were also far more commercially minded. For all their generous coverage of labour matters, they saw their role increasingly as entertainment as much as political education. Their appeal stemmed partly from their interest in gossip, crime, sexual scandal and increasingly sport. It would be a brave observer who could predict just what these papers were purchased for, and just which reports bore the greatest number of thumb-marks at the end of the Lord's Day. All the more perhaps since, at the shabby margins beyond the fiercely political unstamped press of the 1830s, and the relatively serious Sunday papers of later decades, there circulated a thriving host of others, also primarily directed at working men and sometimes their wives, focusing purely upon stories of crime and scandal. These included *The Police Gazette*, with its stories of violent wrongdoing, and *The Town* with its advertisements for

> **Tales of Twilight**... containing the adventures and intrigues of a company of ladies prior to their marriage, as related by themselves ...and **Onanism Unveiled or the Private Pleasures and Practices of the Youth of Both Sexes.**[35]

Nonetheless, one may wonder about how much responsibility the popular press had for the working-class march from militancy after the 1840s. If there was such a shift of opinion, or at least action (as on balance there was), it surely happened for reasons deeper than the commercially-driven policies of newspaper proprietors and editors.

This does not deny these policies, and the changing structures of capital underpinning them, significant background influence. The profit motive's rising importance in newspaper production would have made radical intellectual and political initiative seem decidedly hazardous to Sunday editors, anxious to increase circulation to attract and retain advertising, and thus please proprietors and investors. Certainly, they were more wary than the editors of the 1830s, concerned merely to break respectably even, and who thus had only limited interest in advertising revenue. Anyway, the proprietor they had to please, in so far as he was a separated entity, was himself dedicated to the cause, and had normally founded the paper to advance it. Whilst liberal democracy probably thrives best in capitalist systems – because of the free market and attachment to the more general freedoms often distinguishing them – those systems are not in any sense perfectly functional to the liberal purpose. Indeed, Marxist notions of inner contradictions, dog-eared as they appear after Communism's collapse, seem decidedly persuasive when liberal ideals about freely circulating ideas and information are set against the popular media's profit-driven and apolitical content in early twenty-first century Western Europe, North America and Australasia. Perhaps the trivial character of these media supplies evidence that capitalism is now increasingly failing to service this important sector of liberal democracy.

However, these possibilities were far less evident whilst democratisation was actually occurring. Furthermore, if editorial motivations by the 1860s were primarily commercial, and editors and proprietors had begun determining reporting policy according to its likely impact upon circulation, it seems reasonable to think they would be programmed to follow rather than lead the change in working-class mood. In the long term, this was surely mainly conditioned by the capitalist economy's growing ability to lessen poverty and, from the seventies particularly, to raise real living standards for increasing numbers of working-class families. In the more immediate term, Neville Kirk[36] is surely correct to suggest that a key factor in moderating working-class behaviour was the liberalisation of middle- and upper-class attitudes and actions. National elites became somewhat more accommodating towards the legislative demands of labour – for example, securing the legal status of friendly societies, co-ops and eventually unions, or extending factory legislation. Local employers became somewhat more willing to recognise unions as negotiators; local elites began granting important public status to all three sorts of working-class organisation: opening civic and other ceremonials to their representatives, and themselves attending their meetings. This heightened working-class reformism, and enhanced the priority given to seeking political citizenship for its own sake, a long-central element in working-class radical demands.

Moreover, this tendency to embrace constitutionalism was as evident amongst radical newspapers, even early on, as amongst other radical bodies. This was clear for all the savagery of titles such as *The Gorgon* and *The Destructive*. Many contemplated the use of force as a possibility, but few actively advocated it, and mostly in pursuit of 'constitutional rights'.[37] This radicalism had always probably been susceptible to incorporation of various sorts due to its tendency to identify its friends in populistic and thus inclusive terms like 'the people', and its most central as the 'idle', as much as the employing, classes.[38] Equally, it tended to assume that the misappropriation of political rather than of economic power was what underpinned working-class misery; this would always cause difficulty when life and status began improving in spite of the idle classes' continued political hegemony.[39]

Furthermore, whatever its moderating and depoliticising effect upon the likes of *Reynolds News* and *Lloyds Weekly*, commercialisation was never sufficient to prevent numerous socialist weeklies appearing around the turn of the century, a few arguably national, but most purely local.[40] Although susceptible to the market in that many died each year, their places were taken by many others. They were in fact partly immunised against it because they carried little advertising, and, like their un-stamped radical predecessors, used primitive production technology, enabling them to operate cheaply. In spite of commercial pressures, some newspapers again became vehicles for expanding the working-class political agenda. Meanwhile it is again significant that few such periodicals seriously moved beyond constitutionalism, or otherwise for-sook liberal-democratic values.

There was anyway another highly important carrier of relevant news and argument. In many towns, from the 1870s, even more the 1880s, local weekly papers made determined efforts to open their pages to working-class readers. Liberal newspapers particularly began carrying extensive reportage of co-op, friendly-society,[41] union and trades-council activity. Equally important was the fact that, from the 1890s and in a liberal-democratic spirit of carrying all the news fit to print, such papers also began covering local socialism. There were long, learned articles advocating the relative merits of Liberalism and socialism; extended reports of debates staged between rival local activists on the same theme, along with shorter but still substantial ones about SDF and ILP meetings. There was also increasingly extended coverage of local industrial disputes, rising to a wordy crescendo in the strike-torn years up to 1914. It is hard not to admire these newspapers for their seriousness, and apparent determination, however partisanly Liberal their editorial opinions, to convey all available serious news to the communities they saw themselves as serving. They were probably more important than the overtly socialist press in expanding the late-nineteenth-century political agenda to include socialist-influenced prescriptions for the continuingly-disadvantaged mass of the population.

There was finally another information-carrier for news about working-class civil organisation, this time with a more elevated audi-ence, and thus rather different function. Throughout the century, at least during times of high social and political tension, the middle-class press – both in London and the provinces-also covered working-class industrial and political activity. This coverage was admittedly more intermittent, more restricted and more crisis-driven than the news-papers reviewed thus far. Nevertheless, when it happened, it could be very extensive. Many thousands of words, for example, were expended on the Peterloo demonstration of 1819 and its threatening aftermath. The *Manchester Guardian* filled many column-inches with reportage of Chartist demonstrations, and even more in relation to the 1842 Plug Riots. The London papers spilled vast numbers of words on the 1889 Dock Strike.

The reportage was often hostile, and treatment of working-class leaders and their followers contemptuous and caricatured. Nevertheless, even at its most biased, it could hardly avoid conveying, even exaggerating, the seriousness of the crises being covered. Sometimes, particularly when perpetrators of repression could be portrayed as safely aristocratic, as with Peterloo, the coverage became quite sympathetic. All this must have borne significant responsibility for liberalising middle-class and elite attitudes towards working-class conditions and civil organisation evident particularly from the late forties. In London, where class-relations were largely unconnected by employment, and thus more ignorant and fearful, press reports about 'the foreign country', wherein the 'residuum' was believed to live, helped produce frightened and pacifying waves of charitable endeavour from those living in the West End and fearing the East. Reportage of the 1889 London Dock Strike, and its disciplined and unviolent character, is argued crucially to have domesticated these fears, possibly making the problems seem more negotiable.[42] Perhaps liberalisation took longer in London. Nevertheless, here too newspapers were surely important in producing the more accommodating sorts of attitudes amongst Britain's upper and middle classes, enabling the incorporation of working-class civil organisation into the broader polity.

From all the foregoing, it seems clear that working-class newspapers – at least the political ones – played important roles in attaching their readers to civil society in democratically functional ways. They encouraged and connected working men's organisations of all kinds, and became a focus of agitation in their own right. They purveyed information and debate about the working-class situation. Along with the local weekly press, radical papers became very important media through which liberal as well as democratic values and commitments could be widely spread. Finally, middle-class newspapers were probably important media through which the accommodations that were necessary preconditions for working-class acceptance of, and incorporation into, the developing liberal-democratic system could be achieved.

3. Access to Civil Organisation

We can now examine working-class civil organisation itself. We should note just how formidable were constraints on articulation for this group. Although radical and local weekly newspapers provided enormously important informational networks, the difficult legal context until 1855, limited working-class economic resources, partial literacy, and access to education and to the growing transport system, all meant that organisation, certainly beyond the purely local, was immensely difficult. Thus almost any articulation was probably an achievement, and certainly needs assessing by less exacting criteria than that of groups further up the social scale.

Here, we are concerned with those distinctively working-class bodies whose purposes were not primarily political: friendly societies, co-ops and trade unions, along with that other part of civil society wherein many working men and their wives extensively participated: organised religion. As organs of self-help and thus generators of autonomy from the state and from elites, the first three seem almost archetypical civil organisations. So too do some Nonconformist segments of organised religion – less so Anglicanism if only because of its role as the Estab-lished Church. However, as we have noted, this same self-helping characteristic also labels them natural products of the *laissez faire* state, rather than means of resisting an authoritarian one. Union influence actually heightened after the state, under union pressure, removed the courts from the business of policing industrial disputes in the 1870s. Even non-Anglican religion emerged in the presence of a liberal state which, whilst indulging an official church, made no effort to discourage, still less suppress, the alternatives.

It also bears repeating that all these working-class civil organisations originated and became firmly established many decades before formal political inclusion. Indeed by 1867 and 1884, they were highly de-veloped and well on the way to achieving accepted places alongside the civil organisations of those, primarily middle-class, groups who had already achieved political inclusion. This was a major reason why these latter groups and their elites increasingly deemed working men suffi-ciently 'fit' for political inclusion. They could be included politically partly because, as we shall see, their organisations were already well on the way to social inclusion, and because they appeared attached to social values unlikely to produce political problems affecting the political agenda in unwelcome ways. The growth and acceptance of friendly societies, co-ops and unions accelerated in the decades subsequent to political inclusion, thus reinforcing pre-existing working-class attachments to liberal democracy and enhancing their ability to operate successfully within it.

These developments are firstly observable in terms of organisation and membership. This needs reviewing for its own sake. Quite aside from the positive contribution that we shall later argue active civil participation made to political fitness, affiliation alone could create democratically-functional independent loyalties and attitudes. Furthermore, friendly societies and co-ops, given their investing as well as defensive character, necessarily encouraged people to regard themselves as having a stake, thus an interest, in the fortunes of the society wherein they lived.

Friendly societies, always much the largest working-class civil organisations before 1914, emerged in the later eighteenth century. By 1801, there were probably around 650–750 000 people in approximately 7200 societies in Britain,[43] rising to 925 429 by 1815. By 1830, Eric Hopkins has suggested, 25 per cent of adult males belonged to friendly societies.[44] Others have placed the estimate at 50 per cent.[45] Most were purely local, but the nationally-oriented Affiliated Orders had already begun drawing lodges within their ambit. They did so increasingly rapidly from the late 1830s – such that the two largest Orders, the Manchester Unity of Oddfellows and the Ancient Order of Foresters, had 249 261 and 84 472 members respectively by 1848. By the 1867 Reform Act, their membership had risen to 405 255 and 321 253.[46] Those societies making returns to the Royal Commission in 1872 had known memberships of 1 857 896; the Commissioners concluded the total membership of all societies was around 4 000 000.[47] The rapid growth of this branch of civil society whilst political inclusion continued is clear from the steadily rising membership figures for societies registering under the 1875 Friendly Societies Act. In 1877, there were 2 750 000 people in such societies; ten years later, this had risen to 3 600 000; by 1897, there were 4 800 000 and by 1904, 5 600 000 – rises all substantially above the rise in population. Taking into account the continuingly numerous unregistered societies, and the size of the working population (around 7 000 000 by 1892), it seems reasonable to think that by around 1900, well before the final bout of male enfranchisement, the great majority of working men were linked to this crucial branch of civil society.

The same early origins and accelerating subsequent development are evident amongst bodies serving other needs of respectable working-class life. How soon unions are deemed to have emerged depends partly on how formally and permanently-organised structures of occupational self-defence must be before earning that title. Something very like unions were emerging during the decline of the much older guild system – from the late-seventeenth century.[48] More certainly, John Rule and others have plausibly argued that the intermittent and often informal 'natural associations of experience' emerging in the skilled workplace from the early-eighteenth century should be considered as unions. From our current standpoint, we may want to consider these 'recurrent habits of association' as proto-civil organisations. They had little continuous existence and only sometimes dignified themselves with formal titles, but these '*ad hoc* unions' apparently occurred and recurred. They arose when divisions between masters and men intensified, and when masters felt their profits sufficiently pressured to threaten what journeymen saw as 'customary wages' and other facets of 'the moral economy of the workplace'.[49] Sometimes they achieved county-wide organisation, and from 1720 became sufficiently organised to petition Parliament to reimpose traditional protective legislation.[50] Such associations persisted into the nineteenth century, for several decades co-existing alongside more formal and permanent union bodies.

Even if these quasi-unions are discounted as civil organisations – and they probably should not be given their ability to enhance and protect occupational autonomy from employers in occasional alliance with the state – more formal unions clearly existed amongst skilled artisans from at least the early-nineteenth century. Thus, in the second decade, the makers of women's shoes are recorded as having 'at one time fourteen divisions in London'; and maintaining 'a well-regulated correspondence with the trade of every city and town, of any importance throughout the kingdom'.[51] Names might change, and membership fluctuate, but such organisations existed and persisted, often respectably disguised as friendly societies. Moreover, and this surely highlights the vibrancy of early civil organisation, they continued in spite of the attentions of the Anti-Combination Laws. The very frequency with which this legislation was used, even in the absence of strong determination by the elite, testified to this fact, as did the emergence of the first union periodical, *The Gorgon*, in 1818. Prosecutions certainly damaged unions at crucial points in their existence, but failed to prevent their continued twilight existence, and the achievement sometimes of what Edward Thompson calls 'a very high degree of organisation' with considerable funds.[52] Lord Sidmouth was a Home Secretary rarely inhibited about repressing the lower orders. He recognised 'the alarming extent to which . . . combinations of workmen in different branches of trade and manufactures have been carried', but saw no point in extending Anti-Combination Laws since they were incapable of greater effect.[53] This was so partly because of the limited control any early-nineteenth-century state could realistically hope to exert, particularly given growing social and political complexity born of economic change. However, it is also ascribable to the determined vibrancy of working-class civil combination.

With these laws' repeal in 1824, permanent union organisations became more possible, and certainly more historically traceable. Now, there were clearer signs of regional and sometimes national bodies, however short-lived. At various points in the decade after 1824, this was evident amongst Scottish miners, builders and more enduringly, engineers. Such articulation became more widespread still in the 1840s with county-wide miners' unions appearing in Durham, Northumberland, Lancashire, Yorkshire and Staffordshire. In 1842, a Miners' Association of Great Britain and Ireland began a five-year existence, claiming to represent 70 000 mineworkers, one-third of the total workforce.

Exactly when the first tightly-organised 'new-model unions' emerged is much disputed and need not concern us. However, 'the amalgamateds' were certainly increasingly central features of union life from the early 1850s. In assessing the vibrancy of working men's civil organisations, we should note that it was at this point that organisations emerged, permanent and continuous in reality as well as aspiration. There were enduring and highly disciplined associations – of printers (1849), engineers (1851), cotton spinners (1853), miners (1858), carpenters and joiners (1860), and tailors (1866) and several others.

The 1850s also saw the permanent emergence of wider union organisation – extending beyond defending particular crafts into cross-occupational concerns. In fact, there had been long traditions of co-operation, probably dating back to the eighteenth century. From 1818, there were recurring attempts to organise general unions, including the Owenite Grand National Consolidated Union in 1834, and the more significant National Association of United Trades for the Protection of Labour from 1845. Though lasting only a few years, the Association had three permanent London officials, to conciliate disputes, and lobby Parliament in areas of joint concern. However, only in the 1850s does cross-trade co-operation permanently emerge. The bodies concerned were admittedly local, yet this hardly denigrates the importance of what was happening since economic life in these years was also locally organised. Co-operation during crisis became increasingly frequent in many towns and cities throughout the decade, and from 1858, the first permanent trades councils emerged – in Glasgow and Sheffield, then London (building on long traditions of less formal co-operation), followed by similar bodies in Newcastle, Nottingham and Liverpool. Throughout the 1860s, such bodies appeared at steadily accelerating rates: by 1866, one year before urban working-class enfranchisement, there were at least 24 councils in permanent or semi-permanent existence, and by 1875 approximately 40.

Though these numbers subsequently declined, the period around enfranchisement also saw fairly continuous union co-operation beginning nationally, building partly upon trades councils. These attempts were based first on the personnel (the Junta) and organisation of the London Trades Council, then on the United Kingdom Alliance of Organised Trades in 1866, and the Conference of Amalgamated Trades in 1867. Finally, in June 1868, initiated by the Manchester and Salford Trades Council, there occurred the first meeting of what rapidly became the TUC. By 1871, this body had a permanent paid secretary, and in 1872 began a series of annual meetings uninterrupted down to the present.

By 1880, its affiliated unions had a combined, and mostly male, membership of around half a million. By 1900, this had risen to 1 200 000 (with a further 822 000 in unaffiliated unions), and 2 682 357 (plus 1 462 643 in non-affiliated unions) by 1914. By 1919, one year after the final bout of male enfranchisement, total union membership stood at 7 926 000.[54] In the later stages of this process – first fleetingly in 1889–1890, then far more enduringly from 1910 – the initially skilled and semi-skilled composition of the union movement was boosted by increasing unskilled unionism.

The above story has been told more extensively and more heroically many times. It is related briefly here simply to emphasise the central point that unionisation commenced many decades before political inclusion formally began, and in the years leading up to 1867, working men were drawn into this sector of civil organisation at accelerating rates. Furthermore, this form of articulation was becoming increasingly effective, co-ordinated and permanent. As inclusion continued, with the Acts of 1884 and 1918, so unionisation accelerated further, now reaching more vulnerable and disadvantaged segments of the manual population. By 1918, around 33 per cent of the labour force had some sort of at least minimal attachment to one of the more negotiational bits of civil society.

Similar patterns are evident in co-operative organisation. Since community-building has always had, at best, an ambivalent relationship with liberal democracy, I will restrict the analysis to retail co-operation. Although tradition insists on its commencement in Rochdale in 1844, this form of co-operation had a substantial prior history. Whilst some was conceived as preparational to community-building, other organisations were far more pragmatic – aiming either to support unions during extended strikes or towards entirely retail ends. In Scotland, such organisations emerged from the 1770s. G.D.H. Cole found at least three societies – at Govan, Lennoxtown and Larkhill – with a substantial subsequent history . Of these, the first lasted from 1777 to 1909, whilst the others were both founded in 1821 and still existent when Cole wrote in 1944.[55] Many more shorter-lived societies were founded in the 1830s and 1840s. In England, even in the 1820s, co-operation was clearly often a very specific response to varied local needs – sometimes linked to Owenite objectives, sometimes altogether more pragmatic. Cole claimed some 700 such societies existed across England, Wales and Scotland by 1831; around 380 of these have been positively located by more recent historians – concentrated especially in London, the Midlands and north-west England.[56] The main model for many (particularly in London)[57] was William King's very pragmatic retail and co-operative society in Brighton.

Many early societies existed only fleetingly. However, from 1844, retail co-operation began a continuous and steadily-expanding existence. As with unions and friendly societies, the broad picture is one of accelerating growth in the decades around enfranchisement. This is evident from the number of societies founded. In Lancashire, Cheshire and Yorkshire, 9 were established between 1845 and 1849; 22 between 1850 and 1854; 44 between 1855 and 1859, and 100 between 1860 and 1864.[58] There was then some deceleration, primarily due to the Cotton Famine's depressing effects. Nevertheless, the next twenty years up to 1884 witnessed the appearance of a further 144 societies in these counties. The east and west Midlands show a less spectacular but nevertheless essentially similar picture. Just two societies were founded between 1845 and 1855; 1856–60 produced 16; 1861–5 witnessed the emergence of 29; 1866–70 bred 26, whilst the next five years produced 38.[59] Scotland shows similar growth-patterns. Most societies were still extant when Cole wrote his history of co-operation in 1944. Given the figures for society-foundation, it is unsurprising that membership showed the same pattern of civil good health in the years around political inclusion. In 1873, it stood at 350 000. By 1883, just before the next bout of enfranchisement, 628 000 were co-operative members, and by 1900, 1 707 000. At the time of the 1918 Reform Act, there were 3 847 000, and by 1928, adverse economic conditions in many parts of the country notwithstanding, membership stood at 5 885 000. By 1939, this had risen to 8 643 000.[60] By these latter decades, increasing proportions of members of course were female, and thus of less immediate concern here. Nevertheless, if political fitness is judged by attachment to civil organisation – and with the co-op, contemporaries found this particularly persuasive – the basic point seems clear so far as working men and their families are concerned.

Co-operation, more than other working-class civil organisation, intends for its members some significant degree of financial, as well as just organisational, autonomy. In this context, it is highly important that, by the 1870s, even more the 1880s, in growing numbers of particularly Northern urban and industrial areas, the largest single concentration of capital was not a privately owned business but the local co-op. By 1867, just a few years after the Cotton Famine, the Rochdale Pioneers boasted a share-capital of some £128 000,[61] and spanned the entire range of working-class purchasing – operating ten grocery stores, nine butchers, three shoemakers, three cloggers, one drapers and one clothiers.[62] Like a growing number of locations, Rochdale also boasted a manufacturing society. The same picture is evident nationally: by 1905, the Co-operative Wholesale Society had become one of the largest businesses in the world.

Finally, as some of the foregoing has implied, the enfranchising decades also coincided with growing national co-operative articulation. Local co-ops admittedly were even more resistant to centralisation than union branches or friendly-society lodges. However, as with those bodies, this was less a sign of organisational weakness than commentary upon the localised state of nineteenth-century British life generally. However, even this did not prevent the steady and early emergence of an increasingly well-articulated 'movement'. As early as 1852, the Co-operative League was founded to discuss common problems. During the 1850s, and again in the 1860s, there began a series of national conferences leading to the Co-operative Wholesale Society in 1863, and its Scottish counterpart in 1868. In 1869, less than twelve months after the TUC appeared, and two years after the 1867 Reform Act, there occurred the first Co-operative Congress. This rapidly became an annual representative event, discussing common matters of commercial and defensive concern. The 1873 Congress produced the Co-operative Union, representing the movement right across Mainland Britain. Housed in its increasingly opulent Manchester headquarters, the Union presided over an expanding array of regional sections. These in turn divided into district associations of neighbouring societies, holding regular conferences across the country. As noted earlier, these efforts at national and regional articulation for propaganda and policy-forming purposes coincided with, and drew inspiration from, the emergence of several co-operative journals, especially the *Co-operative News* in 1871.

On the surface, organised religion seems to provide the least convincing evidence of working-class civil integration. As Chapter 4 noted, the link with the state made Anglican Churches unpromising vehicles for the autonomy of any group – from the state, or from national and local elites. At first sight, moreover, nineteenth-century working men seem decidedly detached from any sector of organised religion. Middle- and upper-class contemporaries were much exercised by what they saw as the lower orders' lamentable irreligion. The 1851 Census, with its evidence that many industrial towns could boast no more than 25 per cent attendance on that alarming Sunday, heightened the general gloom. Local surveys later in the century suggested still more widespread paganism.

Historians of the 1960s and 1970s rather confirmed these gloomy prognostications.[63] However, recent evidence suggests a more God-fearing, or at least God-accepting, picture. Working people might not have been formally observant, though often were, but they generally married, died and often baptised their children in church. They also happily celebrated the great Christian festivals – even if, like Whitsun, these were not necessarily the ones churches themselves preferred. Working people also came into more frequent contact with religious ancillary organisations in times of need than any other charitable bodies. Furthermore, though most might be repelled from church services by shame about their tattered clothing, or strong desires to spend their one day of rest in life-restoring torpor, most accepted the basic Christian message. Their Christianity might be indefensibly 'diffusive' and doctrinally innocent, but it certainly included a just, and personable God. Most children were sent to Sunday School – to enhance their basic moral grasp, get them out of the house, or more probably both. Many young adults also attended – partly in pursuit of basic literacy and education, at least until sabbatarians made this harder.[64] Many working people were also caught up in evangelical revivals, regularly sweeping Britain from the later-eighteenth century, particularly in those engineered by the more democratic Methodist sects.[65] Finally, many manual workers, like many social superiors, sufficiently identified with Protestantism, and associated Protestantism with Britishness, to hate Catholics with considerable periodic intensity. Amongst voluntary organisations, religion commanded more contact and attention than any other.

Yet, however much organised religion might give some diffusive point to slum life, and enhance consent for the established order, only some of such contact could have been sufficient to connect working people, particularly less observant working *men*, with the religious sector of civil society in democratically functional ways. For this, some sort of formal membership, and reasonably regular attendance were required. In fact many working men (and even more working women) were regular church- or chapel-goers, particularly outside the largest cities. Furthermore, for all the middle class's fervent observance, workers probably constituted a majority of regulars in most areas, emphatically so in some like south Wales.[66] Furthermore, active working-class participation was most marked amongst Methodist sects, the ones growing most rapidly and where self-governance was most vibrant and self-conscious.

Churches have already been reviewed in relation to middle-class civil association. Thus we hardly need repeat the process here. We need only emphasise religion's importance in the lives of many working-class people by noting the growth in numbers in those segments where working-class adherents were most marked. The various Methodist sects grew from around half a million in 1850 to 860 000 in 1900. Wearmouth estimates 60–70 per cent were working class.[67] The growth was even more marked amongst those sects generally accepted as predominantly working class. Thus the Primitive Methodists increased from 104 762 in 1850 to 196 408 in 1908; the Bible Christians from 16 951 in 1852 to 34 961 in 1900. Both increases substantially exceeded population rises.[68]

All this points to the central fact that, for its working-class, as for its middle-class adherents, organised religion supplied a very successful set of voluntary organisations. This is true even discounting the Anglican Church as a true civil organisation and, given the frequently vibrant and open character of Parish meetings noted elsewhere, we may be unwise wholly to do so. Though probably declining by late-century, religion remained important in the lives of many working people, and certainly significantly influenced them during the long period of political inclusion. Admittedly, religiously observant working men, unlike their middle-class counterparts, were a declining minority of their class. Nevertheless, if we grant civil organisation importance in rendering its adherents fit for inclusion and successful operation within a liberal-democratic system, the minority was sufficiently substantial to be worth having.

However, we should balance this general picture of civil vibrancy by noting a more negative side. In particular, nowhere was participation evenly spread across the entire working-male population. Two generalisations can be made. First, the higher up the scale of male skill, economic and occupational security one looks, the more intense multi-organisational and mutually-reinforcing civil participation seems to become. If this really was the key to political fitness, then Victorian elites were correct to assume this quality was most richly spread amongst the most skilled and secure sections (not necessarily synonymous) of the manual population. They may also rightly have assumed that the further down one looked the less did there seem prima facie evidence of such democratic readiness. Certainly, skilled and secure semi-skilled workers formed a substantial core of political fitness that probably contributed heavily to the success of this phase of democratisation.

However, to be weighed against this is the second point: the fact that some aspects of civil organisation spread downwards a long way, spread into some rather unexpected places, and did so increasingly as the century wore on and political inclusion progressed. Only amongst the most desperate working class (admittedly a substantial group), and perhaps primarily in cities rather than in towns or villages, was civil organisation largely absent.

Let us take each point in turn. Workers who were most skilled and/or secure were also clearly likely to be most fully integrated into civil society. As the most successful working-class voluntary associations (aside perhaps from the churches), it is unsurprising that friendly societies, as we shall see, were least exclusively skilled. Yet even their spokesmen often described them in decidedly artisan terms, as did outside observers. There were significant reasons for so doing, particularly amongst the Affiliated Orders, whose fees tended to preclude anyone who was not reasonably secure, as did fines for falling into arrears. In fact, friendly societies drew members overall from a wide occupational spectrum. All the same, particularly in early-century, one was more likely to be a member if skilled than if unskilled or even semi-skilled. For example, whilst 85 774 town labourers belonged to the Manchester Unity of Oddfellows in 1866–70, 74 760 and 49 076 were carpenters and joiners, or cordwainers[69] – both far smaller occupational groups. Skilled workers were also more likely than other manual operatives to be society officials. Even in those rural areas where friendly-society habits were widespread amongst agricultural labourers, it was the village artisans who generally ran the lodges.[70]

As is well-known, unions also, until briefly in the late-1880s and more enduringly from 1910, recruited most heavily from skilled occupational groups, along with the more secure semi-skilled industrial workers like textile and mine-workers.[71] Indeed, until the 1870s, they did so almost exclusively. Even when unskilled unions emerged, their leaders tended to be skilled workers, their normal exclusivity diluted by socialism and enlightened self-interest. Skilled and secure semi-skilled workers were also probably disproportionately represented amongst working-class churchgoers.[72] Finally and most predictably, retail co-ops recruited very disproportionately indeed from amongst the skilled and secure. Co-ops were well aware of this, and saw it less as a problem than the healthy result of their desire for respectability and financial probity. Indeed, they were resistant to broadening their membership; when attempts were made before 1914, as the Co-operative Women's Guild found, they generally failed.

That participation in civil organisation was most richly evident amongst skilled and secure working men is unsurprising. On the negative side, friendly-society and union membership required the ability to pay regular subscriptions – necessarily if the organisation was to survive and fulfil its functions. Only relatively well-paid, or at least secure, workers could afford these. Friendly societies even fined members for non-payment. Co-operative societies' prohibition on credit, and emphasis upon the quality as much as the price of what they sold, similarly disadvantaged those without secure and reasonably substantial wages.

There were also more positive reasons for the participatory predilections of such workers. Genuinely skilled work required a series of informed decisions about what to do; thus the use of intellectual as well as manual faculties. Once required to exercise them, their possessors were quite likely to apply them to other areas of life. Skilled jobs often permitted some leisure, and thus opportunities to make such applications. Such workers also often saw their skill as a species of property.[73] This produced strong occupational solidarity, pride and sense of entitlement – reinforced in the early decades amongst unmechanised trades by notions of 'customary rights' in relation to things like wages, conditions and consultation, deriving from the long history of such occupations.[74] All this represented something palpable, morally as well as practically worth collective defence. Skilled workshops, along with factories and mines, all with quite high levels of continuity of personnel, were relatively easy places to organise and create solidarity. Skill, whether intrinsic or reputational, along with income-security, also produced a strong sense of status, particularly when set against awareness of the unskilled abyss below. This could be enhanced by membership of friendly-society lodge, Nonconformist chapel, union or local co-op. Skilled jobs were also most likely to offer significant control over the work-process, control with which early employers often found it unpolitic and unprofitable to interfere. If skill was a form of property, the result in small workshops might well be a 'democracy of work',[75] where all were involved in daily decisions about how the job was to be done. Given such autonomy, it probably seemed quite natural to participate in organisations – whether co-ops, unions or friendly societies – likely to enhance this quality and minimise dependency, whether on the state and its Poor Law, employers or private charity. Also important in creating predispositions to civil involvement was the fact that many more felt themselves to be skilled than had intrinsic claims so to be. Overall, skill could generate *interest*: in the twin and democratically-functional senses of being interesting, and creating vested interests worth defending.

For all these reasons, thoughtful observers often saw skilled workers almost as a race apart. Henry Mayhew remarked upon their qualities in mid-century London: 'In passing from the skilled operative of the west-end to the unskilled workman of the eastern quarter . . . , the moral and intellectual change is so great that it seems as if we were in a new land, and among another race.' For Mayhew, this was why they were 'red-hot politicians' whilst their unskilled counterparts were 'as apolitical as footmen'.[76]

However, civil organisation was also maldistributed amongst working men on bases other than skill and job-security. In particular, civil participation was geographically uneven. It was far more vibrant in northern industrial areas, and to a lesser extent in those of south Wales and central Scotland, than elsewhere. Co-ops originated in Lancashire and Yorkshire towns, and more modestly in central Scotland, and continued concentrating heavily in those areas up to 1914. This was evident from the number of societies, and the location of the largest ones.[77] They also developed rapidly in the mining villages of north-east England, and the east Midlands shoe and hosiery district. The movement was most successful in medium-sized industrial towns; least so in large population centres like Birmingham and London,[78] and in low-wage agricultural areas.[79] This broad pattern continued until 1914. Only in the inter-war years did membership explode in major cities, particularly in the south. Similar, though modified and shifting, patterns are also evident with union membership. Like the heavy industry upon whose organisational advantages and solidaristic tendencies it primarily fed, it was most heavily concentrated in Lancashire, Yorkshire, north-east England and south Wales. London, though initially important because of its thriving artisan trades, thereafter declined in relative significance.

The universalistic character of the Established Church, and dedicated church- and chapel-building programmes by all denominations, ensured religious organisation was widely distributed across the country, penetrating even the most slum-ridden locations of large cities by the second half of the century. Nevertheless, it too showed significant concentration, at least judged from our current standpoint. This is certainly evident if we assume Nonconformity to be the supplier of the most democratically-functional forms of civil organisation – on the grounds that chapels placed greatest emphasis upon autonomy and self-government. The 1851 census suggested Wesleyan and other Methodist sects (including the Calvinists) were most heavily concentrated in northern England, the north Midlands, Norfolk, the south west and throughout Wales. These were also areas where chapel-attendance was most assiduous.[80]

Amongst working-class civil organisations, friendly societies were most widely spread, showing least geographical concentration. Like unions and co-ops, they were densest in expanding northern industrial areas. Nevertheless, there were few types of location – city, town or country – and few geographical areas, not exhibiting a reasonably healthy society-presence throughout the period of male enfranchisement. Thus in 1873, alongside the 485 344 and 132 033 and 92 036 registered society members in Lancashire, Yorkshire and Cheshire respectively, there were 173 952 in Norfolk, 151 096 in Middlesex, 77 311 in Warwickshire, 41 557 in Glamorgan and 33 138 in Devon.[81]

This points to our second, and contrary, point – the spread of civil organisation. On the one hand, admittedly, working-class civil organisations were clearly concentrated in overlapping ways amongst the most skilled or secure workers, and in certain areas of the country, particularly industrial ones. Such locations seem likely to produce the clearest evidence of political fitness. Rochdale's working class, for example, was generously supplied with all four sorts of civil articulation – and, given what is claimed in chapter 6, it is perhaps unsurprising that it was renowned for its political liveliness and independence.[82] Other northern towns showed greater deference admittedly, yet once the personal link with the employer began being replaced by the more impersonal ones of the limited company, independent political patterns started asserting themselves.[83] On the other hand, there were few geographical areas, and only diminishing numbers of lower occupational segments, from which civil organisation was wholly absent in the decades of political inclusion.

This can be illustrated by examining the politically crucial decades of the 1860s and 1870s. At this time, unions and co-ops were heavily concentrated in the urban and industrial north, amongst artisans and secure industrial workers. Yet even this leaves them fairly widely spread in occupational terms since claims to skill embraced men like cotton spinners whose dexterity was as much reputational as intrinsic.[84] Such workers were often heavily unionised, as were many secure semi-skilled people like miners and cotton weavers. Friendly societies were also fairly widely spread across the country at this time, and, together with Nonconformist chapels, had penetrated areas like the south-west and East Anglia – where unions and co-ops were fairly thin on the ground. By the 1870s trade unionism was making gains, however briefly, amongst rural labourers. More important, and partly underpinning this, was the fact that chapels and friendly societies had been for several decades strongly established amongst agricultural workers, at all levels of skill and pay, particularly in open villages and in areas like the south and south-west, east Yorkshire, and Norfolk.[85] As the Primitive Methodists discovered in 1896, sadly since village life was seen to be in decline, 'we are a village church. Nearly 75 per cent of our chapels, and a large proportion of our "preaching places", are in the villages'.[86] This was twelve years after rural enfranchisement, but their strength in these areas was hardly new. Indeed it helped underpin friendly society activity.[87] However much urbanised radicals like George Holyoak, even in the 1890s, might despair of the alleged passivity of 'the organised fungi who seem to vegetate . . . in the shape of farm labourers',[88] even this group were not devoid of democratic hope. By 1900, perhaps only the most insecure and residual levels of working men lacked some sort of active contact with civil society. For them, and they admittedly came in quite large numbers, the only points of contact were inert: the collector from the large and often rapacious funeral society,[89] or the church worker with the pacifying charitable handout. Still to come was the massive expansion of unskilled trade unionism from 1910, and the rapid inter-war spread of retail co-operation.

None of this suggests all male urban workers had equal access to the sort of democratic and liberal training that Chapter 6 suggests the foregoing elements of civil society were capable of supplying. Far from it. Many, as noted, had little contact until just before the First World War. Many more had only partial contact compared with what was on offer. Some civil organisations, like unskilled unions and even unrapacious funeral societies, made relatively few demands upon members. Whilst civil organisation might enhance autonomy from the state — hardly needed with *laissez faire* once governments had eased away from automatic repression — it did not necessarily liberate people from the power of local elites, particularly employing ones. Indeed some have argued that, in large factory areas for example, unions, co-ops, friendly societies and chapels were at least partially linked into the deference-inducing networks of employer paternalism.[90] Moreover, even active participation in civil organisations, where the service rendered intimately concerned the participant, did not automatically induce intense political activity, where issues might seem more remote. Nevertheless, by the standards of many societies undergoing more recent democratisation, nineteenth-century British working men were widely endowed with the civil means of procuring liberal-democratic political fitness. What we must now discover is how these organisations ran themselves, and what participation in them actually entailed.

6 Working Men and Political Fitness: Internal Self-Governance

So far we have rather assumed all this organisational participation could produce useful liberal-democratic skills and attitudes. To assess how far it did, we must explore how working-class organisations operated. In doing so, we must again take into account contemporary definitions of political fitness: however value-laden, the possession of such fitness helps explain why working men were allowed within the political pale by groups already included, and why subsequently they were successfully absorbed. Defined thus, fitness seems to involve three closely inter-connected, though uneasily compatible, questions. First, how far were such organisations capable of turning working men into democratically-committed citizens? Second, how far did they enhance their members' effectiveness as a group, or set of groups, trying to advance perceived interests? Third, and this particularly concerned contemporaries, how far did unions, friendly societies and the like arm members with attitudes and values likely to permit their untroubled absorption into the political system, and the industrial capitalist system whose portals it significantly guarded? With qualifications, the answer to all three is broadly affirma-tive. However, as with other groups reviewed here, the version of democracy they eventually became committed to, and for which they were equipped, was the least demanding of those arguably on offer. Let us take the questions in turn.

1. Democratic Citizenship

This is an area where little research is available: historians have trad-itionally been more interested in how unions, co-ops and friendly societies presented themselves to the world than in their internal pro-cesses. Nor, given the sources, is such research easy to do. However, on the available information, it seems clear working-class civil organisations were centres of self-governance, exhibiting considerable internal dem-ocracy, in many respects more determinedly so than their middle-class

183

counterparts. If habits, expectations and skills evident there spread into the broader polity, those affected were likely to become useful citizens. Yet, as organisations enlarged, becoming more complex and bureaucratic, as members perhaps found other more interesting things to do towards late-century, so pressures and demands lessened. The match between what was expected of members within civil society and the broader polity consequently became more precisely aligned.

Significantly, the most extensive of the purely working-class voluntary organisations, friendly societies, were also most democratically impressive. Whether wholly localised societies, or Affiliated-Order lodges, they formulated elaborate rules to ensure their proceedings were democratic, and as many members as possible did their democratic duty. The strength of such characteristics was probably reinforced by being inherited from their much older predecessors, the guilds.[1] Whilst national officials were generally permanent unless de-selected, most Affiliated lodges annually rotated office-holding to ensure all took their turn, often levying financial penalties on refusal. Averaging little more than one hundred even at late-century, lodges probably found enforcement relatively easy, even if key positions requiring expertise remained in more permanent hands. Purely localised societies might have much larger units of decision-making (general meetings of the whole membership), and were thus necessarily less able to insist on rotation. Yet even they tried penalising non-attendance, annually elected their officers, and penalised those refusing responsibility.[2] Major decisions were generally taken, or at least sanctioned, by annual general meetings, and where necessary subject to subsequent popular ballots. Societies often took elaborate care to ensure democratic decorum on these occasions. The West Country's Keynsham Jubilee Society was typical of many:

> in all debates, the affairs in question shall be balloted; the ballot to be collected by the clerk, each person taking his seat, and remaining quiet the whole time; the major part of every ... ballot shall determine the affair; and if anyone interrupt the ballot or make any noise ..., after being ordered by the stewards to keep silence, .. he shall forfeit, for every offence, sixpence or be excluded.[3]

However, whilst testifying to the spread of democratic values, such formal rule-descriptions only give limited evidence about democratic practice. Here, there is difficulty since Affiliated lodges were too numerous, small, and perhaps too secretive, to warrant more than passing mention in local newspapers. Mostly, we can talk only about probabilities. Their intimate size, strong drive towards independence, the very personal functions they enduringly exercised (making regular monthly decisions about benefits and eligibility), determinedly rotated offices, and the tempting ambience of the pubs wherein they met, were all likely to encourage attendance and participation. So too probably were the localised neighbourhoods wherein lodges existed, at least if Lancashire friendly societies are typical.[4] Even the more apathetic lodges, where attendance might slip to two-thirds of membership,[5] would still be envied by most present-day voluntary organisations. As one Druids member told the 1872 Royal Commission:

> We . . . look upon the lodge as a small family party. The lodge to which I . . . have belonged for the last thirty years, consists of about 50 . . . We know each other directly or indirectly . . . we are . . . interested in each other's welfare in regard to health, and sickness and misfortune. There is sympathy connected with those societies . . . adhesiveness . . . [6]

Some evidence is also available from lodge-minutes. Where studied, there seem clear indications of democratic practice. Certainly, there are clear rejections of influence from local elites when attempted. Neave found frequent indications of this amongst lodges in Yorkshire's East Riding,[7] as did Margaret Fuller in the West Country. Here, as early as 1825, and commenting on the relative unpopularity of clubs started by local notables, a Parliamentary Select Committee noticed local workers 'do not like to see the management in hands other than their own'.[8] Such evidence is particularly significant given the dependent image of rural life so often presented.

The evidence from the many purely local societies, still existing even in late-century after the massive accelerating growth of the Affiliated Orders, is rather better. Although often invisible to local newspapers until this time, it is significant that, when reporters did discover them, they were apparently operating with determined democracy. This determination seems doubly important because they were often considerably larger than Affiliated lodges, thus less outwardly encouraging of participation.

Certainly this determination seems very evident amongst Lancashire's local societies. Their offices were annually elective; even lesser posts could attract considerable attention. In 1901, a meeting to elect a collector and committeeman for Rochdale's Bridge Inn Society was

typical of many. It was packed with men and women anxious to vote for
their favourite and 'had to be adjourned to the Public Hall where some
511 voted'.[9] As already noted, these societies' day-to-day processes are
rarely visible. Nevertheless, the point of greatest journalistic attention is
suitably testing since it was, for many, the point of death when greatest
disillusion and apathy might be expected. For various reasons, the 1911
National Health Insurance Act seriously disadvantaged small societies,
causing many to terminate their affairs, and members to 'part with their
dear old faithful friend'.[10] Yet, for all the sadness, the spirit of the
terminal decisions – often taken against officers' advice – was emphatically democratic. Near Bolton, 230 members of the Horwich Parish
Church Sick Society met to terminate matters in July 1912, as did 280
of the 500-strong St Ann's Sick and Burial Society in Turton.[11] Near
Blackburn, 250 conducted the final rites for the St Nicholas Sick Society
at Subden,[12] as in May had 300 of the 420-strong Great Harwood Adult
Sick Society.[13] However, the passionate democracy of these collective
suicides is best encapsulated by the disbandment of Rochdale's New Inn
Sick Society. The issue was first raised at a crowded and rowdy meeting
in a school in January 1912. Here, notwithstanding appeals from
officials, kindred organisations, and the District Union of Friendly
Societies, members rejected a committee motion to become an
approved society under the Act. So impassioned were proceedings
that 'they approached the nature of a Rugby...scrimmage at one
point'.[14] This produced a second meeting in February where more
decorum was observed after appeals from the chairman, 'not to
scramble over the form backs...they had a letter from the vicar
complaining about the damage done to the school'. Nevertheless, things
remained pretty lively when the motion to disband was put:

> There was a shout of 'both hands'...a forest of small hands,
> big hands, short hands, long hands, clean hands, grubby hands
> shot upwards towards the roof to the accompaniment of vocal
> yells.[15]

This meeting led to a third, as the constitution apparently demanded.
This equally crowded assembly decided to poll members. Afterwards the
audience fragmented into groups, 'excitedly discussing the situation'.[16]
Finally, in mid-March, a referendum decided decisively for disbandment. Democratic to the end, a fourth meeting was called to hear the
result and appoint liquidators.

These purely local societies were still quite small – rarely more than 500; their determined democracy might seem a natural product of their relative intimacy, particularly in a world still highly localised in 1914. However, essentiality of function and parochiality of concern could be sufficient to ensure fervent democracy even in much larger organisations. Whilst shading into large, entirely passive and often corrupt collecting societies like the Royal Liver, these were democratically more lively than the vice-presidential charities reviewed in Chapter 4, sometimes remarkably so. Certainly, this is true if we judge by Rochdale's thriving Newbold Sick and Burial Society. Founded in 1841, it had a membership of 16 644 by 1871, and 26 107 by 1903. Though this was drawn from the Rochdale area, the Newbold was not subdivided into more parochial units like the Affiliated Orders. Sociability was evident, but hardly central to its appeal. Nevertheless, democracy, both Athenian and electoral, was strongly evident. For all the supposed changes in working-class life from the 1880s, this was fervently maintained until at least 1914. All offices were elected, and all elections (where members of either sex over 18, and all parents of insured children, could vote) attracted fervent interest. For major offices, polls of over 80 per cent were normal: in the 1910 presidential election, with a 90 per cent poll, the winning candidate actually collected 113 more votes than the three general election candidates combined.

On these occasions, great issues were sometimes involved. In the 1908 presidential election, the incumbent, having tried to turn the society into an insurance company, found himself challenged on the issue by another candidate. The election was first attempted at the annual meeting, but it was so crowded that it was adjourned to the Public Hall. This too rapidly became 'densely crowded. Hundreds still clamoured for admission outside. Most . . . had to go away disappointed. Every corner of the room was packed, and the platform was as thronged as the body of the hall'.[17] After three hours of impassioned debate about 'whether the members were for sale', a poll was demanded. Two weeks of intense campaigning followed where local control became the central issue. Both sides inserted large strident adverts in the local press. The challenger issued a full election address , and his canvassers accompanied the collectors on their rounds. He finally won by 9792 votes to 7453.[18]

Many other issues required no electoral settlement, yet were equally democratic. Crowded quarterly meetings over the years held long discussions about detailed issues of Society business. Many decisions were made on committee-recommendation, yet members could also reject such advice. In fact, the decision most arousing members was outwardly odd. Yet it typifies the determined parochiality, loyalty and passion of this essential and intimate area of working-class life. In 1887, there began a raging dispute about whether the Society should remove its headquarters from the Fox Inn where its life began to somewhere more central and less drink-sodden. Temperance rapidly became the only issue. The initial meeting was adjourned to the cavernous town hall; even here, hundreds could not get in. The *Rochdale Observer* gazed wonderingly:

> Probably no other local issue could have drawn such an audience ... the writer has ... never seen an audience so representative of the homes of the district: fathers, mothers, brothers and sisters with their cousins and aunts, and weren't they excited? A stranger might have thought some great question, on which depended the fate of nations, was to be settled.[19]

Eventually, temperance apparently gained a majority, but the issue went to a poll. In the ensuing campaign, the two sides argued the issue in myriad newspaper-letters, leaflets and crowded rumbustious meetings. Eventually, in January 1888, the reform cause was decisively defeated in an 88 per cent poll. The issue re-emerged at the next quarterly meeting. Here temperance received its final defeat amidst anger from those 'fetched from enjoyment' in the bar downstairs. Afterwards, 'the leading ... reformers were the centre of an abusive crowd ... a Radical councillor surrounded by three loquacious women who gave him a 'piece of their minds ... in very plain language'.[20]

The evidence about friendly-society democracy in action has admittedly drawn heavily on local Lancashire societies – reflecting my own research, and their greater visibility in the local press as compared with Affiliated lodges. Yet with similar predisposing conditions in place – the centrality of sickness and death as working-class concerns, the interest in locality, lodges' small size, pubs' universal availability as meeting-places – there seems reason to think that society operations would have been similar. Certainly the loyalty Lancashire's local societies clearly commanded is equally evident where Affiliated lodges have been studied – say, the towns and villages of East Yorkshire, Norfolk, Sussex or the south-west. Where evidence is available, the attachment to democratic self-government is clear.[21]

As the century progressed, power within the Affiliated Orders, as within trade unions and co-ops, began centralising. Here, societies were urged inexorably forward by their sheer operational scale, the consequent need for security, and the accountability imposed by registration under successive Acts of Parliament, especially those of 1875–6. The results were democratically ambiguous. On the one hand, lodges guarded their autonomy fiercely, and representative democracy increasingly supplemented continuing direct democracy. In the Manchester Unity, the largest, and typical of others, lodges elected District Committees who elected an Annual Moveable Committee (an annual conference moving year-by-year partly to maintain sensitivity to local opinion). This in turn debated policy and elected the Board of Directors. However, whilst remaining democratically vigorous, lodges steadily lost financial control: after 1875, they had to regularly contribute to a central fund, relinquished control over surplus money, lost the right to secede if they disliked central policy. Also contribution- and relief-scales came increasingly to be set by the centre.

Some local societies also expanded, rapidly outgrowing their roots, and becoming regional in operation. By 1904 the Blackburn Philanthropic Burial Society, for example, one of the four largest of its kind, had 239 123 members extending across four counties, whilst the Chorley Funeral Society had around 30 000 across two. Both remained attached to direct democracy in the form of Quarterly and Annual General Meetings. Yet, because these continued being held in their founding locations, their decision-making was beyond the geographical reach of many members. Thus they became even more reliant upon professional, if still elective, leadership than the Affiliated Orders. They were still democratic in that leaders were legitimised by regular popular election, and remained psychologically close at least to their local members. Also, governance rested upon high levels of satisfaction and thus consent. Such societies also still commanded considerable local loyalty, as in 1911 when 5000 members of the Blackburn Philanthropic descended noisily upon Manchester's Free Trade Hall, there, after a spell of lusty community-singing, to defend their leadership from attack. Yet, perhaps because the more successful local societies were often only concerned with procuring respectable death, their popularity increasingly rested upon committed but passive consent rather than active participation.

Government itself further eroded the vibrancy of this segment of working-class civil society via the 1911 National Health Insurance. As noted, this led to the demise of many small local societies. Although registration as approved societies under the Act enhanced their status and at least stabilised their membership, they also lost substantial operational control. Compulsory insurance meant they gained many members wholly uncommitted to their democratic culture and self-helping principles. Finally, they were twinned in approval by the large insurance companies, wholly undemocratic in operation and with immensely superior resources. Whilst friendly societies were probably immensely valuable as vehicles of democratic education during the period of male working-class inclusion, they could not retain this role once the longer term state-expansive consequences of that inclusion began belatedly to bite. While government became more responsive to their perceived needs, if not necessarily their actual desires, many working-class people lost fine control over a key aspect of their lives.

Co-operative societies from their early-nineteenth-century inception were also democratic in operation. Like friendly societies, they emerged partly from a desire to take control of some of the essential features of life. Democracy was also inherent in the ideal of the 'community of consumers' that was central to co-operative culture.[22] It was also central to co-operative rhetoric and argument. The commitment was expressed in both constitutional provision and practice. In constitutional terms, the Rochdale Pioneers, though early in the field, were typical of many who came later. Their initial constitution provided for a president, treasurer, secretary, three trustees and five directors – all annually elected. Major decisions were to be taken in quarterly meetings open to all members where all votes were equal irrespective of custom or share-ownership. The Co-operative Wholesale Society also held quarterly general meetings with one delegate from each member-society, plus one for every 200 members; these meetings elected the directors.

What this meant in practice is hard to know exactly since, like all the working-class civil organisations under review, little research has been done on how they conducted their business. Given their self-generated character, and the fact that the movement developed independently in different parts of the country, high levels of internal democracy seem probable. To judge from local society operations with which this writer is familiar, decision-making remained subject to considerable popular control and participation. Though attendance at monthly, quarterly and annual meetings was only a fraction of total membership it was still substantial – particularly if the additional temptation of a 'tea meeting' –

the Co-op was notably temperate – was on offer. Certainly, from the point local newspapers began recording society activities, attendances of several hundred, or even over a thousand, were quite common. The proceedings might be fairly formal. Yet at other times, there was passionate disagreement on major issues of principle. Decisions about whether to affiliate to the Co-operative Wholesale Society, for example, absorbed many societies in several nights of intense debate.

Yet, here too, centralisation began producing a degree of democratic remoteness. Centralisation was born partly of the sheer scale of operations, and the perceived need for central purchasing and even production. The movement also needed to safeguard its interests against well-meaning governmental regulation, and against less well-intentioned shopkeepers bent on legislatively destroying its tax-exemptions. As with friendly societies, the results were democratically ambiguous. On the one hand, as regional and national organisations appeared in the 1860s, direct local democracy was simply supplemented by representative kinds. Cole makes clear that both the Co-operative Wholesale Society and the Scottish Co-operative Wholesale Society resulted from extensive consultative exercises, unsurprising since they were created from the bottom up by societies immensely jealous of their autonomy.[23] The movement also showed strong desires to ensure accountability in the national organisations thus created. In 1869, there occurred the first of what rapidly became annual Co-operative Congresses, composed of delegates elected by local societies. This was quickly supplemented by similarly representative regional and district conferences. In the twenty years after 1869, a crucial period of enfranchisement, the Co-op thus developed a whole network of elective organisation. Congresses debated and decided upon all aspects of common policy, including establishing a bank (1869, 1870 and 1871), Regional Sections (in the 1870s), and co-operative production (1882). They argued about the role of women and the creation of the Women's Co-operative Guild (fairly continuously from 1883), resources to be devoted to education (from 1882), parliamentary representation and many other issues. However, centralisation, for all the consultative network surrounding it, also involved local societies losing control in areas like purchasing-policy; perhaps too an increasing sense of the movement becoming remote from its members. Co-operation continued growing into the 1940s; yet for increasing numbers of members, membership involved little more than a feeling of community (important to a continuing sense of autonomy and vested interest but less so as a source of democratic training) and the 'divi'. Size and centralisation rendered the movement more politically effective but also more remote.

While much has been written about the external behaviour of trade unions (in relation to employers and government), as with other working-class civil organisations, historians have been less interested in how they conducted themselves. The Webbs, amongst the few observers who were, viewed them benignly as 'thousands of working-class democracies'.[24] Constitutionally, unions appeared thoroughly democratic, with elaborate electoral procedures for most offices at all levels, and for popular consultation about decision-making.

This was evident from the start, partly arising from the origins of many unions as informal and localised 'democracies of work', the means whereby groups of workers controlled how their jobs were done, and tried defending that control against employers where necessary.[25] These early unions were apparently genuine face-to-face democracies. As with friendly-society lodges, all members were expected to take their turn when committees were formed, and fines were levied on those refusing.[26] As with friendly societies, this was due to a mix of principle (genuine attachment to democracy) and necessity (office-holding being costly for men economically hard-pressed and overworked).[27] As the decades passed, and unions became larger and more formally organised, so more representative and indirect forms of internal self-governance had to be established. Yet, as the Webbs noted with disapproval, even at the turn of the century, this step was taken reluctantly, amidst much hankering after traditional patterns of direct control via mass meetings – 'even in so large a centre as London'.[28] Many experiments were tried to avoid ceding powers to representative centres. One was the rotating governing branch, sometimes elected by the whole membership, with the intention of avoiding the dreadful fate conjured up by an Ironfounders' lodge in 1849:

> What, we ask, has been the history of nearly every trade society in this respect? Why that, when any branch...has possessed the governing power too long, it has become careless of the society's interests, tried to assume irresponsible powers, and invariably... opened wide the doors of peculation, jobbery and fraud.[29]

Representative assemblies and permanent officials, particularly General Secretaries, slowly emerged. Yet branches still went to elaborate lengths to try to maintain control, and ensure delegates enduringly reflected the instructions of those sending them, and avoided becoming representatives exercising independent judgement as the result of assembly debate. Other attempts to maintain what has been called 'strong democracy'[30] by limiting official discretion included persistent resort to referenda, and insistence that their initiation should be available not just to executives seeking to legitimise their decisions, but also any branch objecting or wanting to propose alternatives. The frequency of such practice, and branches' eagerness to take advantage of opportunities offered, drove the Webbs to observe:

> Those who believe that pure democracy implies . . . direct decision by the mass of the people, of every question as it arises, will find this ideal realised without . . . limit in the history of the larger trade unions between 1834 and 1870.[31]

The Webbs regarded such tendencies as deeply misguided – hamstringing officials in dealings with employers, and representing a refusal by workers to come to terms with the need for representative democracy in an increasingly complex world. Workers were failing to recognise that policy-making and negotiation must come under the control of permanent and increasingly expert officials if unions were to be effective. Writing in 1897, the Webbs were encouraged to see such vestiges of direct democracy declining, and would have been still happier about their further decay through the twentieth century, until reinvigorated by the state, for reasons of economic management, in the 1980s. Yet, as even they grudgingly admitted,[32] however unrealistic, the resilience of such behaviour[33] was a tribute to the depth and vigour of democratic culture amongst secure working men in the decades around enfranchisement.

Furthermore, if the Webbs were correct in thinking direct democracy was being curbed because 'thoughtful trade unionists' were realising its impracticality amidst increasingly complex negotiation with employers, experience in this bit of civil organisation was arguably producing some sort of education in democratic realities. The Webbs believed members were learning that referenda and the like not merely created administrative uncertainty and inefficiency, but also enhanced the possibilities of personal dictatorship for manipulative General Secretaries. Far more practical in democratically checking official autonomy was longer-term insistence upon regular popular election – particularly for General Secretaries. Here, the Webbs argued plausibly, trade unionists showed not just appreciation of democratic realities, but also deeper democratic reflexes than bank and company shareholders. As a result,

> the general secretary finds himself not at the head of a docile staff of . . . subordinates who owe office and promotion to himself, but of . . . separately elected functionaries each holding his appointment from the members . . . [34]

What unions adopting separate popular elections for their general secretary and executive officials were essentially creating were microcosmic presidential systems with separation of powers. For the Webbs, even this did not answer the central problem of reconciling popular control with administrative and negotiating effectiveness. As they noted, with surprising sensitivity for people so enamoured of expert-rule, the dilemma was peculiarly acute for working-class organisations: the situation inevitably drew union officials away from the cultural world and priorities of those they represented, in ways not experienced by middle-class organisations.[35] The Webbs believed working men's education in democratic realities could produce only one effective solution – representative democracy modelled on the British Parliamentary system. Unions must create 'parliaments' or conferences composed of annually elected representatives from the various districts in proportion to membership. These bodies should then elect executive bodies, or 'cabinets', who would then appoint a professional general secretary. He would be responsible to them, and they would be responsible and responsive to the members electing them, amongst whom they continued to work. Thus problems of reconciling popular control with efficiency, and increasingly powerful general secretaries, would be resolved. The Webbs were delighted to discover two of the largest unions – the Cotton Spinners and the Miners Federation – had adopted this system, or something like it. They were also pleased to note a general trend towards representative democracy, with executive committees increasingly elected by districts. These included not just skilled and secure workers, but also new unskilled unions like gas workers and dockers.[36]

All this suggests that unions, like friendly societies and co-ops, exhibited strong democratic attachments, and could provide their members with significant democratic training. They also shared equally democratically-functional abilities to generate increasing autonomy of local elites. This was eventually evident even in very dependent places. As a disgruntled Dorset clergyman noted in 1913, bitterly remembering the start of agricultural unionism, 'the Revolt of the Labourers began under Arch. And by revolt, I mean the expression by every means in his power of his independence of the classes to whom he had hitherto been in submission.' Alan Howkins has argued such attachments may explain the liberal voting patterns of Norfolk labourers in 1900 and 1906.[37] At the same time, like friendly societies and co-ops, unions were also confronted by problems of size, and needs for efficiency, effective external negotiation and political clout. This produced growing trends towards representative alongside direct democracy, permanent and professional leadership, bureaucracy and remoteness from ordinary members; trends heightened further as the corporate state began emerging during the First World War. From the late 1880s, they were also enhanced by developing unskilled unionism. Low educational levels, little feeling about jobs being sources of pride or status (understandable because they involved neither skill nor security), and more urgent needs simply to survive, all ensured membership would be viewed instrumentally, involving lower commitment, thus less desire for participation than with skilled unions. This was doubly so because membership, though increasingly extensive, was like unskilled jobs also perpetually shifting. Leaders were thus more remote, and sometimes more prone to corruption.[38] Membership, whilst undoubtedly enhancing autonomy and perhaps a sense of stake, was less likely to involve democratic education.

Internal democracy and the potential for autonomy was also pronounced amongst those parts of organised religion where working men (and here also women) most clearly predominated. It is true that only some churches, drawing on substantial working-class support, are clearly functional here. Catholicism, whatever its role in enhancing politicisation in nineteenth-century Ireland, and indeed in the modern Third World, hardly seems a likely vehicle for enhancing democratic culture in Mainland Britain before 1914, given its attachment to hierarchy, and thus to the authority of popes, cardinals, bishops and priests. Indeed, the absence of a dominant Catholic Church would be seen as democratically positive by observers familiar with its impact upon Southern European polities, at least until recently. Nor really, for the working class at least, does nineteenth-century Anglicanism appear a natural democratic facilitator. Given its Established character, the dominant presence of national and local elites in its governance, and the obedience to authority of all kinds its ministers so often preached,[39] Anglicanism seems an improbable vehicle for democratically training working-class adherents. Indeed, particularly in rural areas where it was dominant, and landlords were substantial and resident, the parson was not unreasonably seen as the squire's right-hand man in levying deference from the lower orders. On evidence in Chapter 4, the Church remained an unpromising venue for democratically training working men (or women) even with the emergence of the Church Assembly in the 1920s. Nevertheless, even in Anglicanism, it is significant that working people often actively participated in Nonconformist protests about church rates centring upon elections of churchwardens and overseers at parish meetings. Such meetings also became vehicles for Chartist and other protest. This was why the *Manchester Guardian*, gloomily viewing the aftermath of one such protest, remarked that such occasions were 'highly injurious . . . to good order'.[40]

Far more important for working-class people were the various Nonconformist sects, particularly the Wesleyan break-aways. We have already noted that de Tocqueville saw non-established religion as central to the democratic functionality of civil society in early-nineteenth-century America.[41] There seems good reason for paying it similar tribute in Britain – for parts of the working class as for many within the middle class. Nonconformity had much potential as a democratic vehicle. For working-class people, one attraction, particularly of Methodist sects, must always have been the possibility of achieving a state of grace irrespective of wealth. Equally appetising was Nonconformity's general emphasis upon the laity's importance in all matters of church governance. For all their centralising temptations, this was observed even by Wesleyans. It was enthusiastically embraced by those splitting away – and, if Wesleyans were predominantly working-class as some suggest, this was even truer of some sects. Indeed, fervent self-governance was implicit in the very origins of groups like Primitive Methodists and Bible Christians, concerned as they were about the perceived elevation and separation of ministers from their flocks.[42] The more working-class the sect – and this applied not just to Wesleyan breakaways but also Calvinistic Methodists – the greater the insistence upon self-governance; an emphasis perhaps reinforced by equal insistence upon participatory religious fervour, and the personal and individual character of spirituality.

All this renders sects natural centres for democratic training and producing democratic self-confidence amongst working-class members. Like the other civil organisations under review, chapels ran themselves. Democracy was implicit from conception, decisions to create congregations and places of worship being taken by potential participants, even if increasingly sanction had also to be sought from district organisations and circuits. Once established, decisions on all matters of collective life seem to have been the responsibility of monthly members' meetings, though again increasingly subject to district sanction. These included chapel-building (given the expense, often occasioning long debate), principles for admitting new members, and disciplining and excluding existing ones. They elected their own governing committees; the Calvinistic Methodists[43] also appointed, and occasionally dismissed, their own ministers. The more autonomous the church, the more likely financial management would be included amongst its responsibilities, with decisions taken in the light of what could be afforded. This situation perhaps reinforced lessons available from local co-ops, unions and friendly societies, and thus what we shall see were strong working-class predilections for important aspects of political economy, though chapels' ambitions admittedly increasingly led them into debt and thus primitive sorts of deficit financing.[44]

As activities expanded (into Sunday schooling, for example), some decisions were relinquished to committees. Though this eroded direct democracy, as with unions and friendly societies, it produced representational and office-holding experience. As Smith has commented of the Oldham area, there were often 'so many organisations and meetings that it was impossible to run a new Dissenting church without a massive mobilisation of its ordinary members and adherents'. Even in socially-mixed chapels, this probably militated against middle-class monopoly of office:[45] in West Yorkshire, for example, socially-mixed chapels elected socially-mixed groups of Trustees.[46] Many congregations provided opportunities for the far more onerous and personally developing responsibilities of lay-preaching. Meanwhile, even Wesleyans, conservative and centralised though they were, never felt able, nor apparently wished, to abandon commitment to elective and representational democracy; indeed, attachments grew as the decades passed. The sovereign Annual Conference, always elective, became more representative still under the 1878 constitution. This decreed that conference delegates were to be elected by the May synods. The laity's role was also substantially increased, a significant development in the midst of growing representative democracy. Furthermore, the constitution formalised a practice introduced as early as 1797: holding referenda on major decisions.

Given the foregoing, it is unsurprising that there is considerable testimony implying the democratic functionality of experiences available in many Nonconformist chapels. Significantly, this comes as much from rural areas, like Norfolk, as from the more expected urban ones. In 1887, Revd Augustus Jessop wrote:

> there is no denying that in hundreds of parishes...the stuffy little chapel...has been...the only place where the peasantry have enjoyed...free expression of their opinions, and where...they have kept up a school of music literature and politics, self-supported and unaided by dole or subsidy – above all a school of eloquence, in which the lowliest has become familiarised with...ordinary rules of debate, and...trained to express himself with directness, vigour and fluency.[47]

Bert Hazel, trades unionist and MP, remembered:

> [The chapel]...was the centre of activity, especially in...more remote rural areas...the only place where lads could go...no matter what your background, everybody was invited to participate...it was an opportunity because you were always encouraged...to take part...you gained a degree of confidence...it may have been a load of tripe...you said, but...the fact was you got to your feet, and you discussed afterwards.[48]

Chapels offered self-confidence, self-respect, experience of participation, responsibility, public speaking and leadership. Through Sunday schools, adults as well as children could seek basic literacy and numeracy – at least until the point religious authorities decided provision was becoming over-secularised.[49] In areas where they were strong, the more proletarian sects could also generate islands of substantial autonomy and resistance to the deference expected by local elites. Primitive Methodist strength in areas like Norfolk may partly account for the rapid way some switched allegiance from Toryism to Liberalism after rural enfranchisement in 1884. Equally, Calvinistic Methodist strength in South Wales underpinned Welsh working-class resistance to the social and political power of the predominately Anglican and English mine- and foundry-owners.[50] Nonconformity was also closely linked with temperance,[51] thereby probably helping limit the influence of drink upon elections, thus enhancing their rationality.

Such generalisations, however, require significant qualification. Some historians[52] imply far less democratically functional views of working-class Nonconformity. Wesleyans in particular, especially their central elite, are seen as bearing considerable and willing responsibility for working-class passivity in face of exploitation, the acceptance of hierarchy and the need for obedience. Much of this writing relates to the period of industrial take-off. However, in areas where chapels were socially mixed, and economic dependency a central fact of life, then, even more than other civil associations, they could become part of an enduring deference-framework binding workers to employers. If your employer also built your chapel, then appeared as your lay-preacher or Sunday-School teacher, his ability to influence your view of the world and interests in it was potentially considerable. If accurate interest-recognition, untrammelled by the effects of dependency, is a precondition of 'true' democracy, then not everything that Methodism did – still less Anglicanism or Catholicism – was usefully productive. Admittedly, it has been validly observed that Wesleyanism was insufficiently widespread to fully bear the pacifying burdens Marxists have laid upon it.[53] Yet, this must also limit estimations of its democratic functionality.

Even with these considerations aside, there were other democratically unpromising features of chapel-life, at least if the end-product is *liberal* democracy. Evangelical revivalism, with its encouragement of what outsiders might see as mass-hysteria, seems an unlikely basis for encouraging that rationality many observers, then and now, regarded as a precondition of political fitness. For some converts at least, it also induced an unhealthily unconditional faith in charismatic preachers, and surely contributed to some of Gladstone's popularity. Furthermore, whilst Nonconformity might open the path to God's grace to anyone irrespective of property or station, chapel-goers were often unsympathetic to those choosing not to take it. They could easily become havens for the sanctimoniously-saved, encapsulated from the wicked surrounding world, incapable of spreading democratic culture or anything else, uninterested in secular issues. If they ventured outwards, it might well be as temperance agitators, bent upon curbing working-class pleasure, and thus automatically suspect. This is surely one reason why only some sects proved capable of generating leaders for other, more clearly protective, sectors of civil society in ways explored later.

Nevertheless, even with these reservations, Nonconformity, like friendly societies, co-ops and trade unions, was clearly capable of generating democratically useful skills and commitments amongst its working-class adherents, in the right circumstances counterweighting some of the less democratically functional attitudes that economic dependency tended to encourage.

To some extent, their success here is reflected in equally resilient, if also somewhat ambiguous, commitments to internal democracy and democratic procedures by working-class radicalism. In fact, political civil society did not just reflect its non-political equivalent. Admittedly, movements like Chartism derived their organisational models from sectarian Methodism, unions and even friendly societies.[54] As we shall see, working-class politics also drew many leaders, and some of its skills and self-confidence, from similar sources. Furthermore, as with the middle class, working men's non-political organisation was far more continuous, embracing a far larger committed membership (as distinct from supporters) than their political activity. The demand for citizenship flowed quite naturally from what participation in friendly societies and the like already lent working men – the sense of being part of the society in most other ways. In these senses, the notion of 'reflection' is appropriate. Yet it is also true that democratically-committed political organisation began soon after its non-political counterpart. In this sense, they were both simply part of the same strong and mutually-reinforcing democratic culture. Radicalism's internal democracy flowed from its long-central demand for political inclusion. Doubly significant of this culture's strength is the fact that, though perhaps logical, the commitment was in no sense inevitable – as the far less democratic commitments of the Birmingham Political union, the Anti-Corn-Law League, business organisations and the Suffragettes showed.

Whatever the reasons, radical commitments to internal democracy were strong from the start. Three examples from the pre-1850 period will make the point, this being when political organisation was most intensely difficult. Quite aside from vast problems caused by poverty, lack of time and restricted access to the communications network, there was the fact that most forms of political agitation beyond the entirely localised or totally centralised were illegal – due to Habeus Corpus suspension from 1795 to 1820, the 1799 Corresponding Societies Act and the 1817 Seditious Meetings Act. Yet, though beset by the first of these, and by determined government persecution, Corresponding Societies remained firmly wedded to internal elections and democratic procedures and rituals. All major policy changes were decided by referenda.[55] Francis Place's self-congratulatory account of their activities is instructive:

> The Society assembled in divisions in various parts of the Metropolis . . . weekly . . . Each division elected a delegate, these formed a

general committee which also met once a week; in this committee, the sub-delegate had a seat, but could neither speak nor vote while the delegate was present ... In ... August, it was referred to the divisions as a constitutional question, whether the Chairman of the General Committee should be chosen every time the committee sat, or ... elected for three months. It was determined that the president should be elected for three months. A ballot ... was taken, and I was elected ... by a very great majority.[56]

Equally instructively, even revolutionaries felt obliged to observe democratic forms. As Edward Thompson has noted:

the Cato Street conspirators, while plotting in a garret the assassination of the Cabinet, found it necessary to appoint one of their number as Chairman ... and ... take the question of beheading Castlereagh ... in proper form, with a vote upon the substantive motion.[57]

Given such precedents, and their democratic programme, it is unsurprising that Chartists showed these commitments even more intensely. Chartism desired to render itself 'as democratic in its workings as the principles of it are democratic in their nature'. As Eileen Yeo has argued, Chartists were committed to ensuring internal democracy, and this was reinforced by practical steps to open their ever-broadening activities to all supporters, irrespective of poverty. This partly explained attachments to exclusive dealing and collective self-sufficiency. Alongside desires to keep within the law, or at least to avoid its surveillance, it also underpinned the widespread use of class meetings in members' houses (where small numbers would ensure maximum participation). Chartists also widely resorted to debating societies to try to spread political training. Office-holding was burdensome for those who were not merely poor, but if lucky also overworked. Union branches and friendly-society lodges often resolved this by compulsory election. Chartism tried the opposite course, paying its permanent officials. However, in never-ending attempts to ensure accountability, Chartists insisted upon quarterly elections and short incumbency at all levels, and frequently resorted to mandating delegates, and regular reporting back. All these practices determinedly climaxed in blueprints for the National Charter Association. Indeed, worries about the Executive Committee slipping beyond control produced the Annual Delegate Convention, designed as the movement's elected legislature. Ultimately, NCA attempts to ensure democratic accountability, whilst also avoiding legal prohibitions on branch-based organisations, were doomed to failure. Nevertheless, the repetitive determination betokens the culture upon which it drew.

This culture was still available to socialist organisations and the Labour Party fifty years later. In many respects, these were classic voluntary organisations from democratic perspectives, often growing from the local bottom up. Of the 115 delegates at the ILP's founding conference in 1893, 91 represented provisional branches formed in anticipation of the national party.[58] Yet, even more than previously, we see the increasing tension between stronger and weaker forms of internal democracy evident in the discussion of working-class civil society thus far. We also see the choice participants increasingly felt obliged to make. It is an undoubted tribute to the Labour movement's strong democratic culture, and its commitment to achieving full citizenship for at least its male members, that the character of its internal democracy was the focus of much debate within and between its various branches – trade unions, the ILP, the SDF, Syndicalism, the Fabians and the Labour Party itself.[59] Yet the result was increasing centralisation: leaders and many followers, confronted by realities they perceived as being created by the need to negotiate within the broader polity, increasingly chose weaker, or at least more indirect and leadership-centred, forms of internal democracy

In spite of contrary pressure from *Clarion* intellectuals, the SDF, and many rank- and-file trade unionists, the movement's various segments increasingly rejected delegate-democracy, proportional representation, referenda and recall and more frequent elections – both for their own decision-making processes and those of the wider polity. The TUC adopted the bloc vote in 1895, and in 1899 its Parliamentary Committee persuaded delegates to adopt its own more centralised and bureaucratic federation scheme (NIFTLU) rather than the more participatory alternative originating from the *Clarion*. As this suggests, Labour and socialist organisations also became steadily more attached to permanent leadership. This growing commitment to more constrained forms of representative democracy was never total. The ideal of delegation remains strong amongst union activists even now, and liberal-democratic commitments remained intense. Yet there were clearly interactions between working-class civil society and the wider polity, and indeed with negotiating needs created by increasingly centralised employers' organisations. On the one hand, the movement's internal processes over the years undoubtedly powered expectations of full political citizenship, and helped educate those awarded it. In this sense, they underpinned and strengthened liberal democracy. On the other hand, the elite-centred traditions of the British polity, and of its democratisation, also reflected back on working-class civil organisations. It provided them with limited models and pushed them into negotiational postures seeming to require substantial leadership-autonomy, and thereby trustee rather than delegate forms of representation. The emerging quasi-corporate state from the inter-war years undoubtedly reinforced these trends.[60]

2. The Articulation of Demand

As already evident, the discussion thus far shades into our second and related question: how far civil organisation enhanced working men's ability to realise collective ends once admitted to the polity.

This question has already received partial answer in the sense that good citizens in a political sense are also likely to be effective interest-defenders. As noted, working men's civil organisations were capable of generating democratically-useful skills, ones not just supportive of the polity, but also essential to the group. Such organisations also trained and generated leadership – both within politics and, given minimum government, in the at least equally crucial world beyond. Indeed, this could hardly be otherwise: the Nonconformists aside, these were organisations directed at perceived class or group ends; and friendly societies, unions and co-ops were mostly led either by working men, or people very close to them, socially and sympathetically. Most union leaders, locally and nationally, originated from the ranks of those they led; even leaders of the unskilled at the end of the century tended to be skilled working men, radicalised by socialism. The leadership of friendly-society lodges was, by virtue of their internal procedures, almost definitionally working-class, or in rural areas at least artisan.[61] Only at national level did leadership become middle-class. Local co-ops were also working-class led. The Rochdale Pioneers' founders were all manual workers.[62] As a contemporary noted of the CWS, 'one of the most important facts . . . is that the men in charge . . . are all workers . . . risen from the ranks of co-operation'.[63]

Indeed, the very richness of working men's civil organisation was increasingly self-reinforcing. Different sorts of organisation frequently swapped leadership, and the less directly political segments helped generate leadership for the more political. Friendly-society leadership in some places drew heavily upon Primitive Methodism, as indeed did its membership.[64] As has been widely noted, some local Chartist leaders, and many union officials, before and after 1850, had prior backgrounds as friendly-society activists, and in the chapels, particularly and unsurprisingly, as lay-preachers.[65] Many Lib–Lab and Labour MPs were also strongly rooted in chapel life. So too were many working-class Liberal activists. Numerous working-class councillors and school-board members were local union leaders and activists, Nonconformist lay-preachers, and, in some rural areas at least, friendly-society officials.[66] Most Lib–Lab MPs from the 1870s were leading trade unionists.[67] So too, particularly up to 1945, were many Labour MPs.

Yet there were limits to the ability and willingness of working-class civil organisation to generate political leadership. This was unsurprising. Much nineteenth-century civil association was concerned with, and absorbed by, the need for self-help in a world wherein state-aid, outside the punitive Poor Law, was absent. For reasons investigated later, friendly societies, co-ops and unions had only very limited concerns with politics. Friendly society and co-operative leadership, in particular, showed little interest in moving into politics. So too did Wesleyan Methodism, unlike some of its offshoots. Much early- and mid-century trade unionism was also 'pure and simple', indifferent and mistrustful of political involvement, particularly after the collapse of Chartism, whose links with unions were ambivalent at best. Even much later, when they had admitted the need for political action, unions remained sufficiently indifferent to political priorities to donate only their second-rank leaders to parliamentary candidature. There was also the fact that, for all their richness compared with other later polities, working men's voluntary organisations until around 1850 were too under-developed, too absorbed by their primary functions and too concerned with simple survival to have much time or energy for political activism. There is too the longer-term problem that working-class leadership is socially elevating: even if leaders do not forsake manual ranks, their children generally do. Manual leadership practically never lasts beyond one generation.

For all these reasons except the last, shortfalls in political leadership were particularly pronounced in the early decades of working-class political action. Alongside the need to be taken seriously when confronting aristocratically-dominated politics, the rural origins of many workers, and the potentially inclusive populism of some radical rhetoric, this accounts for the importance of the 'gentleman leader' in mass radical agitation until around 1850. The charismatic oratory of men like Henry Hunt, Richard Oastler, Feargus O'Connor and Ernest Jones was crucial to sustaining movements for factory reform, against the Poor Law, and in favour of enfranchisement. They probably paved the way for the equally charismatic, but even more clearly constitutional, influence of Bright and Gladstone.[68] Such men were probably crucial transitional figures. They helped lead working-class outsiders on to the inside-track, and aided the consequent transformation of working-class politics – from relatively undisciplined crowd-politics into more organised agitations centring upon the mass platform, ultimately opening the way for the respectable channelling of radical action evident from the 1860s.

Equally symptomatic of the relatively undeveloped state of civil organisation until mid-century was working-class radical reliance upon middle-class figures – from professional, lesser manufacturing and shopkeeping backgrounds. Amongst those with a national reputation, were influential figures like Bronterre O'Brien, Reverend J.R. Stephens, and W.P. Roberts, the miners' lawyer. More locally, amongst many others, were equally crucial individuals like Isaac Ironside, accountant and leader of the Sheffield Democrats in the 1840s and 1850s, R.J. Richardson (bookseller), H.W. Hodgetts (manufacturing chemist) in Salford, and Thomas Livesey, a periodically-bankrupt small manufacturer and dominant figure in Rochdale radicalism for the 25 years until his premature death in 1864.[69] To achieve acceptance at a time of intense class antagonism, such men had to identify their lives with those they led, and often partially to detach themselves from their origins. Nevertheless, they did not originate in working-class civil society in the way many were to do after around 1850.

All the same, voluntary organisations were increasing sources of manual political leadership. Their multiplicity was also self-reinforcing in other ways. As often noted, they generated organisational models for each other. Wesleyan chapels and circuits have been seen as particularly prolific lesson-givers about what disciplined organisation could achieve in terms of democratic self-governance and agitational effectiveness, providing examples widely adopted by trade unionism, Chartism and other forms of radicalism.[70] Indeed, such consequences were perceived and feared by social superiors. As early as 1820, Robert Southey noted gloomily how 'Methodism has familiarised the lower classes to the work of combining in associations, making rules for their own governance, raising funds and communicating from one part of the kingdom to another'.[71] Given the way Nonconformity continued to underpin trade-union and political leadership until at least the First World War, such lessons were unlikely to be forgotten by later generations. Given the close links between unions and the Labour Party, and the tendency, particularly at first, for constituency parties to be indistinguishable from local trades councils, we can plausibly believe significant organisational education was also being transmitted across the boundary.

Civil organisation enhanced the democratic effectiveness and clout of working men in three other ways. First, the expanding presence and cohesion of friendly societies, unions and co-ops, and their ambitious representational claims, rendered members and assumed supporters increasingly worthy of appeasement by competing national and local elites. So too, in periods of intense working-class politicisation, did organised political radicalism. As noted in Chapter 3, such behaviour was evident even before enfranchisement, both in terms of rhetoric and some alleviating action: for example the emergence of Conservative Workingmen's Friendly and Burial societies across the North; or more sympathetic administration of the local Poor Law. Appeasement partly underlay increasing desires by local notables to appear on the anniversary occasions of co-ops and friendly societies in boroughs after 1867, and rural areas after 1884.[72] From the 1870s, in areas of high union membership, both Tory- and Liberal-dominated municipalities increasingly granted union rates and conditions to manual employees, and insisted that firms with municipal contracts did the same. The same decade saw successive Liberal and Tory governments expand union legal protection. Finally, the presence and increasing respectability of working men's voluntary organisations induced local elites to offer them increasing status in civic ceremony.

Second, and partly underpinning such behaviour by municipalities often dominated by manufacturers, the increasing union presence in many industries led employers from the 1850s – again before enfranchisement – to offer limited but increasing rights of negotiation over wages and conditions. We should not exaggerate either the novelty or extent of this. Informal conciliation was traditional to artisan life, stemming from closeness between master and man in small workshops, in terms both of socio-economic proximity and common interest. It also flowed from the associated force of custom in determining wages and conditions. This produces the ambiguous point that negotiation was both a long-term habit and, like the artisan economy itself, in some respects part of a decaying system. Indeed, one reason for union growth was precisely the disruption of such traditional relationships. Furthermore, whilst negotiation re-emerged from the 1850s, many sectors of British industry remained only marginally affected, influenced as much by employers' insistence on their 'right to manage', and bouts of mutual savagery.

Nevertheless, negotiation and conciliation were growing features of industrial relations from the 1850s. Initially, they were products of growing union emphasis upon acceptance, moderation and respectable status. Aided by skilful propaganda from groups like the Christian Socialists, and their own desire for predictability, discipline and control of competition, employers, particularly larger ones, began seeing a need to accept unions as facts of economic life. The steadily emerging consensus was expressed in growing pressure for legally-underpinned conciliation, eventually finding legislative form in 1867 and 1872. Far more effectively, there emerged a growing move to establish boards of conciliation and arbitration, starting in Nottingham in 1860, and (very significantly) spreading widely across the country by the time of enfranchisement. In many respects, it is arguable that by 1880, there was a growing culture of acceptance and negotiation in many industries – about wage-rates, conditions and hours.[73] There were obvious limits; the consensus was never total. Nevertheless, collective bargaining became an crucial economic counterpoint to democratisation, not significantly eroded until the Thatcherite years.

Third, and as the second point implies, civil organisations were also important in the non-political areas with which most were primarily concerned. In the *laissez-faire* society heavily shaping their existence and activities, friendly societies, unions and co-ops gave members significant influence over matters immediately affecting their lives, influence partly independent of formal enfranchisement. These included wages, work-conditions, consumption, sickness-provision, sometimes pensions, and far more frequently the centrally important rituals of death. Many now come within the state's purview to a greater or lesser extent. This has happened partly from beliefs that self-helping attempts to control such fundamentals are doomed to failure. Nevertheless, this was hardly how friendly-society members saw things. When the state took over health insurance in 1911, even with societies incorporated into its administration, many felt, whatever the gains in quality of provision, they were losing something important and valuable. In this sense, and because of its very autonomy, nineteenth-century civil organisation was an aspect of democratic control in its own right, one predating formal enfranchisement and ultimately partly eroded by its long-term consequences.

3. Absorbability

This brings us to the final and most contentious way civil organisation enhanced working men's political fitness: it helped render them politically absorbable, arming them with appropriate values and causing them to make acceptable and digestible political demands. As noted, many upper- and middle-class persons feared enfranchisement would inevitably produce irresistible demands for state expansion and redistribution. In the long run, this was possibly true, but in the short-to-medium term, it was hardly evident: what demands for state expansion there were did not emanate from working-class voters. Nor did many come from their civil organisations.

Here, we see how values generated by working-class civil society interacted with the *laissez-faire* state, and the political and legal frameworks we noted in Chapter 3 were being created by national and local elites to reinforce it. From a working-class viewpoint, this had both negative and positive features. Negatively, as we have seen, there were the state's baleful messages to those unwise or desperate enough to seek its protection (via poor relief), or who found themselves on the wrong end of its regulations, thus meeting the magistrate, policeman, sanitary inspector, slum-clearance order, school-attendance officer, or dark vaccinator.[74] Not everything the state provided was so hostile – expanding municipal utilities, for example. However, the further down the social scale one was located, or had the misfortune to slip, the more likely national and local states would seem enemies, agents of interference, disturbance and especially public shame. Yet, this state also had more positive features for those prepared to accept its rules and economic values. For the collectively self-helping, there was legal recognition, protection, even privilege. Alongside this were social and political benefits available to civil organisations, particularly from local elites: formalised incorporation into urban ceremonial, recognition through political rhetoric (both highly important in an age much attached to respectability and other marks of status), conciliation, and willingness to respond positively to acceptable political demands.[75] And for working-class people generally, at least those with some margin beyond subsistence, there was the by-law-created terrace – open to inspection by outsiders, thus less threatening to elites than court-housing, yet sufficiently enclosed and self-regarding to encourage strong attachments to respect-ability.[76] Amongst the marks of respectability, voting itself rapidly became an important part.

There is no doubt on the other hand that working men's civil organ-isations and their values were authentic creations of those they served. They were products of mostly male working-class initiative. Their at-tachment to self-help and respectability substantially emanated from entirely natural working-class beliefs in the value of independence and self-respect. Enough has been written about them in response to histor-ians, perceived overly attached to notions of social control, to show that friendly societies, co-ops and unions were not merely passive products, or recipients, of persuasion from above.[77] Their values derived partly from entirely natural beliefs in the value of independence and self-respect; also from equally understandable attachments to respect by others in inward-looking terraced neighbourhoods. Nevertheless, the framework of regulation, deterrence, recognition, protection and prof-fered incorporation was persuasive, and working men's civil organisa-tions were partly shaped by it. At the least, that framework powerfully encouraged the acceptable and discouraged the unacceptable.

Thus unions emerged from the long-term decay of the guild system,[78] and understandable needs to defend manual interests in a world where custom and mutuality between employee and employer were eroding in face of industrialisation, capitalisation and growing economic competi-tion. They were also responses to the state's consequent withdrawal from regulating wages, conditions and labour mobility. Unions de-veloped and periodically behaved in all sorts of ways deeply frowned upon by national and local elites. Yet, they also greatly benefited in numbers from the legal acceptance and grudging tolerance available from 1824, and then in numbers and bargaining power from the legal immunities the state was prepared to offer from 1869, impelled by competing party elites. They also probably benefited from the status local elites were prepared to publicly accord them in civic ceremonial from the 1860s, highly important in enclosed urban worlds where many watched and civic display was so uninhibited.

Retail co-ops emerged from secure manual workers' reactions to state indifference to the price and quality of essential commodities. Though clearly compromises with the free market, their initial character and aims were significantly influenced by the Owenism of many founding members. Co-ops also possessed a mutuality that, whilst a compromise with individualism, was also far removed from its spirit. Yet they also benefited from the legal recognition, limited-liability protection, tax immunities and investment opportunities the state offered in legislation between 1852 and 1862.[79] This encouraged both their development as retail traders and their move into industrial production. They were helped further by the status local elites, often for their own politically-calculative reasons, were prepared increasingly to give them from the early 1860s – speaking at their meetings, drawing them into local ceremonial life, publicly consulting them over important local issues. This culminated in 1894, when the CWS, a key player, politically and financially, in the Ship Canal Movement, was granted a leading place of honour in its inauguration. Its steamship, the *SS Pioneer*, led the first convoy through the Canal, and the Society's President, J.T.W. Mitchell, was invited to off-load the first cask of sugar.[80]

Friendly societies originated from working people's desire for protection against the consequences of ill-health and for respectable funerals. Society growth was also greatly encouraged by economic and industrial expansion; they emerged most thickly where this was most evident.[81] Their beeriness earned them deep disapproval from elites. Nevertheless, societies were greatly assisted by positive and negative actions from the state and its elites. As we saw in Chapter 3, their popularity was significantly enhanced by the punitive face it turned upon dependency from 1834, and even more from 1871. Poor-Law dependence was rendered shameful; friendly societies helped ensure that independence was a matter for respectable self-congratulation about escape from 'low grovelling depths to cheerfulness, manliness and self-esteem'.[82]

Societies also benefited from state encouragement. So close were they to desired virtue that this began as early as 1834, significantly coinciding with the New Poor Law's commencement. Legal protection and privilege (societies too had income-tax exemption) expanded steadily thereafter. Incorporative invitations from elites into civic ceremonial was evident from around the same time, as noted in Chapter 3, and enthusiastically embraced. Many societies appeared in the 1837 Coronation processions in towns across the country – doubly significant given contemporaneous evidence of class hostility. Where numbers are recorded – as in Stockport where at least 3000 marched behind the various banners[83] – they indicate enthusiasm. Thereafter their ceremonial presence was automatic.

All this suggests working men's civil organisations – and the indications are that Nonconformity was also enthusiastic about self-help – acquired significant stakes in important aspects of *laissez faire* and the free market. In no sense did they unconditionally embrace them. Theirs was collective self-help at best, and for some, particularly some co-operators, was as much about procuring independence of capitalism as compromising with it.[84] Elites often saw union wage-policies as damaging erosions of self-interest's free play. Nevertheless, partly through their own volition, partly by reacting to frameworks created by national and local states and their elites, co-ops, friendly societies and unions derived increasing benefit and advantage from governmental inactivity. Unions benefited from state non-intervention in labour relations, beyond legalising their existence and guaranteeing them against breach-of-contract actions by employers when on strike. The negotiating advantages thus derived may or may not have contributed to unprecedented rises in real wages between the 1870s and 1900, bouts of unemployment notwithstanding, but they agreeably coincided with them. Co-ops and friendly societies were advantaged by legal security, and the ability to invest in capitalist enterprise. They also drew growing status from ever-broadening ceremonial incorporation into national and local communities. Given that friendly societies particularly were deeply satisfying social as well as functional organisations (in an age when entertainment was not generously available), these stakes in the system would be widely felt.

Consequently, after as well as before enfranchisement, these organisations generated remarkably few demands for intervention or provision. By the 1890s, the mood was undoubtedly changing; yet it was doing so in limited ways. Friendly societies, disturbed by the growing costs of ageing memberships, haltingly began embracing non-contributory pensions in the early-twentieth century. Yet even in 1904, Joseph Chamberlain remained wary of the influence and likely reactions of this most organised section of working-class opinion:

> They are in touch with the thriftily-minded section of the working class. Their criticism of any scheme would be very damaging: their opposition might be fatal. They have great parliamentary influence and I should myself think twice before attempting to proceed in face of hostility from so important and dangerous a quarter.[85]

Societies also remained deeply suspicious of health and unemployment insurance through to 1911 – fearing the state and insurance companies as rivals, and their members fearing loss of control.[86] In this they were correct since the Insurance Acts ushered a period of endless decline.

Co-operators too retained their long-term mistrust of state expansion until at least 1914. As purveyors of mutual self-help in areas extending far beyond collective shopkeeping, they had no reason to seek its aid in anything beyond securing the legal framework for their secure existence. In sectors like adult education and library-provision, they were hardly natural supporters even of municipal provision in these areas, as Rochdale's Council discovered in the late-1870s when it sought the Pioneers' support for plans to create a rate-funded library. These local founders of the whole movement initially rejected the proposal because, having created their own library, they saw no reason to 'pay twice' for another – for the benefit, as they saw it, of local shopkeepers who had not been so self-reliant. Pressures for more extensive provision than collective self-help could provide changed co-operators' attitudes in these and other areas. However, reflexes remained strong, reinforced even by class-consciousness itself. The state became seen as an agency of capitalism, hardly therefore a suitable instrument for the sort of collective ownership that socialists in the SDF and ILP were coming to advocate. Some co-operators also came to see the state as an agency bent on rendering workers passive, again in the interests of the capitalist forces it served.[87]

Unions showed more interest in expanding state action, under the inter-linked influence of socialism, periodic unemployment and the intermittently-growing unskilled element. Yet, aside from factory regulation, this interest was barely evident until nearly twenty-five years after urban enfranchisement, and even then unenthusiastic and decidedly qualified. The TUC endorsed the eight-hour day in 1891, but showed little enthusiasm for minimum-wage legislation even after the 1909 Trades Boards Act.[88] It supported fair-wages clauses in central and local government contracts, as did local trades councils. It endorsed pensions from 1896, by which time even the Charity Organisation Society had decided upon their regrettable inevitability. In 1893–4, it passed collective-ownership resolutions, yet reversed them once the Congressional over-representation of trades councils, where socialists were strong, was redressed in favour of a system where unions sent delegations proportionate to their membership. Particularly from around 1900, it showed increasing commitment to work-schemes for the unemployed,[89] but little interest in Lloyd George's 1911 Health and Unemployment Insurance Bills. This was partly because of their contributory character, but also because they threatened unions' hold over their members by undermining the roles they, like friendly societies, had come to play in the absence of the state, and the presence of the baleful

Poor Law. Only when this was partly redressed by allowing unions to become approved agencies for health insurance did union attitudes change. The TUC also intermittently passed resolutions in favour of subsidised municipal housing and a state medical service, though this had little impact upon what was demanded of government. Furthermore, union attachments to 'independence' produced continued suspicions of 'the servile state'.

Unsurprisingly, the various expressions of popular and working-class radicalism down the decades reflected concerns about full citizenship, and their reinforcement by the reception extended to working-class civil organisations by so many segments of national and local elites. In 1831, *The Poor Man's Guardian*, organ of the National Union of the Working Classes, reflecting a trend evident since the 1790s, demanded many things including 'the Extirpation of the Fiend Aristocracy, Establishment of a Republic...Universal Suffrage...Abolition of...primogeniture...Emancipation of...the Jews...Abolition of Tithes'.[90] However, aside from extending the Old Poor Law to Ireland, none involved state-expansion. Chartism's Six Points were primarily about equal citizenship. Aside from a few figures like Bronterre O'Brien, its leaders had no great expectation nor desire that state-induced redistribution would follow democratisation. Nor, the New Poor Law aside, was there much criticism of *laissez faire*. Chartists expected life after the Six Points to improve, but primarily because 'the idle classes' had been robbed of their ability to tax the purchasing power of the industrious ones, and thus their ability to support the armies (both literally and metaphorically) of aristocratic dependants via state patronage.[91] For these reasons, they often eagerly championed Retrenchment. As noted in Chapter 2, the Reform League in the 1860s showed similar priorities. In this, it surely reflected its followers' concerns, evident in the mass outrage greeting Robert Lowe's insult to working-class political fitness in 1866, and the sudden upsurge in Reform agitation thereafter.

Such priorities continued after 1867. The Leicester Democratic Association from 1871 was typical of many in desiring to organise working men, to gain universal suffrage, and 'to educate people in the principles of political economy, moral virtue and social advancement'.[92] The preoccupation with political status (and disinterest in state expansion) were key reasons why popular-radical traditions and categories from the first half of the century could embrace radical Liberalism in the second. It also helps explain why the followers of Hunt, O'Connor and Fielden flocked enthusiastically to later gentlemen leaders, like Bright and Gladstone, far more clearly on the political inside-track, and drew their sons into the same excitedly incorporated crowds. Liberal-Labour MPs from the 1870s were similarly anti-statist Their often charismatic hold[93] over their constituencies rested more upon working-class pride about one of their own making it to the political top than on their attachments to state action, which, beyond desiring protection for trade unions and factory workers, were minimal. The same pride also partly underpinned demands for more general 'direct representation', and their refusal by too many Liberal Associations helped fuel the emergence of the Labour Representation Committee.

Radical feelings about the state were changing significantly by the 1890s, reflecting the influence of organisations like the SDF and ILP, along with that of more middle-class collectivities like the Fabians, and changing trade-union perceptions. All were expansionist in national and even more in municipal terms. The LRC embraced pensions and gave enthusiastic support to agitation about unemployment.[94] Yet many labour and socialist councillors, admittedly partly for reasons of *realpolitik*, spent more time safeguarding the welfare of municipal employees than advancing schemes for municipal welfare.[95] All the same, Liberal welfare commitments owed at least as much to New Liberalism (itself primarily powered by middle-class intellectuals and politicians), and more general elite fears about degenerating national fitness in the face of competition from generously-welfared foreigners, as to pressures from its Labour allies. Only after the First World War, and collectivist experience gained in government during its course, did Labour gain enduring attachment to state expansion, both nationally and especially locally.[96] Even then, it is unclear how far Clause 4 emanated from working-class radicalisation or union desires to give a sop to the movement's middle-class intellectual wing.[97] Furthermore, in the inter-war years, pressures were building on behalf of women, newly enfranchised and, as we shall see, with more reason than their menfolk to perceive the state, particularly the local state, as a source of useful support.

If working men, for their own reasons, were attached to liberal economic values, they also showed enduring and patriotic commitments to liberal civil freedoms. This was evident from the start in mass-attachment to ideas about 'the free born Englishman', and his frequent delineation from less fortunately-endowed foreigners. According to Edward Thompson, the idea embodied all the classic civil liberties.[98] Here, we can see the intersection of popular radical values with the elite responses outlined in Chapter 3: the former were reinforced by the fact that Britain was significantly liberal and only ineffectually authoritarian before it started becoming democratic. Consequently, substantially before democratisation began, radicals experienced the clear advantages available from free access to oral and printed channels of communication. This perception was expressed and reinforced by agitation against the Six Acts and particularly the long campaign, with middle-class allies, against the 'taxes on knowledge'. It was also reinforced by the equal advantages radicals derived from equality before the law, advantages made manifest, in spite of judges' conservative predilections, by early-nineteenth-century juries' reluctance to convict political offenders against blasphemous libel. It was further strengthened by input into popular radicalism from religious dissent. Nonconformist sects had as many reasons as political radicals to think liberal freedoms advantageous.[99] Such attachments produced mass support for persecuted foreigners and hostility to foreign dictators: for example amongst the 200 000 said to have gathered in Hyde Park to protest against the Anti-Conspiracy Bill introduced at the behest of Napoleon III in 1858; or the massive crowds greeting Garibaldi during his London visit in 1860, according to George Holyoak, 'the largest demonstrations ever held' there.[100] From 1861–4, they were evident in widespread demonstrations of working-class support for the North in the American Civil War, even eventually in Lancashire, the Cotton Famine notwithstanding: blacks were enslaved and not yet over here. While Bright used such attachments to help turn himself into a popular tribune, Gladstone exploited them even more spectacularly whilst stumping the country campaigning against the Turkish massacres of Bulgarian Christians from 1876.[101] Perhaps multiple meanings were being drawn by the participants at these events, yet the end-product was mass support for liberal values.

In all sorts of ways therefore, most working men were politically fit, and highly unlikely to disturb any of the fundamental characteristics of the emerging liberal-democratic system. As we shall now see, this was mostly also true of women, the final major candidates for political admission.

7 Women and Political Fitness

We now turn to the last applicant for political admission. How far were women politically fit – either by the standards of those already on the inside-track (by 1885 including not just elites but also most middle-class adult males and around 60 per cent of working men), or by more detached criteria? What access did they have to the media and the rest of civil society; how far did this produce appropriate values and useable political skills; how far were women capable of effectively participating politically and articulating their interests; how far were the resulting demands absorbable by the polity as it then existed? The argument will be that, although women's civil access was clearly more unevenly distributed than men's, and working women were substantially deprived compared with working men, the overall situation remains fairly vibrant, particularly given the constraints, and compared with that in say nineteenth-century Germany or Russia, both then and now. There is much to support Pat Thane's judgement that British women had 'an unusually rich associational life'.[1] Yet, women's perspectives on the state were different from men's. Moreover, by the time of women's political admission, the latter's were also changing. Consequently, women's enfranchisement released significant demands for governmental action. As in previous chapters, these issues will be addressed in four sections. We examine first the context conditioning political fitness.

1. Context

Any discussion must begin with three central points. First, women were not separated from men in the way most middle-class people were from the aristocracy, and the working class. Whatever the effect of separated spheres, marriage, family and social life ensured the two sexes associated together on close and casual daily bases – in homes, on streets, at some public events and, at least in some professional and industrial sectors, in workplaces. Even granting, as we clearly must, that women were wholly or partially excluded from many locations that could produce political understanding and skills for men, it was inherently unlikely that their most basic political values and attitudes to the polity would sharply differ from those of the men sharing their lives. Even if derived partly from civil-society sectors to which women were denied access, it was likely those values would be passed on. Whatever reservations male gatekeepers harboured about women as electors (and they were clearly troubled on this score), there were not the same grounds for worry about shared values that there were about, say, the potentially alienated segments of the lower working class.

Second, there was also little difference between women and men in terms of basic literacy. Those signing their names on marriage registers totalled stagnantly around 50 per cent until the 1830s, then climbed steadily to approximately 95 per cent in 1895. If one could sign, one could probably read at least slightly better. In these respects, women were just as capable as men, indeed if anything slightly more competent, perhaps partly because their occupations were ones where basic literacy was slightly more desirable.[2] As evident later, there were similar doubts about the seriousness of the use to which this literacy was put to what there were with men. Nevertheless, judging by ability to understand basic political messages, there was little to distinguish the sexes.

Third, though philanthropy might mitigate the effects, women were substantially separated from each other by class. To a significant extent, precisely because they did not live separately from men, they probably shared the fitness or otherwise of their economic segment. Though many gatekeepers lumped them together into one vast unfit conglomerate, women varied all the way from formidable and wealthy dowagers policing the entrances to upper-class Society[3] down through the variously secure or anxious middle-class housewives, and through relatively secure, self-confident and unionised Lancashire weavers. Below them were 'dependent' living-in servants; desperate, isolated, often widowed and Poor-Law-dependent outworkers; and equally marginal penny capitalists. For gatekeepers and suffragists alike, one problem of enfranchisement was precisely that they could not easily be collectively categorised, nor could many women be easily persuaded to so label themselves. By contemporary standards, the case for admitting upper-, middle- and respectable working-class women was far stronger than those at the bottom-end. Class also posed problems, difficult for them and analytically nearly irresolvable for us, of assessing political effectiveness: in a deeply deprived and divided society, any woman was presented with a finely-nuanced choice between class and gender as sources of rationally perceived interest.

Women had much in common. Aside from obvious biological com-
monalities, they were all affected, albeit in significantly varied ways, by
the customs and social rules contemporaries intellectualised into the
'separation of spheres'. This, the gendered stereotypes keeping it company, and the broader structures of patriarchy giving it birth, conditioned their lives, education, access to civil society, perceptions and
self-perceptions of political fitness. Theoretically, and in the ideal world
constructed by Victorian men, and consented to, even embraced by,
many wives and daughters, women supposedly presided over, were
confined to, and morally administered the domestic world of home
and family whilst men actively participated in the public one of job,
business, society and politics. As we shall now see, the consequences for
the perceptions and realities of political fitness were complex. In general,
it inhibited access to the services and organisations likely to generate
fitness. Yet, the doctrine did this in ways varying according to class and
time-period. Furthermore, in some respects, and for some women,
separated spheres encouraged access.

Mostly, and over broad ranges of activity, the effects were inhibiting.
In definitional terms, if civil society comprises all associational activity
occupying the space between state and family, then separated spheres
prohibited women from gaining access. In theory, these 'angels of the
house' were denied admission to the corrupting public world, whether of
paid work or politics. It hardly requires saying that the urgent needs of
working-class, and of many lower-middle-class, families, and the bore-
dom and surplus energies of many middle-class women, limited the
doctrine's impact upon the real world of work, social life, even politics.
Most working-class women needed paid work for some part of their
lives. Many middle-class women gained access at least to charitable
parts of the public sphere, and later increasingly to its occupational
sector. Nevertheless, three things remained true. First, until late-century,
beyond areas like Lancashire and the Potteries, and isolated, if substantial, professional sectors like nursing and teaching, most women were
denied access to work as a *career*, and thereby to something lending one
identity. They were barred from nearly all skilled manual work, and
most professional and entrepreneurial activity. Paid work for women
had only negative value: perceived to be performed in search of
'pin-money', something done until marriage and motherhood, or if
continued thereafter, a necessitated contribution to a primarily male-
generated 'family-wage'. The job might not be deemed worthy of census
record. As Edward Higgs has noted, women were often defined as

dependants, whatever their productive functions, whilst men were classified by the nature of their labour.[4] Furthermore, work rendered
women increasingly in need of special regulatory protection, because,
like children, they were not seen as 'free agents'. For men, work had
positive connotations: generating 'independence', 'manliness' and 'self-
respect', all heightened by the new 'breadwinner' tag emerging with the
notion of the 'family wage'. For the most skilled, work had connotations
of property.[5] Thus women had little meaningful access to one of the
most potent generators of identity in men, one highly likely to generate a
sense of autonomy, common interest and independently-arrived-at political opinion. Even the notion of 'the housewife', with her appeaseable
opinions about food prices and other domestic 'issues', was many
decades away. Prior to reaching the wifely state, moreover, she was
liable to a state of limbo without identity: 'waiting for marriage'.

Second, and in turn, this entailed having only partial access to an
immensely potent generator of civil association: at its least organised, the
'democracy of work'; at its more organised, the trade union, the business
association and, most formidably articulated of all, the professional
society or institute. Women might often run small businesses – as
shopkeepers[6] or house landlords – but this provided only partial en-
trance to a segment of society where collective economic activity was
very weak. Few women anyway could legitimately gain access to locations where men had their associational being – not just the workplace,
but also the pub, the club, the inner sanctum of the Athenaeum or 'Lit
and Phil' committee room. Even where this was not so (and some
historians have questioned the pub's strictly homo-social character[7]),
many women even in the 1920s 'do not care to go to a meeting-room
through the bar of a public house'.[8]

Third, even where access to the public world of work, civil association
and politics was available, the separation of spheres maintained sufficient consent across the population to ensure, until at least late-century,
that women's participation was never wholly legitimate. Particularly
where politics was involved, such involvement was always subject to
questioning, criticism and attack – from more elevated persons; from
male and even female peers. *The Times'* famous attack on 'hen Chartists'
had frequently been anticipated by the likes of *The Courier* in 1819
denouncing 'petticoat reformers' for 'deserting their station' and thus
'guilty of the worst prostitution of the sex, the prostitution of the heart'.[9]
It always required special justification of the hopeful and assumption-
granting sort offered by Stockport's female Chartists:

We regret . . . we should be driven by dire necessity to depart from the limits usually prescribed for female duties; but when we find it impossible to discharge those duties . . . when . . . we are unable to provide for the . . . necessities of subsistence, . . . we feel justified in declaring that "nothing less than the . . . Charter can remove the existing distress".[10]

More problematic still was the position of middle-class women, like those organisationally hidden in the Anti-Corn Law League, driven to present their activity as a form of charity.[11] Such caution was well-advised because participation, while useful in some male politics, could always be exploited by opponents to de-legitimise the cause.[12]

Embedded within and underpinning such ideas was an image of the ideal woman. The characteristics she embodied were in many respects the diametric opposites of those contemporaries associated with political fitness: she was submissive, dependent and passive rather than independent and self-helping. What supposedly equipped her for domestic supremacy doubly disadvantaged her in the political sphere: she pulsated with affection and thus emotion rather than rationality; she carried a moral virtue always liable to corruption by politics. Such ideas were necessarily eroded, as time passed, by the behaviour of real women in the real industrialising and urbanising world. Nevertheless, they received later reinforcement from biology and genetics, doubly so as physicians obligingly prognosticated about the menstrual cycle's emotionally disabling effects.[13] It marked the hegemony of such ideas that they received partial consent from the young, but still fact-worshipping, Beatrice Webb (nee Potter).[14]

One could, of course, remain single and, given favourable financial circumstances, independent. If also a householder, one was even deemed fit for municipal enfranchisement after 1869. Yet this was the limit of legitimisation. The characteristics producing political fitness were socially costly. From men and women alike, they were liable to invoke only pity and contempt for under-fulfilment.

The impact of industrialisation and urbanisation here was complex and ambiguous. But, as argued in chapter 4, they did produce or certainly greatly enhance the position of at least one expanding social group with strong vested interests in separated spheres. The well-being of members of the commercial and industrial middle class required that 'a man must act' in the public sphere. For this reason, it also required domestic specialisation from his womenfolk – to maintain and enhance status, maintain the extended family networks upon which middle-class business fortunes rested, and create havens of peace insulated from the exhausting and corrupting public world.[15]

These undoubtedly inhibiting effects upon political fitness notwithstanding, and even when the separated-spheres doctrine was at its most hegemonic, the real situation was always more complicated, even politically enabling, than the foregoing picture. Historians dispute about whether the nineteenth century witnessed separation at its most powerful and all-embracing, or its increasing erosion.[16] Probably, both contentions are partly true. There was certainly nothing new about separated activity along gendered lines. It is strongly arguable that separation, underpinned by patriarchy, and expressed in female dependence, occupational and legal disadvantage, had been characteristic of the eighteenth century and before. Indeed, in some respects, by the early-nineteenth century, women were becoming freer agents than previously. Forced marriages were defunct. They were replaced by more companionate and thus more reciprocal relationships, wherein degrees of negotiation were implied, particularly as husbandly violence amongst at least the middle class rapidly declined. If families were democratising somewhat, it seems reasonable to think that wives would find eventual participation in the wider polity less unnerving than their predecessors from more authoritarian relationships.

On the other hand, the nineteenth century witnessed important changes, ones with potential political relevance. Under the impact of capitalisation and mechanisation, the physical and thus psychological separation of domestic and economic life substantially increased. With more material circumstances to bite on, ever-present separation was now elevated into theory, and moralised by evangelical religion. More particularly, women's domestic role was sanctified by elevating them into carriers and transmission-belts for family moral values. As we shall see, this was not necessarily politically debilitating. However, it deeply affected the middle class from an early stage, received at least verbal support from many working-class spokesmen soon afterwards, and began affecting manual workers' actual behaviour once rising real incomes permitted wives to vacate their mostly unskilled, unrewarding and often unhealthy jobs. There are also grounds for thinking some occupations previously open to women of the middling sort were closing by the late-eighteenth century, as were some roles in family economic activity like farming. So too were the scattering of available skilled manual occupations. Furthermore, the rise of scientific and technical knowledge raised barriers to existing professional occupations, and created many others where access was denied. Women's already peripheral participation in local politics was formally foreclosed for over thirty years by the 1835 Municipal Corporations Act. Meanwhile, their non-existent voting participation in parliamentary elections was formally ruled out by the 1832 Reform Act.

However, even if separation reached a hegemonic peak in Victoria's early years, it was probably short-lived. So far as women's civil-associational access was concerned, it began eroding almost immediately. The very substantial demographic surplus of women over men (already around 655 000 by 1851) rendered total domestic confinement non-viable from the start. Also important here, as in other aspects of British democratisation, were industrialisation and urbanisation. Whilst these forces further separated home and work, they undermined separation in other ways. Not until late-century were working-class real incomes sufficient to permit widespread and secure reliance upon the pay of single male breadwinners. Similar economic necessities, spurred by higher expectations, also weakened the impact of separated spheres amongst the lower middle class. At the same time, demands for unskilled and semi-skilled labour increased far faster than men could, or wanted to, satisfy. Semi-skilled jobs at least required a degree of relatively expensive training. Thus the services even of female incumbents might be required permanently, after as well as before marriage, to points where the practice became normative. If not exactly careers, women's jobs in areas like cotton and pottery-manufacturing could become sources of identity, a degree of equal pay, self-confidence and 'an independent female attitude'.[17] So even more could they in primary-school teaching, long an important occupation for women, and expanding rapidly in the wake of urbanisation and the 1870 Education Act. Such occupations could also generate common interest, thus opening the way for relatively easy union-colonisation.

Accelerating urbanisation and industrialisation also created increasing civil opportunities for middle-class women. These forces intensified, and rendered more visible, social problems and conflicts requiring solution or at least alleviation if existing social and political structures were to be preserved. Their size and complexity, as noted, demanded increasingly organised responses. *Laissez faire*, by inhibiting government, effectively increased the space between state and family: thus responses were necessarily charitable and consequently civil-associational. The very absorption of middle-class males in the public economic world meant the resultant roles were increasingly filled by women.

Here, religion was available to provide legitimisation. If evangelicalism moralised and theorised women's confinement within domesticity, it also helped provide partial escape into civil society through their role as moral transmission-belts. More generally, charity, and increasing numbers of plausibly-connected associational activities, could be portrayed as natural extensions of women's roles as wives and mothers, indeed areas wherein they were uniquely capable.

Furthermore, in the decades up to political inclusion, the contextual situation was changing, and in ways likely to increase the politically-desirable attribute of independence, whilst eroding its opposite. Property-rights within marriage improved in 1870 and 1882, entailing, amongst many other things, the ability to pay associational subscriptions without husbandly permission. So too did access to divorce from 1857. Working-class women beset by violent husbands could apply for separation orders from 1878, and 8000 per annum were doing so by 1906.[18] Meanwhile, industrialisation, mechanisation and expanding government increased the occupations, and thus identities and perhaps interests, open to women. This was particularly evident for the middle class because it included clerical and some professional occupations. Between 1881 and 1901, female commercial clerks burgeoned from 6000 to 56 000; female teachers increased from 123 000 to 176 000. Even the intensely male medical profession had permitted 212 persons of the female persuasion to scuttle into its ranks by 1901.[19] Overall, by 1911, some 260 000 women were engaged in classifiably professional occupations. It was a mark of enhanced autonomy that over 37 000 of these were single women over 45.[20] Admittedly, whilst middle-class women were starting to break away from domesticity, many working-class women began re-embracing it. Yet this hardly eroded autonomy. Rather it was an active and entirely understandable *choice*, given rising real incomes, the unenviable character of most women's manual jobs, and improving respectable working-class housing conditions. Meanwhile, the growing male electorate after 1867 and 1884–5, the 1872 Ballot Act, and the redefining and effective curbing of political corruption in 1883, increased demands for voluntary political labour which men could only partially fill.

As some of this suggests, women's own situation was changing in ways likely to enhance independence and ability to take advantage of these opportunities. The 1870 Education Act, for all its emphasis upon education for domesticity, greatly increased basic literacy-skills. For more socially-elevated girls, secondary education began marked improvement in the same decade. Access to university had begun in the 1860s; by the 1890s, women were being admitted to most faculties in most universities; London had three women's colleges, Oxford and Cambridge six, even if Oxbridge largesse did not actually extend to degrees.[21] Middle-class family size was declining. So too was it in parts of the working class, for example in Lancashire textile areas, a trend widening greatly after 1918. Moreover, this probably partly expressed women's desire for enhanced control over their lives. Independent mobility was improving for middle- and upper-class women, with declining chaperonage and the rise of the bicycle. Finally, and important for some women anyway, this partial escape from domesticity and into enhanced autonomy was underpinned by intellectual revolt against patriarchy – through the 'New Woman' novels of the 1890s, widespread suffragist argument along the same lines in the early-twentieth century, and through productive and long-continuing debate in books and newspapers about the subjugating effects of traditional marriage.[22]

Yet, in some of this, there is the complication already noted for middle- and perhaps working-class men. In a hierarchical and class-bound society, these roads to what some eventually saw as valid sources of political fitness could only be fully travelled by exploiting and emphasising the dependent status of others. If middle-class women, as evident later, gained much of democratically-functional value from charitable endeavour, the recipients of their largesse acquired only dependency. Equally, domestic escape rested upon the labours of the vast servant population, a group, whether male or female, specifically excluded from the franchise until 1918. Mostly, in fact, it was female. Servants constituted the largest women's occupational group until 1939. The 1911 census, the last before political inclusion, recorded some 1 359 359, and there were still 1 332 224 by 1931. In fact, the long term is more complicated. Many servants were under voting age anyway, often regarding their jobs as temporary and transitional. Servanthood has been argued to be a mechanism for the modernisation of rural women: somewhere they could acclimatise to urban life in relative safety (the roving libido of the master of the house notwithstanding) whilst searching for something more attractive and less dependent.[23]

If so, there may be democratic functionality even in servanthood. Yet, its widespread existence points to an even more central characteristic of women's employment: they were mostly located in jobs whose isolation, unskilled or overstocked character, lack of occupational pride or impermanence, rendered them unsympathetic environments for collective protective action. Alongside servanthood, women were heavily concentrated at the domestic and unskilled end of consumer industries like clothing and shoemaking (with work done in homes or sweated workshops) and penny-capitalist trades like charring and washing. Rapidly expanding shop and clerical work in late-century provided environments no more organisationally encouraging – for women or men. Only in a few factory-based industries like cotton weaving and pottery were women located in places where trade unionism flowed reasonably naturally from large and stable workplace collectivities. Also discouraging participation in this branch of civil society were pressures from the double-shift, male union attitudes, as well as women's own feelings that paid work was something undertaken before or between bouts of child-rearing, or to eke out inadequate earnings. These, together with the unpleasant character of most female manual jobs were key reasons why, whilst middle-class women after 1918 somewhat expanded their access to paid work, working-class women increasingly embraced domesticity, an even less promising environment for civil association.

Having examined this somewhat discouraging context, we can explore women's actual relationship to the space between state and family. We start, as with other political entrants, with the media. The general argument will be that coverage of issues and organisations affecting women was increasingly widespread and copious, particularly in the decades around enfranchisement. The content was problematic in some respects. However, commercial reasons, as well as reporting-duty and values, dictated that the printed media were happy to democratise their content when demand required.

2.   Access to the Media

We have noted already that, in terms of basic literacy, women's access to books and newspapers differed little from men's. Indeed, later enfranchisement meant more women could read by the time of their inclusion than male manual workers could by theirs. This was so even if importantly there were fewer means of compensating for illiteracy, fewer locations wherein interests could be easily pursued, and, for working-class though emphatically not middle-class women, less time to do so.

What women primarily had access to was of course male-dominated. Whatever our general argument, we should note that newspapers, periodicals and publishing houses were owned, managed and reported to by men. 'News' might often be non-gender-specific, as we shall argue. Nevertheless, in male-dominated national and international society, most events reported were generated, transmitted and interpreted by men. Obviously, there are questions about newspapers' ability and willingness to respond to events and organisations generated by women.

In one sense, the issue barely arises. However generated, many political events, policies and areas were as likely to be relevant to women and their interests as to men. If foreign policy, much of domestic policy, riots, agitations, sermons, and speeches affected social groups in different ways, this was determined as much by class, religion, region or locality as by gender. Assuming wives could get their hands on the newspaper, there is no prima facie case for thinking them any less interested in these matters than their husbands. What was different, of course, was the legitimacy of their interest. On some readings of separation, politics belonged to the corrupting world from which women needed protection, except perhaps in carefully-modulated doses from some proximate male.

Newspapers, particularly local weeklies, also copiously reported activity in which women were more directly interested because it was part of the public world wherein they could directly participate. Most obvious was the reportage of the burgeoning middle-class-dominated world of philanthropy. This was always generous; as women's charitable activity increased, this too was faithfully set down. It might not receive special prominence, but, given women's participation reached its zenith around the same late-century time that local newspapers reached maximum size and numbers, it would have been hard to miss assuming the absence of deep slumber. Indeed, elite-women became as adept as their husbands at commanding attention from editors in introspective urban localities – through reportage and advertisements of the 'honorary committees' on which 'ladies' increasingly served. So much so indeed that it becomes possible to talk about paternalism being female-transmitted.[24] If they were role models for their lowly sisters, and if indeed they were the mechanism through which deference, dependency and didactic messages about self-help were increasingly transmitted, then local newspapers represented crucial means whereby this was achieved. This was particularly so from the late-nineteenth century as local weeklies began increasingly seeing themselves as family newspapers, beamed as much at women as men, and at all social levels. Moreover, newspapers, again particularly local ones, probably bore further responsibility for charitable growth, and thus women's participation in public life, through their periodic and verbose 'expeditions' into the local slums in quest of shocking copy. Furthermore, as women's activities spread into other areas of social and political life, this too was recorded, if rarely highlighted.

What initially received less attention, but later increasing coverage, were women's 'interests'. These can be defined in two ways: activities which women found *interesting*; and areas and policies that women deemed, or might decide, *in their interests*. Coverage of the first, though evident early-on (via 'conduct books'), was increasingly marked from the 1890s as newspaper editors, magazine entrepreneurs and advertisers began identifying women (especially middle- and upper-class ones) as increasingly important potential readers and temptable consumers. By the 1890s, extended women's columns were almost obligatory in most daily, Sunday and local newspapers. By around 1905, there were also women's pages in the likes of *Co-operative News*, *Labour Leader* and *Justice*. Many newspapers, particularly of the profit-oriented 'new-journalistic' kind, carried increasingly prominent advertising specifically directed at women. 'New journalism' also produced proliferating numbers of women's magazines. Many were edited, if not owned, by women.

The problem for feminists, indeed committed democrats, is three-fold. First, socialist publications aside, most of the foregoing material, in the early stages especially, was aimed at lower-middle-class women and above. Second, the content was determinedly domestic, fashion-oriented, romantic and apolitical. Third, most columns and magazines were beamed at women in the home; few drew them into associational life. Furthermore, they proliferated in the decades up to enfranchise-ment, and with the decline of feminism and many women's retreat from paid work into the increasingly inviting home, did so even more in the 1920s and 1930s and immediately after 1945. By the 1950s, five out of every six women were reading at least one of these domesticated heavyweights.[25] If serious issues were addressed, they were primarily those of household-budgeting, child-care, health, and, before 1914, servant-management. Furthermore, in the early years particularly, be-cause they were edited by upper-class women and directed at social inferiors, their tone was often didactic. They probably caused many readers to feel more anxious, inadequate, and thus less self-confident, within and even more outside, the domestic sphere.[26] What they rarely challenged, and instead celebrated, was separation itself.

Yet such columns and periodicals probably did contribute to one important and democratically-functional development. Housework and motherhood began constituting a sort of profession, in whose skills practitioners could take pride. As a result, 'the housewife' could achieve a viable identity, and acquire a vested interest that, with emerging full democracy after 1918, politicians found it increasingly advisable to competitively appease. Besides government's increasing economic role, this is one reason why prices became an increasingly important inter-war issue.

This aside, what newspapers and periodicals might seem less good at addressing were issues women deemed *in their interests*. Even this is challengeable. Periodicals and newspapers, with their attachment to serious reporting, particularly from the 1880s gave considerable cover-age to women's issues. They were the main means through which the gathering debate about marriage, with its extended reflections on women's disadvantaged and subjugated position therein, found expres-sion: starting with Mona Caird's articles in *The Westminster Review* in 1888, closely followed and to a far wider audience by *The Daily Telegraph* series 'Is Marriage a Failure', with its 27 000 responses.[27] Similarly, *The Pall Mall Gazette*'s sensational 'Maiden Tribute' articles on white slavery boosted the feminist agenda after the campaign against the Contagious Diseases Acts was won in 1886. Daily and Sunday newspapers also extensively covered the Jackson and Lanchester court cases in the 1890s, thus dramatising women's continued legal disadvantages in face of oppressive husbands and fathers.

There was also much reportage of women's and women-dominated political organisations and agitations. To a degree, this was evident even in the climactic period of working-class radicalism before 1850. News-papers noticed women's participation in riots against food prices and the New Poor Law. They also noted female Chartist activity. Such repor-tage was often highly disparaging and patronising, though little more than that covering the activities of radical males. Gender merely added additional excuses for denigration to newspapers not just male-, but also middle-class, dominated. Women's political organisations appearing from the 1870s received increasing, and more detached, coverage from papers even more wedded to verbatim reporting. Indeed, such organisations' ability to reach and inform potential supporters, and influence the political agenda by dramatising issues like the legal disabil-ities of prostitutes and the double-standards these entailed, Social Purity and suffragism, all rested heavily upon male-dominated newspapers and periodicals, with their liberal traditions and increasingly competitive circulation battles. The efforts of women's trade unionism and the Co-operative Women's Guild relied on publicity from union and co-operative house-papers, though the latters' inadequacies also necessitated crucial supplementation from the likes of *The Women's Trade Union Review*. Certainly, the efforts of the Co-operative Union's Central Board to close the agenda of discussion against issues raised by the Guild[28] had little effect on the women's columns of *The Co-operative News*. Indeed, articles and letters there were the main means whereby conflicts between Guild and Union, and indeed within the Guild, over centralisation, relations with the Co-operative and Labour Parties, the 'political rule' and pacifism, were pursued before and after the 1914–18 War.

More problematic was the supply of journals and newspapers directed exclusively at women's and feminist issues, due partly to inhibitions derived from separated spheres, partly women's relative lack of access to capital and partly feminist weakness before 1870. Indeed, before this date, there was nothing, apart from the moderate *English Woman's Journal*, which between 1858 and 1864 determinedly publicised issues of employment, education, training, but not the vote.[29] Nevertheless, after 1870, such publications began emerging in greater numbers; indeed, nearly all the contemporary women's movements produced one or more. The campaign against the Contagious Diseases Acts published *The Shield*. The Social Purity Alliance found expression via *The Vigilance Record*. Women's trade unionism publicised and nationalised its activities through *The Woman's Trade Union Review* from 1876, Annie Besant's *The Link* and *The Woman Worker*. The Women's Co-operative Guild supplemented reportage in *The Co-operative News* with *The Guildswoman* and *Woman's Outlook*, along with numerous pamphlets on more specific issues. Labour and Liberal women also had their own journals. So even more did the various wings of political feminism: *Common Cause* (NUWSS); *Votes for Women* and *The Suffragette* for the WSPU; and *The Vote* (Women's Freedom League). Other suffragist journals included Lydia Becker's *The Woman's Suffrage Journal*, which ran for twenty years from the commencement of enfranchisement agitation in 1869, *The Woman's Franchise* and *The Woman's Suffrage Record*. Equal rights feminism found expression for its views about women's jobs and factory regulation in *The Englishwoman's Review*. Feminism's various branches also expressed themselves in numerous pamphlets, whilst the 'new women' of the 1890s founded a variety of journals.

Some key issues were explored through books. The period between 1880 and 1939 saw unprecedented discussion of marital and sexual relations. Some was via the press, as noted. Some was through non-fiction. This was particularly evident in the years around enfran-chisement. Prominent publications included Marie Stopes' *Married Love* published in 1918 and selling 400 000 by 1923, and *Wise Parenthood* in the same year and reaching 300 000 by 1924. Eleanor Rathbone began her long campaign for family allowances through *The Disinherited Family* in 1917. Other books more specifically focused on marriage itself included Vera Brittain's *Halcyon, or the Future of Monogamy* (1930) and Margaret Cole's *Marriage: Past and Present* (1939).

In fact, there was a more distinctive location for dispersing feminist views, if not activities. Perhaps the place where women's issues were most often, certainly most approachably, addressed was fiction. Gender-identity and grievance found expression in novels far more often than those of class (*The Ragged Trousered Philanthropists* notwithstanding). This is unsurprising for two reasons. First, women read them far more than men; second, novels were highly appropriate, persuasive ways of ad-dressing issues that, apart from the franchise, most often troubled feminists, particularly before 1914. What concerned them most were relations between the sexes, particularly the ways in which institutions like marriage perpetuated women's exploitation and disadvantage. Indeed, even the vote was seen as a means of alleviating such problems. Far more than newspaper articles and pamphlets, novels could effect-ively explore problems that, however much related to societal structures, were enacted at inter-personal levels. Hence, whilst there were 'new woman' journals in the 1890s, this particular attack upon the conse-quences for women of contemporary gender relations, and the construc-tion of alternative models of femininity, was primarily conducted through numerous novels by men and women writers.

Nevertheless, as with men's access to the media, caution is appropri-ate. There were undoubtedly substantial and lengthening avenues through which women's interests and issues could be pursued, and their civil organisations publicised, particularly in the decades around political inclusion. Nevertheless, even more than with men, it is hard to know how many women came across the serious debates being laid before them. For there was much other material at best democratically neutral. Contemporary surveys suggest most working-class women, if they read at all, read romantic novelettes rather than new woman novels. If they were influenced by serious debate, it focused on class rather than gender. Here, as elsewhere, there seems little evidence that feminism touched working women's lives and perceptions in the way class-based radicalism periodically touched those of many of their husbands, and indeed their own. However, to take matters further, we must consider access to civil association itself.

3. Access to Civil Organisation

Three points need making at the outset relevant to the rest of the chapter. First, as already implied, class, and the distinctive ways different classes ordered their gender relations, were far more important in determining access to civil association amongst women than men. As seen in the previous three chapters, though associating together in very varied sorts of organisation, most men, irrespective of class, had some sort of access by around 1900. Moreover, apart from those at the lowest social level, working men were just as attached to associational life as their middle-class counterparts; many, indeed, were multiply attached. This was clearly not the case amongst women. Operative here was the way separated spheres intersected with class. Although separation had far more effect in denying middle- and upper-class women access to the job market, the greater availability of money, education and leisure, and their ability to call upon the services of mostly female servants gave them far greater access than their working-class counterparts to increasing sectors of civil society – initially organised charity and religion, then expanding sectors of politics. Indeed, the suffrage campaign was clearly sustained by expectations of entitlement generated amongst middle-class women by their increasingly rich and overlapping attachment to other parts of civil society, and for some the resultant indignation about enfranchised but allegedly feckless working men. So great was this attachment that, for far longer and more extensively than amongst equivalent men, it was middle-class women who led many working-class women into civil association, particularly trade unionism. Notwithstanding these efforts, working-class women's access to civil society was markedly more impoverished: due to working-class male attitudes, the unskilled and unrewarding nature of women's paid-work, and pressures from the 'double-shift'. Furthermore, although informal street-society might provide useful points of solidarity and support, it was less useful in training women for participation in any broader democracy where formal organisation was increasingly central. However, we can note in passing that street-society was capable of generating effective agitation, given sufficient indignation. Almost certainly, it was the initial basis for the formidable agitation about rents in the years leading up to the 1915 Rent Act.

Second, as this perhaps implies, civil-associational access for many women was increasing and accelerating around the time of formal political inclusion. It was a tribute to the vibrancy of the civil infrastructure of Britain's developing democracy that very significant pockets of organised activity developed even amongst working-class women, and these increased in the decades around 1918. Overall, given the constraints, women's access to civil organisation was arguably remarkable rather than disappointing.

Third, due to separated spheres, much of the civil association to which women had access was initially, and often for some time thereafter, male-dominated. This means the notion of self-governance is partly about influence upon male self-governing processes. As before, we will explore the various sectors of organised civil life in turn.

One area to which women of all classes were drawn was organised religion. Their participation was underpinned by their role as repositories and transmitters of family virtue, perhaps too by their sense of being the bearers of life. For whatever reason, from at least the seventeenth century, more women than men were regular communicants in all segments of organised religion. Amongst the middle class, churchgoing was obligatory, for women as for men. If there was a difference, it was in the number of services attended each Sunday. Amongst the far less observant working class, gender difference was probably markedly more evident. However this may be, though there are few specific studies of women and religion and few useable figures, women probably formed the majority of worshippers amongst most religious groups before and during democratisation. They probably constituted 45–70 per cent attenders at Anglican and Nonconformist churches and chapels between 1700 and 1850.[30] Overall percentages of worshippers recorded in the 1851 Census almost certainly disguise higher proportions of women than men, and the pattern probably continued throughout the century, particularly amongst the working class. Evidence for all denominations in late-nineteenth-century West Yorkshire suggests that women steadily constituted around 70 per cent of membership by late-century.[31] Furthermore, many of the multiple ancillary organisations individual churches and chapels constructed around themselves in the later-nineteenth century were directed at women. In Lambeth in 1899–1900, these included at least 57 mothers meetings, 27 girls and young women's clubs, 21 clothing clubs and 10 maternity societies – along with various others like temperance clubs and bible classes where women probably participated alongside men.[32] In such organisations, women took increasing responsibility, and began exercising significant author-ity.[33]

For increasingly many women, particularly middle- and upper-class ones, commitment to organised religion slipped seamlessly into charit-able activity, both via religious ancillary organisations, and because charity seemed a natural extension of the moral and caring roles of wife and mother. Participation was evident early-on, and charities rapidly became dependent upon their activity. Belfast's Charitable Soci-ety had a Ladies Committee from 1814 for example, and women were evident in Birmingham's philanthropic life from at least the 1830s.[34] By the 1850s, they were not just active in mixed societies, but also in hundreds of women-only charities. Participation expanded steadily through the century, increasingly outpacing men's, rising even more rapidly in the decades around enfranchisement. In 1893, it was esti-mated that approximately 500 000 women worked 'continuously and semi-professionally' in voluntary activities.[35] Philanthropy also attracted working-class women as both recipients and activists: the Mothers Union, founded in 1876 (and building on local unions emerging from around 1850), had 278 500 members by 1910 and 400 000 by 1916, many very poor. It has been termed 'the most pervasive female agency for bringing women together on regular bases outside the home in British history'.[36] From around 1900, new forms of charity began emerging, including many women-only organisations, most notably the Women's Voluntary Service, Townswomen's Guilds, and the Women's Institute whose 1200 constituent units by 1919 demonstrated, in what Alun Howkins has called 'the greatest revolution of all', that women's civil organisation had extended widely into rural, as well as urban, areas.[37]

Philanthropy, then, was one field where women's civil associational attachment was extensive, and, though socially uneven, extended beyond the middle class, particularly by the time of enfranchisement. Things are less clear cut amongst associations broadly classifiable as economic. Participation here was equally uneven socially, though in very different ways. Since nineteenth-century women were excluded from most entrepreneurial and professional activity, it is unsurprising that they were also largely absent from associated collective organisations. In most, aside from teaching, if they participated at all, it was as 'wives and sweethearts' at the dinners, excursions, and other social activities bur-geoning amongst these organisations from the late-nineteenth century. If they had influence, it was over this area: 'the gas engineer is companionable . . . so are his wife and family'.[38] Their absence from professional life excluded them from one of the most vibrant sectors of associational economic activity. Even in small business, where nine-teenth-century women continued participating, they were largely absent from the feeble collective efforts of shopkeepers and house-landlords, also from the more formidable ones of the drink trade and some specialised retailers.

Yet we should note that, as women began emerging in the professions, they also started appearing in the relevant collective organisations. Again, this is particularly evident in the decades around enfranchise-ment. By 1914, there was a separate women teachers' union, and 45 016 women in teaching organisations overall.[39] It is perhaps a significant tribute to the importance of civil organisation, and to the multiple interests that jobs that were genuine careers could engender, that teach-ing was an important recruiting ground for political feminism before and after the First World War.[40]

Nevertheless, middle-class women were hardly prominent in occupa-tional collectivity before 1914. The pattern was somewhat different amongst working-class women. Since the vast majority of the one-third of the workforce who were women were in manual occupations, and since working-class women were the main household consumers, it is unsurprising to discover them in the corresponding protective organ-isations. Yet, they participated far less than their male counterparts, and, in unions, with less apparent enthusiasm.

Until at least 1939, women were consistently seen by male union leaders as unpromising soil for unionisation. Membership figures appar-ently provided equally consistent support for such gloom. In 1886, there were very approximately 36 900. This had risen to 142 000 (around 3.2 per cent of the female workforce and 9.1 per cent of union membership) by 1892, and 433 000 by 1913. These represented around 8 per cent of the female workforce and 10.5 per cent total membership. Nearly half were located in the highly-unionised textile industry. In 1920, unionised women peaked at around 1 341 000, 16.1 per cent of membership and 25 per cent of working women. Even this could be contrasted with the 50 per cent of the male workforce that was unionised. Thereafter membership receded, under the impact of post-war depression, to around 871 000 in 1922, a 35 per cent decline contrasted with 32 per cent for men, and causing the TUC Women's Group to institute an enquiry into the causes of this apparently perennial problem. By 1933, the figure had slipped further to 728 000, still around 16 per cent of total membership.[41]

The reasons for this apparent relative indifference are understandable. As noted, women, due to male attitudes and domestic responsibilities, were located in the least skilled, most impermanent, isolated and overstocked sectors of the workforce, where unionisation even for men was most difficult and insecure. This, together with pressures from the double-shift, and the fact that work was rarely more than a prelude to marriage or supplement to an inadequate 'family wage', even in the burgeoning service industries from late-century, meant unions were unavailable or unattractive to many women. Nor were male-dominated unions necessarily welcoming to female membership, still less to their participation, particularly in the exclusive and long-resilient artisan segments of the economy, or amongst factory occupations where artisan traditions remained strong.[42] Even amongst the steadily multiplying unions open to, or even seeking to unionise, women, the rhetoric was often less than inclusive. It rather assumed the real members, and real owners of the rights and privileges union membership brought, were male. The assumptions that women's employment was a regrettable necessity, and their 'proper place' was at home, were sometimes explicit, often barely implicit. This only confirmed what many women workers, at the nineteenth-century's end, as at its start, tended to believe anyway. Moreover, women's union activity might have unwelcome consequences for husbands, who regarded time off from the family as their property.

Yet, little of this suggests innate female indifference to this branch of civil society, and only some acquired disinterest. In suitable circumstances of job security, where women worked alongside men at reasonably comparable pay-rates, where work after marriage was legitimate, and where workplace situations encouraged solidarity, women could become as enthusiastic about trade unionism as their male comrades. In the manual sector, the most obvious example is powerloom weaving, which women dominated, where they were involved in strikes from an early stage, and attempts to unionise them began in the 1830s. They were substantial components of membership as soon as unionism became a permanent fixture. By 1896, there were 102 847 women in cotton textile unions, and by 1913, some 214 109.[43] Teaching, which had long offered at least unmarried women the chance of careers (after the 1870s, increasingly trained), was also a substantial centre of unionisation as we have noted. Furthermore, figures already quoted show women shared the great accelerations of general union membership, particularly around the First World War and enfranchisement, partly because of the foundation of women-only unions (25 were claimed to exist in Scotland alone by 1895[44]), and partly because more male unions were allowing women entry from the 1880s. In this, they were encouraged by emerging bodies like the Women's Trade Union League, women's trades councils and later women's subsidiaries of the TUC. By 1914, aside from textiles and teaching, there were numerous unionised women (45016) in commerce, distribution and national and local government,[45] and a unionised presence in many other trades. It is also noticeable that, for all the effects of inter-war depression, and the worries of the TUC, the proportionate fall in women's union membership (35 per cent 1920–2) was little different from men's (32 per cent), and membership began rising steadily again from the mid-1930s. By 1948 it had re-attained its 1920 peak of 25 per cent of the female workforce. This suggests that, in the years around enfranchisement, women's attachment to this segment of civil society, if not as widespread as men's, was nevertheless substantial (given the constraints, 25 per cent is arguably more remarkable than disappointing), and equally resilient. Perhaps most significant from our present perspective, women were more evident in British unions than in those of most other countries.[46]

In the co-operative movement, like unions, membership and its privileges were primarily male – at least in the early decades and after Owenism's collapse. However, their role as primary consumers meant women members became increasingly important. Since figures are not categorised by gender, we cannot say how many women belonged to co-operative societies: they seem to have emerged earlier in the South where co-operation was weaker but newer than in the more traditional North. G.D.H. Cole estimates around 100 000 of the Co-op's one million members by 1889 were female.[47] The Women's Co-operative Guild probably attracted only the most active women co-operators, drawn, for all its efforts to extend co-operation to the poor, from the more secure working class. Nevertheless, this is a useful indicator of activism. It is doubly interesting because most Guild members were non-employed housewives,[48] with therefore only limited overlap with women trades unionists, thereby increasing our overall estimate of women's civil attachment. From its inception in 1883, the organisation grew steadily to 12 809 and 273 branches in 1900, 32 182 and 600 in 1914, peaking in 1939 at 87 246 and 1819. From 1890, it began establishing its own regional councils to parallel the Co-operative union's. In terms of geographical spread, the Guild matched the more general co-operative movement except that it was also strong in the south east. Scotland (and Ireland from 1906) had its own Guild, with 24 300 members by 1942, considerably higher proportionate to population than England. By 1939, most of the Co-op's 8 643 000 members were probably female. This might involve most in little beyond shopping. However, since membership implied ownership and of course the dividend, it probably attached them to the organisation in ways shopping at other chain-stores could never do.

Friendly societies, though again predominantly male, also had a significant female contingent and from an almost equally early stage. Many women's societies started in the 1770s. Of the London societies registering under the 1794 Friendly Society Act, 82 (15 per cent) were female. Though these later declined sharply as women became more economically marginal, industrial areas, with many women employed, recorded substantial female participation. One-third of Stockport's societies in the years 1794–1823 were for women. In 1824, the proportion was 16 per cent in Nottinghamshire, 27 per cent in Cheshire, 18 per cent in Lancashire and 35 per cent in Leicester.[49] By mid-century, there were Female Druids, Gardeners, Rechabites, Foresters and Shepherdesses. In 1872, the Friendly-Societies Registrar recorded 283 female societies, of which 237 had a combined membership of 22 690. This probably underestimates even registered societies, and many remained unregistered.[50]

Meanwhile from the early-twentieth century, women figured prominently in another rapidly developing segment of economic self-defence – tenants' associations. These centres of resistance to rent increases became particularly prominent after 1912, especially during the wartime rent agitation. In these, particularly around 1914–15, women played crucial roles.[51]

Women's links to political civil society followed the pattern of the economic and social sectors. For many years, their attachments were weaker than men's. Unlike men's, they were also far stronger amongst middle- than amongst working-class women. However, as has been the general pattern with previous candidates for political inclusion, even these were increasing around enfranchisement. For middle-class women particularly, politics was the most sullying part of the corrupting public world from which separated spheres theoretically protected them. Indeed, for women, establishing political fitness involved not just the vote, but also the appropriateness of any political participation, even for the highly educated. This made initial access to political association crucial to establishing wider legitimacy.

Due to fears about them being ensnared by 'the warfare of political life',[52] women were absent from the many early pressure-group activities that so involved their male counterparts, participating little in the 1831–2 Reform agitation for example. If they joined, women did so with due apology and explanation, and always in ways appropriate to their gender: settling down to organise bazaars and mass 'tea parties' for the cause. Even so, there was an extended succession of moral and politicised philanthropic causes to which middle-class women gained defensible access through portraying them as natural extensions of their caring and virtue-carrying domestic roles. For example, from 1825, nearly a century before political inclusion, many women participated actively in movements against Britain's role in the slave trade. Wilberforce's reservations notwithstanding, one-third of all societies by 1831 were run by women and a similar proportion of petitions against slavery in 1833 came from this source.[53] They also played significant roles in the campaigns for prison reform and, throughout the century, temperance.

Furthermore, building on experience and self-confidence gained in locations like anti-slavery, this participation broadened over time, becoming increasingly feminist, more unashamedly partisan, and then directed at political inclusion. During the 1850s, there emerged societies for reforming married-women's property law, promoting women's employment and (in Sheffield) enfranchisement. In 1866, Lydia Becker founded the National Society for Women's Suffrage, becoming its central figure until her death in 1890, and helping legitimise the notion of women as public political speakers.[54] Equally significant, the 1870s saw the emergence of the campaign against the Contagious Diseases Acts, with its increasingly formidable Ladies National Association. By the 1880s, this was increasingly a nation-wide movement, strongly supported in London, the south east, and northern England, drawing particularly upon Nonconformist women. The LNA, like its male counterpart, was increasingly a mass movement: drawing women into active petitioning and, even more significantly, electoral politics on behalf of parliamentary supporters and against opponents.[55] The double standards involved in the treatment of prostitutes and their male clients so central to the situation the Acts created, and the self-confidence gained by constant campaigning, drew many women into related movements like Social Purity. feminism and ultimately suffragism.

It also probably drew many into partisan politics, particularly on the Liberal side. Women had never been wholly excluded. However, female mass politics really emerged in the 1880s. At this point, the emergence of a mass male electorate, the secret ballot and effective curbs on electoral corruption, combined to terminate the paid canvasser's long and profitable career, and fully inaugurate the activist's. With insufficient men to go round, parties turned to women, in the process fuelling the growth of the Women's Liberal Federation, and accelerating women's increasing domination of the Primrose League. Beginning in 1887, the WLF had 177 branches and around 52 000 women members (an additional 15 000 being supportive or confused men) by 1891, while the breakaway Women's Liberal Unionist Association had 26 and 5000 respectively. By 1897, the WLF spread even more widely across the country, reaching 501 branches and 80,000 members. By its peak in 1912, it possessed 837 branches and 133 215 members.[56] However, women Liberals could never match their less politicised but equally politically loyal Primrose League counterparts. Founded in 1883, but only fully coming into its own after the Tory elite decided to sideline the temporarily troublesome National Union, the League opened its doors to women in 1885. At its peak in 1901, this male-led but female-dominated organisation comprised around 1,250,000 members of whom 700,000 were women, and was 'the largest and most widely spread political organisation of the time'. As Martin Pugh has observed, it covered the entire country, there being no constituency without a habitation, and was often strong in Liberal as well as Tory-dominated areas. Only in Scotland was it consistently weak.[57]

Female party-political participation was not exclusively middle class. However, beyond a few areas like Lancashire and perhaps East London, and except amongst politicised women on the working-class left, like those in the WCG and ILP, suffragism was broadly middle class. Nevertheless, starting in 1866, it became part of what Gillian Scott has called 'a rich culture of organisations, networks and individuals'.[58] Given their rather fissiparous nature, few organisations greatly overlapped in membership, even if they did in activity.[59] By 1907, the constitutionalist wing primarily comprised the National Union of Women's Suffrage Societies, a federation of organisations from all over Britain, whilst the civilly-disobedient WSPU had managed to discharge the Women's Freedom League, and was shortly to eject the East London Federation and the Votes for Women Fellowship. Though few membership figures are available, suffrage demonstrations in the decade before

1914 were regularly drawing crowds estimated in tens of thousands, sometimes up to 150,000, and producing petitions signed by 289,000 (1909). By this time, there were also the Women's Local Government Society and the Women's Guardian Society, dedicated to promoting local political candidature. Meanwhile, WSPU tactics had counter-produced the increasingly formidable Women's Anti-Suffrage League, with 33 000 members and 235 branches by mid-1913, and which in 1908 spawned a petition of over 337,000.[60] Even when fiercely defending separated spheres, middle-class women's civil political involvement was impressive. Meanwhile, after 1918 and with the vote won, the various suffrage organisations transformed and proliferated further into myriad other organisations with varyingly feminist agendas, sitting alongside intermittently political but more conservative organisations like the Women's Institutes.

The separation of spheres was initially less (perhaps *even* less) inhibiting to working-class women's political involvement. However, far less of this was associational rather than 'spontaneous', and separation alongside sheer exhaustion produced considerably more problems in the longer-run than for middle-class women. The late-eighteenth and first half of the nineteenth century saw considerable political activity from working-class women. Particularly where protests were communal, informal, 'pre-industrial' and 'spontaneous', or where their roles as wives, mothers and family-defenders appeared directly involved, women could become very visible indeed. Their presence was strongly evident in the bread, enclosure and Highland-clearance riots to a point where they, and/or men disguised as women, appeared in front, shouting defiance and protecting the crowd from soldiers accurately assumed too inhibited by their presence to attack. Women were evident also amongst early 'industrial crowds': for example at Peterloo, where the Yeomanry appear not to have shared the professionals' sense of propriety; and in early Chartism, which exhibited over 150 female associations in England and 23 in Scotland. Female Chartism in both countries was strongly represented in the textile districts, just as suffragism was to be before 1914. Women were also prominent in the Anti-Poor Law agitation. If Rochdale's experience was typical, they were sometimes highly visible in Anti-Church-Rates agitations. Finally, to judge from parliamentary petitions in 1828, women were just as good as men at hating Catholics in organised ways.[61]

However, most historians have regarded this role as fading increasingly from the 1840s. For some, it did so at the precise point when radical and other forms of working-class politics became more formally organised, thus less amenable to understandings, skills and perspectives derived from women's family and communal roles. Though this may rest upon somewhat dim views of the political capacities of working-class women, the 'double-shift' undoubtedly made it difficult to cope with the time-consuming regularities of 'representative and responsible' political organisation which was the inevitable requirement of mass politics in an urbanising world. Furthermore, street-society, however rich and supportive, provided only limited training for associational politics. Anna Clark may also be correct in ascribing women's political decline to the growing primacy of sexually-exclusive artisan notions of radical citizenship over more community-based traditions.[62] Whatever the reason, women probably faded from Chartism once the National Charter Association got underway, and were largely absent from the 1866–7 Reform agitations. With exceptions already noted, working-class women were probably largely indifferent to all forms of pre-war suffragism.[63] Supported by servants, middle- and upper-class women had no such problems.

However, this impression of working-class disinterest in women's politics can be exaggerated. Participation was significant and increasing in the years around enfranchisement; and again we may wonder whether to be more impressed by its extent or paucity, given the constraints. Working-class women were also probably more politically involved than elsewhere in Europe. There certainly were significant exceptions to the general apathetic picture. Jill Liddington and Jill Norris show that suffragism drew substantial working-class support in Lancashire's textile areas, where it was reinforced by other, economic, forms of civil association like trade unions.[64] The Women's Co-operative Guild was also strongly suffragist, though increasingly within broader commitments to adult suffrage.[65] There was also extensive women's activism in the ILP, not surprisingly because, early-on, the party built its support through local social protests about the Poor Law, housing conditions and similar issues.[66] In 1906, the Women's Labour League was formed. This gave way to the Labour Party's Women's Section in 1918, which by 1926 claimed to have 1656 branches and 250 000 members, located particularly in small towns and villages.[67] One of the most formidable inter-war pressure groups was the National Spinsters Association, with 108 branches, claiming around 1 500 000 members by 1939, and able to mobilise a petition from one million people in favour of pensions for single women in 1937.[68] At the political spectrum's other end, the Primrose League drew support from many working-class women, as did mass Protestant demonstrations against Home Rule 1912–1914.[69]

4. Self-Governance

We must now explore how these various organisations ran themselves. How far were they internally democratic; how far did women's access to sexually-mixed organisations give them genuine influence; how far was any of this experience capable of producing transferable democratic skills and values?

Three points need making at the outset. First, since class importantly influenced women's access to civil society, it also affected the availability of skills and values. If civil society produced democratic training, then this was more readily available to upper- and middle- than working-class women. One symptom was how important middle-class women were even in organisations directed further down the social scale: the tradition of gentlewomen leaders persisted far longer amongst women than their male equivalents. Nevertheless, civil opportunities for political training were spreading across the social spectrum in the decades around enfranchisement.

Second, as with previous political entrants, and unsurprisingly given the manifold linkages between the sexes, women's organisations were not just 'civil', in the sense of being voluntary and occupying the space between state and family. They were also 'civic', in that, almost without exception, they were attached to the broader national and local polities by values, commitment, participation and visible ritual. Women were thereby drawn into electoral and pressure-group politics. Later, they were inducted into national and local legislatures, as well as on to Royal Commissions and the like. They were increasingly represented in national and local ceremonials.

Third, and connectedly, nearly all women's organisations followed the key rituals of democratic accountability – the pre-advertised AGM open to all members, annual reports from officers, annual election rituals. As noted before, these are inherent in the character of voluntary organisation, and there is no reason to think them any more meaningless or oligarchy-concealing than exclusively male associations.

Let us begin with religion. As with men, women's participation varied according to the scope each church permitted its lay members, plus whatever additional inhibitions were incurred as the result of gender. It was most narrowly constrained within the Catholic Church. Judaism, without a clear notion of a priesthood, allowed the male segment of synagogue congregations significant access to self-governance, but far less to their wives and daughters, though women were certainly prominent and increasingly influential in the proliferating ancillary organisations attached to synagogues.[70]

Anglicanism, as noted, offered limited popular participation in Church affairs via parish meetings. Women leypayers were permitted to attend alongside their male counterparts. In some places at least, they participated with some vigour in electing churchwardens and sidesmen. However, since popular participation was most intense over church rates, many, perhaps most, would have been Nonconformists. On the other hand, the rapidly-expanding ancillary organisations attached to all churches especially from the 1870s provided women, particularly middle-class ones, with extensive space for participation, including the decision-making kind. This may well have fuelled their increasing role within the church as deaconesses, and as participants on the parochial councils emerging in late-century, and in the Anglican National Assembly established in 1920.

All dissenting sects from the seventeenth century onwards believed their members were spiritually equal, though few allowed women effective access to decision-making. The Quakers were most open, permitting women to prophesy, speak and participate in charitable and missionary work on the same terms as men. They could even publish tracts and administer funds. Yet, with the Restoration in 1660, even Quakers began constraining what women could do. In 1670, they took the ambiguous step of establishing separate women's meetings, with responsibility for the high-spending area of poor relief, but excluded them from their more general consultative processes. Furthermore, the Quakers were the only group with such roles on offer.

Methodism permitted women to preach, though without official recognition, from 1761. This was an opening particularly for working-class women, and quite large numbers actively exploited it, both in England and Ireland. However, from the late-eighteenth century, they were increasingly marginalised as Wesleyanism sought respectability and professionalised its preaching, banning women from the activity altogether after 1803. Some sects remained more welcoming, notably the millenarians, Bible Christians and Primitive Methodists, whose foundation indeed partly rested upon this right. However, even here, women served only short periods. Again, they had little access to other official positions or decision-making, and their preaching role declined steadily with the demise of cottage and millenarian religion.[71]

Anyway, except perhaps though collective memory, little of this can have had functional consequences for the longer-term democratic future. More significant are the indications of women emerging as chapel officials, in some locations anyway, in the late-nineteenth century.[72] At least equally important was the extensive way religiosity drew them into philanthropy, both that attached to churches and chapels through ever-multiplying ancillary organisations, and the expanding network of more secular charities. Women were permitted, even encouraged, into charitable activism by separated spheres and evangelical doctrine. Equally encouraging was the need to 'personalise' the charitable 'gift' to ensure it attracted proper gratitude and deference. This could only be achieved through visiting. The fact that so many recipients of handouts, advice and missionary endeavour were other women meant men trod reticently here. Thus charities increasingly relied upon female labour, and eventually expertise.

This situation gave women increasing clout within philanthropic organisations, and eventually drew some into politics. David Owen argues women played important roles in managing London's maternity hospitals from the 1770s.[73] We have also noted the creation of a Ladies Committee in Belfast's Charitable Society from 1824, significantly at the urgent request of the male executive committee, and women's real influence in areas like prison administration. Though active and influential, Belfast's committee died later from apathy. However, most charities saw increasing participation at AGMs and on committees from the 1850s: first on women-only sub-committees, then central executives. This gave them real influence on charitable policy, and probably had other democratically functional consequences. Just as women's participation could be legitimised by reference to their caring domestic roles, this participation in turn probably expanded the range of legitimate concerns, particularly as charities steadily expanded their fields of interest. Furthermore, Frank Prochaska argues that visiting areas and people who were dirty, poor and even hostile, along with the need to outface male-dominated executive committees, gave activists self-confidence, personal toughness and negotiating skill that protective separation would otherwise have prevented.[74] Such potentialities were enhanced by high middle-class ambitions about value-transfer, and thus persuasion. For those graduating into service on Boards of Guardians, Education Boards and Councils, those moving seamlessly into the pressure-group activities in which charities increasingly became involved, or for those becoming Primrose-League stalwarts, charity was a source of political training. This was particularly so given that late-Victorian philanthropy and local government expanded contemporaneously and inter-dependently, and women tended to form bridges between the two. This was doubly evident once organisations like the COS, Guilds of Help and National Union of Women Workers began uniting women across the country in common social-work concerns, and became increasingly interested in getting women into local government.[75]

Meanwhile, many women, facing the mismatch between charitable cruciality and votelessness, or the double-standards involved in the treatment of prostitutes and their clients, were drawn into more active defence of collective interest through feminism. Such perspectives were probably particularly available amongst the multiplying women-only charities. These were markedly less centralised, thus more open to membership participation, than mixed charities.

Yet there were limits to the training charity could offer for participation in a democratising polity. Pat Hollis notes that, by 1895, women were entering local government who rejected the whole charitable ethos, a tendency enhanced by the growing influence of labour and socialist ideas and personnel. Furthermore, charity merely extended skills already available through the entrepreneurial and professional families from which many charitable activists came, if only from organising servants. This points to a more fundamental problem, connected to the hierarchical society wherein charity existed. Whatever training it offered middle-class women and men was often denied those below. No recipient or potential recipient was ever consulted about charitable policy, at least until the late-nineteenth century when a few working men (though rarely women) began finding their way on to bodies like hospital committees. The dependency charity implied also raised questions for many about recipients' political fitness, though significantly charities kept many of those deemed deserving from the Poor Law's disenfranchising clutches. Most important, as we have noted, charitable and other civil endeavour by middle-class women rested upon the existence of armies of servants, whose supposed dependence was an enduring source of perceived political unfitness.

Organisations like Mothers Unions may have offered working women more scope for active participation alongside their middle-class leaders. They were certainly formidable organs of self-help, probably too of female solidarity, thus enhancing women's self-confidence and auton-

omy from their husbands. Whether this had implications for their role
and interest in the wider polity is more uncertain. It has been suggested
that Mothers Union literature possessed implicit undertones of women's
rights.[76] Yet the determined domesticity of most Union activities has
more ambiguous implications. On the one hand, it was unlikely to
generate political interest for its own sake, or train working women for
political participation or leadership, one reason why the WCG took
decidedly lugubrious views of the Union's expanding membership. On
the other, Mothers Unions may have been powerful informal generators
of notions that 'housewives' had interests in what politicians did, notions
upon which politicians increasingly believed it necessary to competitively trade after 1918.

Since economic organisation was distributed amongst women in
diametrically different ways from charity, the resulting democratic
training might seem more available to working-class than middle-class
women. Since middle-class women had little access to business organisations, activism, leadership and influence were necessarily also unavailable until well into the twentieth century. Some professional
organisations, those presiding over occupations like teaching where
women were being admitted, opened up significantly earlier. Most
however remained resolutely closed, though in response, women sometimes formed their organisations: the Federation of Women Civil Servants for example.

As already noted, working-class women had much earlier access to
economic organisations, and thus theoretically to their self-governing
processes. Many friendly societies excluded women. However, there is
no reason to think women-only societies were less democratic than their
male counterparts. Indeed, their rule-books carried the same features:
officials were elected; new members admitted by those attending regular
meetings. As with male societies, democracy was further encouraged by
intense conviviality.[77] We know little about the day-to-day operation,
either of these or sexually-mixed organisations. However, judging by
two local societies, women could be significant participants. Although
the officers of Rochdale's thriving Newbold Sick and Burial Society
were exclusively male, women certainly participated in its consultative
processes. This was one reason why election and referendum polls
regularly topped 80–90 per cent. When members joined battle over
removing their headquarters into the town centre in 1887, the first mass
meeting was attended by 'fathers, mothers, brothers and sisters . . . cou-
sins and aunts', and they were equally vocal at later stages in the

conflict.[78]The Blackburn Philanthropic Society had less democratic traditions, and women are rarely mentioned in accounts of its meetings. Nevertheless, when the leadership came under threat from reformers in 1913, many vocal women were amongst the loyal crowd of 5000 assembling jovially in Manchester's Free Trade Hall to defend it.[79]

We know more about women's role within co-operation.[80] As noted, the movement was initially largely male, and its women members, where existent, fairly passive. However, 'women of the basket' were always the co-op's main customers. This, together with the movement's emphasis upon democracy, and democratic training via education, meant their role was always potentially greater than within unions or friendly societies. The Women's Co-operative Guild was founded in 1883 to realise this potential, and counteract what it discovered was co-operative women's firm belief that participation in the movement's affairs was beyond their proper sphere. It tried doing this through consciousness-raising, confidence-building and education, and by seeking to represent the interests of hitherto unrepresented housewives within and beyond co-operation. If anything, the Guild placed even more emphasis upon internal democracy than the dedicatedly democratic Co-op as a whole. Democracy was central to its constitution and rhetoric: 'the great point ... is that we are so democratic; ... all ... take their share of government'.[81] It was even more wary of curbing local guild autonomy than the Union was of its constituent societies. Local guilds long remained primary points of decision-making, and were not bound by central executive policy-decisions. The WCG also successfully insisted upon its own autonomy within the Co-operative Union until the inter-war years. Under its first general secretary, Margaret Llewellyn Davies, the leadership was deliberately self-effacing. It carefully downplayed charisma, only loosely reigned the agenda of discussion, and emphasised members were the main centre of initiative. It also extensively used referenda and polling exercises to discover members' opinions upon issues it planned to campaign about. This greatly strengthened its hand in battles with the Co-operative Union over issues like divorce-law reform around 1914. Before leaders testified before the relevant Royal Commission, the WCG Congress was consulted and there were separate soundings of branch opinion.

The WCG deliberately tried to train members for democratic participation within the Co-operative movement and beyond. Here, it confronted the central problem for all working-class women's organisations – the inhibitions and constraints created by separated spheres, the double-shift and strong predilections towards domesticity, expressed amongst other things in the homely topics often chosen for local discussion. One result was that, particularly in the early decades, its central leadership was heavily middle-class. Margaret Llewellyn Davies (Guild General Secretary 1889–1919) was a Cumbrian clergyman's daughter, and recruited at 27, virtually without previous relevant experience.

The Guild dedicated itself to counteracting this problem by attempting to train women for 'the intelligent management of affairs having a wider significance, and lying beyond the immediate circle of the home and the store'.[82] To facilitate participation, its consultative and decision-making structures carefully paralleled the Co-operative Union's at every level. Local guilds' rapid growth also aided success here: the 600 existing by 1914 required several thousand officers and committeewomen; the 1819 guilds by 1939, two decades after enfranchisement, required many more. In these forums, as in national congresses, working-class women learnt to speak, argue and organise. One result was not merely an increasingly substantial core of guild activists, but their spread into the wider movement's counsels. By 1889, 42 women sat on Education Committees of Co-operative Societies; 73 by 1891. By 1904, the Union's Central Board had a woman chairman; two occupied seats on the Board's Southern Section; two more on the Union's Education Committee; 11 sat on the Association of Education Committees. There were 30 women on the Management Committees of 20 local co- ops, and 238 on the Education Committees of 108 societies. 70 were delegates to CWS divisional meetings, and 16 were Congress delegates.[83]

Partly under determined Guild pressure, its activists also began finding their way into other civil-associational sectors and local government. Some became prominent within the Co-operative and Labour Parties, particularly as links increased after 1918. Some began compensating for the shortage of working-class leadership amongst women trade unionists. Meanwhile, by 1939, the Guild could claim 137 magistrates, two mayors, 18 mayoresses, 24 aldermen, 24 county councillors, and 255 municipal or urban district councillors,[84] thereby rendering it prominent amongst civil organisations that were replacing charities as recruiting-grounds for women in politics. By 1945, three members were MPs.

Women, as noted, were excluded from many unions. The underlying constraints examined earlier also discouraged activism within the growing number where women were admitted. One result was that mixed-union leadership, however substantial the female membership, remained male-dominated. Meanwhile, even more than in the Co-op, many leaders of women-only unions were middle-class. This was unsurprising: the formation of such gender-exclusive bodies was itself a tribute to women's perceived mobilisational weaknesses, and their supposed reticence at mixed-union meetings, preventing them playing full parts in decision-making, still more from standing for office. It was also unsurprising given the unskilled character of most female workers. Thus there was no pool of unionists from skilled trades able to offer leadership to the unskilled of the sort available to male unions from the late 1880s.

Middle-class women therefore filled the vacuum until at least 1914. For these, unionisation became almost an extension of philanthropy, albeit of a radical kind. They dominated the Women's Trade Union League, formed in 1874 to encourage female unionisation. Its long-serving committee included Lady Dilke, wife of the Liberal politician; her niece, Gertrude Tuckwell, a school teacher; Emma Paterson, a headmaster's daughter, and Harriet Martineau, plus a selection of male professionals. Similar, if lesser, figures also dominated nearly all societies organised under League auspices. Meanwhile, Annie Besant, doctor's daughter and Fabian publicist founded the Matchworkers Union in 1888. Women's Trades Councils formed in the 1890s showed similar social characteristics, as did many formed contemporaneously in Scottish textile towns. The Scottish Council for Women's Trades was also middle-class dominated, as was the National Federation of Women Workers formed in 1906.

This characteristic, however unavoidable, caused considerable friction with male unionists. This was partly because socially-elevated leaders were suspected, not inaccurately, of being inherently wary of confronting employers, still more of strike-action – though it was a tribute to the democracy even of middle-class-led unions that the working-class women leaders, who eventually emerged, were equally conservative. Friction was also due to male working-class dislike of those they perceived as bossy middle-class philanthropists.

However, after 1914, such leaders were increasingly rejected. This signified that women's unions, just prior to political inclusion, were finally generating sufficient indigenous leaders, both in mixed and single-sex unions. Amongst female textile workers, the earliest and most resilient unionists, these had been slowly emerging since the 1870s. In that decade, Lancashire weaving unions began electing women officials from their own ranks. Women also began appearing amongst weavers in Yorkshire and Belfast,[85] and local women organisers steadily proliferated in later decades.[86] From the 1890s, indigenous leaders began slowly emerging elsewhere, notably in 1898, when Margaret Bondfield, a West-Country shop assistant, was elected assistant secretary of the National Union of Shop Assistants, Warehousemen and Clerks. However, the real boost to women's union activity developed during the First World War, and the enhanced bargaining position and pride that women, like other unskilled and semi-skilled workers, gained from filling men's jobs and being told they were crucial to the war effort. Hostility to middle-class leadership came primarily from women who earned their organisational spurs in these expanding employment-fields. Indeed, it was partly their influence as TUC delegates that led to Bondfield's election to its Parliamentary Committee in 1918, and further elevation as President in 1923. Her emergence also indicated the growing, if somewhat intermittent, sensitivity of male union leaders to women's expanding role within the movement., as did the inclusion of two women in Labour's International Labour Organisation delegation in 1919. So equally did General Council and Labour Party NEC decisions to establish reserved places for women in 1920, and the all-female Women's Advisory Committee with its own annual conference, in 1931. Although women's trade unionism declined sharply during the Depression, its subsequent recovery in the late-thirties owed much to officials emerging during and just after the War. The fact that, by 1939, this resurrection in turn was producing a further, younger and more numerous generation of working-class activists, in increasing conflict with their predecessors,[87] suggests this segment of civil society was sufficiently healthy no longer to require outside input. This is the more significant for happening against a background of re-invigorated domesticity.

Like co-operation, the union segment of civil society was providing avenues into politics. Working-class women, emerging as union officials, found their way into Labour politics through the ILP and Women's Labour League. In areas like Lancashire and to a lesser extent Yorkshire, where women's unionism was strong, union participation also drew them into suffragism in significant numbers.[88] In the inter-war years, even more after 1945, unions also became channels for some to enter municipal politics, and a few Parliament.

Unions then, like the Co-op and organised charity, drew women from the domestic sphere and into politics – into voluntary organisations like parties and pressure groups, and eventually government. Nevertheless, for many decades, politics remained the public world's most suspect segment, furthest away from the private sphere. Women legitimately participated there over issues most directly related to domestic concerns. Thus one key service of voluntary organisations was not just training women for politics, but also establishing their right to be there at all, and on their own account rather than as male political decorations of the sort represented by Female Chartists and Anti-Corn Law Leaguers. This was certainly one function of later pressure groups, notably the Contagious Diseases agitation. The Women's Liberal Federation and Primrose League played similar roles, greatly helped by urgent needs for unpaid electoral service created by mass enfranchisement, the ballot and corrupt practices legislation, and their own propaganda about women's unique role in political purification.[89] The rapid expansion of more overtly feminist organisations, like the NUWSS, WSPU and the small but formidable Women's Local Government Society, built upon and expanded these areas of political legitimation. The fact that, the WSPU apart, such activity involved both gendered and mixed organisations meant that women's political legitimacy was established amongst increasing numbers of both sexes.

As their role expanded, women, especially middle-class ones, were drawn increasingly into political self-governance, in mixed, even more in gendered organisations. Although segregation arguably sidelined women within political parties, it also enhanced political self-reliance and opportunity, freeing them from the possible inhibitions of male company. Most such organisations had carefully-drawn constitutions and followed basic rituals of democratic accountability: establishment by public meeting; subsequent AGMs, open to all members, that received reports, elected officers and debated policy. As they multiplied and their branches proliferated, so opportunities for political training and office-holding expanded rapidly. This becomes self-evident from contemplating the myriad branches of the Ladies National Association, the Women's Liberal Federation and the NUWSS by 1910, or for working-class women, the Women's Labour League. The Primrose League was a sexually-mixed body, and, at the top, male-dominated. Nevertheless, its female majority were active; women often initiated its Habitations, held top offices there, and took active parts in decision-making. There was also a Ladies Grand Council, subordinate only theoretically to its male counterpart.[90] Furthermore, since these organisations were increasingly national and regional as well as local, what were also available were positions at higher levels.

These organisations heavily emphasised the need to educate women for citizenship, to make them better informed and oratorically self-confident. This, along with passionate political conviction and desire for influence, produced debates at all levels within the WLF on issues like temperance, taxation, employment and trade unionism, land reform, Contagious Diseases legislation, Home Rule and (often and divisively) the terms of enfranchisement. Leadership defeats were common. Members controlled those whom they elected even if their influence over broader Party counsels was, like that of male activists, far more limited. Though less turbulent, more frivolous, and more hier-archical, Primrose-League Habitations also frequently discussed enfran-chisement, even if they steered clear of other women's issues. The NUWSS held twice-yearly national councils, and separate regional ones, both consisting of elected delegates from local societies. Here, participants fervently and frequently debated the terms of enfranchise-ment, electoral strategy and relations with political parties, particularly Labour.[91]

Thus women's political organisations, like their economic and social counter-parts, emphasised self-governance and autonomy. One major exception proves the rule. The WSPU was increasingly a *cadre* organisa-tion, its operations resting upon tight, charismatic, even quasi-military, control by Emmeline and Christabel Pankhurst, first from Manchester, then London and finally (by Christabel alone) from Paris. Its zealous followers neither sought nor obtained consultation. Orders were issued about acts of civil disobedience, and obeyed. Even tactical decisions, like the movement's dissociation from socialism, the shift from 'mild' to full militancy in 1912, or the campaign's abandonment in August 1914 and the descent into alien-hunting, were taken centrally. Though a consti-tution was drawn up by Theresa Billington Greg in 1907, it was never adopted, the Pankhursts simply cancelling the Annual Meeting where it was to be discussed.

Yet the WSPU ran up against the predominant democratic culture. It remained wholly exceptional. The proposed constitution probably re-flected branch-dissatisfaction about centralism, and its non-appearance produced a split and the rival Women's Freedom League. Central directives could not prevent local WSPUs enjoying considerable auton-omy, and some retaining close links with local labour organisations.[92] Moreover, whilst the NUWSS expanded in the two years up to 1914, the WSPU diminished into a violent rump-organisation of enthusiasts.[93] Increasingly, it turned its back upon the surrounding society.

5. The Articulation of Demand

We turn now to the final aspect of political fitness: how far was this last group of entrants capable of interest-articulation within the system; more importantly, how far were the resultant demands absorbable without disruption?

We should note several initial points. First, more than previous entrants, those admitted in 1918 and 1928 were not a single group, even leaving aside those who were men. Objectively and self-perceptively, women were divided by religion, ethnicity, region and especially class. Second, the ambit of what was absorbable, economically and politically, had expanded greatly even since 1884 – under the impact of industrial expansion, New Liberalism, Social Darwinism, Socialism and the First World War. By 1918, far greater government expansion and taxation were possible and conceivable, even for governing elites, than before. This was evident notwithstanding the counter-effects of inter-war structural and cyclical depression. Third, the central thrust of what those purporting to represent women's interests were demanding was changing at the precise point of admission. The was due to the impacts of admission itself, war, women's own changing conception of needs and entitlement, and of post-war government propaganda and intentions. This meant that what women (or at least their representatives), demanded, and were significantly granted, was both similar to what previous entrants had wanted, and more extensive. Women's admission did involve substantial demands upon the state, doing so in direct ways rather than just because middle-class humanitarians perceived certain sorts of state-provision as good for them.

In many respects, women were similar to previous applicants: their demands enduringly involved few burdens upon the state or its finances. As already evident from this and previous chapters, women's perceived interests, like men's, were being politically articulated substantially before formal inclusion. Some mobilisation, of course, especially before 1870, was in pursuit of primarily male, or male-initiated, causes – like enfranchisement, free trade and religious disabilities. For working-class women, even after 1870, this was always likely – partly because class would always vie with gender in their perceived interests. However, there was also substantial articulation of more specifically feminist agendas – and some resulting demands were clearly influential, albeit aided by male allies and intermediaries. Aside from suffragism itself (and women's anti-suffragism), there were successful campaigns over

Contagious Diseases legislation; women's rights to representation in local government, divorce and property reform; factory regulation; education; women's treatment under the Poor Law, and (just before the War) the expansion of local maternity and child-welfare services. In all these, though excluded from the parliamentary franchise, women played substantial and influential parts. Articulation partly grew naturally from women's access to other non-political parts of civil society, and from middle- and upper-class women having time on their hands. Influence was possible because women from 1869 had legitimate local political access; and because many women's leaders before 1918 were drawn from the upper and upper-middle class. Independently of their electoral status, this gave them visibility, self-confidence, skill (greatly enhanced by civil participation), and access to national and local male elites. Equally, they were operating in areas legitimised by their domestic concerns. More uncertainly, they also had useful access to male trade unionism and co-operation, and thus to channels of working-class male pressure-politics.

What women's groups demanded most centrally before 1918 was full citizenship for its own sake via parliamentary enfranchisement. Emerging in 1869, and articulated with increasing stridency after 1900, this was identical to what previous male applicants for entry had demanded. Aside from questions of political practicability and class, this was why so many middle-class suffragists remained so passionately attached to obtaining the vote on the same basis as men, even though it would enfranchise fewer working-class women than it had working-class men, and though it led to intense problems with otherwise sympathetic male (and female) radicals. This was why many middle-class women, voteless yet major community-figures as they were, found the contemplation of supposedly-feckless male working-class electors so outraging.

Little of this involved expansions of, or financial burdens upon, the state. Indeed, the views of most early feminists were strongly libertarian, often remaining so into the early-twentieth century. This was partly born of their middle-class backgrounds; equally, it emerged from understandable perceptions of the state as an instrument of male paternalism, oppression and double-standards in areas like divorce, prostitution and employment-access. Moreover, though working-class male enfranchisement produced no immediate demands upon the state, it still reinforced many feminists' suspicions that government would now be used to express male trade-union hostility to female competition through factory regulation and the like.[94] As this implies, anti-statism was enduringly enhanced for some by equal-rights feminism. This viewed most factory regulation with hostility because it classified women, along with children, as needing special protection. This was paternalist and patronising, legislatively seeming to endorse women's fabled weakness, and employers' consequent refusal of equal pay or proper career status. Here class intersected with gender. Such feminists represented the aspirations and job-perceptions of single professional women. Others shared the business-based reflexes of male relatives. Whatever the reason, many leading feminists were hostile not just to regulation, but also state-aid. Amongst the most dedicated was Milicent Fawcett, long-term leader of the NUWSS.[95] Equally persuaded by such notions, greatly enhanced by involvement with the COS, were many women who sought election to local boards of guardians: although wanting to improve workhouse conditions, they had no interest in out-relief. This was why they, far more than council- and education-board aspirants, aroused hostility from local working-class organisations.[96]

In fact, much that women's groups wanted was also obtainable by securing state-withdrawal or neutrality. The abandonment of Contagious Diseases legislation exemplifies the first; demands for equal property rights during marriage, and divorce or separation at its termination, the second. Even where state-interference was desired, to restrain a violent husband for example, costs were modest.

By around 1890, admittedly, some feminist demands, as several recent historians have established, had radicalised to a point where they challenged perceived bases of patriarchy.[97] Like the Chartists, they came to see the vote as the key to social transformation: equalising political power was perceived as crucial to equalisation elsewhere. Yet, also like Chartism in the 1830s and 1840s, and radicalism in the 1860s and 1870s, the most they required of the state was the equal application of the law, this time between the sexes. What some middle-class suffragists wanted, and expected in the wake of full citizenship, was the transformation and purification of male behaviour and motivation, and the consequent equalisation of gender relations – away from violence, double-standards and sexual exploitation, away from the stereotypes of women that legitimised inequality. Equal political status would automatically enhance autonomy and independence. As Lucy Bland has noted of feminist arguments, 'once women had the vote ... not only would they be stronger, more independent and self-respecting, they would also be able to introduce legislation to deal with male immorality'.[98]

However, though alarming for some men, this was unlikely to burden the economy or frighten the tax-authorities.

Yet, if women had much in common with previous aspirants for political entry, they were also different, and destined to become the focus for more immediate demands upon the state and economy after enfranchisement than their predecessors. Historically, working-class women's relationship with the state had been significantly different from that of their male counterparts. Wives were probably the main direct applicants for poor relief, as for charity. Given the role assigned them by separated spheres (which itself had few problems about dependence), and the often urgent needs of the families they nurtured, dependence on outside sources might have seemed less obviously shaming than it did to their husbands. Admittedly, wives were the key figures in working-class domestic economies of self-help – managing weekly budgets, shopping, paying landlords and funeral societies, negotiating with pawnbrokers. But, for this reason, only they knew how marginal was the business of 'getting by'; and probably found fewer problems about pleading. They also had most intimate connection with children's sickness and death. They were prominent in early demands for the retention of traditional paternalism – via food riots and Poor-Law protests. Though attached, as we have noted, to civil society in significant and growing ways, far fewer women than men had full access to the satisfactions available from working-class organisations of self-help, especially friendly societies. Equally important, the state itself, along with many employers and unionised men, saw women (and children) as proper objects for protection within the labour market. Aside from safety issues, they were the prime focus of steadily extending workplace-regulation from 1833. Historically therefore, women and children were the main source of legislated costs on industrial capital, and for reasons owing little to democratisation. They were also enthusiastic users of some late-Victorian municipal services – for example, water, gas and wash-houses, and pre-1914 maternity and child-welfare services.

Women probably also had more long-term stake than men in the quality and cost of one commodity where the state, especially locally, had long been active, and was to become much more so: that of housing. They spent more time there; used it more; and paid the rent, a fact helping explain their prominence in the pre-1915 Rent Act agitations, and the priority the Women's Labour League gave municipal housing before 1914.[99] With so many husbands away, women were also the main immediate beneficiaries of these and other extensions of state-regulation and provision becoming available during the War.

Whether or not all this rendered working-class women enthusiastic about the state, it certainly predisposed them to offer less resistance to its expansion. It also connected with a major shift occurring in middle-class feminist emphases and priorities during the War. Middle- and upper-class women, through charitable visiting, had long had far more contact than their menfolk with the domestic lives of the poor, the location where deprivation and the problems of escaping it through self-help were most visible. Whilst this led many into ever-more dubious advice about budgeting of the sort reinforced by the COS, it led others like Beatrice Webb, Clementina Black, Eleanor Rathbone and many within the WLF into more state-expansive opinions. This was particularly so, as they perceived the weakness of women's trade unionism, and began seeing governmental protection as a substitute.[100] This was also likely if they viewed women primarily as mothers and protectors of children, rather than just as job-market rivals to men.[101] Another related source of growing sympathy with state-action was the WCG, with its emphasis upon representing the housewife's interest, and its growing understanding of her difficulties – beset as she was by the 'double-shift', dangerous child-bearing and exhausting child-rearing, all within tight budgets, without servants, but with unhelpful and even violent husbands. Strengthened by growing expertise stemming from its membership-surveys, the Guild argued housewives needed special protection: not just divorce reform, but also anti-sweating legislation, sickness, invalidity and maternity benefit, municipal maternity-centres and family allowances. In this, the WCG was far more enthusiastic than the Co-operative Union (still strongly wedded to self-help and hostile to the state) and many Labour MPs, who feared the undermining of male authority implicit in demands for payments direct to women. The Women's Labour League shared this enthusiasm.[102]

Until 1914, this state-friendly feminism was merely one strand alongside more dominant demands for citizenship, equal rights and male-transformation. However, the circumstances of the First World War removed or undermined the latter three, whilst strengthening the first. Citizenship was granted and male transformation seemed a churlish aspiration in face of the Western Front's killing-fields. For all women's job-expansion in the wake of dilution and conscription, equal-rights feminists also found life harder when men returned in 1918, and massive governmental propaganda urged women to settle down to replace those

who did not. They gained the radical-sounding 1919 Sex Disqualifi-
cation Removal Act, but could do little to resist the marriage-bars
employers increasingly used to circumvent it. They had few answers to
the manifest desire of many women to escape from unrewarding jobs
into the home, nor to the wish for legislative protection by many who
remained. For working-class women, outside textile areas, permanent
careers and equal pay meant little, even less once structural and then
cyclical depression began. In this overall situation, Welfare Feminism, as
it was increasingly called, became increasingly dominant, a change
signalled by Eleanor Rathbone's election to the Presidency of the National Union of Societies for Equal Citizenship (successor to the
NUWSS) in 1919, and her success in persuading it to adopt family-
allowances as a central cause in 1925. It was also evident amongst
Labour's increasingly vibrant Women's Sections. Welfare Feminism
addressed women's domestic aspirations, reinforced as they were by
rapidly proliferating women's magazines. It fitted politicians' predilections to have women regenerating the nation, by insisting that, if women
were that important, the state should reward their status through maternity and family-allowances, equal divorce rights, and, as this branch
of feminism became increasingly incorporated into women's Labourism,
decent and affordable housing.

This emphasis upon domesticated women's rights further enhanced
expectations of the state by elevating 'housewives' into a perceived
group with identifiable interests. The WCG's aspirations bore fruit.
'Housewives' were reckoned, probably accurately, to have deep concerns about the prices of essentials, which politicians did well competitively to appease by promises of economic management. Given limited
managerial skill, it was surely fortunate that economic conditions produced sharp declines in food prices in the two decades after women's
enfranchisement. These trends in demand were reinforced by a further
development following enfranchisement. Almost for the first time in its
history, British radicalism, in the form of the Labour Party, began giving
agenda-space to issues created by domesticity. Until now, Labour had
been primarily concerned with pushing workplace-demands which, with
the important exceptions of hours-regulation, occasional minimum-
wage demands and unemployment-support, had only modest implications for the state. The switch produced considerably more.

For some contemporary feminists, and current historians, this represented a loss of direction and accurate interest-perception roughly akin
to the working class's supposed bourgeoisification after 1850. Women

relinquished control over the political agenda, becoming diverted from pre-war battles against patriarchy and male exploitation into domestic issues which accepted the framework enmiserating their lives. This change effectively marginalised women's real needs, particularly if they chose to remain unmarried.[103] However one views this (and it raises similar problems to other versions of 'false consciousness'), there is little doubt that the shift and its underlying causes meant that women's enfranchisement in Britain, just as it did elsewhere,[104] released more expectations of the state than any previous political inclusion. It did so partly because these political entrants had greater expectations and relevant needs involving the state. Yet, the increasing state-protection offered women from 1918 was not just because of pressures from women voters, important as groups like the National Spinsters Pensions Association[105] undoubtedly were. It was also because men's traditional conceptions of women's roles legitimised such protection, as did associated politicians' concerns about national renewal. From the inter-war years, this bore significant legislative fruit. Eleanor Rathbone estimated that around twenty laws affecting women were passed between 1918 and 1925 alone; far more were to come. Some, like the theoretically equal employment-rights granted in 1918, equal divorce-rights in 1923 and 1935, and the 1925 Guardianship of Infants Act, were fairly neutral so far as the state was concerned. However, this was clearly not the case with the 1918 Maternity and Child Welfare Act, inter-war housing legislation and Labour's establishment of the Welfare State after 1945. As Pat Thane has noted, 'To a very large extent the social welfare actions of the British state, as of others over the past century, have been about women'.[106]

8 The Democratisation of Political Behaviour

For several decades after 1832, the results of electoral inclusion were complicated, though not invariably compromised, by the continuing impact of influence, corruption and violence upon voters' choices. Partly, this was what the system's aristocratic gatekeepers intended. The purpose of this chapter is to explore how and why the democratisation of political behaviour – the replacement of the politics of influence and market with those of opinion – took so long, and how and why it eventually occurred. The reason for locating this at the end is to make available perspectives lent by the rest of the book – to see the decline of non-democratic forms of political behaviour, and the rise of more democracy-friendly ones, in the light of relevant social and political changes, as well as legal ones. Legal change has conventionally been seen as crucial: political behaviour was ultimately democratised by law.[1] The intention here is not to deny the importance of legal enactment: the period after the 1883 Corrupt and Illegal Practices Act, normally seen as decisive, certainly witnessed sharply declining corruption and influence. What is argued is the importance of more general social and economic changes, along with more specific developments in civil society, which combined together to create a climate more favourable to legal enforcement from the 1880s than at any previous time. Only then did social development and elite interests fully 'catch up' with legislative regulation and the apparent intentions that underpinned it.

1. The Impact of Legal Change

Attempts at legal enforcement began early. Edward I's Parliaments, and others scattered through the fifteenth and sixteenth centuries, enacted pieties about free and unbribed elections. The 1696 Treating and 1729 Bribery Acts made bribery a common-law offence, prescribing severe penalties for transgressors – fining those who offered; disenfranchising voters and boroughs proved to have widely solicited or accepted, thus setting enforcement patterns persisting until 1854. An Act in 1770 removed election trials from the House of Commons as a whole into special committees of the House. Besides the crucial 1872 Ballot Act and 1883 Corrupt and Illegal Practices, the nineteenth century witnessed attempts to cleanse elections in 1841, 1842, 1852, 1854, 1868 and 1879. Many framers of the 1832 Reform Act sought to eliminate grosser forms of corruption, and believed rather innocently that the £10 householder was a suitable carrier for moralisation. Many Liberals came to think similarly about respectable working men: 'No men are more disposed to receive the truth and act upon it', said the *Salford Weekly News* hopefully in 1873.[2]

The combined effect of these apparently good intentions was outwardly minimal. Though, as we shall see, opinion was always central to the electoral process, 'legitimate' forms of influence, exploited by new urban, as well as traditional rural, elites, retained enduring impacts, partly helped by the Chandos Clause: many voters, particularly in the small boroughs sanctified by the 1832 Reform Act, long remained dedicated seekers after the illicit rewards still generously available. MPs elected in 1841 were known collectively as 'the bribery parliament'.[3] The 1847 and 1852 elections saw even higher levels not just of bribery, but also of violence and intimidation – or what the 1869 Select Committee on electioneering significantly perceived as '*a system* of working upon voters through private considerations, whether of interest, hope or fear... [enabling] undue influence... to be constantly practised'.[4] 1868 produced not merely a Liberal Government, but minor injuries for some, and extended hangovers for many more. Consequently, the election also helped produce the 1872 Ballot Act. However, whilst secret voting and abandoning the hustings reduced the motivation and extent of violence and intimidation, the smallness of many polling districts left voters vulnerable to determined employers, enquiring or guessing about their workers' electoral obedience. Venal electors could also now take bribes from everyone, then consult the remains of their consciences inside the polling booth. The result was that electoral expenditure, rising steadily since 1832, reached a record £752 000 in the supposedly placid election of 1865, rose steeply in 1868 to £1 382 252, and continued climbing in both 1874 and 1880.[5] Corruption levels revealed at this last election led directly to the 1883 Act.

Yet, one should not discount the effect even of this earlier legislation. Moralising electoral regulation may have born resemblance to more recent race-relations legislation, having effect less by directly penalising wrong-doing, than by slowly changing norms of public behaviour. It enshrined a widely-shared elite aspiration, even if few could embrace it in medium-term practice. This effect was boosted, as argued later, by the growing ability to generate and publicise scandal via the Royal Commissions of electoral enquiry, sanctioned in 1852. Also important in this and other respects was the growing precision with which venal behaviour was defined, categorised and ranked in terms of wickedness – precision greatly enhanced by the 1854 Corrupt Practices Act,[6] and culminating in the 1883 Act's distinction between corrupt and merely illegal behaviour. Most important perhaps was the removal, enacted in 1868, of petition-trials from the inevitably partial parliamentary venue into the courts. This was crucial both for its own sake, and for the growing body of electoral case-law that judges then began generating, particularly in fields like the definition of 'agency' – the point where candidates were to be held responsible for corrupt behaviour by persons acting on their behalf. Finally, although the 1872 Ballot Act has been discounted as an immediate curb on bribery, it did lessen intimidation and violence, partly through replacing hustings by polling booths. Furthermore, like the social and economic changes reviewed later, it probably had a major background impact on the context wherein the 1883 legislation had its effect. Venal voters could now accept offers from all sides; their ultimate electoral behaviour was far harder to check; after 1867, there were far more of them, and parties far more competitive for their favours. All this greatly contributed to the rising electoral expenditure underpinning the worries of many MPs voting affirmatively in 1883.

There is also no doubt it was this last Act that was most immediately effective in curbing corrupt behaviour, whether by voters or by their tempters. This it achieved by several means. It carefully categorised both corrupt behaviour (bribery, treating, undue influence and personation) and less heinous illegal practices (paying travelling-expenses or hiring conveyances for example). It levied high penalties upon the former (disqualifying, even imprisoning, agents and candidates; disenfranchising voters or constituencies), and substantial penalties upon the latter – ordering re-election or simply declaring the successful complainant elected. The Act also effectively curbed election expenditure, and thus the means of inducing depravity, by a precise fourfold classification of constituencies, by size and type, each with specified maximum levels of appropriate spending, and careful delineation of types of permissible expense. Its effects were visible from the rapidly declining seriousness of the crimes and misdemeanours specified in election petitions after 1883, and the amount electoral participants spent. In 1900, each vote cost 4s.4d; in December 1910, it cost 3s.8d. All this was notwithstanding increasing electoral competition, a greatly increased electorate after 1884, and increasing price-inflation after 1900. By 1914, corrupt practices appearing normal in 1850, and tolerable in 1868, had become intolerable and eccentric. Legitimate 'influence' had also reached very low levels.

Here, it should immediately be noted that the effects of the 1883 Act were greatly enhanced by the Redistribution Acts two years later, just before the 1885 election whose relative purity is often pinpointed in tribute to legislative curbs on sharp practice. Redistribution moved the balance of representation away from locations where deference and corruption were most prevalent – rural and small-town areas respectively – to those where they were hardest to practise and least likely to occur, cities and suburbs. This was so even though the Acts also attempted to shore up gentlemanly landed influence by strictly separating rural from urban constituencies.

In any case, legal enactment cannot provide the whole story. Legislation, whether ineffective or effective, must be set within wider contexts of social and political change. We must understand both the factors inhibiting democratic political behaviour and those ultimately facilitating it, and rendering legislative enforcement a realistic possibility.

2. Inhibiting Factors

One immediately complicating factor is the ambivalence of many who apparently attempted to reform electoral behaviour. Even amongst those seeking franchise-extension, only some wanted, in our terms, to democratise the behaviour of new or existing voters. Many contemporaries, particularly amongst the elites, both traditional landed and new commercial and industrial, drew what they saw as a crucial distinction between 'legitimate' and 'illegitimate' influence: the first resting upon 'natural' respect for hierarchy; the other upon venality and thus eroding hierarchy. Few beyond the radicals wanted to undermine the first, many wished to encourage it, thereby maintaining social and political stability, and preserving the privileges of people like themselves. Most wanted to rid the country of the second, or said they did. Indeed, one intention informing the 1832 Reform Act was to achieve both. This was to be done by including those, supposedly like £10 householders, likely to retain or acquire proper respect for hierarchy, provided they were not alienated by continued political exclusion; even more, like the tenants-at-will lovingly embraced by the Chandos Clause. It was also hoped that removing genuinely rotten boroughs would legitimise the many small ones preserved and multiplied by the Act, where influence could be decorously exercised by elevated folk. Similar results could be expected from the slow demise of freemen, scot- and-lot, and potwalloper voters in the decades after 1832.

As this already begins implying, the distinction was far harder to operate in practice than in theory. As Frank O'Gorman has noted, deference was nearly always partly conditional: respect was given in return for performing paternalistic duties thought appropriate to wealth and position – farm improvements, rent-remission in hard times, generous contributions to local charity or constructing civic amenities. One can immediately begin seeing how easily the behaviour expected of landowners, borough-owners, or wealthy MPs in between elections shaded into 'treating', bribery and sponsored inebriation during them. The consequently hazy character of the distinction between legitimate and illegitimate influence in terms of both the influencee's motivation and the influencer's actions made corruption hard to tackle. This was so even though, at the far end of what was a continuum rather than a set of polar alternatives, there lay the sort of outright bribery resting upon assumptions far removed from respectful deference to a legitimate hierarchy.

It was this that made MPs' determination to keep election trials in their own hands so problematic. Many found the distinction hard to draw, particularly with minds further clouded by knowledge of the venality of voters in their own small-town constituencies. Equally paralysing was Members' uneasy realisation that, however publicly pious they might be, and however little they might choose to know, their agents were necessarily altogether less scrupulous about constituency management. All this rendered MPs decidedly uninventive in legally defining corruption before 1854, and enforcing its elimination before 1883. By this latter time, legitimate influence was fading fast.

Given such ambivalence, it was unsurprising that some key acts of 'democratisation' made corruption worse and harder to eliminate. Theodore Hoppen has suggested that, in trying to rid the system of illegitimate influence and consequently demolishing most rotten and pocket boroughs, Parliament created many small-to-medium sized constituencies, too large and venal to be controlled by means other than widespread bribery. Automatic control by borough patrons was now impossible. Electors were too numerous to be kept respectful by continuous patronage; too many voters were outside the direct dependency network of borough patrons, and too many believed votes were something to sell. In this situation, the only options were to intimidate, more often to corrupt. Both reactions betokened declining control.[7]

The 1867 Reform Act did little to curb the corruption liberated, and the deference legitimated, in 1832. There was minimal seats redistribution. Many small/medium-sized, and eminently corruptible boroughs remained. The Act also introduced many dependent voters – factory workers, particularly in northern towns, with lives so dominated by employer paternalism as to render deference-voting as natural as it was to many tenant farmers.[8] For all the stringency of its residence-requirements, it also admitted many poor voters for whom a few shillings or pints in return for voting in required directions were very welcome. Significantly, Reform made no difference to Norwich's reputation as perennially corrupt. To the borough's deeply venal shopocracy were added many artisans who, though skilled, were forced into casual employment by emerging mass-production in the clothing and footwear trades. For them, colourable employment made a welcome change from sweated jobs.[9]

Meanwhile, the 1832 Reform Act had also established the electoral registration system that essentially continued in force until 1918. This did not exactly invite corruption, but certainly encouraged widespread sharp practice by competing parties, and enduring unfairness. As noted, constituency advantage went to the party most able to get supporters on to the electoral roll, and eliminate the other side's – by fair means, foul ones, or just means that 'would do'. Those most disadvantaged by the system were the supporters of less organised parties, and the poorest voters least able to counter the ingenious objections of party agents. The same Act also confirmed the forty-shilling-freeholder vote in the counties – a qualification which, though often remarkably open, was also susceptible to manipulation through the creation of obedient 'faggot voters'.

What much of this highlights is the underlying and somewhat surprising fact that, for all the period's moralising rhetoric, many Victorians were fairly venal. Corruption and sharp practice came fairly naturally. Some perpetrators were hardly surprising, at least to Victorian elites. They were drawn from the diminishing, but long-resilient ranks, of the 'ancient-right' voters from the pre-1832 'open' constituencies. They were also recruited from the 'residuum', the working class' lowest and most desperate layers. Whether or not on the electoral roll, these were probably the most enduring source of election riots and inebriation. There also seems evidence that, when corruption occurred in large urban constituencies, the most likely locations were poverty-stricken inner-city wards. For marginal people, politics became another way of 'getting by', alongside pawning, petty crime, and reciprocal corruption with the collectors of large funeral societies.

However, corruptibility was hardly limited to this group. It was widespread amongst the Victorian middle class. This was one reason why the 1832 Reform Act in some respects heightened the incidence of political venality by including as constituencies many small market towns, whose economies were stagnant, and whose shopocratic voters were presented with relatively few opportunities of expanding profit-margins.[10] This was so even though their expectations were probably rising in common with those of most other middle-class people. Politics, if it came with bribes, 'colourable employment' and orders for drink and food, was a reasonable periodic supplement.

Interesting here is the relationship with religious belief. Middling people were dedicated church-goers. Yet, in small towns, they were also apparently deeply corruptible. Significantly, amongst the constituencies whose election results were most frequently petitioned against were almost all the great cathedral towns. Sanctity apparently could be remarkably odorous, perhaps, as Theodore Hoppen argues, because people compartmentalised politics from the rest of their lives which, by implication, were probity-saturated.[11]

In fact, the rest of some people's lives, beyond small towns as well as inside them, also needed insulation. Sometimes events occurred suggesting that rather a lot of middle-class people were attached to various sorts of sharp practice. In 1887 for example, Samuel Hunter, Salford's municipal gas manager and prominent Wesleyan lay-preacher, was found to have been accepting bribes on contracts for equipment and raw materials for the past eleven years. As the scandal unfolded, it emerged that the practice (dignified as 'commissions') was almost normative throughout the gas industry, in both public and private sectors, amongst those making gas and supplying the means of so doing. Many declared commission-taking also to be general elsewhere in manufacturing. Within weeks of Salford's manager being gaoled, the city's town clerk decamped to Paris and then San Francisco with substantial sums of ratepayers' money and even more held in trust for will-beneficiaries in his capacity as a solicitor. In fact, the practice of making creative and personally beneficial use of trust-money was widespread amongst 'even very respectable solicitors' – [12] a fact emerging strongly in the breast-beating following the prosecution in 1911 of Benjamin Lake, sometime President of the Law Society, who carelessly went bankrupt whilst speculating with clients' money.[13] As we shall see, public norms were changing, but traditional forms of behaviour were remarkably long-lasting.

One reason was the landed elite's economic resilience. This was the main purveyor of influence-politics, and as even conditional deference steadily eroded, this increasingly shaded into shameless bribery. Even where not active purveyors, landowners certainly tolerated such practices, perhaps partly because borderlines between influence- and market-politics were so hazy. As one country gentleman demanded as late as 1882, 'I should be glad to know whether the gentry in the neighbourhood have ever withdrawn their custom from a tradesman found guilty of accepting bribes, or whether any gentleman has ever been excluded from society because he has given them'.[14] Given these attitudes outside Parliament, it was unsurprising that, inside, 'a wealthy man, known to have bribed, nay actually convicted of bribery, is not a whit the less respected by the majority of the members of the House'.[15]

Deference, even more corruptibility, thus permeated many segments of British society. We should also note that some aspects of traditional political behaviour could be placed at the service of opinion-politics. One reason why intimidation was difficult to eliminate was that radical groups found it as useful as conservative ones. Particularly during the 1830s and 1840s, borough and municipal electors were often under severe pressure from non-electors to vote in required radical directions. The sanction carrying considerable weight amongst shopkeeping electors was 'exclusive dealing' – against those ignoring persuasion, and in favour of those co-operating. Furthermore, at times of high tension, and in the noisy atmosphere of the hustings, this might degenerate into simple terrorism. It was these pressures that helped produce several MPs and some councillors sympathetic to Chartist and other radical causes, and rather more finding it politic to claim they were. Contemplation of such opportunities rendered radicals decidedly ambivalent about abandoning the hustings and supporting the ballot without significant franchise expansion, since it would effectively close a key entry-point to local and parliamentary politics. *The Northern Star* was very precise in 1839: 'Once pass the Ballot, and no more scrutiny into the acts of your trustees – no more deference by the trustee to popular opinion'.[16] As this suggests, pressurising electors was even legitimised by aspects of the widely-accepted theory of virtual representation – electors were trustees for non-electors, whether women or working men.

Operative here was intimidation rather than bribery, violence and threatened violence. This too was widely evident elsewhere in contemporary society. 'Collective bargaining by riot' was one expression; animal-baiting and prize-fighting another. Yet another (also rather taken for granted) is evident in this 1845 newspaper report of an assault at Manchester races:

> William Whitesides . . . was leaning over the paddock when . . . Owen Fogey came . . . and leaned over him. Whitesides, not liking this, put Fogey's arms down and pushed him away . . . after a few words there was a scuffle; they fell on the ground Whitesides uppermost. While in this position, Fogey, in order to release himself, . . . drew (Whitesides') face close to his own and bit his ear and the greater part of his nose off . . . Mr W.P. Robert, defending, said . . . It was a natural exhibition of a Lancashire temper . . . the Lancashire mode of fighting . . . not looked upon by themselves as brutal.[17]

3. Facilitating Factors

If factors besides legislative inadequacy explain why political behaviour took so long to fully democratise, others besides legislative enforcement explain its ultimate emergence. Oddly, one of these is the factor underpinning elite-reticence about effectively curbing corruption. Increasingly hazy borderlines between legitimate and illegitimate forms of influence undoubtedly inhibited parliamentary efforts to outlaw venal behaviour. However, it also probably facilitated the ultimate transition to opinion-politics.

The implication of recent work on nineteenth- and even eighteenth-century electoral behaviour has been that deference was always laced with conditionality, and implicit or explicit negotiation. Deferential political behaviour continued because of the performance of paternalistic duties in terms of farm improvements, civic amenity, steady charitable contribution, consumption of local merchandise, or simply providing conviviality. Voting, even when resting on deference, still more when responsive to bribery or treating, was often informed by some degree of reciprocity and even calculation. Electors were rarely simply slavish even when casting the first of their two votes, still less when casting the second. Moreover, although eighteenth-century contemporaries had finely graded senses of what counted as legitimate and illegitimate inducements, this probably became harder in the nineteenth century, when life became even more commercially driven. Increasingly, the main difference between influence and outright corruption perhaps rested upon the degree of respect granted the benefit-giver, and the point where benefits were delivered, bribery being recognisable by being off-loaded *during* rather than *between* elections. Frank O'Gorman, indeed, has argued that conditionality was evident even in many uncontested elections. Writing about the century before 1832, he suggests that continued non-contest indicated less electoral torpidity than community satisfaction with the terms of deference set by borough patron or patrons. Contests, or threatened contests, indicated dissatisfaction, producing either renegotiation of the terms of deference or the emergence of new and more generous patrons.[18] This was so before 1832, and probably increased subsequently as social and economic change steadily eroded the bases of deference. If this was so in England, then even more was it true of Ireland, Wales and Scotland, where landed reciprocity was less evident and conflict either latent or overt. Overall, if Tom Nossiter is correct in assuming that deference- and market-politics are situated on an evolutionary scale terminating in opinion-politics,[19] then even deference had what might retrospectively be seen as some democratic potential.

If there was a continuum between influence- and market-politics, so equally was there between those of market and opinion. While some voters were undoubtedly 'anybody's' with loyalties entirely open to the enticements of 'Mr Most', increasing numbers of others were basically opinion-voters requiring bribes simply to turn out, or from custom. Bribery became the means of further persuading voters to do what they had already decided upon by virtue of religion, upbringing, issues or sometimes class. Such behaviour was certainly evident amongst borough electors in the years around 1832. Great Yarmouth and Lewes, for all their fabled venality, had substantial histories of partisan voting, to judge by how consistently electors cast both votes for one party or the other in elections between 1818 and 1841. Issues were important, for example parliamentary and municipal reform, the Anatomy Bill, slavery and the Poor Law. Bribery, although endemic, was also customary: in Great Yarmouth distributed at two guineas per head across the electorate.[20]

As this implies, opinion-voting, whether financially facilitated or not, had a significant history even before democratisation began. In some locations, it was an intermittent feature of eighteenth-century electoral politics – in Bristol for example where partisanship was consistently fierce, and Norwich where Whig-control rested partly on satisfying the needs and interests of the textile trade.[21] Contrary to earlier Namierite agreement that pre-1832 elections were without ideology, thus wholly either paternalist or clientalist, there now seems evidence that partisanship was emerging consistently in some constituencies from around 1780. Analysing behaviour in eight selected boroughs between 1818 and 1841, John Phillips has found partisanship well established in Maidstone, Colchester, Lewes and Great Yarmouth, and significant in Bristol, by 1818. It was also emerging in Northampton, Shrewsbury and Beverley, in the wake of conflicts over either parliamentary or municipal reform. Furthermore, nearly everywhere, one or other of these issues produced significant changes in behaviour, suggesting the presence of opinions, and ones capable of change, even if bribery was required to produce its expression.[22]

This in turn suggests that democratisation itself, and conflicts about it, could democratise political behaviour. The widely spread passion aroused within both the elite and across the population in 1830–2, in venal as in more moralised boroughs, makes this probable. What Phillips has claimed for most of his eight boroughs, Michael Brock has argued for both boroughs and counties across the country.[23] Subsequent issue-based conflicts, again amongst national and local elites and beyond, probably produced similar effects, at least in some places – over municipal reform and free trade in the 1830s and 1840s; temperance after the United Kingdom Alliance's emergence in 1858; religious disability; control of education and Disestablishment right up to 1914; liberation movements and persecutions abroad in the 1860s and again the late-1870s. In all this, and aside from democratisation itself, the most significant generator of issues was religious conflict, particularly that between Anglicanism and Dissent. It did so steadily in the nineteenth century, just as it had been evident at times and in places like Bristol in the eighteenth.[24]

It seems likely that issues themselves, and the intensely political instincts of many within the elite, could push behaviour in opinion-based directions. Many voters probably shuffled between conviction-

and market-voting according to circumstance. If venality revived, as it probably did, in the forties, fifties and sixties, this was partly because national elites found little to disagree about after Corn-Law Repeal in 1846, the Whigs' consolidation in power, and the Conservatives' consequent twenty-year eclipse. Whilst partisanship often remained resilient, particularly in large urban areas, the central elite offered little upon which it, and consequently opinion politics, could grow. Yet, even at the end of this quiescent era, and even in Beverley's seedy atmosphere, the two-thirds of the 1000 voters who were corruptible saw payment as their right, believing this was bribery only if emanating from the party they were not planning to vote for.[25] The revival of fierce partisan competition amongst the elite from 1868, now expressed through increasingly powerful propaganda-machines, could only reinvigorate movement towards opinion-politics, even if for a while still laced with deference and venality.

Thus even corrupt and deferential politics contained considerable democratic potential. Furthermore, however split-minded people were, the nineteenth century contained more genuine religiosity than those preceding or succeeding it. Moralised electoral behaviour was always an alternative, particularly as evangelical revivals took hold amongst all denominations. In this situation, anything clarifying hazy borderlines, posing choices or dramatising hypocrisy was always potentially influential. Here the role of scandals themselves may become significant. Scandals in any sector of life are not fixed entities; they have variable relationships with dubious behaviour; what causes scandal in one generation will leave another unmoved, even though the relevant behaviour is identical. Their occurrence says much about contemporary moral standards, and probably often indicates they are shifting: borderline-behaviour condoned or tolerated in one era scandalises people in another. Yet, if scandals indicate moral change, they also probably accelerate it. By definition, they are intensely public events whereby venal behaviour is identified, dramatised and execrated, providing moral opinion-leaders with opportunities to clarify lines of public tolerability. Given widespread religiosity, and an expanding and vibrant newspaper press, the nineteenth century had considerable ability to generate them. Scandals can make some feel guilty; being public events, they can make far more feel ashamed. They can induce moral panic.

Where electoral behaviour was concerned, there were clear links with legislation. The system established in 1852 whereby fraud allegations were investigated by Royal Commissions created potent scandal-generators. The long drawn-out process whereby Commissions of the great and good repaired to the relevant constituency, exhaustively enquired of candidates, agents and voters, then reported on behaviour past and present, all to extended publicity in local and daily newspapers, was well-designed for public execration and re-defining public standards. Being identified as a notoriously corrupt borough became steadily more worrying in a period increasingly combining widespread civic pride with growing awareness of the broader national ethos, particularly when local newspapers could dramatise both pictures. Commission-generated scandals also affected the governing elite, producing growing shame, if not exactly guilt, and growing compulsions to take remedial action.

The process was hardly rapid; corruption was widespread and deep-seated. Nevertheless, as each general election produced its volley of Commissions, there emerged an expanding public opinion and an increasingly shamed elite prepared to categorise previously tolerated or initiated behaviour as scandalous, particularly perhaps as one generation reacted against its predecessor. For example, the 28 Commissions following the 1880 election, particularly the eight investigating complaints in England, induced widespread anger and shame amongst substantial sections of the public and, partly in reaction, a consensus between Conservative and Liberal front benches about the need to eradicate what was now perceived as 'this foul and loathsome weed'.[26] This eventually produced the decisive 1883 Corrupt and Illegal Practices Act.

However, the enactment, even more the effectiveness, of this legislation was due to more than just scandal. We should first understand its context. It was passed ten years after the onset of agricultural depression; sixteen years after the enfranchisement of part of the male urban working class; some twelve months before the inclusion of rural and urban males; and two years before a substantial equalisation of constituencies. In other words, it succeeded the coming of mass politics, and just preceded the enfranchisement of what many saw as the population's most deferential segment. Politics promised to become ever more expensive, at a time when many landowners were finding it ever harder to bear such expense. The Act also preceded a boundary reorganisation recognising and facilitating the disruption of community-based politics, and extinguishing the small boroughs that had been the primary source of corruption since 1832.

To understand why corruption then rapidly declined, and why deference remained unrejuvenated, we must examine broader patterns of
long-term economic, social and political change, encouraging the emergence of opinion-politics whilst eroding the bases of influence- and
market-politics. Underpinning this was a 'modernisation of social relations',[27] the spread of respectability down and across the population,[28]
and, partly under the influence of scandal, the defining of virtue in ways
increasingly excluding bribery, venality, violence and undue inebriation.

Spreading respectability was certainly one factor. From the later-
nineteenth century, it began precluding certain sorts of electoral behaviour, particularly public drunkenness and political violence. In fact,
politics was only one aspect of what was coming to be seen as disreputable. The same forces precluding electoral violence and inebriation were
probably also rendering unseemly the more brutal popular pastimes like
animal-baiting and prize-fighting, and indeed 'the Lancashire mode of
fighting'. Respectability did not just undermine corruption; alongside
mass education, it also helped eliminate violent and intimidatory modes
of expressing political opinion and persuasion. In labour relations,
collective bargaining by riot was fast retreating in face of an emerging
negotiational culture; the slow but significant incorporation of organised
working men into consultative roles in politics was having similar effects
there. Here respectability intersected with the impacts of the 1867
Reform Act and 1872 Ballot Act. The inclusion of politicised working
men removed the most important out-group with a motivation to
pressurise and intimidate voters. Meanwhile, the spread of respectable
by-law housing began to undermine the street culture upon which
rumbustious electoral politics had so long fed.

Another influence was accelerating urbanisation. Towns had long
formed bases for alternative loyalties to those on offer from national
and local aristocratic elites. The language of civic pride, citizenship, and
rights supposedly vested in ancient charters were available in freemen
constituencies throughout the eighteenth century to boost Independ-
ency by sanctifying a range of grievances against local oligarchs.[29] So
too, and even more widely, were notions of the 'free born Englishman',
and the linkage of ideas about liberty to growing national identity.
Furthermore, cities, defined in demographic rather than cathedral
terms, were always harder and more expensive to politically control
than towns or villages, due to size, anonymity and internal population
movement. In fact, although nineteenth-century urbanisation was rapid,
it often initially enhanced autonomy and local visibility. In some, this

came to underpin factory-based paternalism and conditional deference. However, from the 1880s, urbanisation patterns changed somewhat, with the forces sustaining paternalism being undermined by anonymity and counter-pressures. In 1871, the proportions of English and Welsh urban-dwellers in locations of more than 100 000 topped 50 per cent; by 1901, 51.1 per cent of the entire population were so located. Many formerly self-contained industrial towns like those in Lancashire, the West Riding and the Black Country, began merging, becoming engulfed by larger neighbours, sprouting suburbs of their own, or invading surrounding industrial villages. Trains and particularly trams increasingly enhanced these locality-erosive processes, severing the geographical relationship between home and work. Limited companies replaced one-man firms. Particularly when purpose-created rather than modified family-companies, they were necessarily more impersonal, less local and their labour relations more conflictual. Greater impersonality and bureaucracy made factory-based party attachments less likely, whilst duties to shareholders rendered electoral bribery harder to sustain or justify. Moreover, this was part of a broader regionalisation and nationalisation of economic activity, expressed also in sectors like insurance and shop-keeping.

Industrial, commercial and urban growth also expanded horizons and economic opportunities in some market and cathedral towns sustaining venal politics after 1832. Amongst such locations, Norwich, Ipswich, Lincoln, Gloucester, Oxford, Coventry, Great Yarmouth were all growing rapidly by late-century. Communications, in the form of railways, mass-circulation newspapers or both, were also invading the moral and social autonomy upon which deference and venality rested – in both small towns and countryside. So too was population-movement: from urban to suburban places and from small to large towns, from countryside to town. Partly influenced by agricultural depression, Britain's rural population declined in absolute, as contrasted with relative, numbers, during 1881–91. Affluent urbanites were also moving to become what Alun Howkins has called 'the new countryman and woman'[30] in search of gentility, or economic opportunity in sectors like market-gardening. Finally, and crucial to economic opportunity and moral autonomy in places like Great Yarmouth and Scarborough, was the annual pilgrimage by increasing numbers of urbanites in search of sun and sea.

Underpinning quite a lot of the foregoing, and more directly enhancing political independence, were rising living-standards. Until the

1860s, wages generally simply kept pace with living-costs; at best, they outpaced them on a strictly regional and occupation-specific basis. However, from the 1870s, the agricultural depression and cheap imports produced major declines in staple food prices. Though take-home pay hardly rose, the overall effect was substantially rising real wages for all except those at the working-class bottom-end. Though periodically undermined by waves of unemployment in some areas, this was generally sustained until 1900. Even in Lancashire, cyclical depression did little to curb the relative prosperity that fuelled the rise of mass seaside resorts like Blackpool. Real wages did not begin declining until 1910. Even then, high employment lent considerable protection to living-standards until the early-1920s – when agricultural depression and falling food prices again significantly compensated for the effects of industrial unemployment.

If the urgent desire for electoral remuneration was lessening at the bottom, abilities and inclinations to offer it, and finance deference more generally, was declining at the top. We have already implied this was one effect of replacing the industrial owner-manager, with his mid-century taste for paternalism, by the more impersonal limited company. The disinclination to underwrite electoral bacchanalia was also probably enhanced by many entrepreneurs' perceptions from the 1880s, however inaccurate, about foreign competition and industrial decline. The trend was equally evident in rural areas. The agricultural depression severely undermined landowning incomes, particularly in grain-growing areas (where rental income fell by up to 50 per cent), particularly amongst those without urban rental or industrial income – and grain-based landowners tended to be deprived in this way. Tenants were increasingly unable to pay, whilst many landowners found it steadily harder to remit rents, still more to finance farm-improvements, thus weakening the reciprocity upon which political deference so long rested. In Ireland, Wales and Scotland, it had always been weak, even when relations were not actively conflictual or openly iron-fisted. In the 1880s, deference was wholly overtaken by bitter tenant-right agitations, and in Ireland at least by waves of land-sales to tenants, significantly aided by Conservative governments who had come to categorise Irish land-owners as basket-cases. The agitations even produced strong echoes in England, deference becoming still more conditional and overtly negoti-ated. Good tenants were hard to obtain, vacant farms no use at all. Thus richer landowners found themselves obliged to lower rents, or offer loans to induce continuity or prevent insolvency. If tenants departed nevertheless, often having farmed for generations, their replacements were in even stronger bargaining-positions. They might also have little attachment to traditional hierarchies, if, like many, they were refugees from Scotland or Wales. Many hard-pressed landowners were also disposed to sell all or part of their estates, particularly once this was facilitated by the 1882 Settled Land Act, significantly passed just before the Corrupt and Illegal Practices Act. Only some could do so before the land-sale floods in 1910–14 and 1919–21. Nevertheless, declining commitments to the traditional estate system, with its complex of mutual obligations, were clear enough, a development given concrete form because many land-sales were to sitting tenants, and anticipated a general shift in aristocratic investment from land to the stockmarket. Even where estates were sold to businessmen, new incumbents rarely commanded traditional respect. Also important was declining interest amongst landowning families in parliamentary seats – because they disliked the mass politics universally released by the 1884–5 franchise and redistribution reforms, because they could no longer afford the cost; or due to growing distaste for the attacks to which land was subject within the Commons as the aristocracy lost control over the political agenda.

All this meant landowners were less able, and less inclined, to offer the traditional fruits of paternalist and market-politics (worries about the growing cost of politics after all substantially underpinned the 1883 Corrupt and Illegal Practices Act); and many of those below were less minded to receive or be affected by them. Meanwhile, agricultural depression and growing agricultural mechanisation eroded another link in the rural deference-chain by accelerating urban migration by rural labourers, such that rural dwellers began declining in absolute as well as comparative terms. Skilled as well as unskilled workers were now departing.

What this did, along with several other changes reviewed here, was to further enhance the opinion-generating capacities of industrialisation and urbanisation. In the long run, these forces did not just undermine hierarchy. More positively, they also powerfully generated divisions and identities, and thus vantage-points, from which political opinions and interests were likely to emerge. British society had long been a potent producer of these sorts of divisions, if only because of the fissiparous character of its religion. Being primarily Protestant, this had anyway long placed heavy emphasis upon individual revelation. Even in rural areas and industrial villages (like Wales and Norfolk), it could generate

considerable psychological independence of local elites, where Nonconformity faced Anglicanism. In Southern Ireland, even Catholicism could
reinforce nationalism in generating opinions against Anglican elites. In
expanding urban environments, where social controls were harder, and
which were targets for many sorts of migrants, from the surrounding
area and beyond, the opportunities for religious heterogeneity were
increased. Here, sectarianism simply produced additional sources of
identity, interest and principled behaviour to reinforce or set alongside
those produced by community, nationality, gender, occupation and
class. Indeed, the effectiveness of the final legal attack upon corrupt
and dependent politics was surely enhanced by the fact that the late-
1880s also witnessed the increasingly powerful resurrection of this last
identity. Class exerted increasingly influential effects upon the electoral
behaviour of manual, and even more, white-collar groups until the
mid-1960s. Here, there are distant links with the capacity of political
radicalism, first seen in the late-eighteenth century, to set alternative
standards to the 'Old Corruption' from which to view politics, particularly that of the 'free-born Englishman'.[31] More certainly, this was
happening soon after the 1885 Redistribution Act opened the electoral
system to class-politics.

Finally, these developments were underpinned and stabilised by the
long-term and accelerating emergence of civil society. Much of that said
in previous chapters makes it highly likely that this phenomenon would
erode deference and corruptibility, and enhance opinion-politics. Civil
organisations are produced by voluntary effort. Admittedly, they could
sometimes become mechanisms for perpetuating deference and corrup-
tion-based politics. Charities, though instruments of class-formation for
the middle-class people who staffed them, and confidence-generators for
the women upon whom they became increasingly reliant, also produced
deference amongst some recipients. British political parties, like their
counterparts elsewhere, could become whatever their leaders desired,
and voters expected: instruments of conditional deference in rural
counties and some industrial towns, unashamed bribery-distributors in
many small, and some large, towns. Even Nonconformist chapels could
extend employers' hold over employees, where they embraced both.

Nevertheless, most civil organisations, like the social identities and
solidarities initiating them, were likely to enhance the independence of
their members – of elites; where necessary, of the state; and, where
women were involved, of men. For working men, and in the longer term
women, this was clearly true of friendly societies, co-ops and unions. By

the late-1880s, even the unskilled were starting to unionise, even if unemployment and poverty delayed their more permanent incorporation until 1910. Though involving members less than skilled unions, general unions were capable of generating alternative loyalties. Charities, churches and chapels generated independence and self-confidence for the middle class of both sexes. Particularly where they separated one class from another – as in Wales, East Anglia, or, for the Primitive Methodists, many other places – chapels increased these characteristics amongst working people. Organised pressure groups both expressed independence and generated it for the increasing numbers who participated. As noted, even the pre-1914 anti-suffrage movement could not avoid servicing its female members in this way. Meanwhile, all voluntary societies, with their necessary attachment to democratic rituals, and often practices, powerfully enhanced the normativeness of democratic behaviour in the wider polity. Even political parties, once they became mass organisations found the rhetoric and ritual impossible to avoid; the Liberal caucuses even made a virtue of it. They also drew people into participation: when the Corrupt and Illegal Practices Act rendered 'colourable employment' illegal, the vast resultant expansion of unpaid canvassing had long been in preparation. Finally, no voluntary organisation could long survive if it tolerated corrupt behaviour by its members, still less its officials. Friendly societies had few hang-ups about inebriation: absconding with the funds was another matter.

Conclusion

In this book, I have concentrated on two variables often seen as crucial rival explanations of democratic success or failure: the role of elites and of civil association. Hopefully enough has been said to establish them less as contending and more as mutually supplementary. Here Britain shares much explanatory ground with other polities located in the first phase of democratisation.

Telling the story has revealed other and connected variables – also shared with the same group. Britain's democratisation was evolutionary rather than instant; it happened in stages, and emerged from a system that, while mildly authoritarian, was never efficiently so, and indeed was well on the way to becoming liberal before democratisation began. The pre-1832 system had also long-embraced notions of representation, albeit somewhat narrow if flexible ones; and, partly as a result, already provided entry-points for most important groups. Partly because of its highly varied character, and partly because of its vibrant and self-governing localities, the system overall even proved capable of giving some access to new socio-economic groups as they appeared. These variables are interdependent in that relative liberality and partial representativeness made effective pressure for change, and thus evolution, possible. They also partly underpinned the usefully competitive political instincts of Britain's national and local elites. These first-phase polities were also fortunate in democratising when they did: at a time when democracy was the only available model around as a popular alternative to not very efficient oligarchy. Unlike inter-war and subsequent experience, there were no viable popular alternatives to the authoritarian left or right if things fell apart.

These features reinforced and facilitated the growth and benign effect of civil society. The system's relative liberality, its unambitious state, and the often limited effectiveness of its suppressive forces meant that civil society could develop, and itself follow what is probably the natural inclination of voluntary societies if left to themselves. Given their need to ensure accountability, they tend to operate in internally-representative, liberal and (at least so far as members are concerned) relatively

279

democratic ways. Illiberal or efficient authoritarian systems tend to produce similar civil structures below them. They do this particularly at the highly sensitive political and quasi-political/economic levels, which most worry authoritarian rulers and which are therefore most liable to surveillance and persecution. Voluntary associations tend to become authoritarian in self-defence (democratic associations find it hard to react rapidly to crisis, and to safeguard themselves against spies), and because authoritarian models are the only ones available. This relatively open situation meant civil society could develop before and while political popularisation was underway. As a result, the political ones could add to pressures for change, train participants to act appropriately once included, and begin to effectively represent group interests.

This provided a relatively benign (and as we have seen liberal) context, wherein industrialisation and urbanisation, and the associated communications revolution, could generate and facilitate an increasingly rich associational life, of economic social and political kinds. These two forces necessarily breed social heterogeneity, generate interests in every sense, and facilitate their recognition and mobilisation. Amongst the factors likely to generate interests of the vested sort was of course religion. Here Britain, along with much of north-west Europe and North America, was fortunate in having a Protestant rather than Catholic-dominated culture, one therefore tending to emphasise individual responsibility at least as much as hierarchy and authority. Moreover, however much Anglicanism might erode such trends, vibrant old and new Dissent heavily reinforced them – adding also strong commitments to democratic self-governance. This ensured that the religious segments of civil society reinforced commitments to which the latter was already naturally susceptible. They did this not just for themselves. Because of the nineteenth-century linkage, in terms of both inspiration and personnel, between religion and multiple other kinds of civil endeavour, including those generated by class, they also reinforced such commitments amongst other parts of civil association.

Industrialisation and urbanisation also point to another benign and connected factor, whose impact is also evident from the story told here. Britain was fortunate in having a capitalist market-economy in place before democratisation began. In Britain's case, continued commercial expansion during democratisation, alongside now also industrialisation, generated sufficiently benign economic cycles while democratisation was in progress to ensure it was never associated with economic failure (as was damagingly true of most European polities democratising in the inter-war years, and as threatens many post-Communist states). This also ensured rising real incomes during the crucial periods of mass enfranchisement of the relatively poor – from 1867 and in the inter-war years. Again the early timing of both capitalist development and of democratisation in Britain was fortunate, at least from the viewpoint of its elites: there were few rival economies to raise mass expectations far beyond what the economy was then capable of generating. Where people noticed something apparently better, as in the case of North America, many of the most discontented tended to emigrate there – eagerly assisted by grateful elites, and willingly received by the desired and still relatively empty hosts.

Overall, capitalism may be seen as benign for liberal democracy in the long term because of its capacity to generate wealth, create variety and choices. This of course can be highly problematic if the timing is wrong in relation to democratisation. The contrasts with East-Central European and former-Soviet states since 1989, who have had to democratise whilst simultaneously coping with the social and economic strains of putting a market-economy in place, are obvious. For them, the situation has been the more difficult because democratisation has given all those strains instant and legitimised political expression. In Britain, even economic recession has been democratically benign: the agricultural depressions after 1873 and 1918, helped produce substantial falls in essential food prices, each coinciding with the aftermath of major acts of political inclusion.

Alongside the foregoing, there are other democratically-benign factors, mentioned only in passing. For all the inefficiency of popular education outside Scotland, literacy levels were fairly high, and rose to near-totality whilst democratisation was ongoing. Up to around 1850, around half the population could sign their names, and probably rather more could read; by 1900, the vast majority could do both. Britain was also fortunate in having resolved most of its problems of competing national identities before democratisation began.[1] Thus democratisation did not release the sort of system-threatening stresses evident in East-Central Europe after 1918, and amongst post-Communist states after 1989. The one exception was Ireland whose capacity to disrupt, periodically paralyse, and after 1912 briefly threaten political legitimacy illustrates the potentially high costs of unsolved nationality problems.

All this raises questions about comparisons with elsewhere. In the British case, alongside those of other first-phase polities, the variables seem so benign as to preclude comparisons outside of this favoured group, even though comparisons within it are probably highly informative. There is no doubt that trying to create liberal democracy while contemporaneously initiating capitalist take-off creates major problems. This is doubly so if mature capitalist economies are present to set often impossible standards of expectation. So equally does the attempt to simultaneously create a vibrant civil society, in a context moreover where hitherto it has been discouraged or effectively prohibited. So too does the absence of widely-legitimate and stable elites. Equally problematic for democratising polities are the presence of national identities that are ethnic rather than civic, and non-negotiable other than by national separation. Britain has had few of these; those democratising since 1918, equally since 1989, have had many. Yet one may wonder whether all Britain's benign circumstances have actually been essential, rather than agreeable but luxurious extras. Certainly, the examples of Spain and Portugal who democratised instantly in the 1970s, who possessed a dominant, if now reasonably contrite and self-effacing Catholic Church, suggest it is possible to get by with fewer benign variables, and that, in some circumstances, some may not be actual preconditions. So too does the much less recent experience of Ireland, France and Belgium.

One final question remains. Why, with all these variables in place, is Britain not more democratic than it is, and why does there now seem to be a democratic deficit? Here perhaps we come up against the inverse side of two of the factors reviewed thus far. If capitalist development can breed variety, it can also produce democratic and civil passivity through satisfaction and, due to the now massive leisure industry, distraction. Furthermore, the need to negotiate the needs of the groups thus created, as the Webbs probably rightly perceived, also makes their self-governance harder. As this begins to suggest, there has also been interaction between the two crucial variables reviewed in this book. The fact that elites have played so important a part in democratisation, and that groups have been fairly willingly incorporated, has reacted back upon the civil society that underpins democratising success, causing many to duplicate the representative models produced by the broader polity. The expanded role of government has also undermined several of the most vibrant elements of nineteenth-century civil society – mortally in the case of friendly societies, and damagingly in that of trade unions. Expanded capitalism has seriously undermined the third: co-operation.

This serves to reinforce the general point made in this conclusion. Civil society and benignly behaving elites are important parts of explanations of democratic success; they may even be important preconditions, at least in that they need to be present *whilst* democratisation is under- way, if not before. Here Britain was particularly fortunate. Yet they are also partial explanations. In a sense, their value depends upon what is being explained, and what one assumes democracy to be. If democracy is assumed to be a system showing not just democratic characteristics, but also imperfectly formed ones (therefore elite-centred, bureaucrat- ised, and representative rather than direct) then elites and civil society do quite a good job. This is doubly so if one assumes mutual interaction between elites, civil society and political systems deemed democratic; even more if one takes into account developments in the capitalist system so often seen as underpinning liberal democratic development.

One final point is worth making about the role of civil society in facilitating liberal democracy. Civil society seems likely to have useful democratic-training functions wherever and whenever it occurs. How- ever, this aside, in the ex-authoritarian or ex-totalitarian polities of the twentieth century, vibrant civil associations have functioned as means of enhancing the individual's social and psychological independence of the state. In the first-phase polities of the nineteenth century, where the state was deeply unambitous in social and psychological terms, the role of civil socicty may have been to facilitate independence of elites. Further- more, the original condition of dependence and deference was itself concomitant upon just that type of state.

Notes

Introduction

1. BBC Reith Lectures, quoted Dorothy Pickles, *Democracy* (1970), p. 11.
2. Ghia Nodia, 'How Different are post-Communist Transitions?', *Journal of Democracy*, 5, 2 (1994), 15–33.
3. See review of debate, ibid.
4. See, for example, Guiseppe Di Palma, *To Craft Democracies: An Essay in Democratic Transition* (Berkeley, 1990).
5. Victor Perez-Diaz, *The Return of Civil Society: The Emergence of Democratic Spain* (Cambridge, Mass, 1993). For classic discussion, see Alexis de Tocqueville, *Democracy in America* (1833, 1994, ed J.P. Mayer). For recent discussions, see, amongst many others: Ernest Gellner, *Conditions of Liberty: Civil Society and its Rivals* (1994); John Kean (ed), *Civil Society and the State* (1988); Charles Taylor, 'Modes of Civil Society', *Public Culture*, 3, 1 1990, 95–118; Adam B. Seligman, *The Idea of Civil Society* (Oxford, 1992); Edward Shils, 'The Virtue of Civil Society', *Government and Opposition*; R. D. Putnam, *Making Democracy Work: Traditions in Modern Italy* (Princeton, 1993); Michael Waltzer, 'The Idea of Civil Society', *Dissent* Spring 1991, 293–304; C. G. A Bryant, 'Citizenship, National Identity and the Accommodation of Difference: Reflections on Contemporary European Examples', Unpublished paper at European Sociology Association, 1995.
6. Edward Shils, 'The Virtue of Civil Society'.
7. Keith Middlemas, *Politics of Industrial Society: The Experience of the British System Since 1911* (1979).
8. These ideas are explored more fully, and most availably in A.H. Birch, 1 and 2.
9. Frank O' Gorman, *Voters, Patrons and Parties: The Unreformed Electorate of Hanoverian England, 1734–1832* (Oxford, 1990).
10. *Representative Government* (London, 1960), 300–7.
11. *The Making of the English Working Class* (London, 1964), 90.
12. Quoted Mark Hovell, *The Chartist Movement* (Manchester, 1918), 69.
13. J. Deegan, Stalybridge delegate to the National Convention 1839, quoted in Asa Briggs (ed), *Chartist Studies* (1959), 106.
14. Hovell, *The Chartist Movement*, 68.
15. Mill, *Representative Government*, 193ff.
16. Edmund Burke, *Works* (Bohn's Standard Library, 1887), vol. 1, 447.
17. John Vincent, *The Formation of the Liberal Party*.
18. *Salford Reporter*, 17 November 1894, p. 8; 15 September 1894, p. 7.
19. Jim Openshaw, Secretary of Salford Labour Party, *Salford Reporter*, 2 August 1924, 4.

20. T. H. Marshall, *Citizenship and Social Class and Other Essays* (Cambridge, 1950), 28.

1 The Old System

1.   John Cannon, *Parliamentary Reform 1640–1832* (Cambridge, 1972), p.30; also table 4.2, O'Gorman, *Voters, Patrons and Parties*, p.179. O'Gorman does not accept these estimates.

2.   K. Theodore Hoppen, 'Roads to Democracy: Electioneering in Nineteenth-century England and Ireland', *History* 81, October 1996, 555.

3.   G. Holmes, *The Electorate and the National Will in the First Age of Party* (Lancaster, 1976), p.15.

4.   Frank O'Gorman, *The Long Eighteenth Century: British Social and Political History 1688–1832* (1997), p.369.

5.   Notably O'Gorman, *Voters, Patrons and Parties*; Nick Rogers, *Whigs and Cities: Popular Politics in the Age of Walpole and Pitt* (Oxford, 1989). Also Paul Langford, *A Polite and Commercial People: England 1727–1783* (Oxford, 1990).

6.   See later p.200.

7.   O'Gorman, *Voters, Patrons and Parties*, ch. 4; John A. Phillips, *The Great Reform Bill in the Boroughs: English Electoral Behaviour 1818–41* (Oxford, 1992), p.253.

8.   O'Gorman, *Voters, Patrons and Parties*, ch.4. For similar figures, see much older study by Charles Seymour, *Electoral Reform in England and Wales 1832–85* (1915: Newton Abbott, 1970), p.533.

9.   *Popular Politics and British Anti-Slavery: The Mobilisation of Public Opinion against the Slave Trade 1787–1807* (Manchester, 1995), p.5.

10. Rogers, *Whigs and Cities*, p.240ff.

11. Ibid, p.52.

12. Frank O'Gorman, 'Campaign Rituals and Ceremonies: the Social Meaning of Elections in England 1780–1860', *Past and Present* 135, May 1992, 79–115.

13. Nossiter, *Influence, Opinion and Political Opinion in Reformed England* (Brighton, 1975).

14. O'Gorman, 'Electoral Deference in Unreformed England 1760–1832', *Journal of Modern History* 56, 3, September 1984.

15. Lindsay J. Proudfoot, *Urban Patronage and Social Authority: The Management of the Duke of Devonshire's Towns in Ireland 1764–1891* (Washington D.C.: 1995).

16. E.P. Thompson, *Customs in Common* (1991), p.305ff.

17. *Influence, Opinion and Political Idioms*, ch. 12.

18. *The Great Reform Bill*.

19. Rogers, *Whigs and Cities*.

20. Phillips, *The Great Reform Bill*, p.272ff.

21. Michael Brock, *The Great Reform Act* (1973), p.88ff.

22. Phillips, *The Great Reform Bill*, ch. 2.

23. James Vernon, *Politics and the People: A Study in English Provincial Culture 1815–67* (Cambridge, 1993).

24. On the open features of local government, see ibid; James Vernon (ed), *Re-reading the Constitution: New Narratives in the Political History of England's Long*

Nineteenth Century (New York: 1996); John Garrard, *Leadership and Power in Victorian Industrial Towns 1830–1914* (Manchester, 1983); John A. Phillips, *The Great Reform Bill*, ch. 3; Nick Rogers, *Whigs and Cities*, p.305ff.

25. Quoted Brock, *The Great Reform Act*, p.16.

2   The Process of Inclusion

 1. William Horne, Solicitor General, quoted in Dror Wahrman, *Imagining the Middle Class: The Political Representation of Class in Britain c.1780–1840* (Cambridge, 1995), p.314.
 2. Norman McCord, 'Some Difficulties of Parliamentary Reform', *Historical Journal* , 10 (1967) 24–38.
 3. Quoted R. J. Richardson, *Manchester Guardian* 2 October 1844, p.6.
 4. Quoted, Cannon, *Parliamentary Reform*, p.16.
 5. Quoted E. J. Feuchtwanger, *Gladstone* (1975), p.19.
 6. Wahrman, *Imagining the Middle Class*.
 7. Ibid, ch 9.
 8. Ibid, pp.176, 318.
 9. O'Gorman, *The Long Eighteenth Century*, p.371.
10. I have used O'Gorman's (*Voters Patrons and Parties*, p.179) figures for England and Wales as the basis from which to calculate the UK figures.
11. Estimates vary somewhat. These originate from B. R. Mitchell, *British Historical Statistics* (Cambridge, 1988), p.793f.
12. K. Theodore Hoppen, 'The Franchise and Electoral Politics in England and Ireland 1832–85', *History*, 70, 279 (June 1985) 204.
13. Phillips, *The Great Reform Bill*.
14. esp. Norman Gash, *Politics in the Age of Peel* (1969); D. C. Moore *The Politics of Deference* (Brighton, 1976).
15. Seymour, *Electoral Reform in England and Wales*, p.302. Seymour estimated that these voters represented a small percentage of the post-1832 county electorate, nowhere more than 1 in 6 – though, in tight contests, these could be important.
16. Nossiter, *Influence, Opinion and Political Idioms*.
17. Angus Hawkins, '"Parliamentary Government" and Political Parties *c.*1830–80', *English Historical Review*, 104 (1989) 638–69.
18. For the justice of such expectations, see Patrick Joyce, *Work, Society and Politics: The Culture of the Factory in Later Victorian England* (Brighton, 1980); John Garrard, *Leadership and Power in Northern Industrial Towns 1830–80* (Manchester, 1983).
19. Hoppen, 'The Franchise and Electoral Politics'.
20. W. L. Guttsman, *The British Political Elite* (1963).
21. Duncan Tanner, 'The Parliamentary System, the "Fourth" Reform Act and the Rise of Labour', *Bulletin of the Institute of Historical Research*, 56 (1983) 205–19.
22. H. J. Perkin, *The Rise of Professional Society: England since 1880* (1989).
23. Garrard, *Leadership and Power*, chs. 6–10.
24. Derek Fraser, *Urban Politics in Victorian England* (Leicester, 1976); *Power and Authority in Victorian Cities* (Oxford, 1979).

25. Thomas Thomason, *Bolton Chronicle*, 13 May 1854, p.6. Redesdale, as Chairman of Committees in the Lords 1851–86, was the key figure in negotiations over improvement Bills.

26. John Garrard, 'The Middle Class and Nineteenth Century Local and National Politics' in John Garrard et al. (eds), *The Middle Class in Politics* (Farnborough, 1978), pp.35–66.

27. David Walsh, *Working Class Political Integration and the Conservative Party in the North West 1800–70* (Salford University PhD, 1991).

28. Henry Brougham 1831, quoted Tom Nossiter, *Influence Opinion and Political Idioms*, p.163.

29. Foster, *Class Struggle in the Industrial Revolution* (1974), ch. 4; Gash, *Politics in the Age of Peel*, p.176; Paul A. Pickering, 'Chartism and the Trade in Agitation in Early Victorian Britain', *History*, 76 June 1991, 232.

30. Neville Kirk, *The Growth of Working-Class Reformism in Mid-Victorian England* (1985).

31. Garrard, *Leadership and Power*, ch. 8.

32. Walsh, *Working Class Political Integration*.

33. John Vincent, *The Formation of the Liberal Party, 1857–68* (1966).

34. Garrard, *Leadership and Power*, ch. 11.

35. Vernon, *Politics and the People*.

36. Maurice Cowling, *Disraeli, Gladstone and Revolution* (Cambridge, 1967). Not an uncontested view.

37. Joseph Snape, proposing formation of Salford Constitutional Association, *Salford Weekly News*, 7 February 1867, p.3.

38. Hennock, *Fit and Proper Persons: Ideal and Reality in Nineteenth-Century Urban Government* (1973), p.12.

39. J. P. D. Dunbabin, 'Electoral reforms and their outcome in the United Kingdom 1865–1900', in T. R. Gourvish and Alan O'Day, *Later Victorian Britain 1867–1900*, p.103.

40. Hawkins, 'Parliamentary Government'.

41. Gareth Stedman Jones, *Outcast London: A Story of the Relationship Between the Classes in Victorian Society* (Harmondsworth, 1976).

42. Mary Chadwick, 'The Role of Redistribution in the Making of the Third Reform Act', *Historical Journal*, 19, 3 (1976) 665–83.

43. J. A. Banks, 'The Contagion of Numbers', in H. J. Dyos and Michael Wolff, *The Victorian City: Image and Reality* (1976), pp.105–22.

44. I am indebted to Dr Sandra Hayton for these figures.

45. See chs 6–7.

46. Mill, *Representative Government*, pp.256–75.

47. For the argument, see P. Marsh, *The Discipline of Popular Government: Lord Salisbury's Domestic Statecraft 1881–1902* (Hassocks 1978); Jon Lawrence, 'Class and Gender in the Making of Urban Toryism 1880–1914', *English Historical Review*, 1993, 629–52; Paul A. Readman, 'The 1895 General election and Political Change in Late-Victorian Britain', *Historical Journal*, 42.2 (1999) 467–93.

48. *Rochdale Observer*, 26 March 1867, p.3.

49. Quoted F. B. Smith, *The Second Reform Act* (Cambridge, 1966), p.26.

50. Steadman Jones, *Outcast London*.

51. Didier Lancien, 'Le valeur de la vote: les particularites du systeme electoral britannique, 1918–48'. Awaiting publication.
52. John Carey, *The Intellectuals and the Masses* (1992).
53. Figures compiled from Hennock, *Fit and Proper Persons*; George Jones, *Borough Politics* (1969), and from my own data.
54. Michael Dawson, 'Money and the Real Impact of the Fourth Reform Act', *Historical Journal*, 35.2 (1992) 369–81.
55. See Declan McHugh, forthcoming University of Salford PhD, provisionally entitled, *The Rise of Labour in the 1920s: a Case Study in Greater Manchester*.
56. Ostrogorski, *Democracy and the Organisation of Political Parties* (New York, Haskell House 1902 and 1970), ch. 4.
57. The Reform League, quoted Smith, *The Second Reform Act*, p.188.
58. Vernon, *Politics and the People*.
59. Leonore Davidoff, *The Best Circles* (1973).
60. *Salford Weekly News*, 13 June 1873, p.3.
61. Pat Hollis, *Ladies Elect: Women in English Local Government 1865–1914* (Oxford, 1997).
62. Brian Harrison, *Separate Spheres: Opposition to Women's Suffrage in Britain* (New York, 1978).
63. Martin Pugh, *State and Society: A Social and Political History of Britain 1870–1997* (1999), p.200.
64. Gerard De Groot, *Blighty: British Society in the Era of the Great War* (1996), ch. 16.
65. William Joynson Hick, cited David Butler, *The Electoral System in Britain since 1918* (Oxford 1953), p.31.

3 The Role of British Political Elites

1. Juan Linz and Alfred Stepan, *Problems of Democratic Transition and Consolidation: Southern Europe, South America and Post-Communist Europe* (Baltimore, 1996).
2. Perez-Diaz, *The Return of Civil Society*.
3. Alexis de Tocqueville, *Democracy in America* (1994).
4. Guttsman, *British Political Elite*.
5. W.D. Rubinstein, *Men of Property: The Very Wealthy in Britain since the Industrial Revolution* (1981).
6. Davidoff, *The Best Circles*.
7. Nossiter, *Influence, Opinion and Political Idioms*.
8. Vincent, *Formation of the Liberal Party*.
9. J. R. Parry, *Democracy and Religion: Gladstone and the Liberal Party 1867–75* (Cambridge, 1987).
10. Cannon, *Parliamentary Reform*.
11. Quoted Brock, *The Great Reform Act*, p.152.
12. Ellis Archer Wasson, 'The Great Whigs and Parliamentary Reform 1809–30' *Journal of British Studies*, 24 (1985) 434–64.
13. D.C. Moore, 'Concession or Cure: the Sociological Premises of the First Reform Act', *Historical Journal*, IX, 1 (1966), 39–59.
14. *Politics in the Age of Peel*.

15. Cowling, *Disraeli, Gladstone and Revolution*.
16. Gaythorne, Hardy, and Bagehot (to Carnarvon), quoted in Smith, *The Second Reform Bill*, p.90.
17. Robert Blake, *Disraeli* (1966), p.440.
18. Ibid, pp.453 and 469.
19. Ibid, pp. 278–84.
20. Phillip Magnus, *Gladstone* (London, Murray 1978), p.164.
21. H.C.G. Matthew, *Gladstone 1809–1898* (Oxford, 1998), p.131.
22. Quoted ibid, p.139.
23. Smith, *The Second Reform Bill*, pp.91, 102.
24. Jose Harris, *Private Lives and Public Spirit: A Social History of Britain 1870–1914* (Oxford, 1993), p.14.
25. Smith, *Disraeli and Social Reform*, p.270.
26. Robert Shannon, *The Age of Salisbury 1881–1902* (1996), pp.14, 92 f.
27. Chadwick, 'The Role of Redistribution'.
28. David Cannadine, *The Decline and Fall of the British Aristocracy* (1992).
29. Harrison, *Separate Spheres*.
30. Lancien, 'Le Valeur du Vote'.
31. Matthew, *Gladstone*, p.119.
32. William Howard Greenleaf, *The British Political Tradition* (1983) vol. 1, p.214 f.
33. Nadja Durbach, 'They Might As Well Brand Us: Working-Class Resistance to Compulsory Vaccination', *Social History of Medicine*, 13, 1, 45–62; P.H.J.H. Gosden, *The Friendly Societies in England 1815–75* (Manchester, 1961).
34. Llyn Hollern Lees, *The Solidarities of Strangers: The English Poor Laws and the People 1700–1948* (Cambridge, 1998).
35. Howkins, *Reshaping Rural England 1850–1925* (1991), p.83.
36. Ibid, p.83.
37. Quoted in *Minority Report of the Poor Law Commission*, part 1, edited Sidney and Beatrice Webb (1909), pp.13–14.
38. Ibid, part 2, p.34.
39. Michael E. Rose, *The Relief of Poverty 1834–1914* (1972), p.51.
40. James Schofield, Annual Dinner of Newbold Friendly and Burial Society, *Rochdale Times*, 16 January 1886, p.6.
41. I am indebted to Peter Shapely for this information.
42. A. Denholme, 'Lord Ripon and the Co-operative movement', *Historical Studies*, 17.66 (1976),15–26.
43. Quoted Feutchwanger, *Gladstone*, p.141.
44. *Democracy in America*, p.233.
45. Lord Sandon, quoted Smith, *Disraeli*, p.246.
46. *Blackburn Standard*, 27 November 1839, p.8.
47. *Salford Weekly News* (SWN), 17 February 1872, p.3
48. SWN, 17 March 1879, p.3
49. *Salford Weekly Chronicle*, 23 April 1870, p.3
50. William M. Kuhn, *Democratic Royalism* (Basingstoke, 1996); David Cannadine in Eric Hobsbaum and Terence Ranger (eds), *The Invention of Tradition* (Cambridge, 1983), p.101–64; Richard Williams, *The Contentious Crown: Public Discussion of the Monarchy in the Reign of Victoria* (Aldershot, 1997).

51. *Bolton Chronicle*, 30 June 1838, pp.2–3.
52. Eugenio Biagini, *Liberty Retrenchment and Reform: Popular Liberalism in the Age of Gladstone* (Cambridge, 1992), ch.6.
53. Garrard, 'The Middle Classes'.
54. Jim Openshaw, *Salford Reporter*, 2 August 1924, p.6.
55. *Rochdale Labour News*, April 1897, p.2.
56. John Garrard, 'The Mayoralty since 1835', *Proceedings of the Lancashire and Cheshire Antiquarian Society*, vol 90, 29–53. For similar argument, see Kirk, *The Growth of Working Class Reformism*.
57. Charles Wilkins, quoted Walsh, *Working Class Political Integration*, p 219.
58. Quoted ibid, p.229.
59. Amongst many others, see Cowling, *Disraeli Gladstone and Revolution*; George Dangerfield, *The Strange Death of Liberal England* (1935, 1997).
60. *Liberty Retrenchment and Reform*, p.86.
61. Election address, quoted Walsh, *Working Class Integration*, p.445.
62. Quoted ibid, p.164.
63. Quoted Anthony Howe, *The Cotton Masters 1830–60* (Oxford, 1984), p.103.
64. Letter to Earl of Harrowby, Peel Papers, quoted Walsh, *Working Class Integration*, p.152.
65. Quoted Feutchwanger, *Disraeli*, p.214.
66. Smith, *Disraeli*, p.260.
67. Quoted Shannon, *The Age of Salisbury*, p.356.
68. Ibid, p.362.
69. *Whigs and Cities*.
70. *The British Political Tradition*.
71. Walsh, *Working Class and Political Integration*.
72. Paul A. Readman, 'The 1895 General Election and Political Change in Late-Victorian Britain', *Historical Journal*, 42.2 (1999) 467–93.
73. *The Rise and Fall of the Political Press* (1981).
74. George Jacob Holyoak, *Sixty Years of an Agitator's Life* (1893) vol 1, p.227.
75. Quoted Vincent, *Formation of the Liberal Party*, p.180.
76. Ibid, p.123.
77. For recent persuasive evidence, see Biagini, *Liberty Retrenchment and Reform*.
78. Garrard, 'Middle Classes'.
79. Kirk, *Growth of Working Class Reformism*.
80. Jon Lawrence, 'Gender and Class in the Making of Urban Toryism 1880–1914', *English Historical Review*, CIIX, 431 (1993) 629–52.
81. Biagini, *Liberty Retrenchment and Reform*.
82. Keith Middlemas, *The Politics of Industrial Society* (1979).
83. Biagini, *Liberty Retrenchment and Reform*.
84. Patrick Joyce, *Democratic Subjects* (Cambridge, 1994).
85. Readman, 'The 1895 Election'.

4 The Political Fitness of Middle Class Males

1. See Seymour Martin Lipsett, *Political Man: the Social Bases of Politics* (1960).
2. Isaac Taylor, 1817, quoted in Leonore Davidoff and Catherine Hall, *Family Fortunes: Men and Women of the Middle Class 1780–1850* (1987), p.235.

3. Ibid.
4. Ibid, p.260.
5. *Influence, Opinion and Political Idioms*, ch.9.
6. Thomas Thomasson, *Bolton Chronicle*, 13 May 1854, p.6.
7. Quoted Stephen Yeo, *Religion and Voluntary Organisations in Crisis* (1976), p.43.
8. Especially Davidoff and Hall, *Family Fortunes*, Part 1.
9. Isaac Taylor, quoted ibid, p.235.
10. Lucy Brown, *Victorian News and Newspapers* (Oxford, 1985).
11. Koss, *The Rise and Fall of the Political Press*.
12. de Tocqueville, *Democracy in the United States*, p.190.
13. Quoted Yeo, *Religion and Voluntary Organisations*, op cit., 57.
14. Quoted R.J. Morris, *Class, Sect and Party: Leeds 1820–50* (Manchester, 1990) p.168.
15. Robert Vaughan, *The Age of Great Cities* (1843), p.296.
16. Morris, *Class Sect and Party*, ch 7.
17. S. J. D. Green, *Religion in the Age of Decline: Organisation and Experience in Industrial Yorkshire 1870–1920* (Cambridge, 1996), ch 4.
18. Hyppolyte Taine, *Notes on England*, translated by Edward Hyams (1863, 1957), p.168.
19. Samuel Low junior, cited David Owen, *English Philanthropy 1660–1960* (Cambridge: Mass., 1960), p.166.
20. Eugene Black, *The Social Politics of Anglo-Jewry 1880–1920* (Oxford, 1988).
21. Peter Shapely, *Charity and Power in Victorian Manchester* (Manchester, 2000), p.23.
22. Simon Fowler, 'Voluntarism and Victory: Charity the State and the British War Effort 1914–18', Unpublished paper, Conference on 'The History of Charity 1750–1990', University of Wales, Bangor, 2–3 September 1999.
23. Brian Harrison, 'Pubs' in Dyos and Wolff, *The Victorian City*, pp.161–80.
24. Richard Trainor, *Black Country Elites* (Oxford, 1993), p.314.
25. Quoted by John Belchem and Nick Hardy, 'Second Metropolis' in Alan Kidd and David Nicholls, *The Making of the British Middle Class?* (Stroud, 1998), p.61.
26. Garrard and Parrott, 'Craft, Professional and Middle-Class Identity', ibid.
27. Anthony Howe, *The Cotton Masters 1830–60* (Oxford, 1984), p.163.
28. Geoffrey Crossick, *The Lower-Middle Class In Britain* (1977).
29. Alun Howkins, *Reshaping Rural England* (1991), p.157 ff.
30. J.R.Oldfield, *Popular Politics and British Anti-Slavery: The Mobilisation of Public Opinion Against the Slave Trade 1787–1807* (Manchester, 1995).
31. D.W. Bebbington, *The Nonconformist Conscience 1870–1914* (1982).
32. For endorsement, see Davidoff and Hall, *Family Fortunes*, p.446.
33. Stephen Yeo, *Religion and Voluntary Organisations*, p.11.
34. John Angell James 1822, quoted Davidoff and Hall, *Family Fortunes*, p.130.
35. Quoted Morris, *Class, Sect and Party*, p.254.
36. See for example Perez-Diaz, *The Return of Civil Society*, p.120 ff.
37. A.D. Gilbert, *Religion and Society in Industrial England* (1976).
38. Paul Smith, *Religion in Industrial Society: Oldham and Saddleworth 1740–1865* (Oxford, 1994), p.39f.
39. See Bilston in Trainor, *Elites*, p.187.
40. Philips, *The Great Reform Bill*, ch.8.

41. Barry M. Doyle, 'Urban Liberalism and the "Lost Generation": Politics and Middle Class Culture in Norwich 1900–35', *Historical Journal*, 38,3 (1995), 614–34.
42. Davidoff and Hall, *Family Fortunes*, p.130.
43. Gilbert, *Religion and Society*, p.34.
44. Bill Williams, *The Making of Manchester Jewry 1740–1875* (Manchester, 1976), p.133. I am indebted to Bill Williams for his insights here.
45. Kenneth D. Brown, *A Social History of the Nonconformist Ministry in England and Wales 1800–1930* (Oxford, 1988).
46. Hugh McLeod, *Class and Religion in the Late-Victorian City* (1974), pp.137–43.
47. E.P. Hennock, *Fit and Proper Persons* (1973).
48. Shapely, *Charity and Power*, ch.4.
49. David Owen, *English Philanthropy 1660–1960* (Oxford, 1964), p.43.
50. Keir Waddington, 'Subscribing to a Democracy? Excluded and Included and the Voluntary Ideology of the London Hospitals 1850–1900' unpublished paper at 'History of Charity Conference'.
51. Florence Nightingale, quoted Owen, *English Philanthropy*, p.481.
52. Garrard, *Leadership and Power*, pp.31–5; Trainor, *Elites*.
53. Howe, *The Cotton Masters*, pp.202–3.
54. Thomas Bazely, quoted ibid, p.177.
55. Fraser, *Urban Politics in Victorian England*.
56. Norman McCord, *The Anti-Corn Law League 1838–46* (1968), ch. 7.
57. Harold Perkin, *The Origins of Modern English Society 1780–1880* (1969).
58. Morris, *Class Sect and Party*.
59. Gilbert, *Religion and Society*, p.163.
60. Geoffrey Crossick and Heinz-Gerhard Haupt (eds), *Shopkeepers and Master Artisans in Nineteenth century Europe* (1984).
61. Michael J. Winstanley, *The Shopkeepers World 1830–1914* (Manchester, 1983); G. L. Anderson, *Victorian Clerks* (Manchester, 1976).
62. Amongst many others on this theme, see Oliver McDonagh, *A Pattern of Government Growth: The Passenger Acts and their Enforcement* (1961); A.J. Lee, *Social Leaders and Public Persons* (Oxford, 1963); Garrard, *Leadership and Power*, p.63 ff.

5 Working Men and Political Fitness: Access to Civil Society

1. Lipsett, *Political Man*, p.180 ff.
2. Durbach, 'They might as well brand us'.
3. See Patrick Joyce, *Work, Society and Politics*.
4. See Raphael Samuel, 'Comers and Goers' in Dyos and Wolff (eds), *The Victorian City*, ch. 5; Martin Daunton, *Coal Metropolis* (Leicester, 1977).
5. See Yeo, *Religion and Voluntary Organisations and Crisis*.
6. Martin Gorski, 'The growth and distribution of friendly societies in the early nineteenth century', *Economic History Review*, 51, 3 (1998) 489–511.
7. Shani D'Cruze and Jean Turnbull, 'Fellowship and Family: Oddfellows Lodges in Preston and Lancaster 1830–90', *Urban History*, 22,1, May 1995, 25–47.
8. Mike Savage, *The Dynamics of Working Class Politics* (Cambridge, 1987).

9. On the domesticating effects of larger and more comfortable housing at the end of the century, see Gareth Stedman Jones, *Languages of Class, Studies in English Working-Class History 1832–1982* (Cambridge, 1983), ch. 4.
10. Outside London, geographical segregation was for a long time limited. However, its effects were greatly enhanced by the fact that working people generally journeyed to work before, and left it after, those in the classes above. See Richard Dennis, *English Industrial Cities of the Nineteenth Century; A Social Geography* (Cambridge, 1984), chs 4 and 5.
11. Martin Daunton, *House and Home in the Victorian City* (1983).
12. Harrison, 'Pubs'.
13. For temperance Chartism, Lilian Shiman, *The Crusade against Drink in Victorian England* (Basingstoke, 1988), ch.2.; for some union attitudes, see Anthony Delves, 'Popular Recreation and Social Conflict in Derby 1800–50' in Eileen and Stephen Yeo (eds), *Popular Culture and Social Conflict* (Brighton, 1981).
14. Shiman, *The Crusade against Drink*, ch.2.
15. *Blackburn Times*, 25 September 1875, p.6.
16. *Blackburn Times*, 26 December 1866, p.6.
17. Not all of it, since co-operators rarely met there, and Nonconformists never did.
18. Alan J. Lee, *The Origins of the Popular Press 1855–1914* (1976).
19. Amongst many sources on these, see Virginia Berridge, "Popular Sunday Newspapers and Victorian Society" in G. Boyce, James Curran and Pauline Wingate (eds), *Newspaper History from the Seventeenth Century to the Present Day* (1978).
20. See David Hopkin, 'The Socialist Press in Britain 1890–1914', ibid, ch 16.
21. For references to this behaviour in late-century, see Biagini, *Liberty Retrenchment and Reform*, ch.7.
22. For the early period, see Thompson *The Making of the English Working Class*, p.717 f; Arthur Aspinall, *Politics and the Press* (1949, Brighton, 1973) p.25f, 395f. For late-century, see Biagini, *Liberty, Retrenchment and Reform*, ch.7.
23. Pat Hollis, *The Pauper Press* (1970), p.119.
24. J.A. Epstein, 'Feargus O'Connor and the *Northern Star*', *International Review of Social History*, XXI, 1 (1976) 51–97.
25. Hugh McLeod, *Class and Religion in the Late-Victorian City* (1974), chs 1 and 3.
26. See David Howell, *British Workers and the Independent Labour Party 1888–1906* (Manchester, 1983); also Bill Lancaster, *Radicalism, Co-operation and Socialism: Leicester Working-Class Politics 1860–1906* (Leicester, 1987).
27. Lee, *Origins of the Popular Press*.
28. For this habit in another, much later, context, see Geoffrey Nulty, *Guardian Country 1853–1978 – the first 125 years of Cheshire County Newspapers Limited* (Warrington 1978), p.72.
29. Thompson, *The Making of the Working Class*, p.733.
30. Lee, *The Origins of the Popular Press*, ch.1.
31. Thompson, *The Making of the English Working Class*, p.720.
32. Quoted ibid, p.721.
33. Iain McCalman, *Radical Underworld: Prophets, Revolutionaries and Pornographers in London 1795–1840* (Cambridge, 1988).
34. Lee, *Origins of the Popular Press*.

35. Quoted in G.A. Cranfield, *The Press and Society: From Caxton to Northcliffe* (1978), p.166.
36. Kirk, *The Growth of Working-Class Reformism*, ch.4.
37. Thompson, *The Making of the English Working Class*, pp. 520, 630.
38. See Patrick Joyce, *Visions of the People: Industrial England and the Question of Class 1840–1914* (Cambridge, 1991).
39. For argument, see Gareth Stedman Jones, 'The Language of Chartism', James Epstein and Dorothy Thompson (eds), *The Chartist Experience: Studies in Working Class Radicalism and Culture 1930–60* (1982), pp. 3–58.
40. D. Hopkin, 'The Socialist Press in Britain 1890–1914' in Boyce et al. *Newspaper History from the Seventeenth Century to the Present Day*.
41. This was particularly so when they were strictly local bodies, rather than Affiliated Order lodges.
42. See Jones, *Outcast London*, chs 16–17.
43. J. M. Baernreither, *English Associations of Working Men* (1889), p.162; Eric Hopkins, *Working-Class Self-Help in Nineteenth Century England* (1995), p.9.
44. *Working-Class Self-Help*, p.24.
45. Dot Jones, 'Did friendly Societies Matter? A Study of Friendly Society Membership in Glamorgan 1794–1910', *Welsh Historical Review* (1985) 12, 324–49.
46. See P.H.J.H. Gosden, *Self Help: Voluntary Associations in Nineteenth Century Britain* (1973), p.42.
47. Ibid, p.74.
48. See George Unwin, *Industrial Organisation in the Sixteenth and Seventeenth Centuries* (Oxford, 1904); Henry Pelling, *A History of British Trade Unionism* (Harmondsworth, 1987), p.11.
49. John Rule (ed), *British Trade Unionism 1750–1850* (1988).
50. Pelling, *A History of British Trade Unionism*, p.11 f.
51. Allan Davenport, 'Life' reprinted in *National Co-operative Leader* 1851, quoted in Thompson, *The Making of the English Working Class*, p.254.
52. Ibid, p.508.
53. Quoted in Pelling, *A History of British Trade Unionism*, p.17.
54. Ibid, p.297 f.
55. G.D.H. Cole, *A Century of Co-operation* (Manchester, 1944), p.148; also Robin Thornes, 'Change and Continuity', in Stephen Yeo (ed), *New Views of Co-operation* (1988).
56. John Langton and R.J. Morris (eds), *Atlas of Industrializing Britain 1780–1914* (1986), pp. 194–5.
57. I. Prothero, *Artisans and Politics in early Nineteenth-Century London: John Gast and His Times* (Folkestone, 1979).
58. Cole, *A Century Of Co-operation*, p.177.
59. Ibid, p.177.
60. Ibid, p.212.
61. Ibid, p.176.
62. *Rochdale Pilot*, 6 October 1866, p.3.
63. See K.S. Inglis, *Churches and the Working Classes in Victorian England* (1973); McLeod, *Class and Religion*.
64. Jeffrey Cox, *The English Churches in a Secular Society 1870–1930* (Oxford, 1982).
65. See Eric Hobsbaum, *Primitive Rebels* (Manchester, 1971).

66. E. T. Davies, *Religion in the Industrial Revolution in South Wales* (Cardiff, 1965).
67. R. F. Wearmouth, *Methodism and the Struggle of the Working Classes* (Leicester, 1954), p.110.
68. Ibid, p.104.
69. Hopkins, S*elf-Help*, p.34; see also Shani D'Cruise and Jean Turnbull, 'Fellowship and Family: Oddfellows Lodges in Preston and Lancaster 1830–90', *Urban History*, 22, 1 (1995), p.30.
70. Alun Howkins, *Poor Labouring Men: Rural Radicalism in Norfolk 1870–1923* (London: Routledge, 1985), p.52.
71. For figures, see Hopkins, *Self-Help*, p.121.
72. McLeod, *Class and Religion*, ch.2.
73. John Rule, 'The Property of Skill in Manufacture' in Patrick Joyce (ed), *The Historical Meanings of Work* (Cambridge, 1987).
74. Prothero, *Artisans and Politics*, ch.2.
75. Clive Behagg, 'The democracy of Work 1820–50' in Rule, *British Trade Unionism*, p.160 f.
76. H. Mayhew, *London Labour and the London Poor*, quoted Thompson, *The Making of the English Working Class*, p.240.
77. See maps in Langton and Morris (eds), *Atlas of Industrializing Britain*, pp. 184 and 195; also Cole, *A Century of Co-operation*, p.213.
78. Though this was less evident earlier in the century, with pre-1844 co-ops having a particularly visible presence in London, as well as in the north. See Langton and Morris, *Atlas of Industrialising Britain*, p.195.
79. This was less evident in higher-wage rural areas. Witness for example the movement's rapid growth in Norfolk after the 1870s.
80. Langton and Morris, *Atlas of Industrialising Britain*, p.213 f.
81. E. W. Brabrook, 'Friendly Societies and Similar Institutions', *Journal of the Statistical Society*, 38, 2 June 1875, 204.
82. Garrard, *Leadership and Power*, ch. 7–8; Vincent, *The Formation of the Liberal Party*, pp.131–52.
83. Joyce, *Factory Politics*, p.331 f.
84. Charles More, *Skill and the English Working Class 1870–1914* (1980).
85. Howkins, *Poor Labouring Men*; David Neave, *Mutual Aid in the Victorian Country-side: Friendly Societies in Rural East Yorkshire 1830–1914* (Hull, 1991), p.72.
86. Quoted in Wearmouth, *Methodism and the Struggle of the Working Classes*, p.223.
87. See for example the East Riding of Yorkshire, Neave, *Mutual Aid in the Victorian Countryside*, p.10 f.
88. Holyoak, *Sixty Years of an Agitator's Life*, vol. 1, p.214.
89. See Douglas Kirkpatrick, *The Unfriendly Friendly Societies* (Unpublished BA Dissertation, University of Salford, 1990).
90. Joyce, *Factory Politics*, p.103 f.

6 Working Men and Political Fitness: Internal Self-Governance

1. Martin Gorski, 'Mutual Aid in Civil Society: Friendly Societies in Nineteenth-Century Bristol', *Urban History*, 25,3 (1998), p.305.
2. Hopkins, *Self-Help*, p.18.

3. Quoted Margaret D. Fuller, *West Country Friendly Societies* (Oakwood Press, University of Reading, 1964), p.64.
4. D'Cruise and Turnbull, 'Fellowship and Family', p.44.
5. Gorski, 'Mutual Aid and Civil Society', p.318.
6. Quoted Baernreither, *English Associations of Working Men*, p.293.
7. Neave, *Mutual Aid*, p.92
8. Report from the Select Committee on the Laws Respecting Friendly Societies 1825 p.12, quoted Fuller *West Country Friendly Societies*, p.21. For contrary evidence, see Joyce, *Factory Politics*, p.289–90.
9. *Rochdale Observer*, 12 June 1901 p.2, and 19 June 1901 p.8.
10. All Souls Friendly and Burial Society, *Bolton Chronicle*, 21 February 1914, p.11.
11. *Bolton Chronicle*, 6 July 1912, p.9.
12. *Blackburn Times*, 13 July 1912, p.10.
13. *Blackburn Times*, 25 May 1912, p.9.
14. *Rochdale Times*, 31 January 1912, p.5.
15. *Rochdale Times*, 14 February 1912, p.5.
16. *Rochdale Times*, 2 March 1912, p.2.
17. *Rochdale Observer*, 13 May 1908, p.4.
18. The next election of 1913 was similarly contested on a related issue.
19. *Rochdale Observer*, 13 December 1887, p.3.
20. *Rochdale Observer*, 8 February 1888, p.7.
21. For example, see Neave, *Mutual Aid*, p.92f.
22. Peter Gurney, *Co-operative Culture and the Politics of Consumption in England 1870–1930* (Manchester, 1996).
23. *A Century of Co-operation*, p.148ff.
24. Sidney and Beatrice Webb, *Industrial Democracy* (1897), p.vi.
25. Behagg, 'The democracy of work', p.170.
26. Webb, *Industrial Democracy*, vol 1. p.7.
27. Trevor Lummis, *The Labour Aristocracy 1851–1914* (Aldershot, 1994).
28. *Industrial Democracy*, p.10 f.2. They were referring to district branches of the London Society of Compositors, and the National Union of Boot and Shoe Operatives.
29. Quoted ibid, p.13.
30. Logie Barrow and Ian Bullock, *Democratic Ideas and the British Labour Movement 1880–1914* (Cambridge, 1996).
31. *Industrial Democracy*, p.22.
32. Ibid, p.22.
33. See for example the Miners Federation until at least the 1890s. Ibid, p.34f.
34. Ibid, p.28.
35. Ibid, p.56f.
36. Ibid, p.49.
37. Quoted Howkins, *Poor Labouring Men*, p.83.
38. Derek Matthews, '1889 and All That: New Views and the New Unions' *International Review of Social History*, XXXVI, 1 (1991) 24–58.
39. Jennifer Hart, Religion and Social Control in Nineteenth Century Britain' in A. P. Donajgrodski, *Social Control in Nineteenth Century Britain* (1977), pp.108–37.
40. *Manchester Guardian*, 5 August 1840, p.3.

41. de Tocqueville, *Democracy in America*.
42. Mark Smith, *Religion in Industrial Society: Oldham and Saddleworth 1740–1865* (Oxford, 1994), p.176.
43. Davies, *Religion in the Industrial Revolution*, ch.2.
44. Green, *Religion in and Age of Decline*, ch.3.
45. Smith, *Religion in International Society*, p.143.
46. Ibid, p.202.
47. Quoted in Alun Howkins, *Reshaping Rural England: A Social History 1850–1925* (1991), p.184.
48. Bert Hazel, quoted ibid, p.53.
49. T. W. Laquer, *Religion and Respectability: Sunday Schools and Working-Class Culture* (New Haven: Conn., 1976).
50. Davies, *The Industrial Revolution*, ch.3.
51. Shiman, *The Crusade against Drink*.
52. Thompson, *The Making of the English Working Class*, ch.11.
53. See David Hempton, *The Religion of the People: Methodism and Popular Religion c.1750–1900* (1996), ch.1.
54. Eileen Yeo, 'Some Practices and Problems of Chartist Democracy' in Epstein and Thompson (eds) *The Chartist Experience*, pp.345–80.
55. Thompson, *The Making of the English Working Class*, p.140.
56. *The Autobiography of Francis Place* edited by Mary Thale (Cambridge, 1972), pp.131, 141.
57. *The Making of the English Working Class*, p.673.
58. Logie and Bullock, *Democratic Ideas and the Labour Movement*, p.75.
59. Ibid.
60. Keith Middlemas, *The Politics of Industrial Society* (1979).
61. Neave, *Mutual Aid in the Victorian Countryside*, p.57.
62. Cole, *A Century of Co-operation*, p.403.
63. Cathrine Webb, *Industrial Co-operation: the Story of a Peaceful Revolution* (Manchester, 1904), p.122.
64. Neave, *Mutual Aid*, p.11.
65. For example, ibid, p.98; Kirk, *The Growth of Working-Class Reformism*, ch.4.
66. Neave, *Mutual Aid*, pp.57–64; Howkins, *Labouring Men*, p.52; Michael Winstanley, 'Oldham Radicalism and the Origins of Popular Liberalism 1830–52', *Historical Journal*, 36.3 (1993), 619–43; Robert Colls, *The Pitmen of the Northern Coalfield: Work, Culture and Protest 1790–1850* (Manchester, 1987), p.178.
67. Biagini, *Liberty, Retrenchment and Reform*, ch.6.
68. Ibid, ch.7; Patrick Joyce, *Democratic Subjects* (Cambridge, 1994); John Belchem and James Epstein, 'The Nineteenth Century Gentleman Leader Revisited' *Social History*, 22.2 (May 1997), 174–93.
69. For Ironside, see Derek Fraser, *Power and Authority in the Victorian City* (Oxford, 1979), p.139 ff; for Livesey, see Garrard, *Leadership and Power*, chs. 7–8.
70. Howkins, *Labouring Men*, p.52.
71. Quoted Thompson, *The Making of the English Working Classes*, p.42.
72. Neave, *Mutual Aid*, p.10.
73. W. Hamish Fraser, *Trade Unions and Society: the Struggle for Acceptance 1850–80* (1974), chs. 1–4.

74. On the dire effects of slum clearance, see Stedman Jones, *Outcast London*, part.2; Anthony S. Wohl, *The Eternal Slum: Housing and Social Policy in Victorian London* (London: Edward Arnold, 1977), pp.141ff; 360ff.
75. Kirk, *The Growth of Working-Class Reformism*, p.154; Biagini, *Liberty Retrenchment and Reform*, chs. 2–3.
76. Daunton, *House and Home*; F. M. L. Thompson, *The Rise of Respectable Society: A Social History of Victorian Britain 1830–1900* (1988).
77. See amongst very many others, F. M. L. Thompson, 'Social Control in Victorian Britain', *Economic History Review*, XXIV (1981), 73–97.
78. See George Unwin, *Industrial Organisation in the Sixteenth and Seventeenth Centuries* (Oxford, 1904).
79. Cole, *A Century of Co-operation*, ch. 7.
80. See David J. Dobson, *Weavers of Dreams* (Davis, California, 1994); Ian Harford, *Manchester and Its Ship Canal Movement* (Keele, 1994), p.163.
81. Martin Gorski, 'The Growth and Distribution of Friendly Societies in the early Nineteenth Century', *Economic History Review*, 51, 3 (1998), 489–511.
82. Annual Dinner of Newbold Friendly and Burial Society, *Rochdale Times*, 16 January 1886, p.6.
83. *Stockport Advertizer*, 29 June 1838. A random search also finds them in processions in Bolton, Manchester, Bury, Warrington and Birmingham.
84. Peter Gurney, 'George Holyoak', Yeo (ed.), *New Views of Co-operation*, ch.4.
85. Quoted in Hopkins, *Working-Class Self-Help*, p.62.
86. David Green, 'National Insurance'; Neave, *Mutual Aid*, p.84/5.
87. Gurney, *Co-operative Culture*, pp.180–7.
88. Sheila Blackburn, 'The Origins of the Trades Boards Act', *Historical Journal*, 34.1(1991), 43–64.
89. Kenneth D. Brown, *Labour and Unemployment 1900–1914* (Newton Abbott, 1971).
90. Quoted Thompson, *The Making of the English Working Class*, p.820.
91. Stedman Jones, 'The Language of Chartism', Epstein and Thompson (eds), *The Chartist Experience*, pp.59–86.
92. Lancaster, *Radicalism, Co-operation*, p.79.
93. Biagini, *Liberty Retrenchment and Reform*, ch.6.
94. Brown, *Labour and Unemployment*.
95. Hennock, *Social Leaders and Public Persons*, p.330.
96. Mike Savage, 'Urban History and Social Class: Two Paradigms', *Urban History*, 20.1,76.
97. Ross McKibbin, *The Evolution of the Labour Party* (1974).
98. *The Making of the English Working Class*, p.79.
99. Biagini, *Liberty, Retrenchment and Reform*, ch.4.
100. *Sixty Years of an Agitator's Life*, vol II,123.
101. Amongst others, Biagini, *Liberty, Retrenchment and Reform*, ch.7.

7 Women and Political Fitness

1. 'Late-Victorian Women', Gourvish and O'Day (eds), *Later Victorian Britain*, p.175.

2.   David F. Mitch, *The Rise of Popular Literacy in Victorian England* (Philadelphia, 1992).

3.   Davidoff, *The Best Circles*.

4.   Edward Higgs, 'Women, occupations and work in the nineteenth-century censuses', *History Workshop Journal*, 23 (1987), 60.

5.   Rule, 'Property of Skill in Manufacturing'.

6.   Shoemaker, *Gender in English Society 1650–1850* (1998), pp.174–5.

7.   Anna Clark, *The Struggle for the Breeches; Gender and the Making of the English Working Class* (1997), p.29.

8.   Alice Horan, 1926 TUC Conference on Enrolling Women, quoted Sheila Lewenhak, *Women and Trade Unions* (1977), p.209.

9.   Quoted Thompson, *The Making of the English Working Class*, p.417.

10. Quoted Malcolm Thomis and Jennifer Grimmett, *Women in Protest 1800–50* (1882).

11. Shoemaker, *Gender in English Society*, p.254.

12. Clark, *The Struggle for the Breeches*, ch.13.

13. Lucy Bland, *Banishing the Beast: Feminism and Sexual Morality 1885–1914* (1995), ch.2.

14. David Rubinstein, *Before the Suffragettes: Women's Emancipation in the 1890s* (Brighton: Harvester, 1986), p.8.

15. Davidoff and Hall, *Family Fortunes*.

16. See Shoemaker, *Gender in English Society*.

17. John O'Neill *c.*1856–60, quoted Clark, *The Struggle for the Breeches*, p.256.

18. Geoffrey Weeks, *Sex Politics and Society: The Regulation of Sexuality since 1800*, (1981), p.67.

19. Rubinstein, *Before the Suffragettes*, ch.6.

20. Martha Vicinus, *Independent Women: Work and Community for Single Women 1850–1920* (1985), p.30.

21. Rubinstein, *Before the Suffragettes*, ch.11.

22. Carol Dyhouse, *Feminism and the Family in England 1880–1939* (Oxford 1989); Bland, *Banishing the Beast*; Weeks, *Sex, Politics and Society*.

23. Theresa McBride, *The Domestic Revolution: The Modernisation of Household Service in Britain and France 1820–1920* (1976).

24. Winifred Bridges, *Deference and Paternalism in North-East Lancashire Cotton Towns During the Twentieth Century* (Unpublished MPhil thesis, University of Salford, 1988).

25. Martin Pugh, *State and Society: A Social and Political History of Britain 1870–1997* (1999), p.303.

26. Deborah Gorham, *The Victorian Girl and the Feminine Ideal* (1982).

27. Bland, *Banishing the Beast*, ch.4.

28. Gillian Scott, *Feminism and the Politics of Working Women: The Women's Co-operative Guild, 1880s to the Second World War* (1998).

29. Jane Rendall, 'A Moral Engine: Feminism, Liberalism and *The English Woman's Journal*', in Jane Rendall (ed), *Equal or Different: Women's Politics 1800–1914* (Oxford, 1987), ch.4.

30. Anthony Armstrong, *The Church of England, the Methodists and Society, 1700–1850* (1973), p.55.

31. Green, *Religion in the Age of Decline*, p.206f.

32. Cox, *English Churches in a Secular Society*, ch.3.

33. Green, *Religion in the Age of Decline*, p.197.
34. R.W.M. Strain, *Belfast and Its Charitable Society* (Oxford, 1961), p.112; Davidoff and Hall, *Family Fortunes*, p.66.
35. Quoted F.K. Prochaska, *Women and Philanthropy in Nineteenth Century England* (Oxford, 1980), p.18.
36. Frank Prochaska, 'A Mother's Country : Mother's Meetings and Family Welfare in Britain, 1850–1950, *History*, 74, 242, (1989), 379–99.
37. *Reshaping Rural Society*, p.278.
38. *Journal of Gaslighting*, 6 June 1905, 674.
39. June Purvis, 'Women Teachers in Edwardian Britain' *Twentieth Century British History*, 8,2 (1997), 266–71.
40. Dina Copelman, *London Women Teachers: Gender, Class and Feminism 1870–1930* (London: Routledge, 1996); Allison Oram, *Women Teachers and Feminist Politics 1900–1939* (Manchester, 1996).
41. Figures taken or calculated from Sheila Lewenhak, *Women and Trade Unions* (1977), p.96; Rubinstein, *Before the Suffragettes*, p.123; Pelling, *A History of British Trade Unionism*, p.297f.
42. Clark, *Struggle for the Breeches*.
43. Thane, 'Late-Victorian Women', p.198; Lewenhak, *Women and Trade Unions*, p.198.
44. Ibid, p.88.
45. Ibid, p.96–7.
46. Thane, 'Late-Victorian Women', p.203.
47. *A Century of Co-operation*, p.220.
48. Scott, *Feminism and the Politics of Working Women*, p.21.
49. Robert Glen, *Urban Workers* (1984), p.110.
50. Brabook, 'On Friendly Societies', p.191.
51. David Englander, *Landlord and Tenant in Urban England* (Oxford, 1983), chs.7–11.
52. William Wilberforce, quoted Davidoff and Hall, *Family Fortunes*, p.429.
53. Shoemaker, *Gender in English Society*, 250–1; Clare Midgely, *Women against Slavery* (1992), p.60.
54. Joan Parker, 'Lydia Becker, Pioneer Orator', *Manchester Region History Review*, 5, 2 (1991–2), 13–20.
55. Paul McHugh, *Prostitution and Social Reform* (1980).
56. Sandra Stanley Holton, *Feminism and Democracy: Women's Suffrage and Reform Politics in Britain 1900–1918* (Cambridge, 1986), p.119.
57. Pugh, *The Tories and the People* (Oxford, 1985), p.27 and ch.5.
58. *Feminism and the Politics of Working Women*, p.264.
59. Holton, *Feminism and Democracy*.
60. Harrison, *Separate Spheres*, ch.6.
61. Colley, *Britons*.
62. *Struggle for the Breeches*.
63. See for example Elizabeth Roberts, *A Woman's Place: An Oral History of Working Class Women 1890–1940* (Oxford, 1984).
64. *One Hand Tied Behind Us.*
65. Scott, *Feminism and the Politics of Working Women*.
66. Thane, 'Late Victorian Women', p.206.
67. Scott, *Feminism and the Politics of Working Women*, p.162.

68. Harold L. Smith, 'Gender and the Welfare State: The 1940 Old Age and Widow's Pensions Act', *History*, 80 (1995), 382–99.
69. Pugh, *The Tories and the People*, p.27; A.T.Q. Stewart, *The Ulster Crisis; Resistance to Home Rule 1912–14* (1969), p.65.
70. My thanks to Bill Williams for this insight.
71. Clark, *Struggle for the Breeches*; Shoemaker, *Gender in English Society*; Deborah Valenze, 'Cottage Religion and the Politics of Survival' in Rendall, *Equal or Different*, ch.1.
72. Green, *Religion in the Age of Decline*, p.203.
73. David Owen *English Philanthropy 1660–1960* (1964), p.50.
74. Prochaska, *Women and Philanthropy*.
75. Pat Hollis, *Ladies Elect*, ch.1.
76. Prochaska, 'A Mothers Country'.
77. Lewenhak, *Women and Trade Unions*, p.20; Clark, *Struggle for the Breeches*, p.35f.
78. *Rochdale Observer*, 13 December 1887, p.3, and 8 February 1888, p.7.
79. *Blackburn Weekly Times*, 22 February 1913, p.5.
80. Scott, *Feminism and the Politics of Working Women*.
81. Lancashire millworker, quoted Margaret Llewellyn Davies, *The Women's Co-operative Guild* (Kirkby Lonsdale: Women's Co-operative Guild, 1904), p.35.
82. Midland Section Guild Report 1894, quoted Scott, *Feminism and the Politics of Working Women*, p.75.
83. Cole, *A Century of Co-operation*, pp.219, 225.
84. Scott, *Feminism and the Politics of Working Women*, p.238.
85. Lewenhak, *Women and Trade Unions*, p.85f.
86. Rose, *Limited Livelihoods*, 180–1.
87. Ibid, p.233.
88. Liddington and Norris, *One Hand Tied Behind Us*; June Hanham, 'Women and the West Riding ILP' in Rendall, *Equal or Different*, ch.8.
89. Linda Walker, 'Party Political Women: A Comparative Study of Liberal Women and the Primrose League 1890–1914'; Rendall, *Equal or Different*, ch.6.
90. Pugh, *The Tories and the People*, ch.3.
91. Holton, *Feminism and Democracy*, p.40.
92. Ibid, p.42.
93. Andrew Rosen, *Rise Up Women* (1974); Harrison, *Separate Spheres*.
94. M. J. D. Roberts, 'Feminism and the State in Later-Victorian England', *Historical Journal*, 38,1 (1995), 85–110.
95. Brian Harrison, *Prudent Revolutionaries: Portraits of Inter-war Feminists* (Oxford, 1987).
96. Hollis, *Ladies Elect*, ch. 5.
97. Sheila Jeffreys, *The Spinster and Her Enemies: Feminism and Sexuality 1880–1930* (1985); Bland, *Banishing the Beast*; Susan Kingsley Kent, *Sex and the Suffrage in Britain 1860–1914* (Princeton, 1987).
98. Bland, *Banishing the Beast*, p.183.
99. Pat Thane, 'Visions of Gender in the Making of the British Welfare State' in Gisela Block and Pat Thane (eds), *Maternity and Gender Policies: Women and the Rise of the European Welfare States 1880s–1950s* (London: Routledge, 1991), p.99.

100. Rubinstein, *Before the Suffragettes*, ch.8.
101. Roberts, 'Feminism and the State'.
102. Thane, 'Visions of Gender'.
103. Jeffreys, *The Spinster and her Enemies*; Bland, *Banishing the Beast*; Kingsley Kent, *Sex and Suffrage*.
104. Bock and Thane (eds), *Maternity and Gender Policies*.
105. Smith, 'The 1940 Old Age and Widow's Pensions Act'.
106. *Maternity and Gender Policies*, p.93.

8 The Democratisation of Political Behaviour

1. Cornelius O'Leary, *The Elimination of Corrupt Practices in British Elections 1868–1911* (Oxford: Clarendon, 1962); Seymour, *Electoral Reform*.
2. 23 September 1873, p.4.
3. Seymour, *Electoral Reform*, p.174.
4. Quoted O'Leary, *The Elimination of Corrupt Practices*, p.65. My italics.
5. ibid, pp.15, 50, 56.
6. Seymour, *Electoral Reform*, p.227.
7. 'Roads to Democracy: Electioneering and Corruption in Nineteenth-Century England and Ireland', *History*, 261 (1996) 553–71.
8. Joyce, *Factory Politics*.
9. O'Leary, *The Elimination of Corrupt Practices*, p.102.
10. Nossiter, *Influence, Opinions and Political Idioms*, ch.12.
11. Hoppen, 'Roads to Democracy', 564.
12. *Solicitors Journal*, 2 February 1901, 231–3.
13. John Garrard, *The Great Salford Gas Scandal 1887* (British Gas North-Western, Altrincham 1887); John Garrard and Viv Parrott, 'Craft, Professional and Middle Class Identities: Solicitors and Gas Engineers 1850–1914' in Kidd and Nicholls (ed), *The Making of the British Middle Class*.
14. Seargeant Balantyne, quoted H.J. Hanham, *Elections and Party Management: Politics in the Time of Gladstone and Disraeli* (1959), p.276.
15. Quoted Seymour, *Electoral Reform*, p.407. For earlier examples of upper-class attitudes, see ibid, p.178.
16. Quoted Bruce L Kinzer, 'The Failure of Pressure from Without: Richard Cobden, the Ballot Society and the Ballot Act in England', *Canadian Journal of History*, 13.3, 1978, 399–422.
17. *Manchester Guardian*, 10 June 1848, p.10.
18. Frank O'Gorman, 'Electoral Deference in Unreformed England 1760–1832', *Journal of Modern History*, 56.3, September 1984, 391–429; *Voters Patrons and Parties*. For different view, see Moore, *The Politics of Deference*.
19. Nossiter, *Influence, Opinion and Political Idioms*.
20. Phillips, *The Great Reform Bill in the Boroughs*, ch 5.
21. Nick Rogers, *Whigs and Cities*, chs 1,2.
22. Ibid.
23. *The Great Reform Act*, p.88ff.

24. Rogers, *Whigs and Cities*, ch. 1.
25. O'Leary, *The Elimination of Corrupt Practices*, p.52.
26. *The Times*, 8 January 1881.
27. Howkins, *Reshaping Rural England*, p.215.
28. F.M.L. Thompson, *The Rise of Respectable Society: A Social History of Victorian Britain 1830–1900* (1988).
29. Rosemary Sweet, 'Freemen and Independence in English Borough Politics 1770–1830', *Past and Present* (1998) 161, 84–115.
30. Reshaping Rural England, p.210; P.J. Waller, *Town, City and Nation: England 1850–1914* (Oxford, 1983), ch.5.
31. Thompson, *The Making of the English Working Class*, ch.4.

Conclusion

1. Colley, *Britons*.

Select Bibliography

Democratic Underpinnings

Logie Barrow and Ian Bullock, *Democratic Ideas and the British Labour Movement 1880–1914* (Cambridge, 1996).

Gisela Block and Pat Thane (eds), *Maternity and Gender Policies: Women and the Rise of the European Welfare States 1880s–1950s* (1991).

Anna Clark, *The Struggle for the Breeches; Gender and the Making of the English Working Class* (1997) p.29.

G. D. H. Cole, *A Century of Co-operation* (Manchester, 1944).

Dina Copelman, *London Women Teachers: Gender, Class and Feminism 1870–1930* (1996).

W. Hamish Fraser, *Trade Unions and Society: the Struggle for Acceptance 1850–80* (1974).

Martin Gorski, 'Mutual Aid in Civil Society: Friendly Societies in Nineteenth-Century Bristol', *Urban History*, 25,3 (1998).

P. H. J. H. Gosden, *The Friendly Societies in England 1815–75* (Manchester, 1961).

P.H.J.H. Gosden, *Self Help: Voluntary Associations in Nineteenth Century Britain* (1973).

Pat Hollis, *Ladies Elect: Women in English Local Government 1865–1914* (Oxford, 1997).

David Hempton, *The Religion of the People: Methodism and Popular Religion c1750–1900* (1996).

Eric Hopkins, *Working-Class Self-Help in Nineteenth Century England* (1995).

T.W. Laquer, *Religion and Respectability: Sunday Schools and Working-Class Culture* (New Haven, Com., 1976).

Sheila Lewenhak, *Women and Trade Unions* (1977).

Paul McHugh, *Prostitution and Social Reform* (1980).

T.H. Marshall, *Citizenship and Social Class and Other Essays* (Cambridge, 1950), 28.

R.J. Morris, *Class, Sect and Party: Leeds 1820–50* (Manchester, 1990).

David Neave, *Mutual Aid in the Victorian Countryside: Friendly Societies in Rural East Yorkshire 1830–1914* (Hull, 1991).

Guiseppe Di Palma, *To Craft Democracies: An Essay in Democratic Transition* (Berkeley, 1990).

Victor Perez-Diaz, *The Return of Civil Society: The Emergence of Democratic Spain* (Cambridge, Mass, 1993).

F.K. Prochaska, *Women and Philanthropy in Nineteenth Century England* (Oxford, 1980).

R.D. Putnam, *Making Democracy Work: Civic Traditions in Modern Italy* (Princeton, 1993).

Gillian Scott, *Feminism and the Politics of Working Women: The Women's Co-operative Guild: 1880s to the Second World War* (1998).

Adam B. Seligman, *The Idea of Civil Society* (Oxford, 1992).
Edward Shils, 'The Virtue of Civil Society', *Government and Opposition*.
Malcolm Thomis and Jennifer Grimmett, *Women in Protest 1800–50* (1882).
Alexis de Tocqueville, *Democracy in America* (1833, 1994, ed J.P. Mayer).
R.F. Wearmouth, *Methodism and the Struggle of the Working Classes* (Leicester, 1954).
Sidney and Beatrice Webb, *Industrial Democracy* (1897).

The Democratisation Process

Michael Brock, *The Great Reform Act* (1973).
John Cannon, *Parliamentary Reform 1640–1832* (Cambridge, 1972).
Mary Chadwick, 'The Role of Redistribution in the Making of the Third Reform Act', *Historical Journal*, 19, 3 (1976) 665–83.
Maurice Cowling, *Disraeli, Gladstone and Revolution* (Cambridge, 1967).
K. Theodore Hoppen, 'The Franchise and Electoral Politics in England and Ireland 1832–85', *History*, 70, 279 (June 1985) 204.
William M. Kuhn, *Democratic Royalism* (Basingstoke, 1996).
Frank O'Gorman, *Voters, Patrons and Parties: The Unreformed Electorate of Hanoverian England, 1734–1832* (Oxford, 1990).
John A. Phillips, *The Great Reform Bill in the Boroughs: English Electoral Behaviour 1818–41* (Oxford, 1992).
Nick Rogers, *Whigs and Cities: Popular Politics in the Age of Walpole and Pitt* (Oxford, 1989).
Charles Seymour, *Electoral Reform in England and Wales 1832–85* (1915: Newton Abbott, 1970).
Duncan Tanner, 'The Parliamentary System, the "Fourth" Reform Act and the Rise of Labour', *Bulletin of the Institute of Historical Research*, 56 (1983) 205–19.

Democratisation of Political behaviour

Michael Dawson, 'Money and the Real Impact of the Fourth Reform Act', *Historical Journal*, 35.2 (1992) 369–81.
Norman Gash, *Politics in the Age of Peel* (1969).
Patrick Joyce, *Work, Society and Politics: The Culture of the Factory in Later Victorian England* (Brighton, 1980).
Tom Nossiter, *Influence, Opinion and Political Opinion in Reformed England* (Brighton, 1975).
Frank O'Gorman, 'Electoral Deference in Unreformed England 1760–1832', *Journal of Modern History*, 56.3, September 1984, 391–429.
Cornelius O'Leary, *The Elimination of Corrupt Practices in British Elections 1868–1911* (Oxford, 1962).

Index